FIRE
IN THE
CITY

SAVONAROLA AND THE STRUGGLE
FOR RENAISSANCE FLORENCE

LAURO MARTINES

OXFORD
UNIVERSITY PRESS
2006

OXFORD
UNIVERSITY PRESS

Oxford University Press, Inc., publishes works that
further Oxford University's objective of excellence
in research, scholarship, and education.

Oxford New York
Auckland Cape Town Dar es Salaam Hong Kong Karachi
Kuala Lumpur Madrid Melbourne Mexico City Nairobi
New Delhi Shanghai Taipei Toronto

With offices in
Argentina Austria Brazil Chile Czech Republic France Greece
Guatemala Hungary Italy Japan Poland Portugal Singapore
South Korea Switzerland Thailand Turkey Ukraine Vietnam

Published by Oxford University Press, Inc.
198 Madison Avenue, New York, New York 10016
www.oup.com

Library of Congress Cataloging-in-Publication Data

Martines, Lauro.
Fire in the city: Savonarola and the struggle for the soul of
Renaissance Florence / by Lauro Martines.
p. cm.
Includes bibliographical references and index.
ISBN-13: 978-0-19-517748-0 (alk. paper)
ISBN-10: 0-19-517748-7 (alk. paper)
1. Savonarola, Girolamo, 1452–1498.
2. Florence (Italy)—History—1421–1737.
3. Florence (Italy)—Politics and government—1421–1737.
4. Florence (Italy)—Church history.
5. Reformers—Italy—Florence—Biography.
6. Dominicans—Italy—Florence—Biography.
7. Florence (Italy)—Biography.
I. Title.
DG737.97.M3 2006
945'.5105092—dc22   2005031802

1 3 5 7 9 8 6 4 2
Printed in the United States of America
on acid-free paper

al mio carissimo jairo, un gigante a modo suo

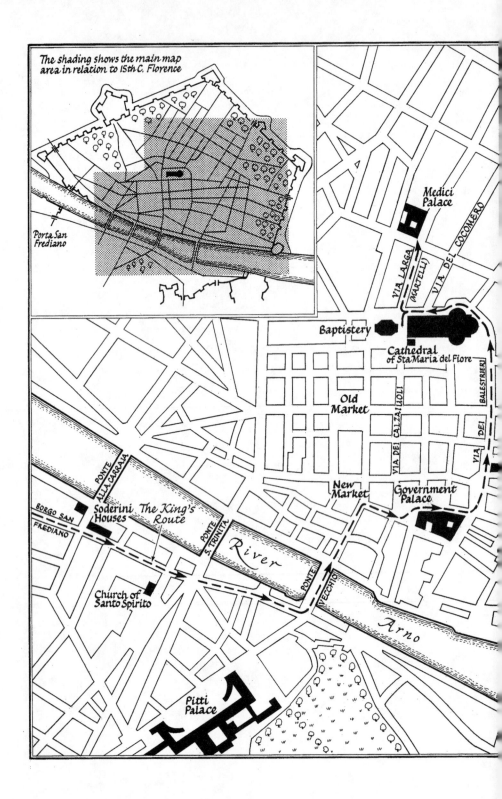

The shading shows the main map area in relation to 15th C. Florence

Porta San Frediano

Medici Palace

VIA LARGA (MARTELLI)

VIA DEL COCOMERO

Baptistery

Cathedral of Sta Maria del Fiore

VIA DEI BALESTRIERI

Old Market

VIA DEI CALZAIUOLI

VIA DEI

New Market

Government Palace

PONTE ALLA CARRAIA

Soderini Houses

The King's Route

BORGO SAN FREDIANO

PONTE S. TRINITA

River

PONTE VECCHIO

Church of Santo Spirito

Arno

Pitti Palace

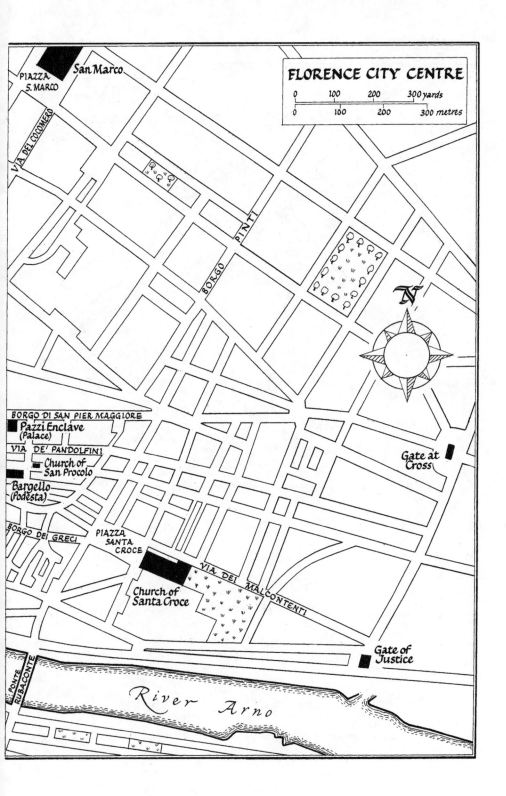

FLORENCE CITY CENTRE

0   100   200   300 yards

0   100   200   300 metres

PIAZZA
S. MARCO

San Marco

VIA DEL COCOMERO

BORGO PINTI

BORGO DI SAN PIER MAGGIORE

Pazzi Enclave
(Palace)

VIA DE' PANDOLFINI

Church of
San Procolo

Gate at
Cross

Bargello
(Podesta)

BORGO DEI GRECI

PIAZZA
SANTA
CROCE

VIA DEI MALCONTENTI

Church of
Santa Croce

Gate of
Justice

PONTE RUBACONTE

River Arno

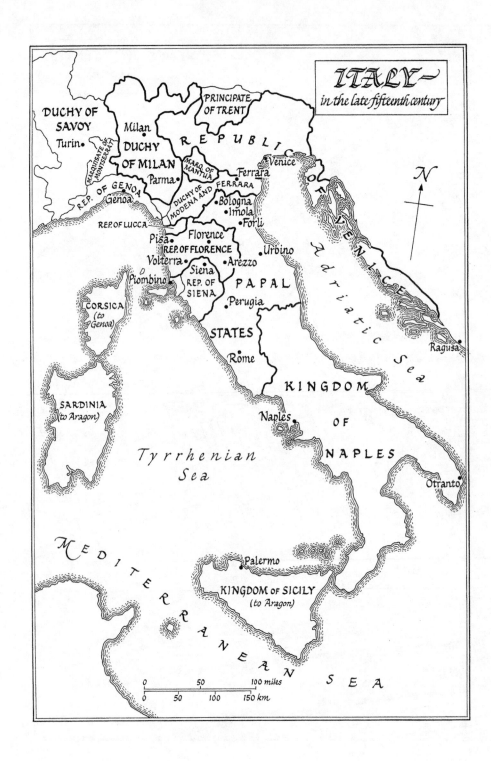

CONTENTS

ACKNOWLEDGEMENTS

MY IRREDEEMABLE DEBT must be to the Savonarola experts living and dead, whose labours and intelligence made this book possible. Without their work, not a single page of what I have done here would exist. They are all cited in the notes, comments, and Bibliography. The writing of history – in the modern world, at all events – can never be anything but a team enterprise. Those of us who forget this belong to the demon of ingratitude.

Yet once more I have the happy obligation to thank my publishers, Will Sulkin and Peter Ginna, superb readers and editors. In my years as an academic, never did I have critics and commentators as alert and perceptive as they. The university world is far from having all the best of what there is in imaginative talent and intellectual rigour.

My friend and agent, Kay McCauley, an ongoing inspiration, knows how much she is appreciated, but an expression of public thanks can never be wrong. My first reader, as always, Julia O'Faolain, deserves all that the heart can offer.

All translations are mine, unless otherwise indicated.

Lauro Martines
London
Autumn, 2005

LIST OF ILLUSTRATIONS

An X-Ray of
Florentine Government

G overnment in Florence was the job of a pyramid of small councils, with the Signoria or Signory – eight Priors and the
Gonfalonier of Justice – at the apex. These nine men held office
for two months, and were then replaced by a new group. The city thus
saw six changes of government per year. Although seemingly unstable,
the system worked very effectively for more than two centuries, because
other councils were drawn in to support the Signory.

Two bodies of counsellors, the Twelve Good Men and the Sixteen
Gonfaloniers, worked closely with the Signory. They spoke for the different
parts of the city and voted on most matters of importance. Their short
office terms were staggered, so that the incoming (new) Signory always
meshed, so to speak, with counsellors who were fully on top of the
current political situation.

In wartime and periods of danger, the Signoria shared *diplomatic* power
with the War-Office Ten, who served for six months or a year and who
conducted the war. If the Ten were renewed, owing to strains in foreign
affairs, they could be re-elected.

The Eight, a political and criminal police, were continually consulted
by the Signory. Like the Sixteen, the Twelve, and the Ten, they met in
the government palace, the *Palazzo della Signoria*.

Everyday Florence, then, was ruled by a cluster of offices. The Signoria
took the initiative and introduced all new bills to the Great Council, but
only after sustained consultation. Offices were filled *by lot* or, in part, by
election in the Great Council. Action *by lot* simply meant the blind
drawing of eligible names from electoral pouches. Political eligibility, in

turn, was based on long residence in Florence (thirty years or more), on the long-term payment of taxes, but most especially — in practice — on descent from a direct male ancestor who had qualified in recent times for the Signoria, the Twelve, or the Sixteen. On these grounds, the men who were eligible for election to office were a citizen oligarchy.

In their habit of close consultation and the soliciting of advice, the Priors of the Signoria captained a collegiate form of government with a relatively wide social base. To help them decide important questions, they could at any moment — and often did — call in and, in effect, take the votes of the city's top politicians and leading public figures: in all, some 200 to 300 men. Just here was the solidity and force of Florentine republican government.

GLOSSARY OF TERMS

Arrabbiati (the Angry Ones, or even 'Mad Dogs'). A porous political grouping, strongly opposed to Savonarola.

Compagnacci (the Rude or Ugly Companions). A company of upper-class pleasure-seekers, founded to fight Savonarola and his movement.

Eight, the. A police council, geared to use spies and to work in secret.

Frateschi (the Friar's Men). Supporters of Savonarola. See also *Piagnoni*.

Great Council (the). Florence's supreme legislative body after 1494.

Parlamento. Assembly in the government square of at least two-thirds of all Florentine political citizens.

Piagnoni (Wailers or Weepers). Ardent Savonarolans, also known as *Frateschi*.

Priors. The eight members (*Signori*) of the Signoria, the city's chief governing body.

Signoria, Signory. Made up of eight Priors and the Gonfalonier (Standard-Bearer) of Justice, the Signoria conducted the daily business of government, held office for two months, and was succeeded by a new group of nine men.

Sixteen, the (Sixteen Gonfaloniers). Counsellors to the Signory, they spoke for the city's sixteen *gonfaloni* (broad neighbourhoods or districts).

Ten, the. The War-Office Ten. They handled war and military affairs, including foreign relations, in times of war or danger.

Twelve, the. The Twelve Good Men. Counsellors to the Signory, they represented the city's four administrative divisions (*quartieri*), three men for each quarter.

CHAPTER ONE

Chorus

I N THE FINAL MONTHS of Savonarola's life — it was early 1498 — a plot was concocted to blow him up in the cathedral of Florence, as his great preacher's voice boomed forth from the pulpit to thousands of listeners. The ringleaders belonged to a kind of fraternity known as the 'Rude' or 'Ugly Companions' (*Compagnacci*). They planned to hire a man named Baia, an 'explosives expert' (*maestro di fuochi lavorati*), and to let him concoct and place an explosive device in the cathedral. If they had carried out their plan, theirs would have been the first 'terrorist' bomb in the history of Europe. Having looked into the particulars, however, they discovered that some of their own friends and relatives, who were likely to be present at the sermon, might 'be maimed or killed', and so they backed away from the idea.

Viewed as a figure of prime political importance, Girolamo Savonarola would be the target of other murderous threats. The Pope himself, Alexander VI, longed to get his hands on him. No wonder, then, that in the 1490s, the people of Florence began to see something that they had never seen before, nor had any other Italian city: the sight of a simple priest, a Dominican friar, flanked by an escort of armed men whenever he left his convent to go out into the streets of the city.

The same friar also attracted acts of sacrilege. On the night of 3–4 May, 1497, several of his enemies broke into Santa Maria del Fiore, the city's great cathedral. They smeared the pulpit with excrement, covered it with the stinking carcass of a donkey, and drove nails up under the pulpit's bookrest, in the hope that if Savonarola managed to preach the next morning, he would impale his hands, as he struck the bookrest in the midst of his fiery delivery. Less than a year later, with government support, his enemies mounted their final attack — an armed assault on his convent, San Marco. After a six-hour siege, which included the use of small artillery pieces, they finally forced him to surrender. And at about 2:00 in the morning, although surrounded by guardsmen, he had to walk through a moving gauntlet that stretched more than 1000 metres, all the way up to the government palace — a gauntlet of screaming and shouting men, who sought to kick and punch the cowled figure, as they spat insults and spittle on him, or tried to poke at his body with torches. Much of the city was awake that night; public fury with the Friar was all but palpable; and many of his supporters were either in hiding or in flight from Florence.

Who exactly was this hated priest, a man previously so revered by the Florentines, that even a few days before he faced the gauntlet, the city's rulers, the Signoria, had not dared to turn him over to the Roman Curia?

In the 1490s, at the summit of the high Renaissance, the most remarkable man in Florence was not the Magnificent Lorenzo de' Medici, nor even Michelangelo or Machiavelli, but — as he occasionally called himself — 'a little friar' from Ferrara, Girolamo Savonarola.

Of small to medium height, dark-haired, grey-eyed, pale, boney-handed, big-nosed, and speaking with an accent that singled him out as a foreigner in Florence, he was the talk of all Italy, as he stood in the eye of a raging political storm. Government officials in Venice studied reports on him. The Pope and the Duke of Milan watched him with an anxious eye. He was to conduct embassies to the King of France, and many of the top men in Florentine government looked to him for advice, while others, including old-line aristocrats and political grandees, hated his guts. Yet he was a force in the shaping of the city's foreign policy and in the reshaping of its morals. His voice as preacher, resounding through the grand void of the Florence cathedral, attracted thousands of listeners, hungry for his guiding words and passionate morality. The faithful and the curious poured in from neighbouring and more distant towns, at times swelling the attendant throngs to 14,000 or even 15,000 people, intent on listening to that stranger, or — given the intriguing rumours — just to lay eyes on him.

Florence, still in the front line of the Renaissance cultural awakening, with Venice and Rome running closely behind, had expelled the

Medici family from the city in November, 1494. An underground of feisty republicans had suddenly surfaced to hail the end of Medici tyranny, to seek open political debate, and to demand responsible government. Now the ascetic Savonarola stepped in to become the city's chief agent of republicanism and the implacable foe of dictatorship. This man was not afraid to speak his mind in a setting in which most prominent citizens, keeping to a watch-and-wait stance, were holding their tongues. Sixty years of bullying Medici rule had taught many Florentines to be silent about politics, or even to slip over into cooperation with those who were castrating the city's republican institutions, leaving only seductive but empty façades.

The talk of all Italy, a friar? Rumour held that Savonarola was the familiar of kings and princes; that he claimed to be a religious prophet in the Old Testament mould; that he was a fiery speaker and rabble-rouser; that he governed Florence from behind the scenes; that he – a man in holy orders – was a scandalous and virulent opponent of the Pope, Alexander VI; that he captained a secret political party; that he had taken power from the nobility and put it into the hands of the lower classes; that he was an ambitious, crafty, and proud overreacher, quietly engaged in piling up a fortune; that he had converted the citizens of Florence, famous for their cunning and business acumen, into a flock of gullible sheep; that he had been vile to his own family; that he had splintered Florentine households, turning wives against husbands, brothers against brothers, and sons against fathers; that he was a holy man, a near saint, and a formidable intellectual; and that he was most certainly a heretic and a schismatic. There was also chatter alleging that he was a hermaphrodite, a homosexual, and even a sufferer of the new European scourge – syphilis. In short, his fames and infamies were many, and historians have remained divided for five centuries – at times fervently so – about his mission, his accomplishments, his influence, his public personality, and even his honesty and sincerity.

Alas for him, the charge of heresy stuck. In May, 1498, before a great crowd of men and boys – women had been barred – he and two other friars, his closest collaborators, were hanged in Florence's government square. This done, their bodies were immediately burned to ashes in a bonfire that also engulfed the gallows. Their charred remains were then swept up into carts to be wheeled off and disposed of in the river that cuts through the city. Rome and the government of Florence feared that the many who still believed in the Friar's words and deeds – people from all walks of life – would rush in to collect scraps of what remained, with an eye to having got their hands on relics. If these should occasion miracles, the Friar would then be looked upon as a saint and martyr.

The drama of Savonarola's years in Florence transcends its time and place, because it links high politics and religious activity in a time of epochal crisis.

Italy had fallen prey to an invading French army, and concerted attempts were being made to subject the peninsula to foreign rule. The entire period is frequently seen as a blotch and turning point in Italian history, especially as there was also a crisis in the Church. Well before Luther and Calvin, many Italians had seen that they lived under a reign of shameless simony and bartering in the papal court and college of cardinals. Poets made blistering attacks on the curial hierarchy, and the angry Savonarola now branded the leaders of the Church as vendors who 'trafficked in' – buying and selling – 'the blood of Christ'. A generation later, in the 1520s and 1530s, Luther and other Protestant Reformers would have little trouble smashing the traditional unity of Western Christendom; and it is arguable that Savonarola had inklings of the coming cataclysm.

Historical writing has two different stories to tell. There is first of all the one that passed before the eyes of contemporaries: a panorama of individuals, crowds, incidents, and dramatic scenes. Anecdote and colour are likely to govern this narrative. Streaming through all of it, however, in shifting forms of consciousness, is the second story: that is, a constant flow of cultural and political phenomena, the so-called impersonal forces. We dare not forget these for the simple reason that they both precede and succeed the life of every individual, every group, every singular event. And the job of the historian, surely, is to weave back and forth between the two stories; or at the very least, to keep the impersonal and seemingly formless story constantly in mind, for there, in and among the 'forces' without faces, is the ground of historical analysis, the social settings that serve to turn the actions of men and women into something more than unrelated fragments – indeed, into tapestries of historical meaning.

It follows that the one thing we should not do to the men and women of past time, and particularly if they ghost through to us as larger than life, is to take them out of their historical contexts. To do so is to run the risk of turning them into monsters, whom we can then denounce for our own (frequently political) motives – an insidious game, because we are condemning in their make-up that which is likely to belong to a whole social world, the world that helped to fashion them and that is deviously reflected or distorted in them. Censure of this sort is the work of petty moralists and propagandists, not historians.

Savonarola has been the property of specialist scholars for too long, especially since the first publication of the great biography by Pasquale Villari, *La storia di Girolamo Savonarola e de' suoi tempi* (1859). Soon translated and widely distributed in the late nineteenth century, Villari's book roused the imagination of historians and sent them searching through archives and manuscript libraries in the quest for more materials on the charismatic friar. In the late twentieth century, the work of scholars so swelled our knowledge of the man, his works, and his religious and political thinking, that it is daunting for any one historian to try to take it all in. In the present day, therefore, the experts – academics and men in holy orders – are all the more given to speaking only to one another.

I propose to carry the factual essentials of their knowledge out to a larger reading public, while also adding, of course, my own lines of analysis. Savonarola himself had no excessive respect for 'the philosophers', that is, the intellectuals who saw learning as an end in itself. He distrusted and assailed the aims of pure reason; but he was even more wary of priests and monks, because he believed that hypocrisy ran deeper in them and was compounded by ignorance.

This book, I should add, is not a biography – an enterprise better left in the hands of the specialists, although (and in any case) far too little is known about the Friar's private life to turn it into highbrow gossip or a tantalising narrative for 'psychobiographers'. What we know for certain about him is chiefly connected with his years in Florence and his time as a controversial public figure. My account is focused there, especially in the years from 1494 to 1498, when Savonarola's life and the history of Florence were so joined together that it is impossible to pull them apart. The result here, therefore, will be the biography of a time and place in the sense of covering a short span, at least in historical terms; and Savonarola is, to be sure, the prime actor. Yet the few years in question hold much of the history of Florence, because they are a critical stretch in the city's tormented passage from republic to princely despotism, from government by citizens to the rule of one man attended by courtiers.

Savonarola was a 'fundamentalist' – if I may use this charged word – in wanting contemporaries to take their Christianity seriously. He wanted it to alter the substance and direction of their daily lives, even if doing so exposed them to persecution, ridicule, or threats. He also sought to keep to the words of the Bible. But he nailed his doctrinal commitment to the ideals of a republic in which all eligible citizens would have their say. Florentine politics, he argued, was the business of a whole community, not the affair of one man, one family, or a tiny elite. Princely rule (hence 'tyranny') of the sort promised by the Medici house had no greater foe than the little friar from Ferrara, especially as he knew that humane and responsible government could not be achieved without a strong sense of morality, of sympathy for the greater good of the community and even for the value of the individual soul. Just here, along the path cut by his moral stance, is where politics and his form of religious fundamentalism broke in to contest part of the same ground of action. The results were to haunt Florence for many years. However they might wish it were otherwise, even Machiavelli and Guicciardini, the two greatest political minds of the age, accepted that the state as they knew it could not stand outside the confines of religion, because it was bound to use God for political ends.

I have begun to touch on themes and hidden questions that will call for sustained treatment, as we move into the book and start to unfold a story that is as tragic as it is astonishing. Here however, at the very outset, we may edge closer to the ways and thinking of the late fifteenth century, if we keep the following disagreement in mind.

Savonarola threw Christian belief into the faces of supposed Christians. They knew, he reminded them, that Jesus Christ was born in poverty, and that the Virgin Mary, a woman of humble social station, if of powerful faith, must have been modest and simple in her dress as well. Why then did painters dress her up to look like a luxurious Renaissance whore? Could such an image be for true believers, or was it firstly an invention for wealthy and powerful men? 'Oh friar, stop there,' he might have mimicked, in one of his imaginary dialogues, planted in the middle of his sermons, 'all the finery is in her honour and in the honour of God.' 'No,' he would instantly have shot back, 'all that finery is for the honour of men, and first of all the patrons, a rich merchant and a bishop who live only to please their senses.'

In many ways, this fictional dialogue catches the clash of basic attitudes between the supporters of the Friar and his enemies. The clash became fatal when it was fought out in the arena of politics.

CHAPTER TWO

Vile Bodies: 1472–1490

H E KNEW LUXURY – there was no doubt of this – having grown up on the periphery of (and almost within) one of Europe's most extravagant spots, the princely court of Ferrara. His grandfather's fame as professor of medicine at the University of Padua had been such as to call forth an invitation from the Marquis of Ferrara in 1440, and from then on, for the rest of his life, Michele Savonarola was court physician to the Este lords of that city. There, as a boy, Girolamo was to see opulence and raw power of the sort that he would come to detest and denounce.

Stemming perhaps from thirteenth-century warriors, the Savonarolas originated in Padua, where one of the old city gates was named after them. The professor's father had been a wool merchant, one of his brothers a canon lawyer; hence there was always room for a brilliant marriage. Girolamo's mother sprang from the Bonacossi, a branch of the old and powerful Bonacolsi clan, once the lords of Mantua. The linking of two such families, Savonarola and Bonacossi, reflected marriage practice of the day, and it is likely that one of the courtiers around the Este set up the initial feelers between the two houses. Naturally enough, therefore, when Girolamo was born, in September 1452, he was held to baptism by the chief secretary to Duke Borso d'Este, Ser Francesco da Libanori.

But after the rich old court physician died in 1468, the Savonarolas of Ferrara gradually lost their wealth and lofty contacts. The Friar's father, who had probably rebelled against Paduan study habits, went into business and money-changing, failed at both, fathered seven children, and left his two daughters without even the means of marriage – proper dowries. Of the sons we know this much only: one became a professional soldier; a second would prosper in the medical profession; and a third, following his elder brother Girolamo, would enter the Dominican Order of preaching friars.

The sources hint that the child Girolamo was much preferred by his grandfather, owing probably to the boy's prodigious intellectual talents and love of study. Court physician Michele, the author of learned medical and scientific treatises, could not but look upon the child with pleasure and favour. Inevitably, therefore, Girolamo's primary subject had to be Latin; his grandfather seems to have been his first tutor; and soon enough, given the new taste of the age, he was reading Cicero, Quintilian, and even the 'lascivious' Ovid. In time, however, he would turn against fashion, as he began to cherish the early Church fathers – Jerome and Augustine especially, as well as their medieval heirs, St Bernard and Bonaventure, the great canonist Gratian, and St Thomas Aquinas, the most ambitious and creative of all Aristotle's commentators during the high Middle Ages.

The young Girolamo's religious and mystical turn may be explained in part by the strong and loving influence of his grandfather, a man of profound religious sentiments who was repelled by the cult of pleasure and sensuality, the materialistic worldliness, of the Este court. About fifteen years before his hiring of the Paduan professor, the Marquis Niccolò III d'Este had insisted on the execution of the princess Parisina Malatesta, his second wife, and one of his own illegitimate sons, because the young prince and mother-in-law, who were nearly the same age and more than twenty years younger than the Marquis, were suddenly found to be carrying on as passionate and secret lovers.

Something of his grandfather's revulsion is thought to have passed to the studious Girolamo. Years later there would be stories to the effect that as a young man he had written idealised love verse in the Petrarchan manner, and that he had once fallen in love with a young but illegitimate noblewoman, a Strozzi from Ferrara. Not knowing of her bastardy, she had spurned his advances by observing that his family was not good enough for hers. Whereupon the stung Savonarola had immediately retorted, 'And do you think it proper that the Savonarola house should give a bastard like you to one of its legitimate sons?'

Since these scraps offer almost as much as we know about the love claims, we may as well drop them. All that can be safely asserted is that something in his earliest years, or in his later adolescent experiences, led him to the conviction that humanity is given over to the base pleasures of vile bodies and to sensuous, material waste. He would find good reasons for his flight from such a world.

Having done a good deal of work in the fields of classical literature, history, and moral philosophy, Savonarola's abilities carried him easily through studies at the University of Ferrara, where he appears to have taken an advanced Arts degree. With the death of his rich grandfather, and his father's failures in business, there must have been talk in the family about what he should do with his life. For a time he even studied medicine. To go into trade, or to seek a secretarial post at the Este court, was out of the question for a young man who already looked upon the world with disaffected eyes, even if his parents had urged him to consider money-making pursuits, as we infer from the reaction he expected when he threw up the ways of ordinary life for the quiet of the cloister.

His poem on the destruction of the world, *De ruina mundi*, written at the age of twenty, begins with a despairing statement about the passing away of everything good, almost despite the providence of 'the supernal King'. Earth, he finds, 'esteems those who are the enemies of God' and Rome is 'in the hands of pirates [captained by Pope Sixtus IV]', meaning cardinals and bishops.

> Ah, look at that catamite and at the pimp,
> Dressed in purple, frauds looked up to
> By the common people and adored by the blind world.

His anticlerical stance leads him to a set of themes that turn up occasionally in Italian verse of the fifteenth century. Thus, the honoured and the happy are the sort of men who live from theft. Wealth acquired by means of trickery and violence is what produces 'noble' spirits. Noble too, in the world's eyes, are the destroyers of people and the disdainers of Christ. Earth honours the keepers of fraudulent account books and the masters of the art of doing evil. Not surprisingly, therefore, 'usury is called philosophy' – meaning, scornfully, that the practice of lending at interest had been converted into a question hedged in by the dense, abstract debates of canonists and theologians.

Earth is so pulled down by every vice
That it will never stand again.
And Rome, the capital, slips into the muck,
Never more to rise again.

The young Savonarola lives with one hope alone: that in 'the next life' all those who were truly noble will be known. He closes the *Canzone* with an envoi, telling it to go forth with his message, but to beware:

Avoid all those who put on purple.
Flee from palaces and ostentatious loggias,
Speaking to the few alone,
For you will be the enemy of all the world.

At the age of twenty, then, he had found his moral voice, which he was putting, interestingly, into a verse form refined by Petrarch for love and for moral rumination about love: a stage on the way to the love of God. But there was nothing revolutionary in his anticlerical outlook. Scorching criticism of the upper clergy, in Italy at all events, came forth in the eleventh century, peaked in the thirteenth century, and continued robustly up to the time of Luther and the Protestant Reformation. In Girolamo Savonarola's time, the tradition of anticlericalism was exceptionally strong in educated circles, such as at the University of Bologna and in Florence, where lawyers and literary men were frequently in close touch with learned clerics, as well as with men in the Roman Curia. They were thoroughly familiar with the chosen enemy. The novelty in Girolamo's indictment of powerful clergymen was to emerge only years later, in the scope of his accusations. Meanwhile, he entered more of the same hard line into his *De ruina ecclesiae* ('On the ruin of the Church'), a poem written in 1475, the very year of his 'escape' to a convent.

Here, speaking to chaste Mother Church, he grieves over the disappearance of all Christian heroism, with its great ardour, love, and piety. Weeping and hiding away in a 'beggarly cave', the Lady tells him that 'When I saw that proud woman [a corrupt papacy] go into Rome' and take over, she retreated into her cave. The real Church, therefore,

Goes about poor, with her parts exposed,
Her hair in strands and her garlands torn;
[. . .]
She is blasphemed by dogs,
The swindlers of our holy days.

For now, at least, 'a false, proud whore' has won out, and all we can do is 'Weep and be silent.'

The young Savonarola had hit his stride: he had just entered the Dominican Order, but he was making a clean distinction between the true Church and the harlot in Rome. He was not, however, proposing to go about trumpeting this claim. On the contrary, the poem ends by saying that not to be heard or understood 'is perhaps better'. His fight at the moment, with himself and with his family, was an internal one, and it was movingly described in the famous letter to his father of 25 April 1475, occasioned by his flight from Ferrara to the convent of San Domenico in Bologna.

Honoured father,
I have no doubt that my departure is very painful to you, particularly because I stole away so secretly, but by this letter I want you to understand my soul and will, so that you may take comfort from it and realise that I have not made this move in so childish a way as some people think. And first of all I want you, as a manly spirit and disdainer of fleeting things, to be swayed by truth, rather than — as women are — by passion, and to judge in accordance with the empire of reason whether or not I was right to flee from the world and to pursue my own calling.

The reason that moves me to enter a religious order is this: first, the great misery of the world, the iniquity of men, the carnal crimes, adulteries, thefts, pride, idolatry, and cruel blasphemies, all present on such a scale that a good man can no longer be found. Whereupon many times a day, while crying, I used to sing this line: Fly from these lands, bolt from this shore of misers. I could not bear the evil of the blinded peoples of Italy, all the less so when I saw virtue trampled and vice elevated . . . owing to which I prayed daily to my lord Jesus

Christ that he pull me up out of this slime. . . . Now God, in his infinite mercy, has shown me the way, and I have accepted it, although I am unworthy of so much grace.

Answer me therefore. Is it not some great good for a man to flee from the filth and iniquities of the wretched world, in order to live as a rational being and not like a beast among swine? And would mine not have been a great ingratitude to have prayed God to show me the straight way to take, he having stooped to show it to me, and then not to take it? Oh my Jesus, rather a thousand deaths than that I should ever be ungrateful to you this way. So, dear sweet father, rather than weep, you should thank our lord Jesus, who gave you a son and then kept him very well until his 22nd year; and not only this, he also deigned to make him his knight militant. Well, then, don't you think it a true [gift of] grace to have a son who is one of the knights of Jesus Christ? But to speak briefly, you either truly love me or you don't. You would not say, I know, that you don't love me. Therefore, if you love me, since I am made of two parts, soul and body, you either love the body or the soul more. You cannot say the body, because then you would not [really] love me, in loving the most vile part of me. If therefore you love my soul more, then why do you not seek what is good for it? You should surely rejoice and celebrate over this triumph.

I know that the flesh must feel some pain, but it should be reined in by reason, especially by wise and magnanimous men like you. Do you think it wasn't painful for me to part from you? I want you to believe that in all my life I have had no greater pain, no greater affliction of mind, than in abandoning my own flesh and blood and going out among people unknown to me, to sacrifice my body to Jesus Christ and to put my very will into the hands of those who are perfect strangers to me. . . . But because I know that you complain of my having stolen away and almost fled from you, you should know that my pain and passion were so great in having to leave you, that if I had shown any signs of this, I believe that my heart would have broken before I parted from you, and you would have impeded my decision and my action, so don't marvel at my having said nothing to you . . . I beg you, dear father, to put an end to your laments, and do not want to cause me more sorrow and pain than I already have: do not grieve over what I have done (for certainly I wouldn't renounce it even if I believed that this would make me greater than Caesar), but rather because I am still flesh and bones like you, and the senses fight off reason. I have a cruel battle on my hands in the fight to keep the Devil from jumping on my shoulders, and all the more so the more I feel about you. These days with their fresh wounds will soon pass away, and I hope that in time you and I will be consoled through grace in this world, and then in the next one through glory [our salvation]. . . . I beg you to comfort my mother, pray you both to give me your blessing, and I shall always pray fervently for your souls.

The letter reveals that Savonarola already knew how his father had reacted, or was bound to react, to his departure and religious vocation. They had discussed the matter; there had been much gentle but firm disagreement about it, and so the young man had resolved that his flight would have to be precipitate. A month or two later, the family were still wailing over his decision, as attested to by his impatience in a second letter:

What are you crying about, you blind ones? Why so much weeping and grumbling, people without light? If our prince [of Ferrara], reaching out among the people, had asked me to strap on a sword and become one of his knights, to what jubilation and feasting you would have treated yourselves! And if I had rejected the request, which of you would not have thought me crazy? Oh you without common sense, oh blind fools and without a ray of faith! The Prince of princes, he who is infinite power, calls me with a loud voice – more, he begs me (oh vast love) with a thousand tears [as on the Cross] to gird on a sword of the finest gold and precious stones, because he wants me in the ranks of his militant knights. And now, because I have not spurned so great an honour, unworthy me . . . you complain when you should rejoice, all the more so in that you claim to love me. What then can I say about you, if this is what makes you sad, but that you are my chief enemies – worse, the enemies of virtue! If such are your ways, I say nothing else to you but this: Away from me all you who work at doing injustice (*Discedite a me omnes qui operamini iniquitatem*, Psalms VI 8).

He now closes this letter, though with a more generous flourish and again in Latin, by urging them to accept joy: 'since the soul is more precious than the body, rejoice and exult that the glorious God is making me a doctor of souls [not of the body]'.

Bologna was the site of Italy's premier university; it continued to attract students from all over Europe, notably for the study of civil and canon law. There was thus a dash of something international about this ancient town in papal territory. Foreign speech was common there, and students from distant shores sometimes appeared as characters in the fiction (tales) of the period.

Savonarola moved on the fringes of this scene, based, as he was, at San Domenico. Here, already the holder of a university degree, his progress over the next four years was swift, owing as much to his commitment and intellectual prowess, as to his immersion in theological study with two or three leading masters, each of whom taught at his convent. He had a phenomenal memory and seems to have got close to memorising much of the Bible. In addition, his devotion was absolute: a year after arriving at San Domenico he took final religious vows. His progress may be marked by the fact that he was transferred in 1479 to the convent of Santa Maria degli Angeli in Ferrara, to be the teaching master of novices there. That a string, however, might have been pulled to get him back to Ferrara and close to his family is a suspicion to be rejected. Social ties between the clergy and eminent local families tended to be close in Italian cities, often too close if the serious care of souls was really primary. But Savonarola's dedication and obedience to superiors were such that he would never have countenanced the corrupt suggestion that he try to pull a string. God came first, not family.

Looking back, some time later, Savonarola surely regarded the years at Bologna and Ferrara as preparation for 'the city of his destiny', Florence, that hard and wordy town which he would know how to conquer, if only briefly, with a cascade of words of his own.

This call finally came in May 1482, when the Order dispatched him to Florence, to the convent of San Marco. His new position would be as chief instructor in theology and lecturer on Scripture. He made the journey on foot, carrying only his copy of the Bible and a religious compendium, a breviary, to be crammed in time with his glossings and reminders. His habit of walking from city to city was a statement of his commitment to poverty and humility (horses were for gentlemen), and years later the habit was revealed even in his attempt to keep to it when serving, temporarily, as a Florentine ambassador. Here, therefore, is the place to note that the Dominican Order was split between the 'Observants' and the 'Conventuals'. On one side were the Conventuals, the friars who believed in the communal and individual possession of property; on the other were those who elected to 'observe' the original rule of their founder, St Dominic, who seems to have put the acquisition and possession of property outside the rule. Savonarola had naturally selected the Observants, and was even opposed to the collective holding of major properties, apart from the sufficiency of lands and buildings needed to carry out the preaching mission of the Order.

The move from Ferrara to Florence, from Santa Maria degli Angeli to the chosen religious house of the Medici, San Marco, was not just a passage from one convent to another, where life would be much the same. Yes, the Dominican rule would be much the same, but the men would be different, and more different still the two cities. As members of a militant preaching order, St Dominic's friars were meant to go out into the world to raise their voices and to catechise; hence there was a continual mingling with the local populace. Savonarola had abandoned the world because of its vile bodies, but only in order to prepare himself for a return to it, with a view to uplifting the spirits of those bodies by his sermons. Now he would find that Florentines were very different from the people of Ferrara, where a princely court and autocratic government had long since driven citizens out of politics and public life.

Florence was still a republic in name, if only partly so in fact. In the 1480s, Lorenzo de' Medici was the supreme political boss, much more than first among equals. He was skilful at getting his own way, but he also had to put up with – and try to manipulate – a tangle of executive and legislative councils; and he had to win friends and influence people, or bully and threaten them. The result was that Florentines talked about men in politics and even – though much more guardedly – about political issues as such. Moreover, the city ranked as an international centre of trade, finance, and industry; and its citizens famously were looked upon as fast talkers – shrewd, spirited, superb keepers of accounts; not courtiers, not haughty noblemen, not soldiers, and not mere landowners who lived solely from rural income. Verbal expression was their forte, not only because their triumvirate of writers – Dante, Petrarch, and Boccaccio – loomed as models and polishers of the Tuscan tongue, but also because the city continued to abound in literary men who drew voice, word, and spirit from the people of Florence. In the fifteenth century, no other Italian city produced a constellation of writers like Leonardo Bruni, Leon Battista Alberti, Matteo Palmieri, Lorenzo de' Medici, Luigi Pulci, Marsilio Ficino, and Angelo Poliziano, not to mention a numerous company of lesser writers whose names are now mainly known to students of the period.

This public world is what Savonarola was going to confront every time he came out of San Marco and plunged into the city to give a sermon, to make a visit, or to carry out some other commission. Better yet, Florentines brought the city to him on their visits in quest of guidance; and in the 1490s they would flock to San Marco.

On his first posting to Florence, he remained for five years, although he made a number of side trips, such as in 1485 and 1486, to be the Lenten preacher at San Gimignano, a neighbouring town under Florentine rule. He arrived there after an embarrassing experience in Florence's San Lorenzo, the splendid parish church of the Medici, where he had been honoured with an invitation to offer the Lenten sermons of 1484. The sermons were a disaster, and the memory of this would nag at him, as he admitted a decade later. Having never before preached in such grand surroundings and to a large congregation, hence nervous and a foreigner to boot, Savonarola all but drove his listeners away by his funny Lombard speech (Italy teemed with dialects), weak voice, ungainly gestures, and poor delivery. Being out of his element, he ended up, he confessed, with 'a few simple men' and 'some poor women' as his only listeners. Lecturing to groups of friars, or teaching them one-on-one, came naturally to him, and they responded warmly to his passionate and gentle manner. But he was not ready for seasoned or sceptical listeners, and especially in Florence, where the populace looked for a performance and citizens were ready to compare preachers, to criticise, or to go to another church for their seasonal homilies. A year later, his preaching at San Gimignano was already much better, to judge by the reception he got on his return there in 1486. He had evidently improved his voice and delivery.

Savonarola made no impression on Florence in the 1480s. Almost no one there was to remember him afterwards, and certainly not the chroniclers or keepers of memoirs. His departure in 1487 went unnoticed. A call had come from Bologna, and he returned to that university city as 'master of studies' at San Domenico, where teaching was conducted at the university and post-graduate levels. A year later he was again moved to Ferrara, but in the next two years he also preached at Brescia, Genoa, and other cities, including perhaps Modena and Piacenza.

The death in 1484 of Pope Sixtus IV, one of the most brazen of all nepotistic pontiffs, and the election of Pope Innocent VIII (not Holy Father but an 'unholy father' of children), brought no satisfaction to Savonarola, as is clear from his poem, *Oratio pro ecclesia*, occasioned by the death of Sixtus. In this verse prayer, he invites Jesus to be forgiving, to look upon papal Rome 'with perfect love' and 'mercy', since it might otherwise perish. The Church would thus be spared a bloodbath, for the devil is knocking it down, 'breaking its nerves and bones'. All good spirits and counsel seem extinct, and 'I see nothing but swords./ Jesus, forgive our iniquities!' Satan's 'armed squadrons' are pitched 'against our holy Mother [Church]', so that unless 'You take up arms for Her' this time, all religion and pious custom will be lost. Lord, 'We are orphans and you our only hope.'

These despairing lines throw light on Savonarola's frame of mind at the time. He continued to hope for God's pity, and had not yet started to expect the scourgings, the armies of dead, the destruction and renewal of the Church that he was to prophesy and call for ten years later. Still, his metaphors and imagery are cast in the guise of an armed struggle, and his view is large: he was looking to Rome and the wide world. He would have to take all Italy into his considerations, and so migrate into politics.

CHAPTER THREE

The Friar Returns: 1490–1491

PRODIGIOUS IRONY ATTENDS Savonarola's return to Florence in the late spring of 1490, because the prime mover was Lorenzo the Magnificent, and behind him in the initiative was the young and glamorous Count Pico della Mirandola, one of the formidable minds of the age. In trouble with Rome on charges of possible heresy, and unhappy about his treatment at the hands of the Curia, the Count had taken refuge in Florence, where he won the friendship of Lorenzo. He also entertained a keen admiration for Savonarola, whom he had first met and listened to, some eight to ten years previously, either in Ferrara or Reggio. They were to become devoted friends. And what bound them together, arguably, was the Friar's evolving anticlericalism: his developing moral critique of a careerist and unscrupulous clergy.

The irony springs from the fact that the Friar would turn into the foremost enemy of the 'corrupt' Medici house, the man who would fight tooth and nail to keep them out of the city after the collapse of the Medicean regime in November 1494. However, in 1489–1490, Lorenzo was not only ready to please the Count by working for Savonarola's return, he himself was also tilting in a pious direction, as his chronic maladies became ever more grave. He was thus emotionally prepared to see a strong religious figure in San Marco.

More than a year before the Friar's return, Lorenzo had sent a letter to the General of the Dominicans, pressing him for the desired transfer to Florence. But the General had been required to work through the Vicar of the organisation's northern branch, the Lombard Congregation, and it was a year before all the arrangements could be made, finally relieving Savonarola of his teaching charges in Ferrara.

If he was little more than an obscure monk during his first period in Florence, now, nearly forty years of age, he came back fully formed as a teacher, theologian, and personality. By election of the friars of San Marco, he soon became Prior of the convent, with the result that he was going to have to engage more directly and face to face with the Renaissance city, not only with the citizens who would come to seek his guidance, but also, for example, in many meetings with some of its more prominent men and intellectuals. Briefly, therefore, let's stand back a bit, and see how Florence came to be as it was in the 1490s.

The roots of the Italian Renaissance were in the upper peninsula of Italy. Here, from Perugia to the Alps, was the most populous part of Europe, a chequered expanse of cities on hill, plain, and valley, trailing an urban history that stretched back to Roman antiquity. Protected by mammoth city walls or natural barriers, such as sea and mountain, inhabitants developed passionate local patriotisms. Cities became the *patria*, the fatherland, of their citizens, strikingly so in the biggest ones: Venice, Milan, Genoa, Pisa, and Florence, as well as in smaller cities such as Padua, Mantua, Ferrara, Bologna, Siena, Lucca, and Perugia. Even lesser places – Pavia, Piacenza, Cremona, Arezzo, and the Romagnol towns – sparkled with heady displays of *campanilismo*, local patriotism.

As Italian cities flourished, driven by trade and a population boom that lasted, roughly speaking, from the eleventh to the early fourteenth centuries, they created their own governments and courts of law, collected taxes, raised armies, fought intrusive monarchs (popes and German emperors) in the twelfth and thirteenth centuries, and turned themselves into petty states. They also grabbed neighbouring towns, in an aggressive process of continual expansion. By the late fourteenth century, the biggest of them were, for all practical purposes, little states, with Venice, Milan, and Florence at the head of the list. They were distinguished by their large and often ingenious ambitions. Here was the ground of the Italian Renaissance, with its associations of merchants and craftsmen, oligarchs and petty warlords, ranks of citizens, priests and friars, and – in the surrounding countryside – a population of peasants whose manual labour produced much or most of the food for the ruling city. The resulting culture was expressed in the energetic building of churches and government palaces, in a body of complex law, in the keen desire for images, in storytelling (often filtered through sermons), in increasing literacy, and in sheer musing or daydreaming. The search for explanations and self-definitions, along with the exercise and justifying of claims of power, meant that a rediscovery of the history and literature of the ancient world – 'the revival of classical letters' – was all but inevitable. Greece and especially Rome had something to say to Italy's late medieval cities.

In the fourteenth century, for reasons that no historian has fathomed, Florence – why not bigger and more powerful Venice? – took the vanguard of the peninsula's high cultural awakening, particularly in literature and the visual arts, remaining there until the sixteenth century. The two centuries from Giotto to Botticelli, from Dante to Machiavelli, also held many other Florentine names of the first rank. But their homeland had other energies as well. A cloth-producing prodigy, Florence was one of the most industrial of Italian cities and more than just a centre of trade. In the early fifteenth century, with a population in the range of 40,000 people, it had, astonishingly, seventy international banking houses – far more than any other place in Europe. Moreover, unlike industrial Milan, which had imploded into a princely autocracy, Florence remained a vigorous republic, governed by a class of citizens who were determined to rule their own lives, and who would pose a dangerous political problem for the Medici, once the great banker Cosimo commenced his rise to power. In the 1400s, Florentine banking and industrial production saw a downturn, but the culture of the city kept its innovative course.

In 1490, accordingly, Savonarola confronted a Florentine upper class whose most alert interpreters and spokesmen often observed relaxed religious practices, were familiar with the world of big business, as well as with papal Rome and other cities, while also knowing something about the philosophies of Aristotle and Plato, and about the history and literature of antiquity. He would also face a strong taste for worldly love poetry, blasphemous satire, and a craze for the building of grand domestic palaces. Questions of private comfort to one side, the palaces had one defining purpose: to assert family identities – that is, to exhibit wealth, authority, and supposed moral worth, and to stand as on-going testimony of materialistic hopes.

From a tepid piety to a craze for palace-building and a taste for worldly literature, the scope of these interests added up to the culture of an elite – a minority – that could not sit well, as we shall see, with the Friar's designs for Florence.

At that moment too, the beginning of the 1490s, politics figured among the most immediate concerns of the city's upper class. Lorenzo de' Medici was ailing. His swaggering son and political heir, Piero, had so far shown little promise of the sort that would satisfy the leading citizens and oligarchs who orbited around Lorenzo. More than fifty years of devious Medici rule had meant a mix of republican and tyrannical government by strong-arm committees, demagogic assemblies, coerced legislative councils, the manipulation of electoral lists and eligible candidates, the corrupting of courts and judges, and the tactics of intimidation, such as the punitive use of taxation. In campaigns to eliminate opposition to the Medici and their supporters, bosses had removed dozens of families and hundreds of citizens from the political scene: they were banished from the city, or stripped of their right to hold important public office. The Medicean regime had thus driven wedges into the large class of political citizens, not only between supporters of the Medici and recalcitrants, but also into the ranks of the supporters, splitting those who began to monopolise the top offices, including easy access to Lorenzo, from the others who were edged out to the periphery of office and honours, and who also lost access to the most lucrative posts. Politically, then, Florence knew the breath of discontent only too well.

If Savonarola had failed to pick up the signs of a political malaise during his first Florentine tour, he would certainly notice them after his return. But first he had to familiarise himself with affairs in the convent, a Dominican religious house, hence a place of learning, of sustained prayer, and of preparation for the preaching of correct doctrine to the laity.

Brought back to San Marco to teach logic, one of his strengths, Savonarola made a swift conquest of the friars, who took warmly to the northerner and elected him their Prior in the following year. Yet even then he avoided doing what all men expected, and that was to visit the Magnificent Lorenzo de' Medici, the living head of the great patrons of San Marco, and to show his appreciation by his gratitude and readiness to curry favour. This did not happen. Savonarola felt that he was in God's debt, not man's; and although the proud Lorenzo resented the slight, he seems to have said very little about it, apart from voicing a cutting observation: 'a foreign monk has come to live in my house and he hasn't even bothered to come and visit me'. Two very different and conflicting views were wonderfully buried here. Lorenzo was making a glancing reference to patron–client relations, to that which a powerful man had the right to expect from his supposed dependants. But Savonarola's distance and silence were also a statement. He would soon be saying, repeatedly, that it was wrong and even wicked for men in holy orders to seek out *gran maestri* (great lords, the top bosses), because the consequent ties could only end in compromises, lies, and corruption for the servants of God.

Meanwhile, if Lorenzo was going to have doubts about the Friar, there would be more to be concerned about. For during his years away from Florence, the militant knight of Christ had found the skill to turn himself into a superb orator and public personality, thus following in the footsteps of the most famous preachers of the age, men such as Roberto (Caracciolo) da Lecce and Bernardino da Siena, who were also, in their fashion, mimes and actors.

Delivered in San Marco, Savonarola's Advent sermons of 1490 (completed on 9 January 1491) had attracted and impressed large numbers of laymen. His success was crowned by an invitation to preach in the city's largest and most important church, the cathedral, where he next offered the Lenten sermons of 1491, the year's principal preaching cycle. And those who launched the invitation must have had a sense of what they were going to get, because apart from treating the nature of Mass and its rituals in fascinating detail, the eighteen Advent sermons turned into a hard-hitting assault on a lax and unprepared clergy, on the sins of usury and fraudulent financial transactions, on the avarice of the rich who corrupt their sons by setting immoral examples, on honouring rich men simply because they are rich, on those who are 'tepid' in their religious commitments, and on the buying of Masses for family chapels. Citing *Matthew* (21:13), he closed his seventeenth sermon by claiming that priests, as well as laymen, had transformed 'the house of God into a den of thieves, especially during holidays'.

Savonarola was denouncing standard practice. Influential families looked to the Church as a source of jobs and income for their sons.

When young men took holy orders, they went through a charade, unless they were driven by a spiritual need, and this had given way to job-seeking. A well-placed priest could expect a comfortable life. For two centuries, moreover, the rich had turned to the buying of private space in the wide public areas of churches. There they built frescoed chapels blazoned with their coats of arms, and paid the local clergy for the celebration of private Masses — ritual prayer for the eternal salvation of the donors or of dead ancestors.

Historians disagree about Lorenzo's attitude toward Savonarola in 1491. But once the 'foreigner' began to hold forth in the cathedral, the supreme Florentine patron very likely began to nurse doubts about him. On the one hand, it seems, he wanted a truly religious monk at the head of San Marco, one whose qualities would help to spread the fame of the convent; and he wanted to keep faith with the brilliant Pico della Mirandola. In addition, Lorenzo himself had drifted toward a more ardent piety, owing, as already noted, to his failing health. But he could not, on the other hand, look well upon a preacher who struck too hard and effectively at the pleasure-loving clergy and the greedy rich, especially in a city where the disparities between rich and poor were striking. Worse still, the Friar began to hint at happenings in the near future — scourges, cleansings, death, and renewal.

One day, five of the city's most eminent citizens paid a visit to the Friar: Francesco Valori, Guidantonio Vespucci, Domenico Bonsi, Paolantonio Soderini, and Bernardo Rucellai. We may as well have these names here, because all five would play leading parts in the events of the next six or seven years. It was alleged that they were acting slyly for Lorenzo, in gently advising Savonarola to stop talking about the future and to preach in a more traditional vein. In view of Lorenzo's pride, however, it is more likely that, knowing him well and knowing their Florence, the five men simply took it upon themselves to confer with Savonarola. In short, a group of influential citizens tried, it appears, to caution him; but he rejected their embassy, as is clear from the content of the sermons. Their protest went no further. As long as he was allowed to preach, he was free to say whatever he chose. He could of course have been run out of town, but that would have required action both by the government of Florence and Savonarola's clerical superiors.

The Latin outlines of Savonarola's fifty Lenten sermons were drafted almost tempestuously between 9 January and 16 February 1491, the Ash Wednesday on which the preaching began. In the words of one historian, they seem 'the explosion of an internal maturing that required outward expression', and are a prelude to the later sermons on the urgent need for a renewal of the Church. But they also target social and economic abuses. The opening sermon stresses the idea that ceremonial externals in religion may betoken an inner void: a people without true faith or commitment. Savonarola then passes to the urgency of his call: 'Do penitence!' The time of renewal has come. 'We must change our way of preaching', and something more: 'I know for certain, as many of you also know, that my being here marks a beginning . . . I shall start a new manner of preaching.'

The succeeding sermons introduce a wealth of themes and often return or allude to the main ones: for example, the evils of a merely ceremonial religion, the doctrinal ignorance of the laity, 'thieving priests' and their cupidity for lucrative posts (benefices), the purchase and sale of Church offices (simony), the lechery of clerics, sodomy, and the oppression of the poor, such as by unjust taxation. The last of these claims is strongly enunciated in the Sunday sermon of 27 February, when the Friar also remembered that the rich in Florence expect to collect interest on their taxes – a customary Florentine practice. God's justice will come down on this, he declared. 'This place will no longer be called Florence but turpitude and blood and a den of thieves.'

Sources say nothing about the reaction, but as these words rang forth, there must have been a stunned silence in many among the great throng of listeners, as well as anger or resentment in others. The preacher was already on his way to evoking praise, as well as indignation.

Keeping in part to the preaching conventions of the day, and moving from his love of Scripture, Savonarola's sermons always began with quotations from the Bible as his springboards for a blistering commentary on the present scene. But his attacks and criticisms were continually spliced with lessons concerning the love of God, the understanding of Scripture, Christ's sacrifice for man, faith and grace, and the example offered by Christian martyrs.

He singled out other targets: priests who seek out and court the powerful, conspicuous luxury as a form of stealing from the poor, the pride and underlying stupidity of the learned and worldly wise, the vanities of women, and time and again the corruption of the Church, with reminders of the need to cleanse and renew it. His picture of the clergy is unrelenting: they have killed Christ 'in their hearts'; they shoot dice, rush through Masses, thirst for money, and accompany the dead for ducats, not out of charity. Some keep boys, while others keep concubines and are the 'slaves of love'. The fact is that 'Priests are all elegant now, with long hair [looking feminine], fine cassocks, and laughing in the choir' or even conducting business there.

But his bravest hour came with a change of venue on 6 April, the Wednesday after Easter, in the fiftieth and final sermon. On that day he preached to the heads of government in the Palace of the Signoria. Here, among 'the lords', the Friar says, 'I am no lord, as in a church.'

His theme was justice. Since, however, the justice of God exists only 'through faith in Jesus Christ', he also has to consider 'faith' and 'steadfastness'. Proceeding to rip into the *Signori* for their many defects and failures, he emphasises the claim that government heads, like the commanding men in the Church, set a kind of supreme example, with the result that 'every good and evil proceeds from the head'. Consequently, if they, the lords, could amend their ways, 'you would turn this into a holy city'. Citing passages from *John* (21), he suggests that they are 'tyrants' because they are proud, love adulation, and do not return ill-got gains. They make secret decisions, favour their own officials, sing the praises of important people, levy immoral or unjust taxes, will not listen to the arguments of the poor, take the side of the rich, and allow their officials to impose unpaid labour burdens on peasants and on the wretched. There were also other complaints: they delay lawsuits, call for unjust war or discord among cities, fail to punish corrupt officials, and even tamper with the currency. Instead, they should attend to making people happy by pursuing peace, by seeking some kind of equality among citizens, and by moving against avarice with an eye to reducing the causes of envy, hatred, and dissent. Finally, 'look up to Christ, who calls out to you from heaven'.

How Savonarola pitched this sermon – his tone, accents, and exact words – we cannot say, because he spoke, as in the previous sermons, from a quickly-drawn-up and concise Latin synopsis. Hence much of what he said, connectives and fillers, examples and vivid expressions, came *ex tempore*. Perhaps he also departed from his summary. But he was coming from a series of sermons brilliantly preached in the great cathedral and before large throngs of people. There *he* was lord. We also know that he was to become – if he wasn't already – fearless, particularly in moments of stress. So if he kept more or less to his synopsis, such as we have it, then he spoke firmly, movingly, and without flinching. Very likely, too, he amazed, silenced, or angered his listeners – the *Signori*, their two bodies of advisers, plus a small assembly of invited counsellors. No Florentine government of the fifteenth century had ever been addressed thus by a monk, who in fact, in his thirty-third sermon (Sunday, 20 March), had already stated: 'I believe that Christ speaks through my mouth.'

The Lenten sermons of 1491 resulted in name and fame for Savonarola, and he now began to enter Florentine public opinion with his stern warnings about rich and poor, with the beginnings of his call for a renovation of the Church, and his implied claims to a form of divinely privileged knowledge.

Lorenzo de' Medici and his leading supporters, as we have seen, were made uncomfortable by the sermons. Savonarola was taking social and political questions directly into the religious sphere, or, perhaps more accurately, he was driving religious values into politics. Yet this 'worldly' sphere, politics, was not devoid of Christian ideals. On the contrary, codes of law in Europe generally, and in Renaissance Florence, tended to link the ends of government to ideas of amity, concord, justice, and the common good among citizens and subjects; and all these were defined in terms of Christian thought.

In the end, Lorenzo refrained from any direct interference, although it is likely, as the chief sources allege, that he was the one who arranged to have another preacher, the well-known and learned Mariano da Genazzano, an Augustinian friar, deliver a publicised sermon in the church of San Gallo, challenging Savonarola, and arguing, in effect, that it was rubbish to pretend to have knowledge of the future. Such pretension, he held, could only lead the populace toward sedition. Here, by implication, was a reproach to Savonarola's attack on the rich. Turning, however, into too crude and personal an attack, Mariano's performance seems to have alienated Florence's intellectual community.

All the same, the new Prior of San Marco went on preaching. He had started to gather converts around himself, including, over the next year or two, the cream of Florentine intellectuals – Marsilio Ficino, Angelo Poliziano, Domenico Benivieni, Bartolomeo Scala, and others. His reputation for holiness had taken wing. In early April 1492, therefore, as Lorenzo de' Medici lay dying, he sent for the Friar, in the desire to have his final blessings. A popular story alleges that when Savonarola entered the chamber of the dying man, he demanded certain conditions, including the restoration of Florentine 'liberty', before he would give his absolution and blessing. This is too good a tale, and peddled by the writings of Piagnoni, Savonarola's close followers. Besides, the claim pivots on an act of bartering, of cutting a deal, and this was simply not the Friar's way in matters of conscience. A long meeting between the two men brought solace to Lorenzo, and the visitor seems to have offered his blessings. But otherwise we know nothing of what went on between the two, even if we choose to imagine a gentle and respectful monk, for Savonarola's one-on-one relations with acquaintances and with his friars suggest that he was likely to be compassionate.

CHAPTER FOUR

The Wait: 1492–1494

S ORROW IN FLORENCE for the death of Lorenzo was confined mainly to his household, to a few of the political men around him, and to others who had profited from his regime, including the families of prominent supporters, in a line running back to the 1430s. But there were no large outpourings of grief. More credibly, his death raised doubts, anxieties, and some republican hopes, because the twenty-year-old Piero de' Medici, heir presumptive and *gaffeur* (blunderer), as he is known by one of the experts, had so far shown no talent for politics. His real passions had already surfaced: horses, fastidious dressing, playing football, and, it seems, showing off his splendid body and good looks. There was reason to suspect that the nobility of his mother's Orsini blood, which ran in the veins of great Roman *condottieri* and prelates, had gone to his head. Nothing of the burgher shone through in him, as it did even in his father, who could look at an account book and worry about the fortunes of the different branches of the Medici Bank. As for son number two, Giovanni, though not yet seventeen, he was already a cardinal and had to be counted out of the Florentine political scene, at all events as an active, on-going presence.

In these circumstances, although an array of Medicean oligarchs moved in at once and recognised Piero as the heir to his father's offices and privileges, they worried about his abilities and about their own standing. The dying Lorenzo urged Piero to seek the counsel of the reigning oligarchs, who had sometimes served as his leading advisers; but whether or not the youth would honour this recommendation was an open question; and Lorenzo appeared to worry, because he had seen that the young man was vain and headstrong. Would Piero take advice from wise and seasoned old politicos?

Within a year of his death, Lorenzo's circle of supporting noblemen had lapsed into strong disagreement. Some were dubious about Piero, but others had turned decidedly against him, and one clique secretly favoured the cadet line of the Medici. Apart from a few hotheads, however, they were not yet ready to take action. Among the more cautious were at least two of the men who had sought to get Savonarola to temper his sermons, Paolantonio Soderini and Lorenzo's brother-in-law, Bernardo Rucellai, who had married one of his sisters. Foreign ambassadors had instantly picked up the signs of disaffection, caused mainly by the fact that Piero was cutting his ties, or distancing himself, from the top men, angling to make his own decisions, and surrounding himself with upstart aides or secretaries — new men of the sort raised by Lorenzo himself. But whereas the vanished master had been able to work with both aristocrats and secretaries, Piero preferred the new men, whom he could begin to look upon as his own creatures. Sensing his own inadequacies or impatience with the tasks of government, he was more comfortable with social inferiors, even when calling on their advice. He could also feel good about piling work on them, and brush aside the crucial details of government, which probably bored him. The drawback was, however, that the oligarchs from the old families could not stomach seeing the new men in high office — men who, like Ser Piero da Bibbiena, were not even Florentines, thereby adding insult to injury. They also began to see that in time — led on by his underlings — he would want to make himself unquestioned lord of Florence. By the spring of 1493, accordingly, some of them had even started to entertain the idea of pushing Piero aside so as to make way for an aristocratic republic: a state or *reggimento* in which a restricted circle of noblemen would draw government fully into their own hands. And over this vision there would be fierce disagreement.

In the years 1491–1493, Savonarola was not yet a political man, or at least not consciously so. He did not measure the world of men in accordance with politics and the daily exercise of power. His view of the Church, however, and of the impact of social life on morals, hence on salvation, was bearing him toward a position in which he would want to have a voice in politics. Later, when pressed, he would often deny this accusation, and saw it as something of an outrage. A profound and sincere mystic, for whom really to love Christ was a rapture, he could not see how he could ever put politics ahead of God, or how he could fail to weigh men in anything but the light of eternity.

Meanwhile, he had to deal with Piero de' Medici. Elected Prior of San Marco in July 1491, Savonarola had chosen to stay away from Lorenzo, but all the evidence indicates that his relations with the new head of the Medici family were good. He certainly did not presume to challenge the young man's primacy. Most importantly, the Friar was able to enlist Piero's continuing and solid support for his plans to reform San Marco, where it became clear that the friars were ready to live more ascetically, even if due mainly to the influence of Savonarola. In any case, by the convent's rule, no friar could have private property, and the new Prior even opposed the ownership of petty items that smacked of luxury, such as silver crosses, fancy rosary beads, or expensive bibles. The friars now began to favour a stricter regimen: more fasting, more praying, less aimless talk, and other austerities, including the wearing of simpler cassocks, made from smaller cuts of rougher cloth. Their plans, moreover, were ambitious. They aimed to reform not only their own convent but others as well, and this required that their Florentine house break with the northern (Lombard) Congregation of Observant Dominican convents – an act requiring Rome's intervention.

Accounts of the break in question get pinned down in administrative details. So let us simply say that in its clash with the northern organisation, San Marco was also seeking to cut ties of patronage, of Milanese influence over the convent, thus challenging the long arm of the lords of Milan. The matter therefore had to pass to the papal court, to be decided by Pope Alexander himself. Since there was a certain fluidity in convent organisation, especially under pressure, the question of a shift in allegiance was not too unusual. There had been changes earlier in the century, when the great banker and politician, Cosimo de' Medici, relying on money and brazen influence, managed to take the convent of San Marco away from the Silvestrines (Benedictine monks) and to transfer it to the hands of the Observant Dominicans. The convent was later put under the umbrella of the northern organisation.

In 1492–1493, Ludovico Sforza, de facto lord of Milan, called on his diplomatic forces in Rome, also roping in his brother, Cardinal Ascanio Sforza, in the struggle to keep San Marco from defecting. His purpose was to keep high the name and influence of the Sforza. But Savonarolan pressures, with the support of Piero de' Medici, were unrelenting; and San Marco's Cardinal Protector in Rome, Oliviero Carafa, was able to swing the Pope in Florence's favour (May 1493). Over the course of the following year, though again in a stubborn fight with the Lombard Congregation, the Friar and his men were able to bring the Dominican convents of Fiesole and Pisa under their leadership; and they had designs on others as well – in Siena notably, but here they failed. With the resounding help of local government and patrons, the Siena Dominicans successfully rebelled against the pretensions of their Florentine brothers. Nevertheless, San Marco became the head of a new monastic alignment, the Tuscan Congregation, afterwards restyled the Congregation of San Marco. And their policies could be tough. When the Dominican convent at Pisa was brought under San Marco's rule, nearly all the friars (more than forty) abandoned it, because they refused to accept the new austerities. Fiesole lost four men for the same reason.

The Savonarolan struggle over organisation provoked venomous resistance, and this reminds us of the vital links between Church and society, clerics and patrons. Owing to the enormous scale of ecclesiastical rights and properties, of profitable office and income-paying benefices, local families and politicians had, as it were, too much invested in neighbouring religious houses to keep politics out of the Church, or the Church out of politics. Ambitious clerics, with the right connections, routinely borrowed money from bankers in order to buy lucrative Church offices – obvious investments. The practice was known as simony; and bishoprics were sometimes passed on, if not indeed willed, to family members.

In the wake of his Lenten sermons of 1491, Savonarola came to be known by friend and foe alike as 'the preacher of the desperate and the malcontent', but his activity and fight with the Congregation of Lombardy had not yet confined him to Florence. He travelled to Lucca to preach twelve sermons in 1491. In May 1492, and again at the beginning of 1493, he was in Venice on convent business, seeking to drum up distant support for his rigorist designs. But he soon made his way to familiar Bologna, where he remained from about 12 February to 8 April 1493, and delivered the city's principal Lenten sermons of that year. There, according to Piagnone (pro-Savonarolan) sources, he had a dramatic encounter with Ginevra Bentivoglio, wife of the lord of Bologna. She and her showy entourage, it seems, took to attending his sermons but often arrived late, whereupon the assembled throng would all rise in courtesy and Savonarola would have to interrupt his sermon in mid flight. On two occasions, therefore, he politely invited the lady and her party to get to the church on time. Ignored, on the third occasion he simply snapped something like: 'You see, here is the devil, here is the devil, come to interrupt the word of God.' Despite a marked taste for seigneurial violence in Bologna, it is improbable, as the same sources allege, that *la* Bentivoglio then called for Savonarola's assassination. But the rest of the account rings true, and it is likely that the courageous Friar did at some point meet her with a sharp remark. The lady and her courtly company were the very type of the rich and powerful (*gran maestri*) whom he was always to criticise.

Meanwhile, for Florence, for Piero, and for Savonarola, the Italian political scene was swerving toward a crisis that would bleed the city, convulse all Italy, topple the Medici, and catapult the Friar to the forefront of events.

At the beginning of the 1490s, Neapolitan exiles in France, with the backing of the lord of Milan, Ludovico Sforza, encouraged the King of France, Charles VIII, to invade Italy and seize the kingdom of Naples. Charles was to base his case for the Neapolitan crown on old Angevin claims. Sforza himself, engaged in a fatal controversy with the King of Naples, and convinced of his own political genius, was not altogether certain that Charles would actually march into Italy at the head of a great army and artillery train. Yet moved by a dream of chivalry and conquest, the King had let it be known, as early as 1491, that he intended to claim Naples and to go on from there to a crusade against the Ottoman Turks. The decision to invade Italy was taken by Charles and his counsellors in the course of 1492, but when the time came, the Ottoman part of his plans was dropped.

CHAPTER FIVE

Fear and Loathing: November 1494

Piero Tumbled

THERE WERE OMENS in the first days of November, 1494, and one of them was very queer. Piero de' Medici was out in the field, negotiating with the King of France, when a large fat falcon, flying at top speed, killed itself by hurtling into the space above the main door of Florence's government *palazzo*. According to a contemporary, this could only portend one thing: 'the death of Piero's great status, reputation, and government'.

An expectant mood for fatal happenings was coursing through the upper classes. Anxieties in the city had been building up ever since the spring, when King Charles VIII began to press the Florentines on the matter of where their allegiances lay. Would they side with him when he came down to Italy to claim the kingdom of Naples, or must he look upon them as enemies and allies of his rival, King Alfonso II? Three French embassies were to make their way to Florence, always with the same question, and all were sent away with evasive replies, although the question was tormenting citizens. Florence had no standing army and was short of money; King Charles needed cash to help defray his military expenses; the Medicean regime and its leading noblemen were deeply (if quietly) divided; and Florentine bankers and merchants, with goods and investments in France amounting to about 300,000 florins, had been expelled from Lyons in June.

Anxieties turned into outright fear at the outset of September 1494, when Charles invaded Italy with an army – it was rumoured – of from 30,000 to 40,000 troops, including a fearsome train of artillery, consisting of light and heavy siege guns, on a scale rarely if ever seen in Italy. Bound to the Aragonese King of Naples by his Orsini blood ties, Piero de'

Medici – against strong feeling in Florence – continued to hold out for the Florentine alliance with that southern kingdom. Privately, however, he was beginning to dither. In early October he held secret meetings with French emissaries. Looking beyond his nearest advisers and a few Medici diehards, he must have had a sense that Florence was now quietly massed against him. Citizens were secretly throwing anonymous jottings – an old Florentine practice – onto the streets of the city, calling for his overthrow and the restoration of 'republican liberty'. But dissent against Piero was also breaking into the open. Men in high office began to murmur. Everything was set for an outburst of public feeling. On 26 October, keeping his own counsel and without any input from the top circle of Florence's political minds, he had bolted out of the city for a secret meeting with King Charles. Four days later, he sent back word to the Signoria, informing the *Signori* that the King was demanding Florence's two seaports, Pisa and Livorno, in addition to the surrender of its great frontier and top-of-the-line fortresses in the north-west: Serezzana (Sarzana) and Pietrasanta. He was also asking for a subsidy of 200,000 gold florins. It went without saying that all this was the King's price to refrain from attacking Florence and ravaging Florentine Tuscany.

The Signoria and its counsellors reacted with shock and indignation. They rejected the demands, and spurned Piero's request for a mandate to negotiate an agreement with King Charles. Nevertheless, 'the boy', as he was seen by some of his critics, proceeded to hand over the ports and fortresses, and the Signoria quickly realised that Piero was in effect buying off the King and trying to save his own neck. Medici authority carried such weight that the young man's word alone got the commanders to give up their custody of the two fortresses. Worse still, during the first week of November, Pisa was overrun by French troops, with the foreigners immediately outnumbering Florence's mercenary soldiers by something like 200 to 1. The surrender of the fortresses came easily and quickly, because one of the Florentine commanders, the Captain of Sarzana, was Piero di Lionardo Tornabuoni, a Medici relative via Lucrezia Tornabuoni, Piero de' Medici's grandmother, while the other, Piero di Giuliano Ridolfi, in command of Pietrasanta, was related to the Medici by affinal ties of marriage.

There was now no salvation for Piero, unless he could seize and occupy the government palace on his return to Florence, where what he had just done was met with an explosion of disbelief and anger. All at once, office-holders and long-time Medicean loyalists began to pass over to the opposition, while most citizens waited nervously and expectantly for what Piero might do when he got back to the city. He had been so much the centre of Florentine attention in these last few days that every move he made seemed to bristle with meaning. Pushing Piero aside, the Signoria sent out an embassy of six of the city's most prominent citizens, including friar Savonarola, to treat with King Charles. Piero himself, returning to the city on the afternoon of Saturday, 8 November, and well-informed about the mushrooming opposition against him, went directly to the Medici Palace. He was greeted at the city walls by about twenty friends, but his arrival took on the colour of something private and almost stealthy. No government representatives were sent out to meet him – a candid slap in the face, since such occasions usually called for officials, horses, livery, and accompaniment to the government palace. Once at home, Piero got his servants to throw *confetti* (sweet confections) from the palace windows out to the poor who had soon gathered outside. Bread and wine were then distributed in ample quantities. He was seeking and sniffing out popular support. But he had also called for the assistance of cold steel: he had ordered Florence's captain (and his close relative) Paolo Orsini to make his way to the city walls with a troop of armed men.

A little later, hoping to re-establish his political pre-eminence, Piero seems to have had a brief, angry exchange with the Signoria. But finding no sufficient support among the men in government, he withdrew from the Palazzo. On the next day, Sunday, after hearing Mass, he went back to the government palace with a small company of armed attendants. Met by two friendly members of the Signoria on the lower stairs of their castellated bastion, he was informed that the *Signori* were at lunch and told to come back in the afternoon. Angry resentments and revived republican beliefs were inflaming all the main actors, with citizens now also driven by a new and concrete dread.

The King was on his way to Florence. His agents had arrived in the city on 4 and 5 November, and working with the cooperation of the Signoria, they set about chalking up the doors of houses to be used for the billetting of French troops. Town criers were sent out to trumpet the announcement that any removal of the chalk markings would be subject to an awesome fine of 500 florins. On the day of Piero's return, therefore, and with the French army soon to arrive, it must have been an uneasy Bargello – Florence's head constable – who chose to ignore Piero's command, ordering him to arrest one of the chief republican firebrands, Jacopo de' Nerli, a well-connected nobleman and one of the counsellors who had called Piero 'a child'. For years now the foreigners (non-Florentines) who held the six-month post of Bargello, also known as the Podestà, had accepted that in emergencies they would be loyal to the Medici family, but this was not to be the case on 8 November.

Knowing that Piero's armed kinsman, Orsini, was already outside the city walls with 500 or 600 mounted men, the *Signori* got ready for Piero's visit, his few loyalists in government now silenced and sidelined. They sent a call out for their counsellors, the Sixteen Gonfaloniers. Armed supporters of the government began to appear out in the Piazza della Signoria. So that when Piero returned, again with his group of armed retainers, including a bunch of friends and relatives, he was rudely greeted at a tiny door or casement (*sportello*) by none other than Jacopo de' Nerli, one of the Sixteen, and told that if he wished to enter he would have to come in alone, unarmed, and through the *sportello*! Cerretani reports that Jacopo then bit his finger 'in sign of a vendetta' [an act of insolence in Shakespeare: see note]. Piero and his men now began to brandish weapons, whereupon, watching the scene from the windows above, one of the *Signori*, another firebrand, a doctor of law, *Messer* Luca Corsini, started to shout 'People and Liberty!', the clarion republican call. The shout was at once repeated down in the piazza, and 'the child', his life in danger, had to be surrounded by his armed men. Retreating from the great piazza, Piero and his company rushed past Or San Michele and moved straight up the Via dei Calzaiuoli to the Medici Palace.

Piero returned to the government *palazzo* because he hoped to win over enough Priors (*Signori*) and counsellors to enable him to seize it. With King Charles due in Florence in the next week or so, and having already bought his support for an astounding price (Pisa, Livorno, and the other sites), Piero could then have retaken Florence. 'But it did not please God', said the most interesting and best-informed diarist of the period (Parenti), 'to tolerate so much iniquity'.

By now the Signoria had ordered the hammering of the great government bell, the tocsin, and many more *fiorentini* were rushing to arms. A small number of Piero's 'plebeian' supporters made their way to the government square, but were forced to retreat by the hurling down of large stones from the palace tower. One of the Bargello's guardsmen was killed for shouting 'Palle! Palle!', signalling the Medici coat of arms and meaning 'I am for the Medici'. The Bargello, a presumed Medici loyalist, was wise enough to withdraw his fifty men from the government square at about the time the young Cardinal Giovanni de' Medici (Piero's brother) was arriving on horseback, attended by a small group of armed citizens. They tried to approach the square, but the Cardinal was cursed as 'a traitor' and repulsed, along with his whole company, some of them coming away with wounds. Riding back to the Via Larga to find Piero, the Cardinal accosted him and reportedly said, 'we're finished!' They had no choice now but to quit Florence. The city Gate of San Gallo, not far from the Medici Palace, was being held by Piero's men, and Paolo Orsini was just outside. When Piero appeared there, Orsini saw at once that he was accompanied by only a few men, and realising that it would be too dangerous for himself and his troops to enter the city, he gave the order for them all to ride away. Piero took the road to Bologna, to seek the aid and comfort of his friends, the Bentivoglio lords. Cardinal Medici, meanwhile, was spotted at his windows, hands joined and praying pitiably. He soon disguised himself in Franciscan garb and stole quietly out of the city.

Events in Florence now moved as in a race. A *coup d'état* had taken place, but who was to be credited with it, and who now controlled Florence? Just back as one of the six ambassadors to the King of France, Francesco Valori — a leading Florentine patrician and soon to be Savonarola's most authoritative backer — led a a group of men into the Palace of the Bargello, where they supplied themselves with arms for use in the defence of the republic. His reputation for honesty lifted him above any guilt by association with the Medici. Three other prominent men, well known as staunch backers of the old regime, and boldly risking their lives, tried to take the government piazza by shouting 'People and

Liberty!', but the barefaced impostors were driven furiously away. That evening a price was put on the heads of Piero and Cardinal Medici. Showing loyalty for Piero, the Eight, a powerful political and police magistracy, were quickly suspended by the Signoria.

Calls went up for revenge against the tyranny of the fallen family. The Signoria therefore had the Medici Palace on the Via Larga surrounded and protected by armed guards. That jewel, with all its treasures, must not fall into the hands of a mob that was ready to sack and then set fire to the building. Officials quickly began an inventory of its contents. Everyone knew already that the family – the Magnificent Lorenzo above all – would be accused of having stolen vast sums of money from the public till and that all their goods and properties would be sequestrated to be put up for sale. Officials even took rings from the fingers of weeping Medici women, who were later dispatched to the convent of Santa Lucia on the Via San Gallo, including Alfonsina Orsini (Piero's wife) and her mother. Yet some days later, when Piero sent a letter to the Signoria, requesting clothing, linens, and wool, the request 'was granted in order to keep him quiet'. Knowing him to be a stickler about his fancy habits of dress, the Signoria slyly concluded that it would be better to let him have that part of his identity than to insist on having his clothing seized and sold, despite the fact that Florence had a flourishing market in luxurious second-hand garments.

On that day or the next, the Cardinal's house was attacked. Piero's minions – his top secretaries and closest collaborators – came under fire. Crowds rushed to sack and burn the houses of Ser Giovanni da Pratovecchio and Antonio di Bernardo Miniati. One of the more servile of Piero's collaborators, born into a well-known family, *Messer* Agnolo Niccolini, would have lost his house and chattels but for the intervention of a prominent jurist, Francesco Gualterotti, and a cluster of noblemen, who stepped in energetically to stop the mob and redirect its fury. Fire had been set to Niccolini's doors.

The moment had quickly come, in short, when the heads of the new regime – young noblemen and disaffected patricians – saw that they must act to protect the most compromised of the old families. Otherwise, in their baying for revenge, unruly bands of men would go on to ransack the houses of all the leading men who had so long been complicit in the tyranny of the Medici. The rebel Signoria now took three of Piero's best-known adherents into the government palace and protected them: Bernardo del Nero, Niccolò Ridolfi, and Pierfilippo Pandolfini – although Pandolfini, it was reported, had repeatedly sworn that any man who spoke out against Piero would have his tongue forced up his arse. Another hunted Medicean, *Messer* Agnolo Niccolini, one of the six ambassadors dispatched to King Charles, seeing that the game was up for Piero, fled north into Lombardy, fearing for his life.

Over the next few days, the Signoria's split with Piero and with sixty years of Medici *prepotenza* (domineering arrogance) was turned into a gulf by a series of other acts and changes. Citizens watched the removal of famous sets of defamatory murals, some with a fret of scurrilous rhymes, painted on the Palace of the Podestà (the Bargello) and on one side of the government *palazzo* – murals that were respectively sixteen and nearly sixty years old, assailing and ridiculing not only the Pazzi-Conspiracy 'traitors' of 1478, but also the foremost opponents of the Medici back in 1434. These images had never ceased to trouble and offend the families in question, many of whom were still in exile or shorn of political rights, while their children were often unable to marry their own social kind. Now full pardons were extended to them all: they were invited back from exile, or restored to their political rights. Within days of the announced pardons, members of some of these families began to return, bearing illustrious old names: Pazzi, Peruzzi, Barbadori, Strozzi, Acciaiuoli, Lamberteschi, Guasconi, and others. There must have been scenes of weeping and great emotion.

To purge the government of its Medicean parts, the *Signori* and their advisers began by suspending two councils: (a) the *Otto di Pratica*, very active in the conduct of foreign affairs, and fully dominated by Piero and his father before him; and (b) the celebrated Council of Seventy, which Lorenzo the Magnificent had established as the prime tool for undermining the city's traditional legislative councils, for keeping the Signoria under a tighter supervision, and for holding the nobility in line. The Seventy included Lorenzo's most trusted cronies – senators, in effect, who sat in the Seventy for life.

Yet all the while the pace of fears and anxieties accelerated. On 9 or 10 November, French troops started to enter the city, and Florentines were preparing themselves for the arrival of King Charles, for a flood of soldiers, and for dangerous negotiation with their royal guest. The new and reformed rulers of Florence – noblemen and others who had been slighted by the old regime – had resolved that the tyranny of the Medici was a thing of the past; but they also knew that Piero had thrown himself into the King's arms in order to save his own neck, and that the King would now importune the Signoria to take Piero back into the city. Worse still, Florence's most important colony, Pisa, had rebelled, and in the years to come would seem lost for ever.

One of the most keen-eyed of contemporaries, Guicciardini, observed that the Medici had been overthrown by *Messer* Luca Corsini and Jacopo de' Nerli, 'young men without credit, without authority, without [political] experience, and of no weight'. Very well, they were the ones who seem to have sparked off the revolt, but behind these alleged lightweights was the fury of a city, appalled by Piero's frivolity, his disdaining of good men, lack of leadership, and craven eagerness to save his own skin at the expense of Florence – that is, by readily giving up two seaports, two key fortresses, and 200,000 gold florins! About this, indeed, Guicciardini had an even more resounding observation: those cities and fortresses 'had given us a sense of power, security, authority, and honourable estate'. And now all this was gone. He goes on to ask the question often put, he claims, by his fellow citizens. Which was greater, the loss of Pisa or the sudden recovery of republican liberty? Putting 'aside many arguments', he simply replies that 'we cannot be said to have "empire" over others if we have no liberty in ourselves'.

But there was more to the restoration of 'liberty' – more inner tumult – than met the eye. For the tearing up of Medicean government also frightened dozens of old families, the compromised houses, putting them with their backs to the wall. Citizens went on crying out for 'justice' (condign revenge); and for the next four or five months, the big colluders worried anxiously about possible arrests, fines, exile, the loss of political rights, or even physical assault in the streets of the city.

In this great and contentious question, whether to punish or pardon those who had most profited from the Medicean regime, Savonarola was to play the leading part. Here, however, there is a different matter to consider first: the tearing up of webs or networks of patronage, caused by the overthrow of Medicean government.

Political patronage under the Medici reached into the civil law courts, the arrest and release of accused criminals, the assignment of personal taxes, the fixing of ambitious marriages, the obtaining of Church benefices, and, above all, election or appointment to public office. It may be taken as axiomatic that high office in Florence made the man, because the honour meant that he enjoyed the approval of the top oligarchs in the city, that he had the ears of judges and tax commissioners, that his sons and daughters would be warmly looked to as possible marriage partners, that he could more easily obtain credit or borrow money, that he himself would carry weight behind the scenes, and that he therefore ranked as an influential patron. Tear up the political system, as happened in late 1494, and you disrupt all the ties that linked patrons and dependants, with consequent moral and psychological confusion, anxiety, and the readiness to turn coats, to accommodate, to be silent, or to watch and wait. Confusion? Suffice it to say that in the late afternoon of 9 November, Bernardo del Nero and Niccolò Ridolfi tried to pass themselves off as republicans by shouting 'People and Liberty' in the government piazza! But they were well-known former collaborators of Lorenzo the Magnificent and were at once thrown back.

In the years leading up to 1494, the centres of the most powerful webs of patronage – the Medici apart – were in the Tornabuoni, Soderini, Ridolfi, and cadet Medici houses, followed by the likes of the Salviati, Capponi, Corsini, Pandolfini, Nerli, Guicciardini, and Martelli. Suddenly, with the flight of Piero and the dismembering of his regime, the political heads of these houses had to draw back and reconsider the political landscape. The question of what to do about the unfortunate Piero loomed nearest. Next came the matter of relations among the designated families and between them and others. Who now were our enemies, and who our friends? What new ties should we be looking for? If the Medici are gone for good, what kind of a regime do we want or can we handle, and must we also satisfy the stirred-up 'people' (il popolo), or at any rate keep them in a state of reasonable obedience? Much of the work that would be needed to content lesser men lay in the resources of patronage, in the ability to dole out favour; and the importance of this was in the fact that the big families, in the quest for office, would need the votes of modest citizens in the republican councils.

These questions continued to harry the great political families over the course of the next generation. Savonarola's impact on the Florentine political scene would complicate matters by introducing new alternatives, as well as by posing and pressing searching moral questions.

Enter the King

I T WAS LATE Monday afternoon, 17 November 1494, as fear snaked through Florence. King Charles VIII of France was about to march through its gated walls, but whether as friend or foe only God and the King knew, and perhaps not even the King, for the republic, as yet, had struck no agreement with him. Just three weeks before, spreading terror, his troops had brutally sacked Fivizzano, a walled-in burg in Florentine territory. And great Pisa, the star of Florence's territorial state, had rebelled with the King's tacit help and blessings. Now the republic was alone in facing the might of France. Its only likely friends, Pope Alexander VI and the new King of Naples, were racked with worries about their own security. Consequently, to demonstrate friendship and good will, although being all but held to ransom, the Florentines had seen to it that France's royal emblems, arranged under a crown, were displayed on banners in different parts of the city.

Charles was to be housed in the palace of the escaped (and now banished) Medici, lying only a minute or two north of the cathedral. The entire circle of surrounding houses had been commandeered for French troops, who would thus form a living fortress around the King. And throughout the city, as we have noted, many hundreds of houses, even some of the poorest, 'including all Camaldoli' (a wool workers' district), had been chalk-marked for occupation by soldiers. A diarist reports that the best rooms were turned over to them, along with beds, tables, and dishes. Many citizens had taken their most precious belongings into the countryside for concealment in farmhouses and trenches. And nearly all maidens 'of good family', as well as young wives, had been removed to convents, so that of the female sex, as one foreign envoy put it, only servants and old women were to be seen in the streets. There was no point in putting temptation in the way of men whom the Florentines, in their desire to see the King as a friend, wanted to like, but whom in their heart of hearts they feared and despised as 'barbarians'. That soldiery, said the eyewitness Cerretani, came 'from cold places that produce animal-like men with strange ugly languages'. They were mercenaries, 'Swiss, Gascons, Normans, Bretons, Scots, and [others] speaking still other languages . . . so that they didn't even understand each other'.

In a gathering darkness, at about 5:00 in the evening, Charles finally rode into the city, displaying exposed weapons, lance on hip and 'bare sword in hand' – a body language of conquest. He entered through the 'San Friano [Frediano]' Gate, on the far side of the river but close to it, at Florence's south-western wall. The Signoria, its two advisory councils, and all the city's outstanding citizens were at the gate to meet him, including a train of forty youths, selected from the richest and most eminent Florentine families, each of them on horseback and expensively attired in 'the French fashion', claimed a contemporary. Signoria and counsellors bowed to the King as he entered the gate. Celebratory constructions ('triumphs'), at two points along the way, gave evidence of the Florentine desire to please the arriving 'guests'. Once in the city, the King rode under a canopy held by the Signoria's advisers, and moved behind a long train, with the forty youths and prominent Florentines at the very front, followed by French courtiers and noblemen. They were followed – according to the diarists – by serried ranks of 7,000 Swiss infantrymen, marching 'with such discipline that only the sound of drums and pipes could be heard'. Behind these, again, came 700 richly armed men, their horses covered with armour of patterned velvet and brocade. Next came 500 mounted archers and another 1,000 on foot. Spearsmen, crossbowmen, long lancers, and cannoneers also filed past. The royal guard, 'men from Dalmatia and other strange places', who were 'much taller and thicker than the ordinary', carried great bows and quivers, or halberds 'and other kinds of weapons, no longer seen in Italy, all borne with striking fierceness'. Charles VIII of France moved in the midst of these, wearing a great beaked white hat, and 'followed by all the men of his council, including relatives of his, [great] lords'.

The King had entered in triumph. Of this there could be no doubt.

But though he was later to be seen mostly in black velvet, it could not be said that he was physically prepossessing. On the contrary, he was almost dwarf-like, with a large nose and a big mouth which often laughed, rather bulging blue eyes, hair colour between reddish and white, and a head that seemed too large for a body propelled by legs that were too skinny. But this King had a sense of humour, an eye for women, a sense of mission, and was certainly no fool, on top of which he was also surrounded by well-informed and shrewd advisers.

His route took him down two long narrow streets, San Friano and San Jacopo, lying just south of the river and running parallel to it. Every eye along the way must have been fixed on that stream of men that was as much a procession as an intimidating march. The flow was briefly broken near the foot of the Bridge of Santa Trinita, where a group of singers and musicians 'were sweetly singing the praises of the King with unheard of harmony'. Charles crossed the river at the Ponte Vecchio, continuing up and past the old headquarters of the guild of silk merchants, Por Santa Maria, and then turned to the right into a short street, Via Vacchereccia, leading directly into the government square. Here the invaders passed another grand construction (a 'triumph') and, 'after more singing, they got a show of fireworks, funny figures on stilts, walking giants, and much noise from the populace . . . all of which greatly delighted and pleased the King, his court, and the army. Trumpets, bells, fifes, and other sounds, the neighing of horses, and artillery pieces with their cannoneers all made the air and land tremble and resound.'

King and soldiers then crossed the great piazza to a long street running north to the cathedral, passing on their right the Palazzo of the Podestà (the Bargello) and the old enclave of Pazzi houses, where the Duke of Ferrara had once owned a small palace. Swinging around the back of the cathedral, the streaming parade reached the small square fronting it, the Piazza di San Giovanni; and there 'nearly all the Florentine people began to shout as with a single voice, "Francia! Francia!" which greatly pleased the King and his people'. Charles now dismounted and went into the great church, its nave illuminated by innumerable candelabra and richly decorated with hangings, banners, and fabrics of the most ornate. He made his way to the high altar, kneeled and prayed, as did all the other lords around him. Afterwards, moving on to the Medici Palace, he and his party rode up the Via de' Martelli (also Via Larga), which was decked out with tapestries and wide arrangements of patterned cloth. In a reprise of his menacing entry, armed guards now occupied the entrance to the palace, backed up by 'many arms and six pieces of artillery [mounted] on small carts'. Guards were also posted at the foot of the palace stairs and outside the King's bedchamber. All the houses, in a circular swathe around the palace, were taken over by royal troops, very likely the most trusted part of the King's forces.

The most civilised city in Christendom – as many then and since have believed – was occupied by an army that was nearly one-fifth the size of its population. Yet what that soldiery might do, and what the King and his counsellors really wanted, or thought they could extract, remained a mystery. Nor was a record set down of the fears and tensions gripping the city, as its inhabitants found themselves sharing their houses with a flood of foreigners armed to the teeth: an extraordinary subject – the charting of a charged mental and emotional time – that the histor- ian must abandon to novelists and to fiction.

Let us not be taken in by the sweet singing, the cries of 'France! France!', the 'triumphal' constructions and street decorations, and the spectacle put on in the government square. Florentines were striving to put the best possible face on things, while standing on the brink of a cataclysm; they were grinning and bearing it, resolute in their efforts to turn a charade into a temporary reality, so as to make their show all the more convincing. For they knew, given the size of the King's army, that they were facing their possible executioner, and so there was a wisdom rampant amongst them. The Florentine people of the late fifteenth century were already an old urban folk, with a vigorous municipal history that stretched back for about 350 years. They could boast of subtle merchants, lawyers, and financiers, of a clever literary elite, seasoned diplomats and astute politicians, as well as of superb accountants and record keepers, and some of the most skilful artisans in the world. Yet the moment also imposed a need for the solace of prayer and piety, and this need would last for years. Crisis had put the Florentines – it must have seemed – up against the face of destiny; with the result that most of them, standing, as it were, at the end of the Middle Ages, looked for their own and the city's salvation in God and in the rites of the

Church. Religion promised an ultimate security, and therefore nothing could have been more practical than for citizens to turn to it in the midst of danger, provided of course that piety was also combined with hard-headed diplomacy and even brinkmanship, as will be seen.

By picking up hints from the diarists (well-educated, upper-class men), but especially by drawing on our knowledge of the ways of Florentine government, of one thing we may be sure: the Signoria was holding continuous consultations, not only with their appointed counsellors but also with most of the city's best and most prominent political minds. Anxious debate and discussion focused on the question of how to deal with King Charles, how far to try to scale down his anticipated demands, and how to face up to his *volte face*, that is, his determined support for Piero de' Medici, who would now be pulling every string to keep the King on his side.

Two days before Charles's entry, the Signoria had summoned a council of 500 men, consisting of citizens who had previously served in (or qualified for) three of the city's highest offices. The purpose? To get their views regarding the King's expected demands. In response, again and again, the dominant feeling, as expressed to the Signoria, was one of 'hatred for the past regime of tyranny. And God was thanked for [our] repossessed liberty.' It was clear that most Florentines now despised Piero for having first held out so stubbornly against the King's previous but more modest requests, and then for his abrupt, pusillanimous surrender to all the man's exorbitant demands.

For the best part of a week, until about 22 November, apart from struggling to keep the peace between citizens and foreign soldiers, the government's primary task lay in resisting the King's repeated requests for the recall of Piero de' Medici. The *Signori* and their spokesmen kept thrusting their new-found liberty into Charles's face. Just a day after his arrival, accompanied by an entourage of 300 citizens, they had gone to visit him in the Medici Palace, to say that they saw him as the liberator 'of our city of Florence'. Three days later, a consultation in the government chambers, convened to discuss the King's plea for Piero, included three of Florence's principal churchmen: Guglielmo Capponi (Bishop of Cortona), Francesco Soderini (Bishop of Volterra), and Cosimo de' Pazzi (Bishop of Arezzo). The first man to address the assembled counsellors was Soderini, and he seems to have made a stirring speech, capturing much of the mood of the moment. He said something like 'hell no' to the King's request; we want our freedom; the King can have money, even lots of it, but not the return of Piero. We must be ready to fight and die, all of us, even sacrificing our families, to keep the Medici out and this city free.

Meanwhile, Piero's relatives and henchmen were working feverishly on the men around King Charles, and particularly on his advisers, urging them to insist that the banished leader be invited back to Florence – a dangerous prospect, opening the way to a possible bloodbath for the republic. The city continued to hold a Medicean constituency, made up of the men and families whose wealth and stature had been tied to their collaboration with the expanding tyranny, and some of them were certainly ready to take back the reins of power. Moreover, by the time of the King's entry into the city, the revolt against Piero had gone so far, so many changes had already been made, and men in government had spoken about the Medici with such brutal frankness, that he could only return to Florence at the price of blood. Sneers and derision must have greeted the fatuous letter that he sent to the Signoria from Bologna, in which he excused himself 'for having been forced to do what he did, considering that his friends had deserted him. However, he wanted only the liberty of the people, and this is what he had shouted in sending the Cardinal out to quiet things [in the government square]. Above all, it grieved him to be called a tyrant, since he had never aimed at anything like that.'

According to contemporaries, the clandestine meetings that went on with Medici loyalists and with the French, plotting the return of Piero, were handled by Piero's wife, the Roman noblewoman Alfonsina Orsini, working out of her convent refuge, and by one of his cousins, the fashionable, 'young, noble, and very rich Lorenzo di Giovanni Tornabuoni'. Parenti claims that Alfonsina and the other Medici women used money and jewels to suborn the King's courtiers, a perfectly credible charge, because such bribery, at the time, was customary practice. Foreign envoys, for example, were often provided with cash for the corruption of influential local men. The young Tornabuoni concentrated on the King's uncle, 'Monsignor di Bles [Philippe de Bresse]', who had been invited to stay in his house; and for this attempt to buy the Monsignor – something that came to be well known – 'many young men from the nobility . . . threatened to burn down his house [Tornabuoni's] and to cut him to pieces'. In their defence of Piero, he and Alfonsina and their accomplices argued that the exile (and runaway) had been 'unjustly' expelled from the city, that the allegation concerning his 'tyrannical' conduct should be examined, and that if it was found to be true, they would all go contentedly into exile. In short, let justice be done: let Piero be summoned back, and the King himself could then settle the differences.

As if, back in the city at last, and with King Charles as his patron, he would ever leave again! Once accomplished, Piero's return would have released a wave of revenge killings, mass exile, and the large-scale confiscation of 'rebel' property – houses, farmland, business assets, cash, credits, and government bonds (investment holdings in the public debt). Florence was a cauldron of fear, anger, and suspicion. Which is why Alfonsina and company had rushed word to Piero, urging him to hurry back to Florence, and to take cover under the long reach of the King. Parenti reports that on seeing the possibility of this, the Priors who still favoured Piero took hope, 'went cold over measures concerning liberty', and began to drag their feet. Fearing the outcome, the other Priors sent for their counsellors, the chiefs (Gonfaloniers) of the city's sixteen districts, and for a group of leading citizens who were dead set against Piero. All now pressured the recalcitrant *Signori* (Priors) to cooperate in the enacting of republican measures.

The fight for and against Piero, conducted under a variety of guises, would go on for the next four years and beyond the Friar's lifetime.

Enter the Friar

S AVONAROLA COULD NOW step up his stride. He was the head of a new congregation of convents; he was known in at least half a dozen other cities, including Genoa and Brescia, where he had given sermons. Thousands of people in the cathedral of Florence had been stirred by his preaching. He had addressed the Signoria; and he already had enemies among both the clergy and laity – strident testimony to his spreading influence. Attended by a reputation for holiness, he had been selected by the Signory at the outset of November to serve in a six-man embassy to King Charles – the six who in effect had pushed the bungling Piero to one side and taken the negotiations fully in hand. In a moment of extraordinary theatricality, they actually passed him on the road to Pisa, but neither he nor they had uttered a word of recognition.

The city's thickening religious atmosphere was attracting more and more Florentines to the Friar, who seemed to ride above daily ignorance and to know more than anyone about the swirl of events, owing – it was rumoured – to a unique connection with God. Already in their first dealings with Charles, on 9 November in Pisa, the ambassadors found that the Crown of France preferred to treat with Savonarola and excluded the five others from at least one round of the negotiations. The King knew that the monk was the bearer of special tidings.

Savonarola told the King that he, Charles, had come to Italy as a servant of God: 'your coming has lightened our hearts' and 'exhilarated our minds', so 'pass on securely and triumphantly, inasmuch as He sends you'. Such missions, however, entail responsibilities. Therefore, 'most Christian King, listen carefully to my words and bind them to your heart', for he (the Friar) spoke as one to whom things had been revealed. He admonished the King to be merciful, especially with Florence, where God has many servants, despite its sins. The warning continued: guard and defend 'the innocents' – widows, orphans, the wretched – and 'above all the chastity of the women's convents'. If Florentines had offended his majesty, he should forgive them, because they had done so out of ignorance, 'not knowing that you were sent by God'. He possibly added: 'God elected you . . . in the interests of his Church', so that while 'you are the happiest of kings', you must obey the Lord and go south to Naples 'as soon as possible'.

What the King himself made of this episode went unrecorded. No doubt he was intrigued and flattered. We know only that he responded with mollifying words and promises. Thereafter, however, he had to be reminded of his promises time and time again. His sense of self-interest had not been spirited away.

In his representations to the King, Savonarola was broaching the dramatic themes of his recent preaching in Florence: namely, that a punishing scourge would come to Italy to castigate the peninsula and Rome for their vices, and that the King was that scourge, hence the whip and servant of God. But there were also wondrous ironies in these claims, particularly for Florence. For if the King was the instrument of God's just punishment, how much punishment would follow? Should one obstruct the King, or not get in his way? And how relieved, unhappy, or terrified should Florentines be, now that Charles had seized Florence's seaports, plus two of its most strategic sites, and was about to occupy their city? Savonarola saw all the slippery features of the picture he had drawn, and therefore was already warning the King to hold his hand, to show mercy to Florence, to get out of Tuscany as soon as possible, and to lead his punishing army into southern Italy.

Later, in his *Compendio di rivelazioni*, the Friar would tell Florentines and the world what he had said to Charles. The fact that he was on the side of the scourger, the King, because it was God's side, may have served to mitigate some part of the fear in Florence. Yet all the slippery elements remained, indeed multiplied, after Charles marched into the city and he and his army settled in for eleven days. The nights at once led to a surge of robberies, and there were fights, woundings, or killings nearly every day in quarrels between soldiers and citizens. In this inflammable setting, two major incidents drew the city toward the brink of disaster.

On 21 November, the consultation capped by the presence of the three Florentine bishops was interrupted by a fierce commotion at the palace doors, set off by two Frenchmen who were determined to break into the proceedings and who had been bribed – it was whispered – by Lorenzo Tornabuoni. The fracas spread alarm; soldiers made for their weapons; on the far side of the Arno, mounted citizens seized control of the bridges; and the King's infantry around the Medici Palace readied themselves for action. 'But divine providence', observes Parenti, 'allowed things to go no further – our government palace sent out no signals [for citizens] to take up arms.' In the meantime, moved by emotion and kneeling before the Signoria, the large assembly of counsellors in the palace suddenly resolved that they would prefer to die rather than to sacrifice the republic and liberty by admitting Piero back into Florence. With the three prelates and Savonarola as their spokesmen, all then went to the Medici Palace to inform the King of their resolution. Charles at last agreed not even to speak of Piero for the next four months.

That very day, the Signoria decided to stock the palace with bread, wine, and arms, and to dispatch skilled agents out into the Florentine dominion to raise an infantry of 30,000 men, who would then be marched to the walls of Florence. In addition, rich citizens were encouraged to keep armed men in their houses, and to come running to the government square at the sound of the tocsin.

On 24 November, a second incident in the Borgo Ognissanti, a long street just north of the river and leading to the Prato Gate, was more serious still, especially if we bear in mind that all the city gates were in the hands of the French. A few Florentine prisoners in French hands, unable to pay their release fines, were being threatened with death as they were led along the Borgo. They were crying and begging for alms, with a view to buying their release from the French, who had arrested them in the neighbouring Lunigiana mountains. Stirred up, it seems, by a crowd of children shouting for their release, Florentine noblemen stepped in and forcibly freed the prisoners. Now, the clamour spreading, men everywhere began to arm themselves. Soldiers hurried to the Medici Palace, and Florentines rushed to the government square. Moving from Porta Prato, their banners held aloft, 500 Swiss infantry tried to enter the Borgo Ognissanti. 'At the entrance to the Borgo, the inhabitants – most of the action being carried out by women – repelled the Swiss by hurling missiles down from their windows and killing a few. They threw chests, bedsteads, ashes, boiling water, stones, roof tiles, and other objects. It was all seen to be a spirited defence, and fear was noticed among the French [sic] . . . since most of them were trembling like women. The tumult was [quickly] brought to a halt by the fear on both sides.'

Spurred on by this bloody encounter, the Signoria sent another embassy to the King, pressing him yet once more for an agreement, and 'after a good deal of dispute', the parties finally reached one. However, on rereading the articles of the draft, the King got up and with menacing words declared that he was not pleased. Now, in an alleged (and celebrated) exchange, one of the ambassadors, Piero di Gino Capponi, 'offended by the ugly words that had been uttered by French lords, tore the agreement up into a hundred pieces and said, "Most Christian prince, we shall sound our bells and you your trumpets and we will show you our armed populace."' He then turned his back to the King and walked out toward the palace staircase, followed by the other ambassadors. At this point, it seems, surprised by Capponi's spirit and 'fearing the infinite multitude of people that the city's great bell could assemble', the King and his counsellors called back the departing Florentines and confirmed the agreement. A day or two later, on 26 November, meeting in the cathedral, the two sides took an oath to the agreement, the King 'swearing personally to its articles at the sacred stone of the high altar'.

Apart from the usual stipulations, such as that the King and Florence were to have the same friends and enemies, the bedrock points of the treaty required (a) that the republic pay 120,000 florins to the King, only 50,000 of which at once, and (b) that Charles return Pisa, Livorno, Pietrasanta, and Sarzana to Florence, once he had completed his conquest of the kingdom of Naples. In short, there was a French climbdown from the sum originally agreed to by Piero de' Medici (200,000 florins). Furthermore, nothing in the treaty met the early demands of the King's counsellors, who had proposed to turn Florence into a kind of colony by insisting that the city have a royal agent or viceroy who would be privy to all government affairs. This demand had stunned and outraged Florentine political leaders.

Guicciardini and all the diarists agree on the exchange between the King and Piero Capponi. But even if the scene was dressed up a bit by patriotic Florentine writers caught up in their own myths, there was a revelatory note in whatever took place during the confrontation. The French, after all, had entered the city as conquerors; most contemporaries believed that their aim was to sack it; and in the days preceding their arrival, a profound dread had passed through Florence, which must have swelled on the day itself, as inhabitants witnessed the marching display of armed might. No such army had ever been seen inside the walls of late-medieval or Renaissance Florence.

But over the course of the next few days something diminished the fear of the Florentines, and the chief cause had a great deal to do with numbers.

Charles entered Italy with an actual fighting force of about 28,000 men, not counting all sorts of non-combatant servants, helpers, grooms, cooks, and hangers-on, who jacked the total up to well over 30,000. On route, however, he divided his army and went into Tuscany with only about 10,800 fighters, though it is highly doubtful – owing to his needs in the field – that all of these actually entered Florence. One of the keenest observers of the day, Cerretani, claimed that royal forces in the city reached a total of 18,000 men – more than a third of Florence's walled-in population. Landucci, the best-known diarist, put the frightening figure at 20,000 men. These overestimates were obviously caused by the awe and fear in the observations of native witnesses. The city's housing resources could not easily have handled such a sudden leap in population. More tellingly, the sums of the other major diarist, Parenti, totalled about 9,000 'men at arms'. And the King himself, in a letter to his cousin, the Duke of Bourbon, reported that he entered Florence with 9,500 fighting men, and 'a large number of mercenaries and other men'. The smaller figures, Parenti's and the King's, were closer to the true mark, something in the range of 10,000 soldiers or a little more – an awesome number still, in adding up to nearly one-fifth of the Florentine population, estimated at not quite 50,000 people.

Yet the French garrison was not large enough to control gates, bridges, and streets, or to monitor secret meetings, arms caches in houses, and the movement of Florentine arms or foodstuffs. What is more, thanks to knowing the streets and ways of the city, and having no choice but to defend themselves if the need arose, the people of Florence, in any encounter, were going to be more resolved and even more ruthless than their invaders. And so citizens began to take heart, in a continuing study of the topography of things, and in gradually realising that the King and his noblemen could not afford a wholesale massacre, ending in the killing, as well, of thousands of soldiers, officers, and perhaps even the King himself. So it was true, the invaders feared the hammering of Florence's great bell.

An indicator of the city's shifting mood was in the details of a lunch planned for 24 November. The King had asked to lunch with the Signoria for a second time, but imposed the condition that the Priors be without arms. Greatly surprised by his suspicions, they agreed to the terms and allowed all their weapons to be passed out of the palace through the main doors, only to have them smuggled back through the windows of the Dogana, the customs part of the palace, which occupied its north-eastern wing. In the end, possibly somewhat fearful, the King cancelled the lunch.

Since Charles's counsellors were urging him to get on with his march to Rome and the seizure of Naples, once the agreement with Florence had been reached and the ceremonies in the cathedral had clinched it, the King himself was eager to get away. Two days later, on 28 November, Charles and his army marched out of Florence, to the infinite relief of its people. Many Piagnoni were to say that the city had been saved by the grace of God and Savonarola's conversations with the King.

The Friar, meanwhile, had made an early start on his Advent sermons, which commenced in the cathedral on Saturday, 1 November. He selected for his themes and point of departure the little Book of the prophet Haggai in the Old Testament, and, preaching right through November, he was thundering out his sermons as Florentines rubbed shoulders with foreign soldiers. Looking back, in the summer of 1495, to the first three sermons of this cycle, he claimed that he had nearly fallen ill from the fervour of his crying out for Florentines to repent, to fast, and to pray. Their scourge, the King of France, was coming.

Savonarola's central metaphor in the Haggai series is the image of the Ark, the boat of true repentence and salvation, to be launched against the surrounding flood of tribulation. He invites Florentines to board it, although the time is late and the doors are about to shut. The unfolding message is directed at the internal, spiritual condition of sinners, so we get almost no concrete sense of what is happening in the world around, despite references to war and flagellations. There was already far too frightening a reality in the surrounding political and military tumult, and any direct reference would have forced him to step into the real mael-strom and to pin himself down. He had good reasons to keep only to worldly generalities and spiritual themes, for he now saw himself as a prophet in the biblical sense, as one who – in voicing the wishes of God – could look into the future and foretell it in general terms.

He addresses Florence, Rome, and all Italy, and declares that the time has come for them to be punished for their sins. But he is harshest of all with the clergy. Their 'unbridled vices' and sins are the main reason for the coming tempest. Next he skewers great lords, rich men and usurers, the learned men who rely purely on natural reason, and not least 'the tepid' – the people entranced by the externalities or ceremonies of religion, but who are neither hot nor cold in their faith. And both directly and indirectly he keeps presenting himself as a prophet. He reminds his listeners that he predicted the coming of the divine sword of punishment less than two years ago. 'Not I but God made it known to you.' And again, 'God has given me as father and mother to you in this time of weeping', and you, Florence, 'have been made a participant through me, by the will of God, in the secrets of God and in future things'.

In his fourth sermon, delivered on about 11 November, after Piero de' Medici had fled from the city and a free republic seemed to be bounding back, the Friar made a glancing reference to the 'revolution'. This regime-change had promised to be bloody, but the Lord restrained himself in mercy. No blood had been shed. 'So thank God, Florence', and we 'shall see whether or not things are going to be this way in the other cities of Italy' – that is, with King Charles and his punishing army on the move. The fifth sermon, delivered on Sunday, 16 November, a day before the King entered the city, also touched on the present scene by 'urging every man to keep his place' and to 'be content with his station'. The point of this recommendation was political, as he makes clear: 'Lots of men would like to help administer the state, but cannot do so because they do not have the aptitude.' 'In the other [Medicean] regime . . . many could and wanted to help administer the state, although they did not belong there, and these also were not in their proper place.'

Political arrangements in Florence had suddenly opened up, and there was a gush of talk about office-holding, about men being eligible for service in public life, and about political inequities and qualified ancestors. Citizens were pressing forward in the councils, as well as in private, angling to make themselves eligible for high office in the coming months. The Friar, therefore, was seeking to make a moral statement about the whole question; and he may even himself have been approached by certain citizens, with the idea of getting him to drop a few favourable words for them in the right quarters. He was to be repelled by this, but could not always stand above that part of the mêlée.

As he was driven (and partly chose) to exercise more and more political influence, his sermons increasingly broached some of the more contentious questions of the day. But he could also dodge solicitations, sidestep challenges, protest, or rise above 'lower' interests to abstract principles, in the effort to maintain his integrity and spirituality. Such efforts were not always successful, nor were his intentions always clear and disinterested.

CHAPTER SIX

Holy Liberty

Creative Florence, artistic and literary, was all politics at the moment, or so it seemed. A few painters went on producing images of madonnas, saints, the holy family, and crucifixions – the ruling themes of Italian (and Florentine) Renaissance art, but there was a marked decline in artistic commissions. It is likely that Filippino Lippi and Sandro Botticelli gravitated toward the ranks of the Piagnoni. Michelangelo himself was won over by the Friar's haunting voice. But another great Florentine master, Leonardo da Vinci, was not even in Florence. He had departed years before. Lorenzo the Magnificent, for all his cultural élan and touted patronage, had done nothing to keep him in Tuscany. Now one of the stars in Ludovico Sforza's train of servitors, Leonardo was at the court of Milan, taken up with designing decorations for masques and courtly theatricals. More importantly, he was also working on models, in drawing as in wax, for a gigantic equestrian statue of Ludovico's father, Francesco, the great soldier of fortune and founder of the Sforza dynasty. Although meant to be cast in bronze, nothing was to come of this commission in the wake of the French invasions and Ludovico's calamitous fall from power in 1499. Leonardo then returned briefly to Florence, found little enough to engage his ambitions there, and soon moved on to other princely courts, beginning with the entourage of Pope Alexander's son, Caesar Borgia.

Ferment: the Great Council

In the weeks after Piero de' Medici's flight and exile from the city, Florentines struggled with conflicting hopes and passions. Families and individuals who had been close to the Medici lived in fear of revenge and reprisals. Ardent young republicans, and old oligarchs gliding over to the republican cause, looked for a new dawn. The desire for vengeance spurred men who had been punitively taxed, kept out of office, bypassed by jumped-up minions, or been made the victims of suborned judges. Mediceans hated the leaders who had tumbled Piero. And resentful exiles hurried or drifted back to Florence, seeking again their place in the sun. Ideas about how to shape and direct the new regime flowed with ease, and into this flow came the input of the Friar's vision.

After the King and his troops departed, Florentines faced the anxious question: now that they had reclaimed their liberty, what kind of a government should they have? What type of men, class or classes of men, ought to qualify for the offices at the head of state? An early Florentine nobility, with lineages stretching back to the eleventh and early twelfth centuries, had been destroyed or incapacitated by civil wars and the triumph of commerce. But over the course of the fifteenth century, Florence had given rise to the sense that the city had a class of political noblemen: a stratum of families whose antiquity of wealth, political eminence, honours, and lofty marriages or kinship ties, lifted them above all the other families. They were a mercantile and banking nobility, whose defining self-awareness was completed by a penchant for leadership and prominence in high public office. There was nothing of horsemanship, war, or feudal courts about them; and any ancient blood in their veins was a ghostly substance.

Regarding themselves as the natural and deserving leaders, they pushed forward in November 1494 to claim authority and pre-eminence. Their view of government and of their role in it was in keeping with a general European situation: with the fact that Italian and other states were ruled mainly by princes, noblemen, or burgher oligarchies. Most of the new republic's dealings abroad would be with princes and aristocrats, and these gentlemen shared a common language of ceremonial gesture and pragmatic politics. Diplomacy was in the hands of seasoned men, ambassadors and secretaries, some of whom were well-trained in Roman law or schooled in the classics. And it was necessary for Florentine statesmen – the oligarchs reasoned – to be at home in the midst of this. They must also, therefore, stand at the forefront of government and domestic politics. The trouble was that sixty years of Medicean rule had given political experience to the collaborators of the Medici, not to the men who had been excluded. Hence, in 1494–1495, the ex-collaborators were the most experienced, the best connected, the most informed; and now, suddenly, they were being looked at with a jaundiced and vengeful eye, particularly the most prominent of them.

Unhappily for the magnates, moreover, they had no unity of political purpose, no sufficient solidarity, because the Medici and their cronies had broken up pre-existing cohesions by favouring some families and not others, by hounding those assumed to be opponents, and by raising new men to top office, thereby turning them into clients and dependants. Consequently, the men from the most distinguished houses now broke up into at least four loose groupings: (1) secret or silent supporters of Piero, (2) haters of the Medici, (3) backers of the emerging (Savonarolan) republic, and (4) those who took a more floating, wait-and-see line. A shadowy clique of prominent patricians even looked to the cadet line of the Medici, to the brothers Giovanni and Lorenzo di Pierfrancesco de' Medici, as possible leaders in an alliance with Ludovico Sforza and Milan. Despite their common class interests, accordingly, the men in the different groupings often failed to cooperate even within the group: and they were riven, in any case, by personal animosities. For them, at least, little Florence was a face-to-face society. They all knew one another by name or face, either from having frequently met in government councils, at receptions for foreign dignitaries, and on embassies, or in the great square of the Signoria and at wedding parties, not to mention meetings in marketplaces or through business dealings.

It only remains to add that the ensuing political struggle was more than a mere contest for an abstraction – power. Taxes, offices with solid incomes, war and foreign policy, the business of the law courts, the shape and content of future legislation, and a citizen's place or concrete identity (achieved through politics) in the world of Florence: all these were on the line.

Over and above the fall of the Medici, November 1494 brought the collapse of webs of privilege and patronage. A sense of strain and distress cut through Florence, aggravated by the sudden hopes of the republican rebels. No group or individual was able to give a direction to events, certainly not the sprinkling of men from the magnate class — Luca Corsini, Jacopo de' Nerli, Piero Capponi, and others — who had put themselves in the front line of the push to topple Piero de' Medici.

In less than forty-eight hours after Piero's departure, three strategic councils, set up to serve the Medici, were put out of action. These changes were not a mere thumbing of the nose at Piero; they were the first dramatic moves in the dismantling of the structure of Medicean government. On that day too, 11 November, an important group of exiles was invited back to the city, and duties on incoming foodstuffs were lightened. At about the same time, two other commanding magistracies were barred from meeting, the War-Office Ten and the political police (the Eight), because they were assumed to be stacked with men too loyal to Piero.

A revolution was unfolding: the Signoria (nine men) and their two advisory councils (the Sixteen and Twelve), thirty-seven men in all, acting as the city's supreme ruling body, had snatched back the dispersed power of the executive cluster of offices and were doing all the governing. It was a daring performance, but fully in line, in a crisis, with Florence's constitutional laws. The thirty-seven men were also consulting closely with select groups of citizens, patricians as well as men of a more middling sort. Hence every day, and almost every hour, they must have had the sense that what they were doing was right, that it was what most of the city wanted, and that in any emergency they would have the bulk of citizens behind them in armed support. This too had given them the courage to stand up to King Charles, to bring pieces of artillery into their turreted palace, and even, on 20 November, to carry out an in-your-face gesture against the King by declaring Piero de' Medici a rebel, in addition to offering a reward of 2,000 large florins for his capture.

All the while political passions were waiting for the more reasoned, long-term assault on the Medici establishment, and this came soon after the departure of the King and his troops. A major all-day consultation took place on 30 November, the details of which were not recorded or archived. They decided to summon a Parlamento in two days' time. This meant a mass meeting in the government square of at least two-thirds of the number of fully-fledged citizens, who would be expected to shout out their approval of the changes to be made by the new government.

A kind of plebiscite, the measure seems to have been recommended by five magnates: Tanai de' Nerli, Piero Capponi, Francesco Valori, Bernardo Rucellai, and (from the cadet line) Lorenzo di Pierfrancesco de' Medici. All, except the last (curiously), were associated with the Medicean regime, and Rucellai was linked to Piero by marriage. But even if they were regarded with suspicion, their knowing ways and experience of politics were such that their voices could not be dismissed; and in the present case, a Parlamento was the best route to take, because its constitutional weight would mark a major break with the past.

When the great bell was rung for the late-afternoon assembly of 2 December, citizens poured into the government square. It was patrolled by armed guardsmen. Facing the populace, one of the chief secretaries of the Signoria read out the intended government changes, and the crowd was then invited to roar back its approval. Although seemingly dry and legalistic, the approved measures were packed with teeth. The chief changes may be pared down to four: (1) all existing laws in opposition to the changes about to be made were declared null and void; (2) the legislative and executive councils established by the Medici regime were abolished; (3) all political exiles and their descendants, in a line reaching back to 1434, were recalled; and (4) there was to be a new commission of electors (*Accoppiatori*), the Twenty, to serve for one year but with a renewable mandate. The job of this commission was to pick or elect each Signoria over the course of the coming year, to have a hand in electing other top officials, and, more sweepingly, to help reshape Florentine public authority.

The complexities of government in Florence were such that many citizens, we may be sure, did not understand all that was taking place in the great square that evening. A group of magnates, however, came away reasonably contented. By a secret arrangement with the *Signori* and their twenty-eight counsellors, they were quickly elected to the commission of Twenty and no doubt hoped to dominate it. The assumption must be that deals had been made, pivoting mainly on the promise of future office for the Priors of the current Signoria and for their advisers.

Let's put our analysis this way: with their new ambitions and freedom, the *popolo* – the middle class of citizens who qualified for public office – was threatening the authority of the nobility, and so a group of magnates was able to convince the government to rein in the rush of change. The consequence of this fix did not escape certain eyes, and within days a party of seven or eight men went to the Signoria to protest, claiming that the new changes were not being conducted along 'popular' lines, and that the 'cupidity' of ambition was what had lodged so much authority in twenty men. Parenti observes that 'the protesting citizens were not heard. On the contrary, frightened and stunned by [an outburst of] threatening words, they came close to being removed [bodily] from the Palace.'

Yet the great and contentious question remained: was Florence simply to return to its pre-Medicean (pre-1434) structure of offices, or was there a new direction to be taken? The next three weeks were charged with debate, as the government prepared to answer the question with new legislation. First, however, it became clear that Florentines were determined – with Savonarola's outspoken support – to have a great council in which all men with political rights should sit for life. This would be Florence's ultimate governing body, the one which, in the last analysis, would hold all sovereign power. The best living example of such a body – and it was often referred to by contemporaries – was the Grand Council of Venice, which held all of that great seaport's aristocrats above a certain age. But the equivalent council in Florence would be different: it was to include large numbers of relatively modest men as well – merchants and little landowners, shopkeepers, prosperous craftsmen, small-time attorneys, and even a smattering of shame-faced poor, that is, men from families once rich or eminent but now fallen and humble. Once again, therefore, despite the new commission of Twenty, magnates and some noblemen saw themselves challenged. The fall of the Medici had released the political ambitions of the *popolo*, and the popular thrust was now too strong to be turned back by the oligarchs, who did not dare openly declare that what they really wanted was an aristocratic state run by themselves. For the encircling political debate was so keen, so acrimonious really, that Manfredo de' Manfredi, Ferrara's ambassador in Florence, writing on 20 December, noted that more armed men and weapons had been taken into the government palace, and that private parties had also armed themselves, in some cases, apparently, even recruiting armed supporters.

If this seems surprising, we need only remember that a government had recently been overturned; houses had been attacked and torched; an invading army had marched through the streets of Florence; the city was stocked with weapons; noblemen themselves were bitterly divided, and many citizens – as the Friar constantly reminded them – were crying out for revenge against the big Medicean collaborators.

Plans for the reform of the government finally came to a head on 22–23 December, in two days of intense legislating. With overwhelming majority votes, the old councils of 'the people' and 'commune' established a new Great Council, for which, in time, the whole of the city's eligible office-holders would qualify, more than 3,500 citizens. If we set this figure up against the total sum of Florentine males aged thirty or more – say about 7,000 or 8,000 men in a population that fell short of 50,000 people – then we find that the new council was going to include nearly half of all men thirty years of age and older, an astonishing number for the Europe of that day, and hence smacking decidedly of something democratic.

The Great Council would be the foundation of Florentine government for nearly the next eighteen years, until the autumn of 1512, when an armed *coup d'état* overthrew the new republic and returned the Medici to power.

The laws of December, 1494, put elections to all major offices in the hands of the Great Council, and the same institution now became Florence's only true legislature. Moreover, to make the Council an efficient body, it was divided into three equal parts; each part served for six months and then left office, to be succeeded by a new group of Great Councillors. Two-thirds of the group in office constituted a quorum; and the approval of bills required a simple majority vote, fifty per cent plus one. However, having taken soundings and advice, only the Priors of the Signoria could convoke the Council, and they alone introduced proposed legislative measures.

The creation of the Great Council underlines the angry discontent with the Medicean regime. It marked a middle-class resolution to hold ultimate power against the pretensions of magnates and aspiring aristocrats, despite the fact that they – the men of a middling sort – were ready to work with aristocrats, or to accept them as leaders, while remaining suspicious of their ambitions. In any case, to work with the ambitious men of the most eminent houses was practical politics, for the simple reason that they were always going to be there: skilful, educated, determined, knowledgeable, insistent, manoeuvring, and often able to pull on vital contacts abroad, in the worlds of diplomacy and business.

Distinction might belong to a surname such as Strozzi, Alberti, Albizzi, and Capponi, but not necessarily wealth. Some houses, their influence vanished, were distinguished in name alone. Many of Florence's illustrious families had poorer, modest branches, ever more distantly related to the leading one; and while their men might be eligible for the most-coveted offices, they rarely if ever attained them. In practical terms, such men truly belonged to the *popolo*. They could therefore easily move and vote with men from the middle sectors; and they were doubtless a strong force in the enthusiasm for the Great Council. Like small shopkeepers or well-off craftsmen, they gave their votes to magnates and lesser noblemen, but they were not cut from the same 'noble' cloth. They were not monied, not travelled, not educated in the classics, not brought up on talk about high politics, and not reared in big business circles or prosperous circumstances. Indeed, at the end of the fifteenth century, many young men from 'name' families were without a trade, minimally educated, and with little or no income, so that they were beginning, more frequently, to go into the Church and even into soldiering.

The Friar Speaks

A s THE CITY tossed about in political passion, Savonarola looked on with alarm and a vested interest. His vision of the future – as he was just starting to reveal – called for him to turn Florence into the spearhead of a spiritual awakening, so that the city could be the great door to the Church's universal renewal. Therefore government and politics had to be driven in that direction, and he had the courage – the 'madness' he sometimes said – to try to take it that way.

By the summer of 1494, his moral stature in Florence and the cadence of his words carried such authority that from the outset of November, when Florentine relations with Charles VIII reached a fever pitch, he was to have a part in every embassy to the King, including the ones conducted in Florence itself, after the entry of the French army on the 17th. There were moments, indeed, when the *Signori* and their counsellors seemed to think that Savonarola alone, that queerly intense and prodigious friar, had the power to prevent a horrendous sacking and to get the King and his troops out of Florence. For some time, most Florentines believed that his inspired words to the King had held back a massacre, that as a prophet sent by God he had managed to instil fear in Charles by reminding him of his role as a divine scourge. But the truth behind the French departure from the city, we have noted, was almost certainly another (unless God had a hand in that too), and it was linked to the insufficient size of the French garrison, to the imagined nightmare of a cataclysmic bloodbath, and to the remonstrances of royal advisers, who persuaded the King to save his troops and to get on with his real mission, the conquest of Naples.

Savonarola's Advent sermons, which began in November and ended on the Sunday after Christmas, were given to a people disoriented by political fears and hatreds. Nursed on a late-medieval religion for which miracles, wonders, absolute evil, and the deeds of angels and devils were real, thousands of Florentines were ready to believe in the Friar as prophet, and wanted to see him so, because he offered a gateway to salvation for Florence, as well as for the individual.

The impact and style of Savonarola's sermons must be saved for a later chapter. Here, standing closer to politics, we do best to concentrate on a select range of his ideas.

He always stressed the overwhelming importance of repentence for sin, for evil done. Hence he encouraged Florentines to confess and to take communion at least four times yearly, rather than once a year, at Easter, in accord with conventional practice. He could also make a complex doctrine seem simple, such as in asserting that 'the sum or gist of the Christian religion consists in the knowledge of God and of oneself'. This, in turn, came down to 'the love of God and hatred of [one's sinning and carnal] self'. In these sermons, as in all his preaching from this time on, there is a searing indictment of the unprincipled clergy (*Chierica*), whom he often holds responsible for the horrors of the oncoming 'tempest', the divine scourge. More specifically, the leaders of the Church and the rulers of states had set such appalling moral examples, were so steeped in vice, that they, more than anyone else, had corrupted the great mass of Christians. Salvation for them was going to be difficult. The consequent ties with politics were easily pointed out: Savonarola was ready to argue that the evil man is a servant to his sins, is not free, and so cannot be a good citizen and cannot properly serve his city.

Again and again the sermons link mercy to civic peace and unity. The Friar pleaded with Florentines to seek civil harmony, to forgive the collaborators of the Medici, and to show them mercy, just as God had been merciful to Florence by drawing the French army away and preventing a holocaust. Those who call out for justice in the matter want no justice, he tells them. They want vengeance, and they are giving voice to their hatred. If servants of the old regime pilfered money or goods from the Florentine commune, let them restore their thefts, of course, but let there be no use of torture, for the instruments of physical pain often force men to confess what is false.

One of his most repeated precepts is that men in public life should serve the common good, never their own particular interests. Precisely this is what had gone wrong with the Medicean oligarchs, in their selfish piloting of government. Renew yourselves on the inside, he cries out to the assembled throng on Sunday, 7 December, for Florence 'is the Lord's'. Therefore, he continues, make laws that will permit no one man to make himself boss or tyrant (*capo*) of the city.

On the following Sunday, 14 December, he preached almost exclusively on the topic of government and politics, and the cathedral was packed with high office-holders, including all the top officials in the state. Only the Gonfalonier of Justice and a single Prior remained back at the palace. And since the subject, politics, was the business of men in the universal assumptions of the day, women were not allowed to attend the sermon, especially as Savonarola also proposed to get into theoretical questions.

Moving quickly by way of St Thomas through Aristotle's view of the state, he notes that since man is a social animal, men necessarily congregate and hence need speech, rules, government, and leaders. He grants that the best form of government is the rule of one man, but only if he be a good man, and this of course is rare. He now broaches a pet theory, which he was to take a little further in his *Treatise on the Government of the City of Florence* (1498). In hot climates, he argues, men are more pusillanimous, have little blood, and so are more easily ruled by one man. In cold climates, men have a great deal of blood, but not much intellect or wit, and this allows others to subject them. 'But in the middle regions, such as Italy, where both blood and intellect abound, men do not readily put up with being under a single ruler. Instead, each man, so as not to be bossed about, would be the one who rules the others.' This was the condition that brought 'the rise of discord and dissension among the citizens of [Italian] cities, where individuals want to make themselves big and dominate others'. Consequently, the 'sacred doctors' of these parts have recommended that citizens choose a form of government in which groups of men are the rulers, 'and most of all' would this 'be suitable for the city of Florence, where blood and intellect greatly abound in the nature of men'. Such a state, however, must be well regulated, or it will generate extreme discord and break up into political 'sects' of the sort that struggle to banish one another from the city.

'O Florence,' he exclaims several times, 'I cannot tell you everything I feel in me. . . . above all because you would not believe me'. All the same, 'Don't consider me, this poor friar, an inept little man full of sins. God has wanted you to see and to try my ineptitude, so that you will the more clearly understand that it is He and not I who does things, and He who reveals doubtful and secret things to me.' The Friar reminds them that they would not believe him when he foretold the coming of the present tribulations, before there were any signs, but now they see that the troubles have started. 'Listen to what I have to say to you this morning . . . to that which God has inspired in me.' He then invites them to confess, to purge themselves, and 'attend all of you to the common good of the city. If you do this,' he goes on, Florence 'will be glorious . . . and become richer and mightier than it ever has been.' If not, God will favour the troublemakers, 'and this will be your final destruction'.

Conspicuously implicit in Savonarola's argument – and all his sermons *are* arguments – is the idea that a state is necessarily stronger when it is more spiritual, because spirit is more powerful than anything physical or sensual. Such a state, in addition, is more likely to enjoy God's grace. Hence the falsity of the vile Florentine proverb, possibly first uttered by the founder of the hated Medicean regime, Cosimo de' Medici: 'States are not governed by means of prayers and paternosters.' On the contrary, said the Friar, they should be, even if government also requires practical prudence. It follows that Florentines should demand more from their clergy; they should get ecclesiastical superiors, even the pope, to correct and discipline the army of wayward clerics. Looking to the moral betterment of the city, Savonarola then calls for a new law against the unspeakable vice of sodomy. 'Florence is infamous for this throughout Italy.' He wants the law to be 'without mercy', even to the point of having 'such persons stoned and burned'. Here was a judgment that reflected the spirit of the law codes of most Italian cities, which tended to stipulate the penalty of death for the second or third sodomy conviction, although, in fact, it was seldom imposed.

Turning to the grievous question of taxes, Savonarola holds that 'The men who govern a well-ordered city should see to it that taxes on property both in the city and outside it are justly levied, rather than left to the will of commissions (*per arbitrio*) . . . in order that men may busy themselves [get on with their trades] for the general good. Furthermore, care should be taken to see that taxes levied on property are rightly weighed, so that the tax is not greater than the income from the property. Similarly, the indirect taxes [on foods and services] should also be moderate. Let the public and private need each get its due share.' He closes this part of his sermon by passing over to the question of marriage dowries. Since they can be the ruin of families, he would put a ceiling of 500 ducats on dowries for girls from the upper classes and 300 for girls from the class of artisans and petty tradesmen.

Seeing his announced subject slipping away, even though his concern is the city as a whole, he gets back to politics by returning to one of his refrains. Above all, he intones, allow 'no man to make himself the head or dominating superior of others. Such men are without the grace of God and His special providence, and they are generally among the worst of men, void of intellect and faith . . . [They] have no true friendship with anyone; they trust no one, although human affairs require true and joyful friendship, which also helps to preserve virtue.' How do you keep tyrants out? 'I will tell you, as I have been inspired to do by God.'

He passes next to his most significant statement of the morning. With a glancing reference to the Parlamento of 2 December, he simply asserts, 'The form you have started with cannot stand, unless you organise it [your new republic] better.' In what is nearly a throw-away line, he then invites his assembly of politicians and office-holders to draw on the model of Venetian government, but to omit certain features, 'such as the office of Doge, which would not serve us'. He has no need to say that membership in Venice's Grand Council was hereditary; this was well known, and the equivalent in Florence could not be so, not, at least, in the same manner.

All of a sudden we realise that he is fully aware of the debate going on around him, regarding the virtues of a great council, an assembly that would hold all potential holders of public office. He does not elaborate and he need not, as this would lead him into a maze of particulars and make him seem too interfering. He is, after all, both an outsider and a priest, a man for eternity, not for the here-and-now windings of politics. Yet he cannot resist an additional observation, which is at once moral, social, and political. He wants to see modest men in that council: 'To encourage each man to behave more virtuously, I also believe that it would be a good thing for artisans to be privileged [made eligible for office] and tempted in some fashion to conduct themselves well, so that they can be honoured [by being elected to office]. It would also make sense to fill the major offices by election and the lesser ones by lot.'

Savonarola's sermon is so laconic and fleet here, as he urges his listeners to speed up their reforms, that he is necessarily taking many details for granted, knowing these to be in their minds. By 14 December then, in private as in public, Florentine talk about a great council had gone very far, and the Friar was already saying that this body, which would hold the power of all the Florentine people, hence its sovereignty, should have a democratic component and *not* be like its Venetian counterpart.

Not surprisingly, therefore, during the next two or three years, the Friar would be accused of striving to put power into the hands of Florentine 'plebeians'. This was a slander, but for princes and aristocrats abroad, the accusation was much like saying that Savonarola wanted Florence under the control of 'mob'; and Florentine noblemen, Arrabbiati, might themselves give voice to this mendacity, in order to stir up feeling against the Friar in Rome, Milan, and Venice.

He moves toward the end of his political sermon by returning to his plea for the pardon 'of all the old things', that is, the doings of the Mediceans, and he concludes by calling for the captains of the city's sixteen districts (*gonfaloni*) to hold consultations with local men, concerning the best form of government for the new republic. Here was yet another approach to the *popolo*. The sixteen Gonfaloniers were then to meet, to pick the four plans that they considered best, and 'to submit these to the Magnificent Signoria'. After hearing 'the sung Mass of the Holy Spirit', the *Signori* should finally 'select one of the four, and you can hold it for certain that the one thus chosen will be from God'. In a closing reference to the Great-Council idea, he adds: 'as I have said, the form of government of the Venetians is very good. Don't be ashamed to learn from others, because their constitution was also God-given.'

In the remaining sermons of the next two weeks, Savonarola returned repeatedly to his major themes – the common good, forgiveness, political renewal, repentance, the dark menace of aspiring tyrants, the grace of God, and indictment of the 'tepid'. At times he touches on these themes fleetingly, but more often he sustains points and adds new colour or particulars. To the objections raised by certain patricians, alleging that this was not the time to establish a new government, he replies that the change is God's will: 'your city is now the city of God and no longer the city of Florence'. The Lord wants Florence renewed because He means the renewal of the Church to begin here. Voicing a messianic vision of Christendom, Savonarola notes that the Church had passed through four different stages; a fifth is now commencing, opening the way for Florence to be the vanguard of renewal and a new Jerusalem. 'People [of Florence],' he ends this sermon of 15 December, 'I love you, and everything I do is for the good and redemption of your city.'

His sermons often carried personal claims: 'the will of God is that the city of Florence be ruled by the people (*popolo*) and not by tyrants. Let no man contradict this; and if what I have said is not true, I am ready to stand before God on the day of judgment, to render a good account.' In a still more personal vein, on the Sunday of Advent, 21 December, he reviews his whole career as a friar, doing so rather movingly. Again, it was a sermon for men only, and at certain moments he speaks directly to the Lord, as though no one else were present. 'Why have you made me a man of controversy and discord in the land?' And a minute or so later: 'Since I was born and reared in Ferrara, what have I to do with Florence?' The Lord replies that he had been called to preach there. 'But what business is it of mine to be preaching about the government of Florence?' God's answer is that Florence is to be a spiritual city, that the foundations must be laid, and that He has picked the Friar as His instrument, not in the least caring about how base or noble the instrument might be, for He is master here. Very well, comes Savonarola's reply, 'I am at your will.' A brief exchange follows, in which the Friar wants to know what awaits him, and suddenly there is a dramatic turn which must have startled his listeners.

Christ reminds him that he was crucified. ' "Thus will it be with you and not otherwise." "O Lord," I then replied, "give me this martyrdom, grant that I should die for you, as you did for me. I see the knife already sharpened for me." "Wait a bit", said the Lord. "Let those things be done that must be done, then draw on the fortitude to be given you by God." ' With his deep mystical bent and love of Christ, Savonarola had so closely identified with the Son – and this, after all, is what Christian theology called for at the time – that he had no trouble desiring a similar martyrdom.

So soon in his Florentine ministry, Savonarola had just foretold his own willing death, and many listeners, in wonder and admiration, now surely began to swing over to his side in sympathy.

His imagined conversation with God at an end, Savonarola turned to the throng in the cathedral: 'Now you have understood, Florence, that I see and know what my condition is.' Although not quite half way through this sermon, it is hard to see how he was able to carry on, having made such a spectacular announcement. He was, however, vastly resourceful as a preacher, so we must assume that a pause of some sort, as he waited for his words to sink in, soon enabled him to continue, and he then passed on again to his remaining themes.

The sermon of Saturday, 27 December, includes a sustained assault on the tepid, the believers whose true commitment was in their attachment to material superabundance and to external trappings. He argues that they have to be removed or eliminated, if the Church is to be renewed. Trappings, however, we may wish to remember, included the remarkable frescos in the family chapels of churches such as Santa Maria Novella, Santa Croce, Santa Trinita, and Santa Maria del Carmine. The love of externals had issued in something other than the merely pious. Savonarola's spirit would have reduced religious commissions for artists, yet it was certainly not the iconoclastic spirit of the great Protestant reformers of the sixteenth century.

The final sermon of the cycle, offered the following day, was more openly political. Injecting a bit of play-acting, as he does in so many of his sermons, and bordering on humour, Savonarola mimics some of his imagined critics: 'Must we all be friars and priests, we who have no wish to be tied so tightly?' The claim was that he meant to impose too harsh a regimen on Florentines — prayers, fasts, self-denial. 'Let's take the yoke off our backs which this friar now wants to strap on us!' Savonarola's reply to this mimicry is that the Lord will make fools of them and dole out his punishment in the coming tribulations. Passing next to one of the highlights of the sermon, he praises the revolutionary government, the Signoria that is to leave office in three days' time. He wants his multitude of listeners to revere this group of *Signori*, who merit entry in the city's chronicles and who 'have gained a great crown in Paradise'. Their work 'was done by the will of God and was more the work of God than of men'. The new *Signori*, due to take office on 1 January, are also present, and so he now tells them that 'God wants you to continue this work with fervour and charity . . . Christ is your King, and you his ministers.' He closes by condemning the rise of political sects, the 'Whites' (supporters of the new republic) and 'Greys' (obstinate Mediceans). Sects and parties bring 'ruin and destruction' to a city.

Savonarola had cut right into the thinking and conscience of that anxious and massed multitude. Woodcuts indicate that the men would have been divided from the women, most likely by railings or long hangings. We may suppose, too, that there had been no small talk in the crowd, because the Friar spoke with too much intensity, and he sometimes (like preachers in seventeenth-century England) held his listeners for two or more hours. The grasping of crucifixes and rosary beads, sighs, cries of mercy, tears and sobbing, the name of Jesus — these were the stuff of the morning's sights and sounds. Here and there, moreover, a few men, their hands racing, had sought to write down Savonarola's words, in at least one case for publication, but in others in order to send reports or manuscript copies out to interested parties.

With Savonarola's message and words of hope echoing through their thoughts, the congregation filed out of the cathedral to face a winter season of uncertainty.

CHAPTER SEVEN

Stamping out Tyranny: 1494–1495

OR ALL HIS certitudes, God's prophet in Florence did not himself stand outside the storm of tribulations foreseen in his prophecies, and it is curious to note that historians have sometimes expressed surprise, or have accused the Friar of cynicism, when finding that he engaged with the forces around him. He was given no choice. He had plunged into politics, so how could that tug of war not pull at him too? Enemies quickly sprang up everywhere, and among them were the gifted preaching friars, Mariano da Genazzano and Domenico da Ponzo, recruited by Savonarola's foes to speak out against him from Florentine pulpits. He was now a man embattled, as he himself proclaimed, and the imagery of combat would often blaze through the language of his sermons.

The city was awash with weapons, and the scrum of emotions in that walled-in space often seemed to contemporaries to be bearing them to the edge of civil war. In the immediate wake of the Pazzi Conspiracy (1478) against Lorenzo de' Medici and his family, a plot that came very close to eliminating him, Lorenzo and his satellites sought to disarm citizens and to locate caches of secret weapons. Thereafter, only Lorenzo, his escort of bodyguards, and a clique of friends were licensed to bear arms. The feared Eight stepped up their vigilance; and the stores of arms controlled by Lorenzo came to be seen as yet another aspect of his unfolding tyranny. But by the early 1490s, the strict monitoring of weapons had been relaxed, and when the republic stormed back in 1494, with King Charles just outside the city gates, the government encouraged the influx of arms. Reacting to the King's return to Tuscany from southern Italy in June 1495, as he made his way back to France, the Florentines brought in armed men from the countryside and again transported more weapons into the city, including stones to be thrown from windows by women, all with a view to defending Florence against a possible assault.

If Savonarola found himself in a tempest on the high seas (his metaphor), with nothing but the voice of God to guide him, many Florentine magnates and lesser noblemen, struck by the buffetings of crisis politics, gave way to bewilderment and fear, especially because there was such contention amongst them. The painful uncertainties are strikingly evident in their upper-class chroniclers, Parenti and Cerretani, who are riven by contradiction in their attitudes toward the Friar. The demand for public office by modest if privileged men was the one threat that should have served to pull the aristocrats together into a daunting political bloc, but it failed to do so. In fact, the threat deepened their fragmentation, and a large number of them passed over into the camp of the Frateschi.

Savonarola, apart from loving God absolutely, or seeking unity with Him, knew one other absolute, and this was the precept that the good citizen should love and serve the common good, not his own private interests. The Christian emphasis on charity and loving others as oneself gave powerful support to this political ideal with a long past, the very ideal that had been increasingly perverted during the fifteenth century. Hounding the opposition and grabbing the spoils had been the way of the victorious Medici. Two generations of Medicean rule, however, had not sufficed to expunge all higher political principles in Florence, especially because the city had a large pool of men who longed to see political power more widely distributed. Then Savonarola moved in with his ardent vision of a new republic and the Christian doctrines of charity and self-denial. The many who had been kept down by the Medici, including numerous men from the old families, were now free to stand up for liberty, for 'the people', for the republic.

But the question remained: how inclusive, in social or class terms, should the sweep of republican offices be? At the extremes were republicans of two sorts. One pole held Bernardo Rucellai, Piero Capponi, Francesco Valori, Paolantonio Soderini, and others of their ilk – men who had worked with Lorenzo the Magnificent, but who could not stomach his 'child' Piero. They wanted a republican oligarchy which they and men like themselves, seasoned in politics, would dominate.

The other pole held men of a more modest social stripe, a multitude who would look upon all citizens in the Great Council as potential holders of the highest offices. These were petty merchants, down-at-heel noblemen, or even prosperous artisans who could claim that a direct ancestor of theirs in the male line, reaching back to the generation of their great grandfathers, had sat in one of three major offices, or had been formally 'drawn' by name for one from the electoral purses. The three offices were the Signory and its double council of advisers, the Sixteen Gonfaloniers and the Twelve Good Men.

Standing somewhere between the two poles was the diarist, Piero Parenti, never an oligarch, but an occasional top office-holder and related to the illustrious Strozzi clan on his mother's side. Parenti distrusted all the magnates; he believed that they were strictly devoted to their own selfish ambitions and families, and so held that a larger circle of citizens should be made eligible for the highest honours.

From the outset, January of 1495, the men of the two poles would begin to look at every major political question – taxes, war, leaders, foreign policy, the hiring of troops, the structure of offices, modes of election, and even religious matters – in the light of how decisions would affect the fortunes of the kind of republic they had in mind.

Manfredo de' Manfredi, the Duke of Ferrara's ambassador to Florence, knew and often met the city's premier citizens. He was in close touch, as well, with Ferrara's distinguished citizen in Florence, Savonarola, whose piety was greatly admired by the duke. Manfredi thus had a working familiarity with the uppermost levels of the Florentine political scene. Like all ambassadors of the period, he was also a spy. His job was to converse as often as possible with the top tier of the city's politicians, with a view to compiling a picture of the political situation in Florence for the benefit of his duke. In some cases, ambassadors were prepared not only to pay for information, but also to try to influence the course of events by means of bribery. While Manfredi's natural sympathies were with the aristocrats, being one himself, his conversations with (and admiration for) Savonarola enabled him to see the virtues of the Great Council, and to intuit the horrors of what might follow from any attempt by the commanding group of oligarchs to snatch power back from the *popolo*. The only way to do this would have been to suppress the Council, and that way lay civil war.

Two other Renaissance republics, Siena and Venice, had nothing in their political anatomies like the dynamism to be found in Florence. Siena's five political blocs had jelled into micro-oligarchies in the late fourteenth century, and no new blood, so to speak, circulated through Sienese republican office. In the city of the great lagoon, Venice, the political class had been frozen in the first years of the fourteenth century, thereby putting a nobility at the head of an hereditary republic. The members of this privileged order were alone entitled to sit in the Venetian Grand Council, and only they qualified for the high offices of state. While great disparities of wealth, rank, and distinction cut through the Venetian nobility, the differences were not allowed to find their force or shape in politics, because the ruling oligarchy of nobles created a system of state jobs, sinecures, and handouts for the needy members of the noble order. The rich nobility, in short, in a kind of welfare state for aristocrats, paid off their 'shame-faced' bretheren; and at the end of the fifteenth century, in rivalries for election to high office, they continually bought the votes of poor noblemen in the Grand Council.

By comparison, then, Florence's Great Council was the foundation of a bona fide republic in which any oligarchy of noblemen could be foiled or beaten down. And the shifting patterns of votes cast in this council was the true expression of social and economic differences.

Was Savonarolan Florence the birthplace of the modern political party, as some historians have argued? The question strikes me as poorly conceived, because the matter of context and constituencies is all important for the modern party, which is nothing – it cannot exist – without large numbers of voters and mass constituencies whose support it is striving to enlist. Florence had no such framework in the 1490s. Instead, it had political currents, groups with common interests, and candidates for office on the lookout for votes. More specifically, the Great Council held the proponents of restricted oligarchy, the secret allies of the disgraced Medici, the men who sympathised with Savonarola, and even those who cherished the Council while rejecting Savonarola. Of all these, only the Frateschi approached being anything like a party, because the leaders of this current had a meeting place in the convent of San Marco. But San Marco was a religious house. Laymen went there to hear sermons, to receive spiritual advice, and occasionally to listen to the expounding of religious doctrine. In the whirl of such encounters, some of them no doubt expressed political views. That they used San Marco as cover for making political plans was certainly possible, but if discretion or secrecy was their aim (since the employment of spies was common knowledge), then it would have made more sense for them to hold such conversations in private, or even, with voices lowered, in a public square, where they could look out for interested eyes and ears.

Florence had strict laws designed to destroy *intelligenze*; groups of electors and office-holders held together by secret agreements to vote for certain men. The penalties for violations of these laws were severe, ranging from heavy fines and loss of all political rights to exile and life-long prison sentences. The common opinion was that political sects were subversive and divisive, that they caused conflict, and were hence bad for the city. Savonarola was one of the leading opponents of such secret clusterings, and from time to time his sermons rang out against *intelligenze*. Renaissance states, Florence included, could not begin to imagine the legality of organised groups in political opposition: this was treason.

The fight for the establishment of the Great Council was immediately succeeded by the controversy over the power of the Twenty Electors, a control-group established by the Parlamento of 2 December 1494. Taking the form of heated private debate, the quarrel went on everywhere. The Twenty faced resentment from the very start, but in the five months that followed the Parlamento, opposition to them turned into an avalanche. Men who had taken up arms against Piero and his supporters on November 9th came to feel that they had risked their lives only to be cheated by the Twenty's powers to elect the Signory, to exercise a critical influence in the election of other leading officials, and to be participants in all major political consultations. The office of the Twenty even divided the most prominent aristocrats, because one of the Twenty, the influential Piero Capponi, driven by private rancour, had cleverly manoeuvred to keep Paolantonio Soderini from gaining a place in that office. Both men came from the far side of the Arno, but evidently hated one another; and some contemporaries believed that this enmity drove Soderini into the ranks of the Savonarolans, where he could more readily use the Great

Council as a stick for beating certain noblemen. The Twenty sparkled with the names of the city's political grandees – Capponi, Bernardo Rucellai, Francesco Valori, Tanai de' Nerli, *Messer* Guidantonio Vespucci, Braccio Martelli, and the cadet-line Medici with a changed surname (*Popolani*), Lorenzo di Pierfrancesco. Only the names of Soderini and Bernardo del Nero were missing.

The Twenty were fated to be disposed of, owing to their being so torn by disagreements that they seemed the looking glass of the fractures within the order of patricians. Capponi and Valori were fierce rivals, equally ambitious, each pulling for his own friends or interests, and each had been courageous in the face of Piero de' Medici's intimidating powers. Yet even as enemies they shared an interest which earned the resentment of those who opposed the Medici. Like Savonarola, they sought to protect the families and men who had colluded with the disgraced house of 'tyrants', in the conviction that to unleash such hatred would issue in bloody strife. Seeing that all sides were armed, their political sense, more than solidarity with the threatened noblemen, enabled them to measure the dangers more or less accurately. But they were opposed, within the Twenty, by Rucellai and Lorenzo di Pierfrancesco, who had their own agendas and circles of supporters; and there was no way to conceal the extent of these differences, as they spilled out into the city and the Great Council.

The anger of the Council with the Twenty Electors moved by word of mouth through the whole class of citizens, until their flaring unpopularity, noted also by Savonarola, led one of them, Giuliano Salviati, to go to the Signoria and resign in mid-May, 1495. Kneeling before the *Signori*, he explained that there was too much quarrelling in the Twenty, especially over the business of elections, that these were more effectively handled in the Great Council, and that he wanted 'to live as a republican'. He was at once regarded as a hero. But the other nineteen members, feeling foully betrayed by his resignation, and accusing him of undermining the work of the Parlamento, resolved to hang on in office, only to find that popular feeling against them swelled more menacingly, until they too were driven to resign on June 7th. Their electoral powers passed to the Great Council.

The voices of obscure men had triumphed. The act abolishing the

Twenty, dated 10 June, flickers with Savonarolan language. Great Councillors are urged, when in the act of voting 'for the honour of God and keeping our liberty', to rid themselves of 'every hatred, [partisan] love, fear, pleading, price, and every other [biased] human grace', and to favour only 'those men whom they know will be useful to the good government of our city'.

Meanwhile, in a parallel development, Savonarola and his 'party' were fighting a related battle on a different front. The Twenty, in any case, would never have got their mandate renewed in December, 1495.

The phrase, 'the six beans', employed to designate a major controversy, was a typical down-sizing, throw-away expression of the Florentines, the seeming triviality of which concealed the penalties of death, exile, mutilation, and crushing fines. By a two-thirds vote of six black beans (yes) against three white ones (no), the Priors of the Signoria could condemn citizens to those penalties. With six beans they could also order the Eight, the other feared magistracy, to inflict the same punishments on any prisoners in their custody. Yet neither the Signory nor the Eight was a court of law. When sitting in judgment on a case, the Signory functioned as a summary tribunal. In jurisprudential theory, this meant that the *Signori* moved in the guise of the all-powerful prince, as laid down in Roman law. In effect, in certain situations, the Priors suddenly seized and exercised the absolute power that belonged to the emperor in Roman law. No lawyers need be called in, and regular judicial procedure, or 'due process' in our terms, was cast aside. However, the Signory took action of this sort only in exceptional circumstances – in emergencies, acts of treason, or in cases involving political grandees. And this power had not been challenged in recent times.

Savonarola took it upon himself to do so, thereby hitting on an explosive issue and immediately attracting support, as well as angry opposition. Believing that in the field of capital crimes the power of the Signoria was too awesome for the new republic, and really too vulnerable to private interest and passion, the Friar called for a law which would allow any person condemned by the six beans to appeal over the heads of the Signoria to the Great Council. There the case would be heard and determined by a two-thirds vote. His opponents argued that the proposed change was an assault on the traditional powers and dignity of the Signoria. To take away parts of its authority was to diminish it and to weaken the power of government. This was especially resented by some of the aristocrats, who aspired to hold the major offices, and who saw any diminishing of these as an attack on them, on their honour, and on their position in the city. Medicean colluders, however, some of whom had been forced to make large obligatory loans to the government, tended to favour the Savonarolan measure, because they saw it as a route to their own amnesty.

On 19 March, a law granting the right of appeal against the six beans was passed in the Great Council by an overwhelming vote of 543 to 163. In his sermons over the next year or two, Savonarola would often refer to this triumph. The measure stripped the Signory of a competence which had lodged frightening authority in six men.

Savonarola's battle for the appeal measure should be seen in the larger context of the republican campaign to break up the pockets of concentrated authority in the small councils at the head of state. It was easily understood that the greater their power, the lesser that of the Great Council. Relying on a variety of such councils, the ruling elite of Medicean Florence had managed to pilfer more authority for themselves, while seeming to do so by constitutional means. The most important of the small councils, the War-Office Ten, preceded the political rise of the Medici and could be more than a match for two-month Signories, especially in wartime, because it operated for renewable six-month terms and was inevitably captained by two or three of the foremost patricians. The Ten also conducted foreign affairs, a charge they shared with the Signory, although in wartime, or in times of danger, they dispatched ambassadors and were more likely to run the show, not the Signory.

Two months after the six-bean appeal became law, just as Salviati was tendering his resignation from the Twenty Electors, the Great Council deprived them of their right to elect the Ten, now known as the 'Ten of Liberty and Peace', and took over this power itself. The Twenty opposed the change, because of course they saw the Ten as a dignity that was tailor-made for men like themselves. But there was nothing they could do against the vastly popular Great Council, particularly in view of their own blossoming infamy.

Florence, in the meantime, was at war with Pisa, struggling to repossess it, and the Ten in charge of the war, nicknamed 'the big spenders', were being seen as shamefully unsuccessful. Already unpopular, their current failures generated a quiet debate about the scope of their authority, and in late 1495 popular voices began to demand controls on their activity by proposing to define, and thus to limit, their powers. The aim was to pin them more firmly to war and military matters. Once again the grandees and eminent men stepped in, seeking to head off the new proposals. The whole question divided the Savonarolan leadership. In late April 1496, a law aiming to regulate the Ten was opposed by the Signory and even by its top executive, a Savonarolan, Domenico Mazzinghi. But it was vigorously supported by the Signory's counsellors, the Sixteen, and was approved by the Great Council with striking majorities. Yet the strictest part of the measure did little more than to seek a rule of behaviour. Hereafter, on taking office, the Ten were to swear to observe 'the constitutions and laws pertaining to their office', and each of them, in turn, had also to take an oath 'to hold no private discussions with any prince or great prelate, either in Italy or outside of Italy, regarding the affairs of your city, without the express commission of the whole office [the Ten] or of at least two thirds of them'.

How very revealing. Men of the sort elected to the Ten frequently moved in a world of *gran maestri*, great lords, and could draw upon contacts in Rome, Naples, Milan, and elsewhere, including France. The *popolo* suspected and resented these men; feared that they were often in contact with Mediceans and might be subject to irresistible bribes; knew that in their heart of hearts most of them wanted a tight oligarchy for Florence, out of which they could more readily assist their families, friends, and dependants. Yet citizens also recognised that such men were highly informed, and that Florence needed their skills and experience in foreign affairs, and even on the field of battle, where they could keep a trained eye on the city's hired captains and professional soldiers. There seemed to be no way out of these conundrums. And here too was the ground of the ambiguities that would stalk the emerging Savonarolan leaders – Paolantonio Soderini, Giovanbattista Ridolfi, and Francesco Valori. No private and simple citizens these. Eminence and experience raised them above other Florentines, with the exception of those from backgrounds like their own, citizens such as Tanai de' Nerli, Piero Capponi, and

Bernardo Rucellai, who opposed Savonarola. All these men moved through the city with an aura of honours, wealth, and friends, dependants, supporters, and imagined secret influence.

The struggle to define the operating sphere of the Ten, and to enforce that definition, was to go on for years and would peak again in 1499–1500.

The first year of the new republic saw another remarkable change, also inspired by Savonarola and distinctly revolutionary, because it flew in the face of an ancient Florentine institution: the occasional practice of having recourse to a Parlamento. I refer to the Signory's right to summon all political citizens to the government square, with a view to holding a popular referendum. Though seldom employed, this constitutional resource went back to the twelfth century, to the earliest years of the Florentine commune; and we have seen that it was invoked on 2 December 1494, to confirm the exile of the Medici and the restoration of republican freedoms.

For more than 200 years, however, *parlamenti* had usually been summoned by victorious factions to manipulate the populace, to banish and destroy political enemies, and to install the triumphant faction in power. Openly challenged, the Medici had used the stratagem on two different occasions, in 1458 and 1466, to overwhelm a swelling opposition, to regroup, and to re-impose their panoply of controls. The fearless Friar turned briefly to the subject in a series of sermons, deftly but firmly touching on it on each occasion. His argument was an article of simplicity. By the grace of God, and without the spilling of blood, thus almost miraculously, Florentines had regained their republican liberty. This grace now reposed in the regular and rational functioning of the Great Council, an assembly – as its history was to show – that could not be truly manipulated. Consequently, any change hereafter sought by means of a Parlamento could only signify a lurch towards tyranny. In this light, the dramatic summoning of the Florentine people to an assembly in the government square could have nothing good about it; and therefore it was best to suppress the possibility altogether.

The remedy and Savonarola's effrontery seem extreme, but he knew perfectly well – the knowledge was emblazoned in the chronicles – that the urban history of later medieval Italy had been plagued by the demagogic use of popular assemblies, the inveterate aim of which had been to impose tyrannies and one-party dictatorships. More immediately, the Friar's remedy was dictated by fear of the Medici, of their secret supporters in the city, of their lordly friends in Milan, and of Piero's relentless diplomatic activity in Rome, Naples, and Tuscany, where he continued to importune King Charles and Pope Alexander to call for his return to Florence. The main image of the deposed boss, as reported by ambassadors and agents, had him at the side of the great mercenary captain, his relative Virginio Orsini, who was often in command of large numbers of cavalry and foot soldiers. If Piero could but get into Florence and enlist, buy, or coerce the support of the Signory, there was no question of it: the next step would be to summon a Parlamento. Within an hour of its assembly, surrounded by armed horsemen, foot soldiers, and a unit of crossbowmen, that throng would have shouted 'yes' to a series of measures, putting decisive power back into the hands of a small council of Mediceans, who in turn would then absolutely control elections, the key offices, the public purse, the dispatch of ambassadors, and the hiring of more troops. Mass exiling and a number of executions would follow.

The Savonarolans got their way. On 13 August 1495, the Great Council enacted a law against any and all attempts to summon a Parlamento. It was passed by a crushing majority of 618 votes to 73. The Friar had even provided a jingle to help remind Florentines of the tyrannical designs of *parlamenti*, and he wanted fathers to pass it on to their children:

> Chi vuole fare parlamento
> vuol torre delle mane [sic] al populo il reggimento.

> Anyone who wants a Parliament
> aims to take power from the people.

CHAPTER EIGHT

God and Politics

THE CRISIS IN Florentine politics, with its undertow of financial uncertainty, cut down on the construction of new domestic
palaces; and Savonarola's call for charity, along with his attacks
on conspicuous opulence, moved public opinion against the display of
big and fancy stonework. The agonising loss of Pisa and of swathes of
Pisan farmland also had the effect of checking private building. Grand
architectural commissions, with their in-built sense of optimism, needed
a secure moral and political climate. A tremendous amount of domestic
construction had gone on in Florence during the 1300s. The great Spini
Palace, commenced in the 1290s and perched beside the river, at the mouth
of the Via de' Tornabuoni, exemplified the grandest features of the
pattern of building in the fourteenth century. In Savonarola's day, the
great Strozzi Palace was still under construction, but the imposing palaces
of the Uzzano, Buondelmonti, Rucellai, Medici, Gondi, Pazzi, Pitti
(though much smaller then), and others were all in place. The biggest of
these had been paid for by profits from international banking, and all
were fine examples of the new Quattrocento fashion for more distinctive building. Not until after about 1520 would large-scale investment in
private palaces again take off, although the new structures would have
more classical lines, hence more sobriety, as in the Pucci, Pandolfini, and
Bartolini-Salembeni *palazzi*.

The 1490s, accordingly, with their economic hard times and chronic
fears, were an interlude, as Florentine ruling families, old and more recent,
drew in on themselves and strained to reach more clearly defined positions in politics and society. They were on a slippery path, stretching
between loyalty to an elitist republic on one side and, on the other, resignation to a princely state. In the one, they would hold the key positions

in government; in the other, they would be servitors at best. But it is likely that they seldom, if ever, saw the alternatives in so clear a light. Some noblemen even wanted to believe that it would be possible both to have the Medici and something of an aristocratic republic. In other words, hope and illusions obscured the way to self-definitions, quite apart from the fact that Savonarola's message had converted many of them to his vision of a New Jerusalem.

Fighter and Prophet

O NE OF THE first great propaganda wars of the early-modern world was fought between Rome and Florence in the wake of the Pazzi Conspiracy against the Medici (1478–1479). The great rewarder and coddler of his relatives, Pope Sixtus IV, had secretly connived with a circle of conspirators. Captained in part by the Pazzi, a family of influential Florentine bankers, the group sought the assassination of Lorenzo the Magnificent and his younger brother, Giuliano. When the conspiracy failed, despite the murder of Giuliano, war broke out and papal troops marched into Florentine Tuscany. Now Sixtus not only excommunicated Lorenzo but also put Florence under an interdict, denying the sacraments and all religious services to people in the city. Lorenzo and his friends fought the Pope's circulating accusations by issuing printed tracts, letters, a scathing account of the conspiracy, a soldier's confession, and even poems. It was an onslaught of the printed word, intended to win the sympathies of Italian ruling elites, and it was done with a view to triumphing on the field of battle, as well as in the coming tangle of negotiations.

Already a young Dominican, and horrified by the web of papal nepotism being spun in Rome, Savonarola saw – must have seen – the importance of reaching minds with a version of events that was not otherwise available: that is, of taking control away from the controllers. This meant recourse to the new printing press.

In Florence, as it happened, the new technology made its appearance in 1471, with the founding of the city's first press, six years after the establishment of the first presses in Italy. The Friar realised that print was the only way to get a mass circulation of sermons, treatises, hard-hitting letters, and other written matter. Contestants suddenly stood in the first phase of an emerging public consciousness. With the incidence of simony in the clerical hierarchy and an acute sense of the world's army of lost souls as his points of departure, Savonarola had no need of lessons in the art of propaganda. He belonged to the Order of Preaching Friars: his distinctive office was to preach, to propagate the word of God. But he wanted more. Evil men and liars in holy orders were propagating a false model – an external, pompous, and heartless religion. It was time to speak the truth, and the Florentine clash with Pope Sixtus had pointed to the best way of doing so – print.

Not until Luther, in the early 1520s, would a member of the regular clergy come forth to exploit the resources of print so effectively as Savonarola. In 1490 and 1491, with his more forthright criticism of the rich laity and lax clergy, the Friar spawned enemies, who then doubled and trebled in 1494 and 1495, when he pushed brazenly into politics. Lies about him, as well as truths, began to do the rounds; and as the vehemence of the charges grew, so too did his need to defend himself. Now, first editions and reprintings of select sermons, individual letters, and his doctrinal works began to pour from Florentine and other presses. Later, to the mendacious charge that he was a heretic, he would repeatedly respond by saying that he preached out in the open to crowds, not in secret places or conventicles, and that all his views were in public, in his printed works, where they could be easily checked.

To reach the largest possible audiences, Savonarola had his doctrinal works, which were first issued in Latin, then brought out in Italian. Although he translated one of the best of them, *The Triumph of the Cross*, the rest of his writings in translation came from the hands of others, and in this regard he was especially blessed with the superior skills of the brothers, Girolamo and Domenico Benivieni. He himself was a scrupulous editor of his writings, as well as a conscientious corrector of proofs before the final printings. He even seems to have invented the genre of the circulating open letter, put out with an eye to forging public opinion. Eleven of his letters were printed during his lifetime, including two addressed to women and a threatening missive to the King of France. His *On the Simplicity of the Christian Life*, for example, was brought out in Latin at the end of August 1496, and published two months later in Girolamo Benivieni's vernacular translation. We may thus assume that the translator worked either with the Friar's manuscript or – as it came from the printer – with page proofs in hand. Seven editions of his little treatise on *The Love of Jesus Christ* were printed between 1492 and 1496. Rather more dramatic, however, was the fortune of his sermons. His two hugely political ones of 8 June and 11 October 1495 were quickly printed. The Amos and Zechariah sermons of 1495 were issued early in 1497; and three homilies from the final series (11, 18, and 25 February 1498) were individually printed at once. Remarkably, over a period of eight to nine years (1491–1500), his writings were issued by the presses of at least six different Florentine printers – Bonaccorsi, Libri, Miscomini, Morgiani, Petri, and Tubini.

Yet the foregoing catalogue does no more than scratch the surface of the numbers of works and editions printed during the Friar's lifetime. He was almost certainly the most published writer in Italy at the end of the fifteenth century; and his 108 items (incunables) printed in Florence alone far exceed those of the city's best loved poets, Luigi Pulci (with eighteen) and Dante (with only ten).

Regarded as a prophet and near saint by many thousands of Florentines, the Friar had been so well trained in logic, philosophy, and theology, that for years he was, as we have seen, the master in these studies for Dominican novices at Bologna, Ferrara, and Florence. He combined two sensibilities, the one emotional or affective, and the other more strictly rational, detached, and even cold. Swooning for the love of Christ was a condition that he could both long for and advocate. But with his prodigious memory and his steeping in Scripture and in theology, he could also be a formidable opponent in debate, as observed by one of the best minds of the age, Count Giovanni Pico della Mirandola.

An 'intellectual' then, a man who trafficked in words and ideas; but this most certainly was not the way Savonarola saw himself, particularly if the term implied a dedication to anything strictly rational, such as in inquiry to be kept wholly within the bounds of 'the natural light of reason'. For him, without 'the supernatural light of grace and faith', pure reason and its ends were driven by pride, by the greatest sin of fallen man; and therefore even Plato had less wisdom than 'a little old woman' with her faith. However fleetingly, the claims of faith over 'natural' reason run through most of his sermons, so that in this sense he was very much a man of his times. The unquiet twins, faith and reason, provided the way of intellectual Europe in the fifteenth century, a Europe that drew its philosophic styles not from Plato, but from the magisterial thinkers of the high Middle Ages.

Yet the designated abstractions – and they are nothing else – were life, heart, and sinew for Savonarola, who could transform philosophy into an incandescence, into something passionate and almost tangible, by wedding it to the love of Christ and the blood of the Crucifixion. Reason raised man above all brute animals, but only faith and grace enabled him to hurtle over the earthly barrier of sin to reach salvation and identity with Christ. With this vision in his mind's eye, the Friar could be fearless: he could face any danger, any martyrdom, and indeed occasionally long for death in order to be united with God.

If – as Auden said of Yeats – 'mad Ireland hurt you into poetry', then we may say of Savonarola that the riches and ostentation of the lords of Ferrara hurt him into a kind of divine madness. Voicing the feeling in his poetry and earliest letters, he was to detest luxury for most of his life, especially because of the greedy and impenitent self-indulgence that went with it. His friars at San Marco found him considerate and kind, and with a gentle manner that won them over to his asceticism. For the sake of a spiritual nobility, they too were soon prepared to give up even the few physical pleasures that might be available in a monastery.

Trained in medieval Christian philosophy, Savonarola fully accepted the notion of the nobility and perfectability of man, who had been created, after all, in God's image. 'Man is a noble creature, with an intellect, free will, and reason.' Or again, 'Man is the most noble of things, a wonderful thing' – a view that followed from the assumption that 'the omnipotent God put man in the middle [of the universe], so that he may contemplate his Creator by considering the created world'. In the hierarchy of created being, man holds the place in the middle; above him are only choruses of angels. But by the power of his free will – a capability made possible by the providence of God – man can raise himself to the highest heavenly planes, where his office is both to contemplate God and to be one with Him.

Strikingly, like Luther and Calvin, the Friar believed in predestination: in a small army of the elect, destined for salvation, and in the multitudes who would be damned for all eternity. He did not however – as others were to do later – turn this conception into an elitist social view. And despite the logical problems in this position, he also held, unlike the Protestant Reformers, that men and women could will and earn their own salvation. The two conditions, predestination and a free-willed salvation, run through his sermons. He was fully aware of the ensuing logical difficulties, and tried on occasion to show that they could be resolved. His essential solution was to distinguish between time and eternity and to hold that the grace of God was somehow – at least in time – not fixed.

Drawing from Aristotle, Albertus Magnus, St Thomas Aquinas, and others, he never tired of saying that we know the world through the evidence of our senses, and that the intellect, or intellective soul, is what enables us to pass beyond sensory experience to a zone in which we begin to have knowledge of God. Elements of this knowledge could be obtained through the exercise of natural reason, but anything deeper required God's input, rays of divine illumination, which in turn had to be based on faith; and the more fervent this faith the better. God is good, perfect, all-knowing, all-powerful, eternal. All these claims were the given; they were generally accepted; but they were also in Aquinas and other thinkers. And Savonarola was well acquainted with the notion, again fully laid out in the philosophical tradition, that it is all but impossible really to know what God is, because the Prime Mover, pure act, eludes the experience given to our senses. At the same time, there was another line of thought, running through medieval mystics – Anselm and Bonaventure pre-eminently – back to St Augustine, to disperse itself in Scripture. This line claimed that everything seeks its own perfection, that this principle permeates all being, and that man's end is unity with God. However, how were 'little women' – in an expression of the patriarchal male of the day – to know all this? Through philosphy and theology? Savonarola transposed the question: '*How shall we learn Scripture?*, the women will say. *We don't know how to study.*' Hence there had to be a very much simpler and more direct way to God, and this was provided by the bridge of faith, wholly available to the most humble and simple souls, including the women and peasants who came in from beyond the walls of Florence to listen to the Friar and to set eyes on him. If you are good and have the grace, he added, 'you have in you that which makes Scripture, and you [also] have the commentary in you'.

A burning faith then, a passionate belief that was called upon daily: this was the best way to God, our true and longed-for destiny, if we could but see rightly. And so to nuns, for example, Savonarola's message was that they should be so much in love with their heavenly spouse as to be 'drunk' or 'crazy' with God. To the sprinkling of illiterate men and women among the thousands who stretched out before him, as he looked down from his pulpit, the call to seek God was less mystically pointed; but the overriding stress on faith remained, and he combined it with the strong plea to confess and to take communion at least four or five times yearly. It went without saying that daily prayer was essential.

Savonarola's journey to his prophetic mission may be traced back to his reasons for fleeing into a monastery: the horrors and turpitudes that he claims to have witnessed in the 'vile' world. Having no wish to step into the shifting sands of psychoanalytic psychology, which would lead us away from history and toward Sigmund Freud, I conjecture that the Friar was turned against the swagger of power and riches by the stories he heard from his pious grandfather, Ferrara's court physician, and by what he himself saw of the Este princes and their courtiers in the streets of the city. He was perhaps too sensitive a child and young man. Yet he did not go into the more docile Order of Franciscans, whose emphasis on poverty would have drawn him closer to one of his capital commitments. Instead, he chose the great preaching order, the Dominicans, because he saw himself as a fighter from the very start – a militant knight of Christ, as he put it, determined to transform people by disseminating the word of God. No wonder that he soon saw the combative power of the new printing press.

During his first dozen years as a monk, he was primarily a teacher to other friars, as he himself gradually learned – and it came slowly – the art of preaching. We know that in his first Florentine period (1482–1487) he was a miserable failure as a preacher. Voice, accent, manner – all went against him. But there was also the political Savonarola: the moral agitator who needed the allure of politics, something come from a fissure in public life, to help galvanise him into action. Florence offered nothing like this in the 1480s, nor did any princely city, and certainly not the two that he knew best, Bologna under the mighty Bentivoglio family and the Ferrara of the Este princes, because preachers there were under the thumb of the ruling lords. This was doubly true if a preacher wandered away from the homiletic conventions regarding vice and virtue, and began to take up such novel themes as the influence and ruthless greed of the rich urban elites. Even in Florence, Lorenzo de' Medici easily got a disturbing preacher, Bernardino da Feltre, expelled from the city, although the action was sharply resented by the populace. They wanted to go on listening to his words on the ways in which the poor were particularly subject to the alleged wiles and extortions of Jewish moneylenders.

If we cast an eye on Venice as a possible site for Savonarola's crusade to reform the Church, we see at once that the closed Venetian patriciate would never have put up with his mobilising of a whole population. They would soon have had him in chains, or rushed him out of the city. But the Florence of 1492–1494, with its unnerving political and moral malaise, provided Savonarola with an ideal opportunity, as the city hung anxiously between a republic and a Renaissance dictatorship. The city's deepest political roots and loquacious populace pulled it toward a republic, but the connivance and servility of a circle of upper-class families pulled it toward a half-disguised Medicean despotism, where honours and offices could be more securely theirs. The pull was not so much a matter of modern sleaze as of the Renaissance susceptibility to the powerful family and its 'natural' quest for exalted place.

For nearly four years (1494–1498), Savonarola's enemies accused him of butting into Florence's affairs of state – he, a foreign monk and priest who therefore had no right to meddle in politics. His reply to this bitter refrain varied from denial to the outright assertion – justifiably made – that he had a line of predecessors, that certain Dominicans before him had also thrust themselves into public life, and that he made recommendations only for 'good' laws, or for general policies regarding the common good of the Florentine *popolo*. He gave no personal support, he insisted, to any political sect, group, or individual. There was truth on both sides. But there was also a larger, oblique truth, never clearly seen by either side.

Savonarola's view of the Church and of society was both moral and political. The corruption of the Church, as he saw it, was so complete and had so contaminated Italian society that only a divine scourging – punishment by murderous war and 'barbarian' armies – could cleanse and renew Rome, the Church, and Italy. The same armies would overthrow Italian princes and governing elites, and the people of Italy would then pass over into a new age. In effect, he was talking about an all out assault on authority, on rulers whom he considered rotten to the core.

Whatever its theology, how could such a vision not be political too? This was why Florence's anger and passions in 1494–1495 offered the Friar his needed setting: a great city-republic, confused and frightened, but also furious with its leaders, the disgraced Medici, while the big men sought to hang on to (or climb on) the unsteady governing saddle. Even if they had not been confronting an invasion, the people of Florence longed for honest government.

The scene, in short, held the makings of a political revolution, and its central force was a demand for moral principle. Stepping into it, therefore, Savonarola had to be more than a mere monk who gabbled about vice and virtue. Now at last he was able to let himself go, rushed along by a feeling that had been with him for years, the feeling that he had a special relation with God, enabling him to peer into the future. His sermons of November–December 1494 candidly carry this claim; and it would soon emerge that he also heard heavenly voices, God's and the Virgin Mary's. The prophet had arrived.

Charismatic Preacher

SAVONAROLA'S LIFE PASSED into mortal danger in the winter of 1494–1495, never again to be safe; and with each season the dangers grew. Haters of the Great Council blamed him for its success. Florentine clerics feared and loathed his diatribes against a materialistic clergy, especially as his convent was soon attracting more and more charitable donations, leaving that much the less for other religious houses. There were even those, as we shall see, who said that they longed to kill him with their own hands. Many a blasphemer, gambler, and sodomite must have detested the Friar, as he kept up his campaigns against them. And all the while there was his great nemesis, Pope Alexander VI, who had a reputation for hiring assassins, as in the case, it was whispered, of Giovanni Gatto, 'the first citizen of Viterbo', murdered in a castle in June 1496. Savonarola soon came to be flanked by an escort of armed men whenever he went into the streets of Florence.

The raw power of his sermons enraged his opponents, making them the more willing to see or to plot his death; but it was a power that also guaranteed his stature and influence, and he would do everything possible to hold on to it. Preaching, he declared ardently, was his life. Let's see him working at it.

His sermon of 21 September 1494 so terrified Count Pico della Mirandola as to make his hair stand on end. Now lost, the sermon was delivered in the midst of strong rumours, alleging that the King of France, at the head of a great army and on his way down the length of Italy, had just entered Genoa. Michelangelo, it appears, was also present on that September morning, and shortly thereafter, in October, fled from the city in a panic, frightened by the Friar's dire predictions. Condivi reported that the artist was to be haunted by that voice for the rest of his life. Citing *Genesis*, Savonarola seems to have ended the sermon with a cry: 'I shall spill flood waters over the earth.' On another occasion (8 March 1496), he ended a sermon by turning to the crucifix with such vehemence, exclaiming that he was ready to die for the truth of God, that the great throng of listeners began to shout and cry out loudly, 'Mercy! And long live Jesus Christ, our King.'

We begin to make out the alarming impact of Savonarola's preaching, and while we lack descriptions of his delivery, we must assume that he used every available means, rhetorical and theatrical, to strike at the hearts and minds of the listeners massed before him. He had to sway a people who were not 'obedient sheep, meek and innocent', but rather 'proud lions, cruel bears, rapacious wolves, dishonest pigs, and other wild beasts', as the Archbishop of Florence, Antoninus, had described Florentines a generation earlier. Even the sceptical and worldly Machiavelli, who heard a number of the Friar's sermons, had to admit that without performing a single miracle, he had persuaded a 'vast' number of Florentines 'that

he spoke with God'. The whiff of holiness and the power to force conviction could only have come from his bearing, sermons, and delivery.

Since Savonarola did not step out of a vacuum as a speaker, a few
words about fifteenth-century preaching will throw light on his methods.

When Renaissance preachers journeyed from one part of Italy to
another, a land of dialects, they had to learn to alter their voices and
diction, if they were going to achieve any kind of stature as speakers and
religious figures. The towering men of this sort – San Bernardino, Roberto
Caracciolo, and perhaps Giacomo della Marca – were in constant demand.
Princes and cities competed for them, and the generals of the different
mendicant orders were bombarded with requests for their best speakers,
above all for delivery of the two most important sermon cycles of the
year, at Lent and Advent. It was almost never the case that a local figure
could satisfy the demand. The talent in question, a strong and eloquent
voice, was too rare; and an industrious city, with its sharp-eyed elites and
populace, longed for that very gift, rousing oratory, in the weeks leading
up to Christmas and Easter. Not a single native Florentine appears in a
conscientious listing of the city's foremost preachers in the last third of
the fifteenth century. Offering summaries of their sermons too, the
account names Caracciolo (from Lecce in the far south of Italy), Mariano
da Genazzano (from near Rome), Giovanni da Piemonte (Piedmont),
Agostino da Pavia (Pavia), Vincenzo da Narni (Narni), Antonio da Vercelli
(Vercelli), Francesco da Viterbo (Viterbo), and other outsiders.

Savonarola's failure as a preacher during his first Florentine residence
must have been due in part to the fact that he had made too little effort
to change his speaking ways and words. In a grammatically refined Florence,
the key city in moulding the Tuscan tongue into Italy's literary language,
and where people were surpassingly proud of their habits of speech, he
came through as rather a lumpy northerner. On his return to Florence,
therefore, having logged in more experience in a half-dozen other cities,
he sought to 'Florentinise' his delivery, not necessarily by striving to
assume a Florentine accent but rather by cutting down on his distinctive
northern sounds. He certainly took up the use of popular Florentine
expressions, such as *moccicone* (snotnose), *sta cheto* (be quiet), and *beccarsi il
cervello* (to peck away at one's brains).

Since sermons might last for two or even three hours, the outstanding preachers had more than something of the stage about them. Savonarola watched and heard Florentine 'bench singers' in performance – men who would mount a bench and recite verse in public for the entertainment of the populace; and he wanted this frivolity banned. But he would not have minded any of their ploys if used in sermons for the greater glory of God. He displays his theatrical sense in a rich collection of outline notes for himself, rounded sketches of Lenten sermons, the *Quaresimale of 1491*, where he observes, 'Take the Crucifix [at this point] and lifting it high, cry out, *Misericordia!*' Or again, 'Take out a nail from the Crucifix, letting his [Christ's] right hand fall, and cry out, O Lord.'

Halfway to being actors, preachers might suddenly weep, cry out, strike at the air, fall to their knees, thrust up a cross, tear at themselves, or invite their listeners to shout 'Mercy!' Caracciolo, for instance, preaching a crusade against the Turks, once suddenly threw off his Franciscan tunic, 'and showed himself off to the faithful wearing complete body armour'.

But in the end, of course, the efficacy of the preacher had to be in his voice, words, and gestures.

The Imaginary Dialogue

ONE OF THE principal devices for preachers in the art of holding the attention of listeners was the imaginary dialogue, the exchange with a fictitious heckler or interlocutor in the assembled crowd. Savonarola was extraordinarily fond of this ploy. He used it to explain doctrine, to accuse enemies, to defend himself, to fix attention, to win sympathy, to answer likely questions, or to add touches of lightness, humanity, and even humour to his preaching. Intriguingly, his fictitious exchanges also hinted at the whole spectrum of his anxieties: madness, pride, the inspiration of the devil, illness, lack of sleep, and the sense of cutting a ridiculous figure.

The desire to slide over into a possible dialogue was often present from the very start of the Friar's sermons, such as when he said, 'I don't want to preach this morning, Florence, but rather to talk to you a bit.'

Or, 'I've come this morning more to reason with you than to preach.'
Far more often, however, early in a sermon, he would single out a
listener or class of listeners, address each for a while, as indicated in
the following forms, and then move on to another: 'You, O tepid one',
or 'you, people of Florence', 'you, merchant', 'you, sodomites', 'you,
miser', or 'you, big shots and great lords'. The very first sermon of his
Haggai series (1 November, 1494) has at least twenty-nine shifts of address,
of changing personal pronouns declared or implied, as he calls out – his
head surely turning – to the individual sinner in the throng (*tu*, thou)
or to 'citizens' (*cittadini!*), and more pointedly to office-holders, priests,
nuns, merchants, rich and poor, mothers of daughters decked out in
finery, usurers, the receivers of alms, the Florentine people, to Florence
itself, to the clergy, or even to God, as in the apostrophe, 'Forgive this
popolo [O Lord].'

The Friar was conducting an emotional movement in listeners, as he
passed more or less swiftly from one group or class of persons to another,
and signalled the change with an exclamation ('blasphemer!', 'gambler!',
'wicked old man!'). He continually alternated between the singular 'you'
(thou) and the 'you' for a plurality – the 'thou' being the familiar pronoun
used by the morally-superior confessor with his penitent. However, he
often spoke in such a way as to insinuate that the addressees might reply,
were almost being needled into replying. Hence the imaginary dialogue
with a person in the throng already seemed on the point of taking place,
and so was fully expected when it came. A cascade of examples may
convey the purpose, sense, and feeling of the staccato-like dialogue.

'O Florence, O Italy, O Church,' he calls out, indicating by this manner
of address that he, the preacher, has the standing to speak to all Italy.

Savonarola had just urged the Eight to be severe, even cruel: '*O friar,*'
he guys himself, '*what are you saying? Do you want men to be cruel?* – I tell you
that this cruelty is [now] a great mercy. – *Oh, you're meddling in affairs of
state.* – No, the state says do it this way and that way, and then this and
that. I am not saying this.' And again, having announced that he would
like to see the members of the Signory living more simply: '*O friar, you're
looking for a blow on the head one of these days!* – I think you're right.'

'*Come now, friar, what do you really want to do?* – I have so preached and strained for you, Florence, that I have shortened my life by many years. . . . — *What prize do you want?* — I want no prize from you, Florence, but you Lord, my Jesus Christ, I pray that you give me that prize that you gave to your holy apostles and to your prophets and to your other holy martyrs.'

'Do what I've said. Carry out the reform of morals, or Christ will do it for you. — *O friar, are you supposed to command us?* — No, I'm not here to command you, but Christ is King of the city and I am his ambassador.'

'You [Florentines] seem to me all crazy. Florence strikes me as full of devils; that [government] Palace is full of devils; the angels have gone away. You do not want to believe. — *O friar, we want a miracle from you of some sort, then we'll believe.*'

He mimics those who accuse him of craft, or who affect false sympathy: '*This friar speaks as he pleases; he moves with art; he speaks with caution; and he is tricking us.*' '*O, poor friar . . . you have so many enemies, in the city and outside, men and women, priests, friars, nuns, and every sort. O poor friar.* — No, you are the poor one.'

One of his shafts plays with the metaphorical links between heaven and earth: 'Florence, Christ is your King. — *O friar, do you think I don't understand? You want to say that Christ is King, so that you can be his minister and do as you like. You've really ensnared this people.*'

'*Friar, you're going to find it very hard to win this thing. You are alone, so you'll have lots of trouble . . . You want to take light to all the world. You are at war with great lords. The whole world is against you: priests, friars, monks. Every one says, let's get this scoundrel. Come now, how do you mean to win?* — By means of what Scripture says: put your hearts in the goodness of the Lord.'

Savonarola's solitude and dangers in Florence often troubled him. Here, therefore, above and below, he was making light of his anxieties, while also challenging and even taunting his adversaries.

'Up now, Satan, where are you? Come on, get all your wits together. Call up your forces, use all your tools and devices, send out all your members against me. I am afraid of nothing. If a man is not afraid to die, what else is there for him to fear? What will your answer be, Satan? — *O my friar, listen to me a bit.* — I am not yours . . . — *Come come, friar, rogue of a friar, would you like some good advice from me? Don't touch painful things, if you want to live in peace.* – I don't want your counsels or your peace, because your peace is never peace and your war doesn't disrupt my peace.'

'*O friar, you're talking very boldly this morning. You're not crazy, so why are you talking like that? You're putting yourself in Christ's place, and what he said of himself you are saying of yourself.* – I'm talking in this brave manner because of the solid grounding I know we have and which no human power can destroy. He [Christ] is the one who speaks in me.'

Savonarola comments on the fact that all Italy is against his preaching, and yet his whole operation proceeds: 'What miracle other than that do you want. You get up here [to the pulpit] and try, and see how well you do. – *O, you praise yourself, you do, friar.* – No, I don't praise myself, because it is not I, a lowly little friar, but God [who is doing these things].'

Having pointed out that Christ intended to conquer the world by means of his message and through faith, he continues: 'Now, if you should ask me, *what do you want, friar?* – I want men to be illuminated by truth. I want to fight the whole world and win. I want the citizens who are against this [republican] government to perish. I want Florence to extend its empire and preserve this government. Oh, if I should say to you, this is what I want to do, you would say, *O crazy friar.* And I tell you that I want to do it, and we shall do it. . . . *Do you want to claim, friar, that you have as much grace and Holy Spirit as the apostles had?*'

Above, as elsewhere, Savonarola glances off the theme of his own madness, only to convert it into a vision of faith with both rational and mystic dimensions.

Next he imitates 'a foxy priest' talking to a woman: '*You believe in the Friar? Beware of what you're doing. If you go to his sermons, I won't absolve you.* – And thus do they [foxy priests] eat chickens, that is, they seduce the simple little women [against me].'

'Oh, friar . . . *they say you are a heretic.* – Throw any low insult at me, but don't call me a heretic.' Again: '*They say you're crazy.* – Oh, now there you've said something beautiful. . . . [As sinners] we're all a bit mad. – *Ah, but you've said that the Church is a whore. O father, the Holy Church? What have you said?* – You're a fool . . . go and do some more studying.'

Expelled from the Church in May 1497, Savonarola's challenge to the Signory was more than matched by his candid dismissal, in the winter of 1498, of the brief that had put him outside the body of Christians:

'Well, you'll say: *come here, friar, do you think this excommunication is valid? Clarify this point for us.* – No, it has no value. – *Oh, who told you so?* – God told me. I say to you God told me. See how I speak to you. – *O friar, if your God has told you that it has no value, our God has told us that it is valid and we say that Christ is with our God.* – Well, now, let's look into this a bit.'

Income-enjoying (beneficed) clerics say to the Friar: '*O father, it's true that the excommunication is not valid, but we're afraid to lose our benefices [if we support you].* – So then, you love your benefice more than you love Christ and his truth. You're meant to risk your life for the truth and for Christ, not for your benefice.' Again: '*Oh, if I should die [in this battle], how then would I win?* – I answer that to die for Christ is the supreme victory.'

'Who has forbidden me to preach? – *The pope.* – I reply that this is not true. – *O friar, there are the papal briefs. What do you say about them?* – I tell you that those briefs are not from the pope, and here are the reasons.' Savonarola then spins a short but subtle argument, terminating: 'Thus the pope as pope cannot err. . . . But when he errs, he is no longer pope; and if he commands something erroneous, he does not command it as pope.'

Coming in the middle of sermons that were often very long or packed with argument, the imaginary dialogue, as illustrated above, lightened Savonarola's load, injected a liveliness of spirit, and brought out the man's fallible qualities, while also revealing the ascetic and moralist. The preacher who could be thunder in his words could also be self-mocking, 'O poor friar', 'O lowly little friar', as he attempted to see himself through the eyes of others. He was too forceful a speaker not to have acted out the imagined scenes. And as this protean side of his character adapted itself to his vast audiences, he was more able to reach out to different sorts of people – highbrow intellectuals, peasants, rich merchants, 'little women', artisans, clerics, officials, and so forth.

On the whole, however, he pitched his sermons chiefly at the propertied middle classes, and at literate men and women, while never overlooking the highly-educated men among the mass of folk before him. And we must wonder about the extent to which his theological mode of argument, with its lashings of philosophy, introduced a whole treasury of words and concepts to men and women who had no other access to higher learning. The history of rational discourse in Italy is hugely indebted to the likes of San Bernardino, Caracciolo, Savonarola, and other preaching friars.

Themes

To MOVE IN on the main themes of a thinker like Savonarola is to rob him of his wealth and sophistication, because the selecting of basic or guiding ideas must omit complexity and lesser themes. This is the diminished destiny of all thinkers who are subjected to summary discussions. I offer this warning as a corrective at the points where our friar may begin to look less than rich in theme and attitude.

Savonarola proceeds from the fundamental assumption that in the coming of Christ (the Incarnation), followed by the Crucifixion, God revealed his love of humanity and the promise of everlasting salvation. He takes for granted that all Christians accept this revelation. Since death is a passage, a bridge to hell or heaven, it follows that human life is 'a life of soldiering' (una milizia): one in which the war is all about the struggle to enter heaven through the soul's triumph over sin. The field of battle, however, is so set out that salvation requires not only the grace of God but also the sacraments of the Church, such as baptism and communion, and hence a vital moral leadership. Savonarola concludes that the overwhelming problem of the age was precisely here, in the moral turpitude of those who governed the Church and administered its sacraments.

For him, therefore, the Church verged on a state of revolutionary renewal. As he saw it, there had been four ages in the history of Christianity: (1) the age of the apostles, (2) the age of the martyrs, (3) the age of the heretics, and (4) the current age of 'the tepid', a time now of such rapid transition that the fifth stage was already beginning to take shape. Savonarola drew some of these ideas from the tradition of so-called 'Millenarian' thought, which highlighted crisis, charismatic leadership, the ultimate clash between good and evil, the coming of a final age, and the end of history. A famous Cistercian monk and mystic, Joachim of Flora (c. 1132–1202), was one of the principal figures in this line of reasoning.

Almost everything else in the mosaic of Savonarola's thinking about the Church was applicable to his vision of renewal: even, for example, his call for the banning of the silver or gold clasps that were used to secure the veils on the heads of women of means. They were a 'super-fluity', a luxury that pointed to a denial of charity to the poor. In a time of transition and great misery for poor folk, when 'tepid' religious feelings continued to prevail, rich ornaments, on men as on women, were a sign of the corruption of the age. On women, moreover, such finery too easily became coquettishness, and this increased sexual desires. Since renewal meant a cleansing first, and first of all in Florence, the world's spiritual vanguard, here too was the explanation for Savonarola's campaigns against sodomy and against the horrors of blasphemy that accompanied gambling. He gives the example of the gambler who, in losing, suddenly cries out (with the opposite meaning in mind), 'Bless Christ's soul!'

With corruption and renewal as his central themes, Savonarola trained his sights on the enemy, the 'tepid' both among the clergy and the laity. In the last year of his life, however, as his domestic enemies and the Roman Curia closed in on him, he intensified his campaign against the flagrant cynicism and materialism of the upper clergy. The tepid were the multitude of half-hearted or lukewarm believers, who looked and sounded and seemed to carry on like Christians, but whose faith was shallow, and their love or charity a meagre thing indeed. They were dedicated to the externalities of religion: church ornamentation, costly chapels decorated with family coats of arms, fancy dress on their priests, a sensuous and distracting kind of song, and a formulaic partici-pation in the Church's sacraments. Either you took Christ seriously, or you did not. If not, you had no business seeing yourself as a Christian. But if you did, then the consequence had to be in measures of self-denial, in good works, prayer, fasting, and the correct use of the Church's sacraments.

One of the accusations often hurled at Savonarola was that he wanted to convert all Florence into a convent. The charge elicited one of his imaginary dialogues:

'*Well now, what are we supposed to do?* – Prayer: this is our sword, and with it we shall always defend ourselves. – *Friar, you've now worn us out with so many prayers. The whole day prayers and fastings, and fastings and prayers. We can't go on this way any longer. We're the talk of Italy. Our neighbours ask, are they doing more Lents in Florence? Everyone is after us with this business about many Lents, and they say: Florence has become a friar; that people has become a friar. We can't stand it any more, all this jeering about our Lents and prayers.'*

Savonarola sought a wholesale reform of morals in the city, as expressed in his assaults on vice, usury, and corruption in public office. If Florence was to be the New Jerusalem, from which the universal renewal of the Church would be launched, then the city had to become a model for all other cities and peoples. In 1495 and 1496, at the crest of his optimism, the Friar frequently saw Florence and Florentine Tuscany in this light.

A man of his times, with a strong stamp of political realism, Savonarola was never a leveller. He accepted the prevailing social hierarchy, with its tiers of princes, noblemen, rich bankers, wealthy merchants, lesser tradesmen and shopkeepers, craftsmen, and peasants. Immoderate ambition repelled him, for here was rampant, self-regarding pride: social-climbing peasants, uppity women, artisans too-well dressed, and scheming politicians. People, he believed, ought to keep to the social stations into which they were born. Yet he often turned to criticism of the rich and powerful: of their palaces, ornate chapels, costly dress, and their eating orgies at banquets. There is little evidence to show that with the passage of time he modified his stance against showy wealth. Like the great riches of the Church, the flashing of wealth was tantamount, he held, to a ritual of thieving from the poor, or at least a denial of charity, and no way could this be reconciled with the teachings of Christ. It is no wonder that he was horrified by the sale and purchase of Church offices, and the piling up of income-bearing benefices by influential clerics. Aside from opening the way to absenteeism (how could a priest be in six or seven different places at one and the same time?), simony turned the offices of the Church into merchandise, and this was doing business with the blood of Christ. If the Church, with its instruments, was crucial in the fight for salvation, it was only because Christ's blood – in the verbal usage of the day – had 'bought' us back from sin.

The Friar's conception of leadership in Church and society enabled him to lay a heavy charge on the backs of *gran maestri*: great lords, rich patrons, and powerful men. The expression, literally 'great masters', runs through the body of his principal sermons and refers not only to cardinals, prominent noblemen, and leading soldiers, but also to urban magnates and city bosses. Leaders stood in the public eye; they set an example; if they were violent or corrupt, their vices spread down and infected the whole society. In this view, the heads of the Church were bound to be the chief villains, because their vows and duties were the supposed seal of their honesty and rectitude. No, argued the friar: look at the rotters in the college of cardinals; look at the Pope; look at the bishops and other top clerics, using their offices as sources of income for pursuing the easy life. ['Lord, why do you not strike them down now!'] And he would never have called St Mary Magdalen a *gran maestra*, as his great adversary does, the Augustinian preacher Mariano da Genazzano, who alleged that she had 'castles, possessions, and great riches'. The heroic age of the Church had been the first, when Christ and his disciples had worked with poor men.

Gran maestri used their influence for self-serving ends, not for the good of the community. They expected and constantly got a rich flow of flattery. On these grounds, all men in holy orders, and especially preachers, were well advised to stay away from them. Even to approach such men could not but be the beginning of corruption. Savonarola came close to defining the good preacher as the sort of man who avoided *gran maestri*, and he pointed to the fact that he himself had no subservient contacts with princes and bosses.

Throughout his years in Florence, Savonarola's hard attacks on 'natural reason' and 'worldly wisdom' were so continuous as to border on pleas for irrationalism. His references to Aristotle, present in most of his sermons, dismiss the philosopher's attitudes just as often as they lean on his arguments. The result is a complex and contradictory friar, a rationalist and a thinker who leaned toward mysticism. The rationalist mounted arguments studded with logical sequences, propositions, distinctions, refinements, and refutations. His training in philosophy ripples through his sermons, and he loved to present arguments in this style of discourse. In the end, however, the mystic always surfaced to insist on the crucial importance of faith and the light of supernatural reason; and now he argued that philosophy as such journeyed out into a field of endless debate, where there could never be any final resolution or agreement amidst the babble of philosphers. Pure reason ended by capsizing into clashing opinions. And what we need is certainty regarding God and salvation. This is where faith and revelation stepped in: they completed the tasks of Christian philosophy, leading directly to God.

But Savonarola's insistence on revelation took him further, to a position that was more properly mystical. He wanted to envisage the road to God, and so — with a rush of feeling — he saw a path that led to a melding and union with divinity, a process built on contemplation and on something like a drunken or mad love of God. The journey was facilitated by study of the Bible, the matrix of all true wisdom. From here, the idea of living for God, the ideal end of man, is only a step away from the readiness, if need be, to die for God, and more specifically for Jesus Christ, because his blood had redeemed us. This idea winds through his sermons like a refrain, and in it we begin to see the willing, fearless martyr, the man who glories in the idea of dying for Christ. Yet the rationalist in Savonarola picked out the straining extremes of this position with such clarity that — swerving shrewdly — he also sought to make light of it, and often threw in the notion of madness, *pazzo*, with a self-mocking charm. No, he wasn't mad. Could madness accomplish what he had done in Florence? Yes, all sinners are somewhat mad; or, best of all, how can it possibly be mad to die for Christ, the *raison d'être* of our mortal journey? It is astonishing to note how often the word *pazzo* turns up in his sermons, as though he were pursued by it, nagged by it, accused by it, and yet he is never afraid to play with the idea.

Savonarola would have been horrified to hear himself called a dualist — a heresy that had long since been vanquished by the early Church; and there was nothing in his theology that stripped the world down to a struggle between the two equal but opposing principles of Good and Evil. There could not be an evil God or a God of evil. However, in his sacred enterprise to renew Christianity, as in his intensifying clash with enemies in Florence and Rome, and with the duke of Milan, he was rhetorically driven to see the world as a field of battle between good and evil, with the armies of God, as he said, ranged up against the armies of the devil. If he was to unify and inspire his Florentine followers, then he had to have recourse to every resource of oratory. With the crescendo of Rome's threats against the Florentine republic, the anti-Savonarolans were simply waiting for a favourable Signoria and the right moment to pounce. In this charged climate, the Friar's denunciations began to sound very much like the words of a dualist. Even in the spring of 1495, he had already conjured up an image of the world riven by two armies, one captained by God and the other by the devil.

Political Views

WE HAVE SEEN that Savonarola fielded an elaborate argument for why Italy, and Florence most especially, were naturally best governed by regimes of 'the people' – meaning the order of citizens long resident in a capital city, and made up largely of the propertied middle and upper classes. Climate, 'an abundance of blood', and a quick intelligence made the Italians into a people with a natural penchant for wanting to govern themselves and for spurning the government of tyrants or narrow oligarchies. And since the Florentines, 'the most quick-witted of all Italians', as Savonarola put it, occupied the heart of Italy, they had the city-state that would best serve as the ideal model of the well-governed and God-fearing city.

In the Friar's manipulation of these notions, the continuing attack on would-be tyrants became as important as the fight for the Great Council, for the appeal against the six-bean majority in the Signory, and for the outlawing of demagogic assemblies of the people (*parlamenti*). With a proper method of voting in the Great Council, whether by ballot or by randomly drawing names from electoral pouches, a regime of the people gave large numbers of men the opportunity to serve in government and to circulate through the city's rich arrangement of public offices. There was no better barricade than this against the ambitions of any strong man who might seek to muscle his way to the top.

As noted earlier, these were unusual views for fifteenth-century Europe, and no less so for Italy, a land chiefly under the rule of princes and war lords, with the exceptions of Venice, Florence, their subject territories, and the dwarf republics of Lucca and Siena. Most educated contemporaries, on the contrary, would have argued that 'the people' – whether broadly or narrowly understood – could simply not be trusted as a responsible force in politics: they were too naïve, too fickle, too unreliable, and really too stupid politically to have a significant voice in the state. In this view, princes and oligarchies were the 'natural' and 'rightful' holders of political authority.

Savonarola's vision of the Florentine republic spirited the subject away from run-of-the-mill political discussion, and put the city on a different plane. Let's recall that he and many others in Florence, including the worldly political diarist, Piero Parenti, believed that the fall of the Medici and the rebirth of the republic had been the work of God, a bloodless revolution achieved by means of His grace, not by the prowess of the Florentine people. Such a judgment, in the world of Renaissance Europe, was not in the least strange. The citizens of Florence, Venice, Genoa, and other city-states had often felt and claimed that God had given them a triumph or rescued them from an evil. In 1447, when the last Visconti duke of Milan died and the Milanese people rushed to establish their Ambrosian Republic, looking back to the old days of the city's republican commune, they held that they owed this 'grace of liberty' to God.

If we cast back to the November days of 1494, when Piero might have held out in the Medici Palace and the King of France marched into the city, we can see how Savonarola, who helped to plant the belief in God's intervention, now leaned on the idea, nourished it in his sermons, and carried his arguments to the point where he could proclaim that Christ was King of Florence. Of course he meant Christ as a divine force, a heavenly *éminence grise* operating through the spirits of men. Over the next two years, his sermons returned to this notion again and again. The streets would resound with it, as his troops of children called out *Viva Cristo, nostro Re*, 'Long live Christ, our King!'

He was most certainly *not* talking about a theocracy. Christ as 'King' was a slogan and a rallying cry. The idea could have no reality in the cockpit of politics, and Savonarola was perfectly aware of this. There would be no clerical hierarchy on the necks of Florentines. On the contrary, that very order was under attack. Hence, speaking from the pulpit as a political realist, he was even able to urge his listeners to elect prudent citizens to office, not 'good' men who would be foolish and a disaster in the affairs of government. The Friar did not for a second think that politics unfolded on the plains of heaven. When he said, 'Florence, Christ is your King!', his imagined heckler rightly threw back: '*O friar, do you think I don't understand? You want to say that Christ is King so that you can be his minister and do as you like.'* Of course, but in politics, this conclusion could only mean government by the Great Council, by citizens, and by the Frateschi.

Over the course of 1491–1492, the Friar's sermons won an astounding reputation for him as a holy and learned man, and by the autumn of 1494, even before the revolutionary events of November, many Florentines already saw him as a prophet. This judgment grew and spread in the weeks that followed the flight of the Medici and the arrival of the King of France. And while occasionally denying that he was a prophet, Savonarola moved emphatically into that role, as he continued to say things showing that he did so see himself. The role meshed with his political concerns. Biblical prophets were historic guides to their people, and their lessons were meant to reverberate throughout the land.

From November 1494, and up to the time nearly of his execution, he gave voice to his political ideas in scores of sermons. Then, at the outset of 1498, the new Signory, headed by the Gonfalonier Giuliano Salviati, invited him to write a work setting forth his views on Florence's 'new government', and he quickly produced his tract *On the Regime and Government of the City of Florence.* Here was his chance to pull together his political thoughts, and here, yet once more, he argued his case for the Great Council, for government by citizens ('the people'), and for the ideal of the common good. But he made a point of rejecting the idea that 'plebeians' might have any voice in government. Frequently charged with having robbed the nobility of power for the sake of the lowly multitude, Savonarola had crossly and constantly denied this. Now he was confirming his view that power in Florence belonged rightly to the propertied men of the middle and upper classes. It went without saying that leadership was bound to be the privilege of the uppermost social tiers.

The Friar then added a sustained attack on the dangers and vices of tyranny, and underlined his claim that the new republic had been the gift of God:

> 'Every Florentine citizen, wishing to help his city and to be a good member of it . . . should first of all believe that this [Great] Council and civil government were sent by God, as is indeed the truth, not only

because every good government proceeds from him, but also because God holds this city in his current and special providence. It must be clear to those who have been in Florence these past three years, unless they be blind or devoid of judgment, that if it had not been for the hand of God, such a government could never have been established in the face of so much mighty opposition, nor could it have been maintained up to our day amongst so many conspirators and with so few helpers. However, because God wants us to use the intellect and free will that he has bestowed on us, he renders the affairs of human government imperfect, in order that we ourselves may perfect them with his help.

God had set up the new republic, and a Dominican from Ferrara – by manifest implication – had been his mouthpiece. The Lord wanted Florence, his 'most loved of cities', to be ruled by citizens and the Great Council; hence any opposition to the 'popular' republic turned into activity that was aimed against the will of God. Or, as Savonarola had stated in a sermon of October 1495: 'I say that any who fight against this government fight against Christ.' In effect then, divinity's plans for Florence as the heroic front line of a religious awakening required a republic, so that Savonarola, acting as God's tool and prophet, could set it on its true way.

In the context of the age, no prince or tyrant would have lent himself to the announced union of political and heavenly designs. The greatest obstacle to these and to the Savonarolan programme, apart from Pope Alexander VI, reposed in the Medici and particularly in Piero, who strained to get back to Florence, but who could only return as a despot. So, if ardent support for the Great Council ran through the Friar's sermons, more persistent still – it was part of the same battle – was his running polemic against the typical tyrant. Part 2 of his tract on Florentine government is entirely taken up with the vision of such a monster, although he had already prepared this portrait in a stinging sermon of 26 February 1496, much of it an essay on the psychology of the tyrant.

In the tract, as in the sermon, the monster looks very much like a cross between Lorenzo de' Medici, Giovanni Bentivoglio of Bologna, the Baglioni of Perugia, and one or two of the early fifteenth-century lords of Ferrara. There are, it is true, legitimate tyrants (i.e. princes), 'but owing to their vices, from being legitimate they become illegitimate tyrants'.

Loving himself above everything else, the tyrant's fundamental policy is first of all to serve himself, and next his family and hangers-on. Being wedded to all the pleasures of the world, as attested to by his lust for honours and power, he is driven by pride, sensuality, and greed. He lays hands on the city's monies for the sake of his swaggering mode of life, and to buy the needed support that will keep him on top. Worst of all is the tyrant recently risen from the nobility or people (the Medici by obvious implication), for he must exile or wipe out not only all his adversaries, but also all who are his equals in nobility, wealth, or fame. Moved by vain and criminal fantasies, as well as by fears, he is suspicious, brutal, and always on the lookout for distractions or pleasures as medicine for his afflictions. It follows that he is beset by 'virtually all the sins of the world, above all because of his pride, lust, and avarice [in thieving from the public purse], the roots of all evil'. Savonarola pours it on, as he fills out the picture by drawing attention to the tyrant's hypocritical piety, his doling out of Church offices to favourites and accomplices, hiring and befriending of war lords (top *condottieri*), so that they may rush to help him in his time of need, and the scattering everywhere of his coat of arms. The tyrant also raises up trusty but servile new men, knocks down the houses of the poor in order to build new palaces, eliminates excellent men, manipulates and controls upper-class marriages, employs spies and informers, and corrupts the courts of law. Moving still closer to the Florentine model, with Lorenzo de' Medici in mind, Savonarola claims that the tyrant wants to be superior in everything, even in little things, such as in speaking, jousting, running race horses, and in the realm of ideas. If he is learned, he needs to shine; and if he writes poetry, he must be first and even be sung. But one of the worst things about a tyrant is that he renders a people pusillanimous and servile. Consequently, 'If a man deserves to be hanged for [the robbery of] a hundred ducats, just think of what the usurper of a kingdom [or city] deserves!'

In Savonarola's view of the public world, tyrants and lecherous, money-loving churchmen represented all that was evil in the modern world, because, although charged with the gravest responsibilities, they were hopelessly turned away from Christ, from the meaning of the Cross, and dedicated to the physical world at its most vile levels.

CHAPTER NINE

Angels and Enforcers: 1496–1498

F LORENCE HAD NEVER seen the like – the sight of thousands of Florentine children, well organised and streaming through the streets in pious processions, or massed on tiers of benches, theatre-like, in the cathedral, listening attentively to a preacher. The years are 1496 to 1498. Plague afflicts the city, especially in the summertime; and a fearsome shortage of grain is imposing such a famine that even peasants press into Florence through the guarded gates of its great walls, in search of bread. Many will die of disease and hunger, sometimes in the streets.

Yet in the pages of the best chroniclers and diarists, the death of starving beggars is little more than a smudge in the background to the city's political animosities, prominent personalities, and religious awakening. It was a hard time, bleaker by far than any period in living memory. But people knew – the Bible proclaimed it – that the poor you have always with you.

Religious companies (confraternities) for boys – serious catechising groups – first made their appearance in Florence in the early fifteenth century, but there were few, if any, ties amongst them. The Savonarolan movement and leadership of the 1490s went around these sodalities, took in children from all over the urban space, organised them according to the city's four administrative divisions, got them to appoint officers to manage their proceedings, provided them with flags, pressed the habits of confession and communion on them, and hammered away at the message that the time had come to turn Florence into a godly city, a New Jerusalem. This would be done by promoting action and talk against gambling, blasphemy, sodomy, 'pagan' revels, and the flaunting of luxury in dress and accessories.

Working as a foil for San Marco's emphasis on children, Savonarola's sermons sometimes skewered 'wicked old men' — all those contentedly entrenched in their vicious habits and nearly impossible to correct. The innocence and 'purity' of children served the Friar as a kind of cleansing force and a stick with which to beat the debauched adults. Their 'fresh' faces also served as a suggestive mode of symbolism. And historians have argued that Savonarola was utilising youth groups to press home his message of renewal.

On 3 September, 1497, in the midst of an epidemic of plague, fra Domenico da Pescia, assigned to work with the children, sent a letter to the pious boys of the Savonarolan movement. Printed in 200 to 300 copies, or possibly more, couriers took the letter out into the Florentine countryside, where many or most of the boys were safely lodged in the villas of their parents or close relatives, far from the mortal dangers of pestilence in the walled-in streets and spaces of the city. They were not, therefore, a rabble of poor children.

Fra Domenico's letter addresses the boys as the elect of God, reminding them of heaven's promised rewards, and urges them to keep a strict routine and lifestyle. But the communication is also a summons to action: the boys are to fan out to other villas and into the villages, to 'purge and sanctify' the face and ways of rural life. The chief moral scars and dangers lay in the 'superfluities' of the men and women who were well off. An extra warning was added: they must guard against letting themselves be seduced by evil company, elders or other boys. The letter's highlights are revealing:

'Fra Domenico da Pescia, your servant in Christ Jesus, [invokes] grace, peace, and health to all you faithful children of Florence, now scattered through the countryside. . . . Having predestined you as His adoptive sons through Jesus Christ . . . our Lord has again elected you first to be holy and immaculate in the presence of His purity, truth, and charity, and then, in His chosen time, to make you participants in and possessors of the great riches, power, glory, and other preordained prosperities . . . that have been promised to your city many times. . . . But because your fathers have not appreciated the promises — indeed, believing very little in them, they have not behaved in such a way as to deserve so much good in your city. You, therefore, in keeping with God's will and to His praise and glory, will soon possess the blessings of this great legacy . . . by the merits of the passion of His son, your Emperor, and by the intercession of your glorious Empress, mother of our Saviour.'

The friar interrupts the letter to say that in desiring to convey certain orders, he was forced to write to them, owing to the dangers of plague; but this reason is not altogether convincing. More likely, he also wants the circulating letter to fall into the hands of enemies, so as to underline or even exaggerate the continuing influence of San Marco. Singling out the little boys (*figliuolini*), the adolescents (*giovanetti*), and the older boys or young men (*giovani*), Domenico encourages them to stand robustly against the 'calumnies and impediments to [Savonarola's] preaching', for these will swiftly pass away, to 'the honour, praise, and glory of God and your salvation'. The letter continues:

'I beg you . . . to live as is right and proper for the elect children of God, observing His commandments, not playing and joking about, and not losing yourselves around your villas in hunting, hawking, fishing, and in pursuing other vain and disorderly pleasures, in the ways of children who have not seen the light. On the contrary, sober, modest, and quiet, as well as prudent and moderate in all your approved amusements, stick to your God-fearing habits, such as by saying the office of the Virgin Mary every day; often confessing and especially during this feast of her glorious birth; keeping your hair cut to measure [above the ears]; fleeing from [country] dances and from every other lasciviousness and turpitude; and do not mix or converse with vain children of the sort who perish [spiritually]. . . . I beg and command [on your faith, piety, love of honesty, virtue, rectitude, love of Florence, of the salvation of souls, compassion for the poor and afflicted, love for the grace of God, appetite for eternal glory, and zeal for the Immaculate Mother] that you go out and cleanse the countryside, all the villas, all the houses outside Florence, just as before Lent you purged this city of the tools of gambling, of all dirty and vain paintings and sculptures, and of all the other useless, vain, and lewd things of the same sort. Now is the time for this laudable undertaking, now that the real heat [of the summer] has passed, and finding yourselves, by the providence of your King [Christ], rather like his envoys and spies, go out to all the villas of your city, so that you can more easily and perfectly carry out this great Christian enterprise.'

Fra Domenico then reaches for a comparison in the Old Testament, and likens their assigned mission to the separate labours of Joshua and Ezekiel, who, although eight centuries apart, set out to purge their people of 'idols and other forms of filth'. In short, as 'emissaries and ambassadors' of God, the *fanciulli* may now carry out what they were unable to do during the previous winter.

Assemble often. You know what to look for and collect; you know the way; you know the blessings to utter at the villas and to the families of those who will want to offer you all their surplus and harmful household belongings for sinning and whose effects make the lands, vineyards, and olive groves sterile and accursed. Therefore get together, so that everything is done in an orderly manner, and obey your officers . . . if there be any among you. If not, then elect one [amongst you] as your head, along with three assistants. And let all the others be obedient to these four . . . in the work of purging the villas (thus sanctifying them) of all their instruments of iniquity and of hail, of other disturbances in the air, and of malign influences, famine, pestilence, and various illnesses that affect men and their livestock. The collected instruments of evil and vanity . . . you will then inventory and store, under lock and key, in a safe and well-guarded place.

Of the several striking features in this letter, including the militant tone, there is the assumption that the Friar's boys were able to act as exorcists, as agents whose purity and faith could ward off spirits and evil influences, if they but rightly applied themselves and acted to remove 'the instruments of evil and vanity'. Such indeed was the power of healing which San Marco, with Savonarola as its head, believed that it could impart to the boys.

In addition to showing political and religious foes the persisting power of the brigades of boys associated with San Marco, the September letter flaunts the striking deployment of the new printing press and the tenacious energy of the Savonarolan movement. It was a leap into early modernity.

The main sources (chronicles, memoirs, letters) tend to note the processions of the *fanciulli*, the Savonarolan children, only on certain high-holiday occasions, such as Palm Sunday, Easter, the festival of the city's patron saint (St John the Baptist, in late June) and, actually, Carnival. But Savonarola's sermons indicate that the *fanciulli* were also out in the streets on other occasions, such as Corpus Christi and in ritual efforts to put an end to famine.

The most condensed picture of what the children were up to may be got by zooming in on their activities in the winter and early spring of 1496.

Known by San Marco as a vile pagan festival, Carnival, the kingdom of the devil, was cleverly converted into a Christian celebration on the back, so to speak, of expectant energies. Traditional and ancient customs called for street revelry, obscene antics, lewd songs, wearing masks, the murderous 'game' of rock fights between boys from rival neighbourhoods, the placement in streets of long wooden crossbars (*stile*) to harry passers-by for money, and the making of local bonfires. In the 1470s, Lorenzo de' Medici himself had happily produced scurrilous rhymes and songs for Carnival.

The boys of San Marco came along to change all this. Ranging, most of them, from about twelve to nineteen or twenty years of age, they erected altars at the corners of main streets, each with a crucifix and candles. Like their 'pagan' predecessors, they also put up street barriers, in some cases using long staves, but their purpose was to collect alms from pedestrians for the 'shame-faced' poor. Instead of rock fights by lower-class boys, which inflicted deaths and terrible injuries year after year, the adolescent converts from the middle and upper classes helped to bring an end to those cruel encounters. They moved out into the neighbourhoods, knocking on doors and looking for the main objects of pleasure or of evil ('vanities'); and these would be fuel for the great bonfire to be held on the day of Carnival (16 February). In this fashion, whether by means of sweet or importuning politeness, they amassed a small mountain of playing cards, dice, gaming tables, chess sets, wigs, mirrors, dolls, fancy veil holders, cosmetics, jars of scent ('lascivious odours'), musical instruments, 'dirty' books in Latin and in the vernacular, pictures and statuettes of nude women, as well as masks, lengths of luxury cloth, and jewellery. The habit of local bonfires was thus morphed into a taste for one gigantic fire in the main government square, the Piazza della Signoria. All the 'loot' was brought here on the day of Carnival, piled up into a great pyramid, carefully guarded, then crowned by a figure of the devil and finally ignited. The children even sang or recited sneering rhymes attacking Carnival and the devil, as if in reply to the lewd street songs of tradition.

In one composition (a *canzone*), Carnival's flight from Florence begins with a Piagnone, a 'wailer' or fervent Savonarolan, calling Carnival 'a madman who does not believe' and who 'has his brains in his sandals'. The madman says that he is off to Rome, because Florentines have promised to burn him. Red crosses and cries of 'Long live Christ!' have won out here, on the banks of the Arno. The Piagnone asks Carnival: 'Where are your children, / straw huts, crossbars, stones, / roisterings, jousts, and so many merriments?' All have turned against me, comes the answer from Carnival. 'The children are my death, / they have taken away my glory.' In Florence, 'everyone has become a friar' and 'I don't want to eat like a friar.' Tell them in Rome, says the Piagnone, that 'Christ has become King of Florence; / we respect no other power.' And arriving in Rome, tattered and 'plucked', Carnival finds, of course, that the high clergy take his side against the Florentines.

The theology behind burning 'the instruments of vanity' was uncomplicated. Pride, self-regarding pride, was the cardinal Christian sin, a turning toward the self and away from God. In a time of universal corruption, in high place most especially, the instruments that catered to pride, or that caused Christians to lose their way, called for demolition. This meant everything from mirrors, whigs, and lecherous books and pictures to games of chance. Gambling fostered blasphemy, violence, and the ruin of families, while lechery led to self-abandonment in base pleasures, and hence to a falling away from God.

Savonarolan street processions were usually preceded by the children's attendance at Mass and a sermon in the cathedral, after which they went home for a light meal. They would come together later, now wearing white smocks over their ordinary clothing, so that all appeared in the colour of purity, and their meeting point might be in front of the convent of San Marco or the neighbouring church of the Most Holy Annunziata. The massed procession, headed by a large crucifix and an image of the Virgin Mary, would then make its way up the main street, the Via Larga, to the front of the cathedral, cut south across the city to the Bridge of Santa Trinita, traverse the river and then cross back again at the Ponte Vecchio, to halt in the great government square. The singing of hymns, punctuated by shouts of 'Long Live Christ' or 'Hurray for Christ the King', were a continuing feature of the proceedings. Organised and arrayed according to Florence's four municipal divisions, the boys marched behind their district banners, moving three abreast and holding hands. On certain occasions, processions were also preceded by drummers, pipers, and government mace-bearers.

The apothecary, Landucci, estimated that on the day of Carnival, 16 February 1496, some 6,000 boys made up the most striking part of the march. Piero Parenti offered the figure of 4,000, although, for the Palm Sunday and Easter festivities, he sets the numbers at 6,000 to 7,000. Cerretani, on the other hand, also an anti-Savonarolan like Parenti, speaks of 10,000 children, but he includes the ranks of girls who had managed to find their way on to the scene. The Milanese ambassador also put the figure at nearly 10,000 children, adding that the eldest were no more than fourteen years and that about 4,000 of them ranged from six to nine years of age. But his age figures are in all probability unreliable. The different estimates bring to mind the conflicting reports regarding mass street demonstrations in modern times.

When we remember that Florence in the 1490s was a city of fewer than 50,000 souls, any number we fix on, be it 4,000 or 10,000 children, yields a total of about eight to twenty per cent of the population: figures large enough to bring the city to a halt in its ordinary business activity. And any Florentines who were not out in the streets, watching the processions, were at their windows doing so, women especially.

For Palm Sunday and Easter, the children wore olive wreaths on their heads and carried a small red cross in one hand, the colour proclaiming Christ's passion. In the other hand, especially in the last year of Savonarola's ministry, they sometimes carried the olive branch of peace. All the boys had their hair cut above the ears. Long hair, a signifier of superfluity and ambiguous sexuality, had been banned from the ranks of the reformed boys and young men.

By transcending or circumventing the pre-existing adolescent companies, and by erecting a city-wide organisation, the Savonarolan youth movement broke out of the networks of local power relations, and San Marco thereby took firmer control of the boys and their allegiances. That is, ties between local bosses and youth groups were severed, most notably as seen in the largest of the boys' companies, the Confraternity of the Purification, which had been drawn under decisive Medici influence ever since the 1440s.

Yet no social movement is ever likely to mark time. Florence fluctuated in its moods and was very sensitive to political pressures. At its peak, the wave of young converts, ranging in ages from about twelve to their early twenties, produced boys who could be aggressive and even intimidating, all the more so in seeing themselves as a kind of morals police. Richly dressed women, when seeing them, turned and tried to get away. Card and dice players, as well as prostitutes, would flee as the white-clad boys wound their way through the streets, in search of gamblers, blasphemers, and obvious turpitudes, including male urinating-points that might be located haphazardly near religious images. Moreover, being made to appear wicked in a setting that had rapidly turned openly pious, people were more likely to surrender 'vanities' when importuned at their doors by groups of earnest boys.

But the climate of feeling gradually changed, and particularly in the last year of Savonarola's life, as his Florentine enemies, with the backing of Rome and the cardinal clergy, increased in the city's governing councils and intensified their attacks on the Piagnoni. Now the marching and scouting boys' groups confronted a growing resistance, including abuse, threats, and outright assaults. Gamblers might reach for knives or even swords, if San Marco's children happened to come on the scene. The boys began to go out into the streets in fear of danger, and they complained to their spiritual directors, with the result that Savonarola, in his sermons, had to pull in his horns and urge them to go about more politely, gently, and 'fraternally'.

Owing to the religious and moral assumptions of the age, fifteenth-century Florence had an unsavoury reputation for homosexuality and the practice of sodomy. San Marco, as we have seen, counted anal intercourse among its most detested sins and mounted a campaign against it. Unsurprisingly, therefore, in view of the Savonarolan troops of 'angel-like' boys with 'lambent' faces, the charge of sodomy was cunningly directed against the convent. On 23 July 1497, in the most dramatic instance and punishment of this 'lewd' accusation, a priest in the church of Santa Maria Maggiore was arrested by the political and criminal police, the Eight, for having declared that Savonarola and all his friars were 'Sodomites'. In retribution, he was made to mount a pulpit on the steps of the cathedral, just beside Giotto's great bell-tower and facing the Baptistry. Here, in front of a multitude, he confessed his wrongdoing and admitted that he had told lies. He was then put into a cage in the city's infamous prison, le Stinche.

Florence was a city in which political standing, wealth, and class were supremely important in the question of who exactly a man or woman was, whom they could hope to marry, how they dressed, and how they were treated in the streets and squares. The class origins of the teenagers and others in the Savonarolan youth movement should, therefore, be correctly understood. If youth was to have the kind of social weight and authority that we have seen above, then they had to show more than mere piety and be more than the bearers of religious symbols. The real setting, after all, was patriarchal. In law, the power of Florentine fathers was exceedingly strong; older men tended to monopolise the chief government offices; women's rights were sharply restricted; and in the propertied classes, men often found themselves, deep into their twenties, greatly dependent on their fathers. The results pointed to a society in which the young could not throw their weight around easily; the poor and the humble had no weight at all, except in sudden explosions, such as food riots or lynchings. Youths from rich families might make their weight felt, but only in exceptional circumstances and if they were well organised.

Contemporary observers pick out and emphasise the socially-superior origins of the Savonarolan fanciulli. And we may easily infer that most of the boys sprang from the property-owning classes: from old families, from the households of rich merchants and rentiers who lived off landed income and investments, and from the class of substantial petty merchants and artisans. Hence in that patriarchal society, the Friar's leading boys – say a Salviati or a Canigiani – were most likely to come from the eminent or old families. Even as reformed and fervent Christians, they would not readily have taken orders from their social inferiors; and their education (most were privately tutored), like their more worldly and self-assured ways, would soon have surfaced. Fra Domenico's letter of September, 1497, was directed at boys who were well-schooled in reading a highly Latinate vernacular, and a smattering of them would have had a good deal of Latin.

Seen in this social context, the intimidating aspects of the Friar's *fanciulli* can be more fully appreciated. Since they were easily recognised or typed in the city's public spaces, the sons of prominent men in the Florentine community could bring fear to women, to the men of the lower classes, and, being well organised, even to adult men of their own stripe. And they would have carried much the same weight when serving as the 'custodians' or 'correcters' of a mix of boys, many of whom came from more modest backgrounds.

CHAPTER TEN

The Pope and the Friar: 1495–1497

Enter Rodrigo Borgia

O N THE FACE of it, the match seemed ridiculous: a contest between a giant and a dwarf, Pope Alexander VI against 'the little friar' from Ferrara. And the wonder would be that the bout could have gone on for so long, with Alexander commanding the might of the papacy, in addition to the wiles of his amazing charm and diplomatic skills. Savonarola, however, had the protection of the Florentine republic and of something more – a strong whiff of the holy, so strong indeed that it made the Pope himself uneasy. In the end, Alexander could not fail to win, but his successors, two Medici popes and a line of others, would pay a delayed price in the shattering of the Christian world by Luther, Calvin, and the Protestant Reformation. The Friar's passionate pleas for a renewal of the Church were, after all, on target. He had seen deeply.

The name of Rodrigo Borgia is a byword for the corruption of the Renaissance papacy – corrupt in its unconcealed practice of simony and nepotism, no less than in its sexual laxity, careerism, and easy sale of indulgences for release or remission from sin. In the 1490s, Rome had – in the words of one wag – 'more whores than all the friars in Venice'. It was also the venue for a parade of anonymous poems, frequently affixed to, or near, the marble statue of 'Pasquino', in the old Piazza di Parione, or to other points in the city. The poems were laden with gross insults and cruel satires, savaging the conduct of popes and cardinals – justly so in the eyes of many of the most educated men, for it was also a time when the bastards of popes Innocent VIII, Alexander VI, Julius II, and two others before them were married off to princes or became the lords of cities and provinces.

Borgia therefore was a man of his day, if more extravagant in his ways.

Spain had a minor Catalan nobility which traditionally sent its men into the Church and into soldiering, much like the Roman Orsini and Colonna families. Springing from that stratum, but falsely claiming descent from the old kings of Aragon (de Borja), Rodrigo was born about 1431 in Aragon, near the seaport of Valencia. Although endowed with surpassing natural abilities, he was to have as a catapult his mother's brother, Alonso, who hailed from a different branch of the Borgia family and who was a leading canon lawyer, Bishop of Valencia, then Cardinal, and finally Pope Calixtus III (1455–1458). Favoured with Church offices by his uncle, Rodrigo followed him to Italy and for a number of years (until 1456) was in and out of Bologna, at the University, engaged in the study of canon law. Obviously intended for high priestly office in Rome, he had not long to wait. Less than ten months after Alonso's coronation as pope, Rodrigo was made a cardinal deacon, along with his cousin Luis Mila, in a secret consistory and by a unanimous vote; and in November of the same year, 1456, their elevation to the college of cardinals was publicly confirmed. That year too Rodrigo received his doctorate in canon law, which he then followed up with a swift accumulation of more benefices, including seven bishoprics, in addition to the most lucrative of all curial offices, the post of Vice Chancellor, yet another gift from Pope Calixtus, made over to him in May 1457. A contemporary calculated that the young man had quickly become the second richest of all cardinals, the first being the great French nobleman, Estouteville.

Calixtus made him, but soon enough Rodrigo's brilliant negotiating of the Roman scene was driven by his own skills. Curial Rome was a city of numerous nationalities, strutting aristocrats, ambitious climbers, and dedicated careerists, many of them well trained in law or grounded in the eloquence and literary masterpieces of the ancient world. At the top, such men often had the backing of princes and city-states, and these voices carried much weight with popes and cardinals. But talent always counted, particularly if placed where it might be strategically used. Such a place was the office of Vice Chancellor, making its holder second in authority only to that of the pope. Here the young Borgia presided over the twelve judges ('auditors') of the papacy's highest court, the Rota; he headed one of the Vatican's largest departments, employing a major team of attorneys, notaries, scriveners, and specialised clerks who issued some 10,000 letters a year; and most importantly – from a personal financial standpoint – when rich benefices were suddenly vacated by a death, he was the first curial official to know.

Rodrigo also logged in other important experiences along the way, as an energetic papal envoy (1456–1457) in the March of Ancona, on the Adriatic flank of the Papal State, and briefly (1457–1458) as the 'general commissary' of papal troops in Italy. But all such offices were waypoints. If a cardinal's loftiest ambition was fixed on the Church's supreme dignity, then his essential business was back in Rome, in personal relations with other cardinals – more bluntly put, in the art of wheeling and dealing.

With the knowledge gained from his position in the Chancellery, and loaded with wealth, Rodrigo Borgia was soon dispensing influence and was already a significant voice in the election of the next pope, the Piccolomini nobleman from Siena, Pius II, who was not blind to the Vice Chancellor's love of money and luxury. Being on the side of winners was to be Rodrigo's way. He became a key figure in the election of the next two popes, Paul II, and the first truly great nepotist, Sixtus IV. But on the death of Sixtus, in 1484, he was ready to intrigue for the papal tiara for himself, and so, like several other cardinals, canvassed hard for it and without scruple – in vain. He lost out to another lover of the easy life, an Italian from near Genoa, Innocent VIII, whose illegitimate children would marry well – his dissolute son, Franceschetto, a compulsive gambler, to a daughter of Lorenzo the Magnificent.

Every papal election was about politics, and often about money too, as Italian princes and city-states sought to pull strings with cardinals, and the group of eighteen to two dozen red hats in the conclave broke up into three or four factions. The contending parties charmed, bargained, bullied, and compromised, or simply bought and sold votes. In this role, the future Alexander VI was one of the most brilliant of players, and in August 1492, 'by the rankest simony', he finally triumphed over Ascanio Sforza, brother of the Lord of Milan, and over the formidable Giuliano della Rovere, who was to succeed Rodrigo and become the so-called 'warrior pope'.

If bribe monies, plus the promise of offices and benefices, won the election for Borgia, the charm and affability of his manners also worked to seduce his colleagues. Of a most 'dignified bearing', 'tall and power-fully built', he 'took pains to shine in conversation' and knew all about etiquette. He was exceptionally handsome, as well as cheerful and easy to talk to, but also quick witted, versatile, well read, and an eloquent speaker. Back in 1449, his tutor in humanistic studies had observed that 'beautiful women were powerfully attracted to him', and the great Catholic historian of the popes, Pastor, concluded that 'to the end of his days he remained the slave of the demon of sensuality'. But in the summer of 1492, as Pope Innocent lay dying, Borgia used every ploy to get things his way, throwing in, as well, the wholesale distribution of his lucrative offices and benefices. In Spain alone he had sixteen bishoprics.

Savonarola, then, in his fight against the official Church, was not really facing a religious man in the Pope, and he knew it. He had come up against a prince and dynast, a superb diplomat, a manipulator of men, and a handsome charmer to boot. 'Oh,' as he was sometimes to say of himself, 'poor little friar.'

Yet many cardinals of the period believed that just such a wordly figure — a consummate politician — was precisely what the Renaissance Church needed in the existing European situation, and particularly in Italy. Having been broken by three contending popes in the late four-teenth century, the unity of the papacy was not restored until after 1417, with the pontificate of the Colonna pope, Martin V. And it was to be another thirty or forty years before popes, now fully re-established in Rome, had the wealth, organisation, and soldiers to stand up to the other Italian states in countless disputes over territorial boundaries and intru-sive armies. These matters, and governing the Papal State, were a pope's most immediate concerns, not the condition of the clergy in Germany or England, and still less the task of meeting the spiritual needs of the people of Christian Europe. Somehow — it was supposed — the spirit would look after itself. Income, soldiers, courts of law, diplomacy, and an elaborate structure of offices would engage Rodrigo Borgia's excep-tional skills and talents, not a gift for piety or love of Christ.

And then there were his beautiful women (Vannozza Cattanei, Giulia Farnese, and others), his children (eight at least), and his boundless love for them. Florentine ambassadors noticed that when talking about his children he could be carried away, almost embarrassingly so. Not surprisingly, therefore, on hearing that his eldest son, the Duke of Gandia, had been mysteriously murdered and thrown into the Tiber River, he gave way to 'cries of anguish', was inconsolable for weeks, and at one point, in a formal meeting with cardinals, reportedly declared that he would have given 'seven papacies' for the life of his son. Here then, in his family, was yet another set of worldly concerns for Pope Alexander; and these, we can be sure, were taking precedence in his daily agenda over all the contentious questions that Savonarola was broaching back in Florence.

A Certain Girolamo Savonarola

ALEXANDER VI DID not begin to take any real notice of a certain friar until after the fall of the Medici and the march of the French army down the leg of Italy. Even now he had too many other worries: the intentions of King Charles VIII, the revolt of the Orsini lords in their castles outside Rome, a cabal of eighteen rebellious cardinals, and the future of his beloved children, not to mention governing a state. Savonarola's words and antics were therefore small beer, until they began to jar with his foreign policy, one key to which lay in the Holy League. Ratified in Venice at the end of March 1495, this alliance of Italian states, not including Florence, aimed to sweep the French out of Italy, so that Italian princes and city-states could get on with their own affairs. The French invaders, moreover, had the support of cardinals headed by the redoubtable Giuliano della Rovere, and they all spoke of Alexander's simony, sometimes questioning his legitimacy as pope. The times had now thrown up this annoying Dominican friar, who insisted on claiming that God had sent King Charles to cleanse Italy of its horrendous sins and who was also predicting a revolutionary renewal of Christianity. Rome, that capital of vice, he kept announcing, would be scourged without mercy.

If Alexander even bothered to give words to the matter, he perhaps asked himself something like, how can an overwrought simple friar amount to anything more than a local pest? But Savonarola's leading Florentine enemies, with their grand contacts up and down the peninsula, set out to change this opinion. They needed all the help they could summon to get the Florence they longed for, whether by restoring the mainline or cadet Medici, by humbling the Great Council and establishing an oligarchy of grandees, or by simply flattening the city's swell of piety, so as to bring back carnival, gambling, horse races, and – the Piagnoni alleged – untroubled anal sex. It was not male friendships that disturbed the so-called 'bigots' (*pinzocheron*), but rather what men and boys got up to in secret.

Since Alexander was the natural and obvious prince to turn to for help, the Friar's opponents soon took to dispatching tell-tale letters to their contacts in Rome, to leading merchants, bankers, and well-conncted clerics: men with friends and patrons in the papal court. The Pope thus began to get a flow of oral and written reports, highlighting Savonarola's repeated claims. In turn, fully informed about this by his own contacts in Rome and Florence, Savonarola rounded on the unknown letter-writers, the informers present at his sermons, and often knocked them for getting their facts wrong, for defaming him, for being troublemakers, and for working to subvert the new republic.

Meanwhile, the Lord of Milan, Ludovico Sforza, was also getting at the Pope through Cardinal Ascanio Sforza, his brother. Now anxious about the French, despite having been the first heavyweight to invite their attack on the Kingdom of Naples, Ludovico wanted them out of the peninsula and he wanted Florence in the Holy League. The Friar, however, was squarely in the way. The Milanese ambassador to Florence, Paolo Somenzi, plied Sforza with reports on the Florentine political scene, as in a letter of 27 January 1495, where he writes: the Dominican 'persists in his bad attitudes and works, because of which I am doing things to turn people here against him. . . . I hope in the next few days to make this people really understand how this Friar is their enemy and is deceiving them.' Three weeks later, noticing the confusion and discord caused by the Friar, Somenzi steps up the charges: 'he all but rules this govern-ment. He is the one who makes *Signori* [Priors] just as he pleases, and similarly all the other offices and magistracies . . . He has said in public, that is [while] preaching, that this people need not obey the Holy Father; and if His Holiness should issue a prohibition barring this city from celebrating Mass, he has said that it should not be observed because it would not be valid, he not being a true pope.'

The rumoured interdict did not arrive; Savonarola thus far had said nothing of the sort in his sermons, at least not as they have come down to us; and he was most assuredly not picking men for high office. Yet the atmosphere in Florence was so charged emotionally, that these were the sorts of allegations that were reaching Rome and being whispered into Pope Alexander's ear.

Eight months after first bursting on to the historical stage in the Florentine events of November 1494, Savonarola heard directly from the Holy Father. He received a friendly letter, dated 21 July 1495, bearing a firm invitation. The Pope was being a diplomat. Having heard that the Friar was able to foretell the future by divine revelation, he invited and indeed ordered him to come to Rome to tell him about this unusual gift. But our man, no innocent by now, and suspecting the ways of His Holiness, feared a harsh Roman trial, prison, or even assassination along the way. He therefore refused the invitation, in effect rejecting the command, with an apologetic letter of explanation (31 July 1495). Owing to his hard labours for Florence, he wrote, he was ill with fever, dysentery, stomach and other ailments. The doctors prescribed rest. Despite all his efforts to secure peace and amity in Florence, there were evil men about, conspiring both against the city's freedom and himself. 'Often they have even intrigued to kill me with poison or swords, because of which I cannot go out safely [into the streets] without armed guards.' Moreover, urgently-needed reforms required his presence in the city. It was God's will that he remain there for the moment, and prudent men urged him not to leave. Regarding his ability to foretell the future, particularly with reference to scourgings and the renewal of the Church, he was about to publish a small book on the subject (the *Compendio di rivelazioni*); it told all; 'and I will be most careful to send Your Holiness a copy'.

There was cheek in this letter, as well as a tincture of Savonarola's whistling in the dark. On his retreat from Italy, King Charles had been boldly engaged by Italian forces at the famous battle of Fornovo (6 July 1495), and while no side could justly claim a victory, the Italians had demonstrated that the French were not after all invincible, despite their fearsome artillery and fighting skills. This had encouraged the Friar's enemies, and the word was that if they could get him to travel to Rome, his assassination would be no difficult matter. For the same reason, Lorenzo the Magnificent had adamantly refused to go to Rome, in the long aftermath of the Pazzi Conspiracy (1478–1480), to beg Pope Sixtus IV's promised pardon for the Florentine Signory's murder of the Archbishop of Pisa and of a half-dozen priests. He had no doubt that if he went he would never leave Rome alive.

The bombshell of a reply to Savonarola's brave letter was penned by an important clerk in the papal bureaucracy, Bartolomeo Floridi, afterwards a well-known forger. Dated 8 September, the original of this reply was perhaps not even seen by the Pope. It was addressed to the Florentine convent of Santa Croce — mistakenly so, it is always said, thereby supposedly underlining Floridi's crass carelessness. Not at all. Arguably, the papal brief was deliberately sent to the Friar's foremost Florentine enemies, the Franciscans, in order to telegraph its contents to the entire city. A day or two after its reception, the letter would be on every Florentine tongue.

The brief quickly proceeds to note the 'schisms' and 'heresies' that may arise from 'a feigned simplicity', when this is used as cover for innovations in dogma. It then names 'a certain Girolamo Savonarola' who has been 'dragged to such a grade of madness as to proclaim himself sent by God and to be speaking with God', though on no canonical grounds whatsoever. 'Any heretic can say the like.' He has also declared that 'Jesus Christ and God lie if he lies . . . a horrendous oath', in addition to stating that anyone who refuses 'to accept his claims puts himself beyond salavation'. Consequently, to fight the danger of his evil ways, Rome is reuniting San Marco and the Dominican convent of Fiesole with the Lombard (northern) Congregation; Savonarola is to be under the orders of the Lombard Vicar General, Sebastiano Maggi, who will also preside over an inquiry into his activity and writings; and he, meanwhile, is suspended from all preaching until the inquiry has been completed. Furthermore, his three assistants are given nine days to move to Bologna, from where Maggi will dispatch them to different convents, none however in Florentine territory. Automatic excommunications will ensue for all who refuse to comply with the letter's demands.

Whether partly or not forged, here was a papal brief designed to be a knockout blow; and horror was the only possible reaction at San Marco, quite apart from the sting and scandal of its having been delivered to the Franciscans of Santa Croce. Everything that Savonarola had put together over the previous five years was suddenly to be dismantled by the removal of his top lieutenants, by putting San Marco under the command of the Lombard Congregation, and by silencing him. Yet one of the points that weakened the brief was the threat of excommunication *latae sententiae*, meaning, in effect, that disobedience or infractions automatically incurred the penalty. Canon law called for 'sobriety and great circumspection' in the use of such threats. And even if the severity of the brief was not all his doing, the Pope was cheapening the penalty by throwing it about a little too easily, such as with his mistress Giulia Farnese. After having promised not to return to her husband Orsino Orsini, she then did so, whereupon Alexander replied with the threat of an 'excommunication *latae sententiae* and eternal malediction'. That September he also threatened Florence with excommunication, unless the city stopped offering aid to the King of France.

Challenged by the brief, the Friar was not going to take the threat lying down, and he replied at once, on the day after receiving it, although it had been en route, curiously, for nearly three weeks. San Marco did not get the brief until the end of September. Was Rome slow in dispatching it, or had the Franciscans of Santa Croce their own reasons for holding on to it?

Savonarola's reply refutes the brief point by point, treating the nature of prophecy, the slur regarding his errors in dogma, his being a messenger of God and talking to God, the statement about Christ's lying, and so forth. Here, as in all his letters of self-defence to Alexander, he bases his pleas in canon law and concise argument. But one of his supporting columns is also the testimony of 'the ten thousand witnesses in Florence' who are ready to attest to the rectitude and orthodoxy of what he has preached. Another is his expressed conviction that the Pope has been misinformed and misled by dishonest men. He recapitulates his reasons, as laid out in the letter of 31 July, for not repairing to Rome in obedience to the papal command. 'In the judgment of all the citizens here who know them, I have capital enemies who are such that they would not have permitted me to get as far as Rome', and he repeats his claim about being unable to leave his convent without an armed escort.

The matter of the Lombard Congregation raised a painful subject, because the original break with them, Savonarola notes, led to quarrels so sharp — and the troubles with them continue — that 'we hold' the Vicar General and his friars most suspect; and all civil laws concede that a man is not compelled to appear in places where he is in danger of being killed. The danger of death — should Savonarola move about unguarded or leave the city — is mentioned in the letter three times. 'And I have such enemies because of the truth I preach, for the truth provokes hatred.' He is not afraid, he adds, but neither does he wish to tempt God.

Although Savonarola does not refer to the incident, some months previously, on a Sunday evening (24 May), he had managed to escape a bloody assault on the Via del Cocomero, as he was on his way back to San Marco from the cathedral, where he had just delivered a sermon.

The men of the Lombard Congregation, he continues, are too lax about their rules, and the friars of San Marco could not possibly depart from their more 'perfect' ways for the sake, by implication, of a worldly life. Surely the Pope would not desire this. The northerners have possessions in common, which is not the case at San Marco, where the friars are also more frugal about food and dress. The same rigour and commitment apply to their observance of silence and the frequency of prayer. Our friars, continues Savonarola, have made vows to God about their austerity, and they cannot now go back on these. In short, he and his brothers cannot believe that it is truly the Holy Father's intention to force them to rejoin the northerners and to have their three leading friars depart for Bologna. Next, referring to his enemies, who include the Pope's malicious informers, Savonarola asserts: 'They want my head . . . / They want to tear me away from this city, not so that I may come to the feet of Your Holiness, before whom they know that I would certainly know how to defend myself, but rather to kill me on the way. Their goal is a tyranny [in Florence].' He closes the letter by inviting His Holiness to send out a trusted cleric to examine him, or to tell him where he, Savonarola, is in error, 'and I will recant all, in secret and in public, in front of all the people'.

The antagonists were now all but face to face, with a known forger on the papal side, bribed — it seems likely — by enemies of the Friar into sending out a more menacing brief than was at that point intended by Pope Alexander. The brief of 21 July included a command that was put in polite and friendly words, whereas the brief of 8 September was gratuitously rude, referring first to 'a certain Girolamo Savonarola', then to 'Savonarola', and finally to 'Girolamo', on top of which, as already noted, it was sent to the Franciscan convent of Santa Croce.

The friars and Prior of San Marco had an official patron in Rome, the influential Neapolitian Cardinal Oliviero Carafa. This nobleman at the papal court was in deep sympathy with Savonarola's call for a renewal of Christendom. The brief of 8 September, prepared in the midst of a hot Roman summer, was kept a secret from him. Now Savonarola's pleas, doubtless by special messenger, got to him as well, and looking into the exchange of letters, he was able to argue the case with Pope Alexander, which helps to explain the succeeding events.

A remarkable reversal followed, and a return to Alexandrine politeness, in a papal brief of 16 October. This communication cancels the command of 21 July, ordering Savonarola to go to Rome, suspends the censures of 8 September, but repeats the order that he desist from all further preaching until his case has been more fully considered. The Pope chides Savonarola for purporting to foretell the future, since doing so can lead 'simple people' away from the true path and obedience to the Church, and these are contrary times for such preaching. At any rate, Savonarola's letters and messages, and the different views of certain cardinals, expressed since the brief of 8 September, had brought a change of heart. He is delighted to learn that the Friar is ready to submit to the Church's correction and that perhaps he did predict 'those things not from malice but rather from a certain simplicity and zeal, with a view to increasing the yield in the vineyard of the Lord, despite the fact that appearances suggest the contrary'. And finally the admonition: 'We order you . . . from this point on to abstain from all preaching, public as well as private, so that you may not be charged with having turned to secret conventicles, after having ceased to preach publicly.' The Prior of San Marco was to observe these restraints until he could 'come to our presence safely and honestly, as befits a cleric, not surrounded by armed men'. Should this turn out to be impossible, he was to wait until the Pope had time to consider the matter more fully, which might even entail the dispatching to Florence of an examining papal envoy. 'If, as we hope, you do as we say, we suspend as from this moment our previous briefs, and all that is contained in them, in order that you may tend to your conscience with tranquillity.'

The diplomatic Pope Borgia had now managed to silence the Friar, while keeping outrage in Florence to a minimum, and temporarily satisfying Milan, Venice, and the cardinals who wanted Savonarola out of the way or at least quelled. With such a clearing of the stage, Florence could be more readily drawn into the Holy League against France. The several cardinals who sympathised with the Friar were also mollified. Interestingly, too, the Pope did nothing to prevent him from publishing his works and was silent about the reasons for this, though I suspect that he was trying to avoid scandal, to keep from being plagued by a chorus of insistence that the man's teachings and doctrine were absolutely orthodox. If they were, and his writings were made the test of his orthodoxy, then he might be able to triumph in the teeth of any examining commission.

Savonarola, meanwhile, had found a respite in the brief of 16 October. He was now in a position to play for time. To be banished from his beloved pulpit was a setback: he saw preaching as his life. But he was free to go on writing; he and his men would remain in Florence; and he could continue to be the living icon of a powerful religious and political movement.

An Anxious Year

WHAT DID RODRIGO Borgia, a proud Catalan nobleman and career cleric, know about communities of active citizens, about political liberty, about a modest man's right to have a voice in sovereign affairs or a vote in the election of candidates for high office? And how could he care about such matters? He was surrounded by armed noblemen, soldiers, and clerics who were absentee holders of rich benefices. Hence he could easily enough understand an aristocratic caste of the sort that governed the old republic of Venice, and as a trained jurist even see a modern reflection there of Rome's ancient senatorial class. But as a princely priest who was looking to dynasties for his children, he could never have a visceral understanding of the politics of petty merchants and small-time attorneys in Florence, where a *fraterculus*, a little friar, had succeeded in turning the population of a famous city into a throng of curious believers and fierce republicans.

If Renaissance Florence was about artists and patrons, and even about the Medici, it was also – and far more deeply – about getting one's daily bread, about heartfelt pieties, families, community life, republican politics, small-time intrigues, and the honest or ruthless quest for honours.

Savonarola was to hold his official silence for 120 days, from shortly after the middle of October 1495 to 17 February 1496. But soon after he had stopped preaching, and given himself over to a period of intense writing, Florence, working through its agents and emissaries, began to nag the Pope for a restoration of the Friar's right to preach. On 17 September the Signory had written to Pope Alexander in Savonarola's defence. In early November, seeking continuous contact with the pontiff, the new Signory appointed an ambassador to the Pope, a Florentine prelate and apostolic *scriptor* already in the Curia, *Messer* Ricciardo Becchi. On 13 November, they sent missives to Cardinal Carafa and to the Pope, pleading the case for the Friar's resumption of preaching. 'Most Blessed Father, he is truly a good man and of a holy life, irreproachable customs, upright faith, and admirable doctrine . . . Blessed Father, we have need of him, we need this man of God and his preaching.' In January 1496, the War-Office Ten were pressing Becchi, and recruiting the help of others at the papal court, to urge the Pope to permit Savonarola to deliver the coming season's main cycle of Lenten sermons. But the opposition never slept. When rebellious Pisa was drawn treacherously back into French hands, bitter feelings in Florence erupted against Savonarola, heard in cries around San Marco: 'That pig of a friar, we'll burn his house [convent] down!'

All the while, working quietly behind the scenes, San Marco's Neapolitan protector, Cardinal Carafa, was treating the Pope to a flow of good words about the Friar, and at a lucky moment, sometime between 10 and 15 February, he managed to procure Alexander's cagey and almost secret oral consent to Savonarola's return to the pulpit. That the scene actually took place is sometimes strongly doubted, but two considerations vouch for it. The astute pontiff was here eating his cake and having it too. Consent was granted in a back room, as it were, and this would satisfy both Florence and the remains of a papal conscience; but it would also be possible, along the way, to renege on the consent, by claiming that no document existed to validate the alleged right, in accord with a Curia that was notoriously bureaucratic and document-mongering. In addition, although he would often protest and complain thereafter, Alexander allowed Savonarola to go on preaching for another year.

Had a deal been made? On 11 February 1496, in a cunning act of stagecraft, the Signory ordered the Friar to give the cathedral's Lenten sermons. It goes without saying that he hungered for that invitation, which was made to look like a command, and he immediately threw himself into the working up of a new cycle of sermons, building them around Amos, the Old Testament prophet of the 8th century BC.

All too soon, however, Alexander was the recipient of letters and reports detailing the contents of the Lenten sermons. Florence's busy-bodies were at it again. And at the outset of March the Pope began complaining to Becchi and to others that he was not in the least happy about the Friar's preaching. He admitted that the allies of the Holy League – Milan and Venice most notably – were also much opposed to the sermons. The objections thus lay in politics, not in religious doctrine.

In a letter to Becchi of 9 March 1496, the Ten rejected 'the false calumnies that are daily invented against fra Girolamo by perverse men'. No, Florence does not suffer him to attack the Church and the Pope. This would not be allowed. Instead, as is the custom of preachers, he strikes at vices and at the faults of princes in general, and he threatens divine scourgings. So let His Holiness not credit the words of his detractors and evil men. Three days later the Ten wrote again, saying that in view of their problems, the Pope should have compassion for the Florentines. This city threatens no one in its pact with King Charles, and the Friar brings immense comfort 'to our people'.

On 18 and 20 March, Becchi reported to the Ten that the Pope was putting up with Savonarola's preaching against his will, and deeply resented his 'meddling' in Roman affairs, which were no business of his! The result was that 'he will listen to no one who speaks up for us' and pays heed only to the calumnies mouthed by the Friar's enemies and ours. Florence can expect absolutely no favours from him, not even the indulgence for Santa Maria del Fiore (the cathedral), which he had promised to Becchi before Lent.

The Florentine ambassador next relayed a string of charges and accusations, beginning with the Pope's astonishment that the city could have put so much authority in the hands 'of the Friar, the children, and the people'. This sort of information, notes Becchi, comes from so many important men in Florence that 'it is hard to try to reject or excuse it'. And here, more particularly, are the objections: (1) that the city should allow Savonarola 'to preach against the will of the Pope, a thing unheard of'; (2) that he should 'speak openly and publicly against His Holiness, the cardinals, and the whole Curia'; (3) 'that he should write, speak, and declare that he is a prophet, that he speaks with God, Our Lady, and saints, and predicts future events with such assertiveness'; (4) 'that by giving such boldness to the people and to children, he hijacks the freedom of those whose business it is to deliberate, to discriminate, and to judge'; and (5) 'that even if these claims were a thousand times false, it is an infamy and a dishonour for the city that a friar should rule and dispose, and embolden children in such a way that here and the world over it should be said that fra Girolamo and children govern Florence, that they act as the Signory, the Eight, the Ten, and the [Council of] Eighty, that they are the ones to punish vices; and that citizens should be afraid of them and have not the courage to speak up or to recommend measures against his [Savonarola's] will; in short, that just to hear such things is a shame and a disgrace. The truth is that all this court laughs at such things, and many who love the city regret and are pained by the claims . . . and it seems to them that you have lost your minds and reputations by not knowing how to look after yourselves.'

Becchi then winds toward his conclusion: 'It is enough that you are sneered at and derided for letting yourselves be governed by a friar, and that children should act as the *Signori* . . . moving about the city with such audacity and temerity.' Yet all this 'is the least of what I hear every day. In looking to the honour of the city and of the citizens who rule it, my biggest problem lies in trying to defend and make excuses for fra Girolamo. And know, my Lords, that I have written the present letter with the greatest displeasure, but solely to discharge my office, so forgive me. I commend myself to your Lordships.'

Being a papal official, hence with a dual allegiance, the ambassador, *Messer* Ricciardo Becchi, had let himself go: he could not be hurt by his 'Lordships' back home, and anyway he had no sympathy for Savonarola. Trying always to remain in the good graces of the Signory and the Ten, Florentine ambassadors were rarely so outspoken. They were more likely to resort to flummery when conveying unpleasant information. One of the more fascinating features of Becchi's letter, therefore, is in what it reveals about the world of the Curia. Here were aristocrats and an order of well-educated men who could not but look down with derision and laughter on the supposed power of a friar, of children, and of 'the people' (*il popolo*). They must have had jolly lunches, leavened by wit in retailing the stories that came out of Florence – caricatures for the most part, but cleverly utilised against the Savonarolan republic by the friends of the Medici, the supporters of the Holy League, and the grandees who believed that a small oligarchy was the only viable government for Florence. They were of course right about the Friar's assaults on the Curia and the organised Church, about his proclaimed stance as prophet, and his supposed conversations with God and the Virgin Mary. But when looked at in the fiercely hostile and sneering context of the papal court, the truth in the charges was bound to take on grotesque features.

Savonarola's enemies could not bear his refusal to be humble, to be afraid, to toe the line, to pay his respects to the high and mighty. And in fact in his first sermon, delivered on 17 February, he came forward in a fighting mood that would carry him right through the series to Sunday, 10 April 1496. While fully accepting a conservative notion of social and universal hierarchies, he also held to a doctrine of 'the elect', of the men and women with the grace of God and destined for salvation. Here was a body of believers that was likely to exclude most of the powerful, rich, and comfortable (but 'tepid') folk of his day, clergy as well as laity. The Amos sermons frequently lash out at 'big bosses' and 'great lords' (*gran maestri*) for 'drinking the blood of the poor', at the enemies of the Great Council, unscrupulous prelates, tyrants, and the vile Roman clergy happily ensconced in a city of '10,000 whores'; but he also, if less often, assails the many secret senders of tell-tale letters to Rome, corrupt old men, and the usual array of gamblers, usurers, blasphemers, and sodomites. Certain refrains run right through the series, as in the claims that he is not afraid, that he will not be quiet, that he knows he is in trouble, that the enemy conspire to murder him, and that he is almost certain to be killed or exiled. Savonarola gave no quarter.

Having delivered his Lenten sermons, he rested for about a month. As late as the beginning of April, the Pope intimated that he was determined to have Savonarola declared a heretic and a schismatic, but the members of a shadowy examining group, although rather critical of the Friar, failed to overcome Cardinal Carafa's strong advocacy. And thanks to additional promises from him, as from others, Alexander temporarily dropped his protests. Becchi quickly informed the Ten about this. Here was further evidence to support the view that the Pope had given his devious oral consent to Cardinal Carafa, permitting the controversial sermons that followed. Consistent with his pre-emptive ways, the Friar's reaction back in February had been to say that the call for him to preach (and the authorisation) had come from God.

Was a new phase possible in relations between pope and friar? Alexander VI had his share of late-medieval superstition, was certainly uneasy about the Friar, and had been moved by him at different moments. It is therefore possible and even likely – though the proposition is contested by Arrabbiati historians – that in the summer of 1496, the General Procurator of the Dominicans, Ludovico da Ferrara, in Florence on a mission for the Pope, sought to tempt Savonarola with the secret offer of a red hat, a cardinalate, on the understanding that he accept certain conditions. This alone makes sense of one of Savonarola's most famous asseverations, uttered in a sermon of 20 August in the Hall of the Great Council and cast directly at the Signory: 'My Lord [God],' he apostrophises, 'I want only you . . . It is not my habit to seek human glory. Away with that! I seek no glory but in you, my Lord . . . I want no hats, no mitres large or small. I want nothing, unless it be what you have given to your saints: death. A red hat of blood: this I desire.'

We may conjecture that a shiver of silence went through the Signoria. The year 1496, though a triumph for Savonarola, as 1495 had been,

saw the city slip toward more serious economic and public-finance problems. The armed struggle to recover Pisa was turning into a nightmare
in war costs. Florentines had lost large tracts of productive land around
Pisa. Companies of foreign soldiers, assisting the Pisans and paid for by
Venice and the Duke of Milan (two of King Charles's foremost opponents), raided parts of Florentine Tuscany. Later in the year, Florence
would begin to suffer grain shortages and famine. The production of
silk and fine woollen cloth – mainstays of the city's industry – was in a
downturn; and money was tight, largely, I suspect, because fear had induced
many rich Medicean collaborators to move a hoard of gold florins out
of the city, following the flight and expulsion of the Medici. One result
was that in its chronic – sometimes desperate – need for cash and war
loans, the republic was at times driven to borrow money from its own
citizens at exorbitant rates of interest – for a form of profiteering that
was sharply denounced by Savonarola as heartless greed.

The Friar's relations with Pope Borgia reached their next critical stage
in the late autumn, with the unexpected arrival at San Marco of a papal
brief dated 7 November 1496. It announced the establishment of a new
congregation of convents, reaching from Lucca and Florence down to
Perugia and Rome, and linking all the Roman and Tuscan houses of the
Dominicans. The Pope himself was the initiator of the reconstitution.
The reason for the change was bureaucratic – it was the search for a
smoother functioning, and there was to be no discussion about it. The
brief closed with the threat of excommunication *latae sententiae*, to be
levelled against anyone who contradicted or impeded or tried to work
against the new arrangement. Taking for granted that San Marco and the
other Dominican houses in Tuscany were still in the Lombard
Congregation, the brief thereby flagged the presumption that the earlier
break with Lombardy had been illegal, as already alleged in the brief of
8 September 1495. The vicar of the new congregation was announced in
December and he was a Sicilian.

Savonarola now held his silence. He did not respond for more than
seven months, not until after his excommunication; and the reply, dated
19 June 1497, went out, courageously, as a public letter to 'chosen' or
'loved' supporters. He argued that the decision about whether or not to
enter the new Roman–Tuscan Congregation belonged entirely to the will

of the friars of San Marco; and since they had chosen excommunication, or even death, over entry into a union with the other houses, then so it would have to be. He himself could not impose obedience on the other friars, although he of course agreed with them.

What Savonarola did not know was that his Cardinal protector, Carafa, seems to have supported the new brief of 7 November 1496. Historians argue that Carafa desired the change not to see San Marco absorbed by the other houses and thus tamed, but rather to enable it to extend the scope of the Friar's reforms. Yet there had been no discussion of the question between the Cardinal and the Friar, nor was there any afterwards. Rightly suspicious, Savonarola opposed the change from the very start. This angered the Cardinal and was to turn him against the Friar, although the likelihood is that he, Carafa, had either given in to wishful thinking or he had been manipulated. The new brief, announcing the decision to draw together sixteen different Dominican houses, was so clearly cut and tailored against Savonarola, that everything he stood for compelled him to reject it.

The Friar's fight with Pope Alexander – a fight between two priests – may be seen in religious terms first, with the focus on the Friar's egregious insubordination and alleged heresy. What made the clash more inflammatory was the fact that certain cardinals thought they saw something illegal, not to say heretical, in the simony that had procured the papal tiara for Rodrigo Borgia. They even raised the question of a general Church Council that could depose a pope. But local and international politics had also been flung on to the great stage. At the end of 1496, Savonarola was still committed to seeing King Charles and 'the barbarians' return to Italy to complete the 'scourging'. In Florence, the aristocrats who wanted his head were seeking, on the contrary, to draw the republic back under their control or under the domination of the Medici, whether by pressing Florence into the Holy League against France, by gradually dismantling the Great Council, or by means of a coup d'état.

CHAPTER ELEVEN

The Savonarolan Moment

King Christ

F LORENCE WAS HIS, Savonarola's. Speaking into the faces of thousands of Florentines, he had claimed it again and again for God. But he alone was God's spokesman in the most civilised of European cities. And if the Pope was the vicar of Christ on earth, Savonarola was Christ's vicar in Florence. His vision and magnetism gave birth to a series of Carnival hymns and street songs, sung both by children and by adults, hailing Jesus Christ as Lord and King of the city, as in this anonymous laud:

> 'Live, long live in our hearts
> King Christ, Leader and Lord.
> (Viva, viva in nostro core
> Cristo re, duce e signore.)

One of the songs, probably from the pen of Girolamo Benivieni, repeated the Friar's promise that Florence would soon be more powerful and glorious than ever:

> 'Long live Christ our King, and the happy
> Virgin Mary, Queen, who says that Florence
> More than ever will be richer, mightier, more glorious
> And soon the worker of miracles.
> (Viva Cristo re nostro et la felice
> Maria regina, che in fiorenza dice
> Più riccha, più potente e gloriosa
> che mai fussi hor farai mirabil cosa.)

Savonarola's followers often referred to the new hall of the Great Council as 'the Hall of Christ' (*sala di Cristo*), and they occasionally spoke of 'holy liberty', even when serving in high office.

If there were men and women among the Friar's followers who in some fashion seriously accepted the idea that Christ was their King, their spiritual King, we dare not assume that the leaders of the political wing of the movement shared the same feeling — seasoned politicians such as Giovanbattista Ridolfi and Francesco Valori. Knowing the knavery of politics all too well, never for a second could they truly have credited the words, 'Hurray for Christ our King', or 'Jesus, King of Florence', except as slogans to be chanted or shouted in order to inspire and unify followers. All the same, no political movement in Florence, or indeed in Italy, had ever inspired such verve and fervour, but it was because the Friar had succeeded in spearing politics with his religious message, or, if we like, in pulling the great issues of politics into the middle of his religious vision.

During the Savonarolan historical moment, lasting from November 1494 to the spring or summer of 1497, no other man in Florence, or group of men, could begin to rival his stature. In December 1494, he already enjoyed such popularity that the leading figures did not dare stand up to him in public, despite the fact that some of them, in private, were very critical of his peace-and-pardon campaign for all the men who had colluded with the old (Medici) regime. His popularity was based entirely on his preaching, on his compelling mix of gentle words and fulminations. He had convinced large numbers of Florentines that God had willed the bloodless overthrow of the Medici; and the 9th of November, the day of their flight from the city in 1494, was turned into a holy day, to be celebrated every year. He was the foremost defender of the Great Council; he had won a practical if resentful pardon for the collaborators of the Medici regime; he had been the key force in snuffing out the awesome power of the Signory's 'six-bean' rule; he had encouraged modest men to seek office and enter public life; and almost single-handedly he had levered the republican political establishment into the outlawing of *parlamenti*. Moreover, in the eyes of his enemies, the citizens who orbited around him had illegally organised the city's only political 'sect', thereby — it was claimed — giving his circle an unrivalled superiority in the governing councils.

As the Friar's celebrity spread, there was a growing curiosity about him, and more people sought to lay eyes on the man, foreign travellers as well as Florentines. Soon they began to seek him out along the Via del Cocomero (now the Via Ricasoli), a long street that ran from the convent of San Marco to the cathedral, for this was his route when going out to give his sermons, and it was sometimes packed with people. But his notoriety also generated hatred and murder threats, alarming his supporters, with the result that in 1495 he soon came to be flanked by a company of armed volunteers; and even as early as March, 1496, contemporaries cited figures ranging from 100 to 300 men. Savonarola claimed to be against having such a guard, but opponents held that he invited it in order to promote his self-importance.

His ranks of converted children, as we have seen, patrolled the streets at Carnival, high holidays, and at other times. They swooped down on gamblers and well-dressed women. They knocked on doors and had even gone into houses in search of 'vanities', owing to which the Friar himself had been forced to tell them, in the middle of sermons, to avoid scandal and to rein in their zeal. Among the boys was none other than the fourteen-year-old Francesco Guicciardini, who would later stand out as the only contemporary with a political and historical mind sharp enough to match Niccolò Machiavelli's. In this light, it becomes plausible to suppose that Machiavelli himself might very easily have sympathised with the doings of the Savonarolan children, had he not been brought up by a father, Bernardo, whose diary reveals that he was most likely a religious sceptic, as indicated by his systematic refusal to invoke God's name at those points where doing so, in diaries, was all but *de rigueur*. By contrast, Guicciardini's father Piero was definitely a pious man and a moderate Savonarolan leader.

Before the middle of the fifteenth century, San Marco had lost much of its earlier status as a convent, with its depleted numbers of friars and only two novices in 1456. Cosimo de' Medici, however, Lorenzo the Magnificent's grandfather, was reported to have poured some 36,000 gold florins of usurious guilt money — and money to buy name and piety — into the convent, and this had turned its fortunes around. The alleged sum was vastly exaggerated. It was not, in any case, until Savonarola's arrival, particularly after his election as convent prior, that San Marco became the spiritual centre (however much contested) of the city, and then soared to a peninsula-wide eminence, while also attracting novices and friars from elsewhere. In Savonarola's time, the numbers of 'professed' in the convent rose by more than 130 friars, reaching nearly 250 in all.

Since so many of its recruits were drawn from among the educated boys of the upper classes, San Marco became the most fashionable religious house in the city. A passing remark in at least one of the Friar's sermons reveals that the convent had turned away many applicants from the more humble social ranks, because they were untutored in Latin and the house had limited daily needs for service jobs and physical labour – routines that were mostly carried out by Dominicans of the sort who were less inclined to study and preaching. Given the doctrinal and educational aims of the Order, the prior of a Dominican convent was more likely to be on the lookout for articulate young men with Latin and a penchant for learning. Under Savonarola, therefore, a remarkable number of San Marco's friars were the bearers of some of the more illustrious names in the history of Florence: Acciaiuoli, Albizzi, Strozzi (with six friars), Medici (three), Rucellai (two), Soderini, Gualterotti, Tornabuoni, Tosinghi, Salviati, Panciatichi, Davanzati, Boninsegna, Gondi, Vettori, Ubaldini, Ughi, Bonsi, Biliotti, and Busini. More and more women from among the patriciate also turned to the monks of San Marco for moral and spiritual guidance; and right through the years of the Friar's Florentine primacy, large numbers of women would always be associated with San Marco's Savonarolan ideals. In addition, the convent had two scholars who had been trained in classical Greek, and one or two others who read Hebrew. Savonarola's teachings and manner even attracted noblemen (e.g. Malatesta da Rimini) from other parts of Italy. Pico della Mirandola and Angelo Poliziano had been tempted to take holy orders, so as to serve under him.

San Marco was soon taking in charitable gifts from all over Florence. Many men and women abandoned their parish churches for the Friar's premises; and money that would once have gone – often passing through the hands of women – to the Franciscans and Augustinians, or to local churches, now went into San Marco's coffers, whence it was quickly distributed, through the *Buonomini di San Martino* (a religious confraternity), to the poor and the 'shame-faced', or used to take in more novices.

Quite apart from Savonarola's brooding anticlerical preaching, as expressed in his assaults on a 'lukewarm' priesthood, here was a prime reason for the Florentine clergy's opposition to 'the little friar' from Ferrara.

More than the changes in San Marco, however, for most observers in Florence and beyond, the real change in the city after 1494 had to do with its habits and morals: hence the common charge that the Friar was striving to turn the whole of Florence into a convent, because of which Florentine merchants and travellers abroad were often met, allegedly, with derision and laughter.

The city's leading chroniclers – Parenti, Cerretani, Landucci – agree that Savonarola's impact brought about a fall in the incidence of gambling, sodomy, and ostentatious finery, and for three years his angels and enforcers transformed the nature and intent of Carnival from a 'pagan' festival to a Christian celebration. In view of the strong divisions within families, pitting sympathisers of the Friar against those who resented his strict piety, we may take for granted that the consequent changes in the patterns of urban life cut more deeply as well, affecting habits of prayer and fasting, blasphemy, confession, and communion. There were times when much of the city seems to have accepted three and even more days of fasting, such as in May 1496, or in November 1494, when, with the French army in Florence, Savonarola had Florentines fasting on bread and water, or on bread and wine. He began by calling for confession and communion twice yearly, but by 1497 he had upped this to four and five times per year, or even bi-monthly. Judging by the great throngs of his devotees, and his self-assurance when urging the increase in such devotion, we may suppose that many Florentines attempted to turn his teachings into practice.

Behind Savonarola's achievement was the astonishing sense, at all events in the eyes of his army of followers, that he had moved Florence to the centre of the Christian universe. Like the Venetians and Genoese, for example, the Florentines had long seen themselves as a special people favoured by God. But in these years, many of them believed that the city had become God's elect. The Lord had chosen Florence, just as he had once chosen the Jews, for a unique destiny. At this moment, therefore, Florentines stood at the fulcrum of all created being, if for no other reason than that the universe – the Friar often argued – existed for the

Interior of Florence Cathedral, Savonarola's great preaching venue.

Florence, *Palazzo della Signoria* (the old Palace of Government) in 1890.

Profile of King Charles VIII.

Pope Alexander VI.

A detail from the Nerli Altarpiece depicting the City Gate of San Frediano by Filippino Lippi. This was the entry point of King Charles VIII and his army.

City Gate of San Frediano, Florence's southwestern edge, near Arno River.

Domenico Ghirlandaio, detail from Sassetti Chapel (Santa Trinita, Florence). On the stairs, behind Poliziano (first figure), Piero and Giovanni de' Medici (right to left).

Medici Palace.

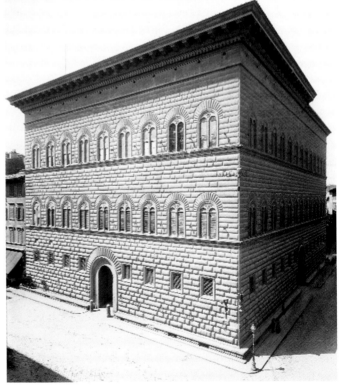

Strozzi Palace, the biggest
construction site in
Savonarolan Florence (1490s).

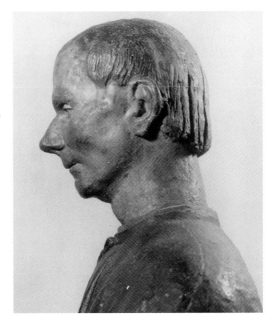

Profile of Niccolò Machiavelli.

The Bargello (Palace of the Podestá), head-quarters for Florence's major criminal court and the main seat of capital punishment inside the city.

Savonarola's execution: hanged and burned, 23, May 1498.

Portrait of Cecilia Gallerani (1496),
mistress to the Duke of Milan,
Ludovico Sforza.

Bust of Cardinal Giovanni de' Medici,
later Pope Leo X.

sake of God's elect. The great task now was to purge and renew the Church; and in this divine appointment, Florence was to serve as the capital from which a war would be launched against the corrupt and the tepid, the wicked, the Turks, and all other unbelievers. This Tuscan capital, however, had to be a city of God and to exhibit such virtue that no other city could even begin to rival it. In effect, then, we also get a sense of how finite the conception of the universe was until the sixteenth century, if rational and practical men and women, in one of the most literate of cities, could come to believe that their time and place, their city walls and their very lives, were so much at the forefront of God's concerns that a stage of human and universal history might be seen as coming forth from them.

In this scheme, the Friar's mission naturally required that the imagery and rhetoric of battle pervade the entire course of his preaching; and the *Exodus* sermons of his final days are particularly scarred by such language, as he finds himself at a turning point in the war, one in which he knew his head to be on the line. But war — a war of words and ideas, of accusation and rebuttal, of insult and pointed logic, and finally of steel and fire — elicited his fearless side. Hence in his peak Florentine years, when stating the aims of his mission, he turned readily and repeatedly to a martial language — to the words for battle, war, armies, soldiers, captains, slaughter, and mass death, all employed to describe the confrontation with evil. And since his charisma and fervour communicated this sense of battle to his friars in San Marco, as well as to groups of nuns around the city, and particularly in the cloister of Santa Lucia, which fell strongly under his influence, it is easy to understand why they ran into the problem of demon possession and rioting devils. Savonarola had filled their imagination and prayers with the spectre of a surrounding, pressing, invading evil.

The story of assaulting devils is retailed by the so-called Pseudo-Burlamacchi, one of the Friar's earliest and most complete biographers, but it is also touched on by another contemporary, Giovanfrancesco Pico della Mirandola. In the winter of 1495, as the Friar's message seemed to fan out in triumph, some of the monks of San Marco, especially the ones charged with nocturnal prayers, were assailed by demons at night: 'diverse figures and monstrous animals would appear to disturb the sweetness of their prayers, and they often spoke ugly, dishonest, and filthy words to the friars, along with certain expressions exhorting them to seize the sensual pleasures of this life. Then they would suddenly vanish.' The clash between sin and purity was frequently envisaged in black and white: 'Sometimes three or four Ethiopians would appear, and give a thrashing to a friar, and having on one occasion really injured one, his cries woke up the entire convent. Fra Lorenzo da Petriolo . . . then told them about how he had been beaten on the head, I believe because he was the one who used to summon the friars to morning prayers in praise of God, and so he was particularly hated by the demons.'

For about six months the whole convent seemed to be in a continual battle; demons took on the shape of ugly 'salamanders'; and in the effort to purge the convent, the Friar not only chanted psalms but also threw about a good deal of holy water. Then just as mysteriously the demons departed and went into the city to get at 'virgins' and nuns, notably in Santa Lucia, an enclosed cloister. Savonarola, fra Domenico da Pescia, and perhaps other friars visited the besieged nuns, seeking to help them by tending to the women who had been possessed and on whom they must have used forms of exorcism. The anonymous Burlamacchi also tells us that the demons insisted on using Savonarola's first name (Girolamo), but, hating and fearing him as they did, they garbled its pronunciation, such as in 'friar Agira' (friar Turnabout) or 'friar Giraffa' (Giraffe). Something about names as a handle was part of the whole magical process of demon possession.

By the spring of 1498 the city's moral climate had changed, and when, under arrest and torture, Savonarola was questioned about the rollicking of demons in Santa Lucia, he claimed to know little or nothing about the matter. He wanted to distance himself from anything connected with demonic forces and from any hysteria that might be especially associated with women. Yet fra Domenico da Pescia's letter of September 1497, addressed to the Friar's boys, took for granted that their purity and special grace enabled them to work as exorcists and to ward off evil spirits.

Political 'Parties'

R EADING AND WRITING history pivot on acts of reason and imagination. With the mind's eye we try to see what happened, and we
reason about why. We may even (perhaps too ambitiously) look for historical lessons. In this sense, every reader of history is also an historian.

Once again we must imagine Florence in its walled-in urban space:
a social world in which the political men of the leading families all knew
one another, had studied each other in office or in consultative bodies,
and were in many cases related by blood or marriage. In addition, they
were often linked by business or other ties, such as through memberships
in the city's scores of religious confraternities.

In late 1494 and 1495, scores of men and families, exiled by the
Medici regime, returned to the city, some nursing rancour, others, like
members of the Pazzi clan, still driven by a keen ambition. In certain
cases, men prominent under the Medici had now lost their high profiles
and were often uneasy, being prey to the resentment and suspicion of
fellow citizens. Yet thanks to the Friar's passionate campaign for reconciliation and forgiveness, they were able to retain an honourable place in
the city and to gain entry to the Great Council. A number of leading
lights under the Medici, in fact, having quickly stood out in defence of
the new republic, again enjoyed political prominence, notably Francesco
Valori, Jacopo Salviati, and Giovanbattista Ridolfi. Hundreds of citizens,
previously of no political weight, some with grand old names and others
from middle-class lineages, now sat in the Great Council, figured as candidates for higher office, attended political discussions at the summit of
government, and cast votes in important elections. Savonarola was their
most powerful defender, thanks to his pleas for free speech and free
discussion. Meanwhile, the multitude of manual workers and poor families, often under-employed, seldom far from hunger, and without the
whisper of a political voice, looked on anxiously, especially because 1496
and 1497 brought soaring bread prices, acute famine, more unemployment, plague, and even an influx of starving country folk.

The rebellion of the seaport of Pisa, the republic's prize jewel in its
little Tuscan empire, turned into such a costly, divisive, and humiliating

affair, that it became the key to anger and exasperation in the city. And as it pursued a desperate war to reconquer the Pisans, Florence's public debt climbed dramatically. In 1496 and 1497, the republic even went to war with Siena, because a Florentine town, Montepulciano, had rebelled in 1495 and put itself under Sienese rule, to the fury of its former masters. After the removal of the French garrison in Pisa, Milan and Venice threw their support behind the Pisans and successfully angled to keep that ancient seaport from slipping back into Florentine hands. It was a policy of blackmail. The Duke of Milan and the Venetian republic were punishing Savonarolan Florence for being allied to the King of France and refusing to join the Holy League against the French. This alliance had been signed in Venice at the end of March 1495, and included the Venetian republic, Milan, the Papacy, and Ferdinand and Isabella of Spain. It was meant to last for twenty-five years.

Florence, in a word, was haunted by rising taxes, war, famine, unemployment, disease, and severe political strains, although of course there were ups as well as downs. Savonarola's solution was to call for repentence, for more prayer, faith, charity, generosity from the rich, and commitment both to the Great Council and to King Charles VIII. His prophecies and his vision of Charles as 'the new Cyrus' – an allusion to the founder of the ancient Persian empire and conqueror of the Babylonians – had pinned him to French ambitions in Italy. A small circle of citizens believed – but they had to hold their tongues – that a solution would lie in the happy restoration of the Medici, and some of these men were secretly in touch with Piero de' Medici, his agents, and his spies. Another group, headed by the influential Guidantonio Vespucci and Piero Capponi, held the view that a simple adherence to the Holy League, and a rejection of King Charles, would soon restore Pisa to Florentine rule and reduce expenses. Others again, from among the old families and former Medicean bosses, saw a solution in government by a small elite, with the outstanding patricians at the helm, since this, they opined, would bring superior leadership, more secrecy in state affairs, and swifter decision-making. Others still, sharing the views of Piero Parenti, gave their ardent support to the Great Council, but opposed the Friar's voice in politics and had no love for his chief backers, Francesco Valori, Paolantonio Soderini, and Giovanbattista Ridolfi. And a few even fixed their hopes on the cadet branch of the Medici, Giovanni and Lorenzo di Pierfrancesco, who had strong ties with the Duke of Milan. But many, I suspect, were moved by the dominant voices, occasionally changed their coats, and played a waiting game.

Florence, we may remember, had stiff laws against 'intelligences' – secret agreements among groups of men, binding them to decisions about how they would vote in elections, whether in the Great or in smaller councils. Laws of this sort went back in Italy to the late thirteenth and fourteenth centuries, to an age of rampant political faction, when conspiracies had been rife in all the peninsula's major cities. The ferocity of those conflicts had spawned tyrants who promised peace, but whose way to it had been through the use of exile, execution, fines, prison, and threats. In the fifteenth century, therefore, law codes and traditional practices were massed against the rise of political parties. Such clotting – 'parties' – smacked of civil discord and even conspiracy. Now and again, in some dozen sermons, Savonarola himself attacked the evils of 'intelligences', denouncing them as plots against the common good.

And yet private political meetings certainly took place in town and country. Cosimo and Lorenzo the Magnificent had met with cronies in the Medici Palace and elsewhere, not only to discuss tactics and proposed legislation, but also to single men out for office, to bully and twist arms, and to drum up support. Their veiled dominance, however, enabled them to enjoy a stolen *carte blanche* for their illegal activity, although in law, as Pope Sixtus IV reminded Lorenzo, the Medici were no more than mere citizens of the Florentine commune.

When dealing with political differences among social groups, observers of the period speak of 'sects', 'intelligences', and 'parts', or they use nouns such as 'Whites', 'Greys', and 'Wailers' to refer to the groups of men who shared certain political views and feelings. This or that 'part' of the whole class of eminent citizens was, say, for or against the Friar. And though we may use the word 'party', we must beware of being corralled by it, of confusing the implied meaning with anything like the anatomy of a modern political machine. Nothing in the make-up of Renaissance states could accommodate mass electorates, well-organised political groups, ideologies, party workers, or even – as an acknowledged right – peaceful opposition to a governing clique. Florence had none of these in the 1490s, and the attempt to grasp its politics with the help of the modern notion of party instantly dissolves in the face of two-month Signories, frequent shifts in alliances between prominent men, ties of kinship among the great families, and the webs of patronage spun by the principal oligarchs. With remarkable exceptions, allegiance to political ideals was too easily broken by the force of loyalties to family groups and patrons. Moreover, to speak out sharply against a leading political figure was to court disfavour or even arrest, torture, prison, exile, and punitive fines. It was alleged that doing the like was 'scandalous', and scandal both undermined reputations and generated civic discord.

In June 1496, a certain Ser Giuliano da Ripa, an attorney in the offices of the Archbishop of Florence, made a sharp attack in the Great Council on some of the city's most eminent politicians. He particularly nailed *Messer* Domenico Bonsi, who had just delivered a report, and accused him of having uttered 'much beastliness' and many lies, with a view to frightening a people already overburdened with taxes. Bonsi and the others, he alleged, meant to drive citizens towards their own wicked aims and a change in government. An order soon went out for the arrest of Ser Giuliano, who took refuge in the convent of San Marco. Negotiations ensued; the leading oligarchs split on the case; but the attorney was forced to give himself up, and there was then sharp disagreement over what to do with him. He was eventually questioned about political activity at San Marco, tortured, ordered to keep his nose out of high questions of state, and banished from Florence for two years. Parenti noted that 'the case was much discussed in the city' and claimed that the men who went after Ser Giuliano were really getting at Savonarola and San Marco. Two months previously (April, 1496), the government had exposed and punished the members of a secret 'intelligence' directed against San Marco and the Friar's adherents. Three men had been imprisoned, stripped of their political rights, and exiled.

From the outset of 1495, and for the next three years, the opponents of Savonarola and what he stood for began to complain that the Wailers or Frateschi constituted an 'intelligence' – a circle of citizens who had a regular meeting place in the convent of San Marco, who were therefore organised, and who held views on elections in the Great Council, on foreign policy, and on all other public affairs of major interest, including the reform of morals in the city. But there was nothing modern in that alleged circle, as a few recent historians have argued, even if we choose to argue that something akin to a modern political grouping came through their conduct and through the 1490s sword-play of ideas.

Savonarola's enemies burned to bring him down for a variety of reasons: some because of his brilliant defence of the Great Council; others because they saw him, in his incessant attacks on tyranny, as the chief obstacle to the establishment of a Medicean dictatorship; still others because in their eyes he had divided the city from top to bottom; and others again because his pious crusade felt like a noose around their necks ('*Oh friar, you want to turn Florence into a convent.*'). Many more, however, desired his destruction because they wanted to break with the King of France and enter the Holy League, persuaded that this reversal would quickly return Pisa to Florentine hands. There were also the citizens who were outraged by his relentless assaults on an immoral clergy, and others again who wanted to stop his diatribes against gambling, blasphemy, sodomy, horse racing, unveiled young women, and ribald literature, such as the best of Luigi Pulci's poetry.

While all the Friar's opponents had one thing in common, the wish to see him exiled or even murdered, they fell out on many other matters of importance. Their hatred of the Friar was not strong enough to pull them together as a party or even a consistent pressure group, because their differences — of class, rank, morals, and loyalties in the tug of patronage webs — were more considerable; and cooperating on one matter today could not guarantee their cooperation on something else tomorrow. In the face of these frustrations, the anti-Savonarolans took the Friar's Men to be more organised than any such grouping among themselves, when in fact the men who admired Savonarola were in some ways almost as divided as their enemies.

The three Florentines most often seen at the head of the Friar's Men were Francesco Valori, Paolantonio Soderini, and Giovanbattista Ridolfi. All sprang from distinguished political families. In addition, the Soderini and Ridolfi had been closely linked to the Medici as protégés, collaborators, and by marriage. One other Savonarolan leader, Jacopo Salviati, also had ties of marriage with the disgraced ruling family.

Supremely talented in the crafty world of high politics, the main-line Soderini were constantly in the limelight during the 1490s, owing to the activity of three brothers: Paolantonio, Piero, and Giovan Vettorio. A fourth brother, Francesco, was the prestigious Bishop of Volterra (later a cardinal), and his diplomatic skills were occasionally called on by the new republic. Yet the first three split over their attitudes toward Savonarola. Paolantonio passed into the Friar's camp because – it was alleged – he had been denied a place among the Twenty Electors by a group of grandees in December 1494; whereupon, to spite them, he took up the popular cause. The jurist, Giovan Vettorio, more of a sceptic than Paolantonio, drifted toward the enemies of the Friar; while Piero, a politician to his finger tips, stole back and forth between the two sides, and consequently was more often in office, in addition to being a more frequent speaker in the rounds of consultation with the Signoria. On the face of it, the brothers observed no family solidarity: each seemed propelled solely by his own motives. Yet later, when Paolantonio's politics put him in mortal danger, the Soderini brothers cast faction aside, closed ranks, and resolved to do everything they could to save him. Steeped in the relentless quest for worldly honours, the great families, as Savonarola often warned, were bound to desert the common good for the sake of kinship ties.

Francesco Valori, possibly the most powerful politician of the Savonarolan years, presented a different problem for the 'intelligence' that supposedly met at San Marco. A man of gravity and few words, with a long reddish face, he is described by Cerretani as having had 'a giant of a spirit' (*animo vastissimo*), 'great presence', and 'extraordinary courage'. Although ambitious and 'austerely proud', he was generally regarded as a man of exceptional honesty and integrity, a judgement reinforced by the fact that he lived sparely, dressed modestly, and had no children to whom he could pass on his political fortunes. But he had a reputation for speaking out too sharply in government councils, and for being proud, cold, and austere – so much so, it seems, that the Frateschi refused to have him as their recognised leader. Furthermore, the other two 'friarly' chieftains, Paolantonio Soderini and Giovanbattista Ridolfi, found it difficult to work with him. Savonarola himself could not throw his weight around with Valori; and if now and again he was able to use the politician, it is equally clear that Valori knew how to make use of the Friar.

The charge that the convent of San Marco was home to a secret 'intelligence' angered Savonarola, and he occasionally poured scorn on it in his sermons. Post 'guards' at 'our three doors', he cried out. And he declared, repeatedly, that he was not one to speak secretly, that everything he had to say had been expressed in public. He was repelled by the words of advice rumoured to be circulating among particular citizens in the Great Council: 'Vote for the Friar's Men.' Never, he crossly asserted, had he ever said or encouraged the like. Vote for 'good men'; vote for 'prudent' men and not fools: this he had said. But he had uttered no names and never used party tags, such as 'the Greys' and 'Whites' – terms which he also denounced. A few times in his sermons, he threw in the disparaging term *Arrabbiati*, meaning 'the Rabid' or 'Angry Men', the label for the chief enemies of the Friar, but they were a loose and fluid grouping, without any organisation or positive policies, unless it was to eliminate Savonarola.

The shifting anatomy of Florentine politics in the 1490s made for strange bedfellows. Parenti asserts that many crypto-Mediceans found their way into the ranks of the Frateschi, the current most strongly in favour of the Great Council and hence against the restoration of the Medici. This claim could be reconciled with the view that the 'friarly' Mediceans had passed over to Savonarola's side in gratitude for his successful campaign to win a pardon for them. They were seen by others, however, as cynical turncoats who hoped to conceal themselves among the Friar's Men, but who would be ready, when the right moment came, to abandon Savonarola and hail the return of the Medici.

Clearly, then, issues and men in politics took on bewildering shapes. Where were the blocs of citizens united by worthy causes? Here, suddenly, the social analysis of politics verges on becoming nothing more than a game which assumes the worst about men.

Since Savonarola always denied, even under torture, that San Marco harboured a political sect, why did the charge stick? The enemy continually levelled the accusation, with an eye to having the top Frateschi arrested and their followers hounded. Determined to destroy the charismatic preacher, they pointed insistently to the fact – most suspicious, in their view – that some of his supporters went to confession or to Mass at San Marco, while others occasionally turned up at the convent to take religious instruction, to hear talks on Scripture, or to attend a sermon. It followed, of course, that such men recognised one another by sight and often by name, and in the convent it must have been difficult, at times, for them to avoid talk about politics. Still, they could as easily have held such chats in their own houses. One of Savonarola's two assistants, friar Silvestro Maruffi, seems to have listened to a good deal of political talk; but the bulk of the evidence indicates that the Friar himself made a point of avoiding it. His communications with Francesco Valori and Paolantonio Soderini often went by word of mouth, as messages relayed by a third party, usually Andrea Cambini.

On reflection, it becomes clear that the Frateschi did not need a meeting place. Scanning the whole of Savonarola's life, I find it hard to believe that he could have tolerated the occasional assembly at San Marco of say a half-dozen to twenty or thirty men, for the mere purpose of discussing political tactics. Not a shred of hard evidence, even from the enemy side, may be called in to underpin this possibility, which ran against the whole style of the man. Far more important to the cohesion of a Savonarolan party were the ideals at the core of the Friar's political programme: his campaign against 'bosses' and tyranny, his zeal for the Great Council, and his incessant pleas for the common good. These were the central points in the galvanising of the Frateschi. Other points counted for less. Savonarola's claim to be a prophet and his call for a renewal of the Church engaged many men but repelled others. More contentious still were his unswerving commitment to the King of France and his angry attacks on gambling, sodomy, and richly-dressed women.

All told then, the Frateschi had a set of policies that were solid enough to give them a semblance of cohesion in the Great and lesser councils. The Greys (Mediceans), Whites (anti-Savonarolan republicans), and Arrabbiati could find no unifying purpose except in opposition, and on many issues they might even be moved to vote with the Savonarolans. Result: they could not stand up to them as a bloc. For three years, accordingly, elections to the ever-changing two-month Signories tended to favour the Friar's men. Although the results occasionally swung in a more neutral direction, they rarely issued in the Frateschi's defeat. Even in March–April 1497, with the old and brilliant statesman, Bernardo del

Nero, Savonarola's great enemy, at the head of the Signory as Gonfalonier of Justice, the Signoria could not muster the support to block the Friar's doings or, at the end of April, to assist Piero de' Medici in his plot to take the city by armed force.

If the Frateschi were little more than a loose aggregate of pious men and some opportunists, what were Savonarola's chief opponents, the Arrabbiati (the Rabid), if not a looser and more formless constellation? Among these, at any rate, two of the top leaders, Guidantonio Vespucci (a formidable jurist) and Piero Capponi, were ready to desert the King of France for the sake of the Italian League, while also looking to the Duke of Milan, Ludovico Sforza, for assistance. However, the other leading Arrabbiato, Bernardo Rucellai, who had once worked hand-and-glove with Lorenzo the Magnificent, was a supporter of King Charles, in part at least because he feared that reliance on the Duke would prepare the way for the return of the Medici. Such division over one of the most important of all questions revealed the group's crippling lack of unity.

In the last year of the Friar's life, the city finally gave birth to an anti-Savonarolan group that looked more like a political sect or 'party' – the Rude, Rowdy, or Ugly Companions (Compagnacci). Even more than the Arrabbiati, they had their being in – and were defined by – their visceral hatred of Savonarola and his policies. Captained publicly by the Florentine nobleman and Friar-hater, Doffo Spini, in secret, it seems, the financial captains were the two Medici brothers of the cadet line, one of whom had married a Sforza princess and was living in Forlì. The Compagnacci were a circle of determined pleasure-lovers who made a point of dressing splendidly, banqueting to the accompaniment of music, and generally 'living it up' in a style that meant to say 'in your face' to the pious Frateschi. Although numbering about 150 men, they could count on many other supporters, such as in street demonstrations, and were also able, in due course, to win votes in the Great Council. In the early spring of 1498, with Pope Alexander VI closing in relentlessly on the Friar, they were to play a critical part in his downfall.

CHAPTER TWELVE

Wailers and Bigots

T HE MOST LITERARY of Italian cities, with its circles of poets, highbrow humanist scholars, and its public recitations of verse, Florence had taken to the Friar's eloquence. His Florentine enemies, therefore, fully appreciating the power of his words, were the more ready to fear and condemn him. They had pejorative names for his followers.

Wailers and bigots (*piagnoni* and *pinzocheroni*): these were the most common of the insulting names for the admiring supporters of Savonarola. They themselves were to make their peace with the name *piagnoni* (wailers or cry-babies), and would be almost proud of the sobriquet, having been tagged with it because some of them wept or 'snivelled' at sermons. But they always and angrily rejected the name of *pinzocheroni*, bigots.

Savonarola had foes from the earliest days of his charismatic Florentine preaching. Having them, as he saw it, was his God-given destiny. When facing a multitude in the cathedral, how could he do battle with a mercenary Church or with unscrupulous political leaders, and not call forth an army of enemies? He knew that they would soon be crying out for his pelt. Towards the end of 1497, as the Frateschi moved in a slow glissade toward crisis, the abuse gathered force and the Savonarolan children were insulted, spat upon, or screamed at in the streets. Opponents accused the rank and file of his supporters of being a credulous and superstitious lot, misguided fools, and he himself was taunted with having been inspired by the fatuous visions 'of little women'. Since he was often seen as the one man who had divided Florence and provoked bitter quarrels that reached into the very heart of families, no insult or accusation was too vile or grotesque when levelled at Savonarola, even the charge of his being a hermaphrodite and a syphilitic.

A poetry of abuse, running back to the time of Dante in the 1290s, was one of Florence's 'glories'. No other city in Italy could match it, but neither could they rival the rest of the city's literary legacy, whether in short fiction, historical writing, love poetry, or narrative verse. Florentines were a wordy lot. And if the Savonarolan movement was the first to produce songs that were necessarily political as well, particularly at Carnival time, it was also the first to elicit a stream of abusive poems from local writers, including one or two Tuscans based abroad. Rhyming verses were more easily remembered and were more effective in pouring hatred and sneering ridicule on the enemy. Most of the poems and short ditties, however, were lost, because they went out as one-page flyers, were thrown around anonymously on bits of paper (*polizze*), were affixed to major public buildings, such as the cathedral and government palace, or did the rounds by word of mouth. Foreign ambassadors reported their circulation, and the news reached distant cities, including Venice, where the chronicler Sanuto noted the fact and reproduced a sonnet.

One anonymous poem invites the city to silence Savonarola:

> Close, O my Florence (time flies)
> This mortal mouth that is destroying you.

Another simply says:

> I say there comes a wind from Rome
> That will soon blow out your name and light.

A tailor who turned his hand to poetry writes of 'the thieving ugly deeds/ of your little friar'. And the poet, Tommaso Baldinotti, sizes up the Friar's sermons as 'barking' and him as the 'seducer of the Florentine people'. Indeed,

> You are the man who has pushed this land of Italy
> To the precipice and ruined all.

Ruined all: that is, sided with our scourge (King Charles VIII), preached against Florence's entry into the Italian League, and kept us from getting Pisa back.

Although their language is tame, the foregoing verses rather sum up the attitude of the Friar's foes in 1497. The samples that come down to us impugn his entire enterprise: his prophesying and ascetic religiosity (called hypocrisy), as well as his disastrous foreign policy and meddling in affairs of state. They pillory him with insulting names such as 'Friar Big Onion', 'awful evil onion', 'the little unhooded one', and 'lowly little friar' (*fratuncolo*). He is accused of 'arrogance' and of appealing mainly to women and plebeians. In a clever sonnet, mimicking the mode of the fictional dialogues in his sermons, he is even seen bragging about his armed personal escort of ninety-six men ('six men per *gonfalone*').

Paying these assaults back in kind, one poetaster from among the Wailers issued a scurrilous verse reply, ordering the anti-Savonarolans 'to get up' so as 'to scare away big flies', and to get back 'into your stalls'. The fight went on to the fiery end.

In January 1497, with Francesco Valori as Gonfalonier of Justice, the Signory cracked down on the anti-Savonarolan scribblers. One of them, Girolamo Muzi, was arrested by the Eight, sentenced to a fine of sixty gold florins and stripped of the right to hold public office for five years. He had hired a man to post his insulting rhymes (a *frottola*) in the cathedral, the New Market, and either in the government square or the palace itself. Another citizen, Francesco Cei, a more serious poet and later on one of the noisiest of the Compagnacci, was banished from the city.

But the most serious attacks on Savonarola and his supporters came from the pulpit and the pens of other friars, one of whom, a Dominican of a different stripe, Giovanni Caroli, was at least as learned as his observant colleague. Augustinian and Franciscan friars also entered the lists against the Prior of San Marco. In the spring of 1491, possibly put up to it by Lorenzo the Magnificent, or by a group of Medicean oligarchs, Mariano da Genazzano, a well-known preacher and Augustinian, seems to have been the first critic to raise his voice in public. He sought to refute the Friar's case against the army of unprincipled priests and clerics. Although the custom in such ripostes was to withhold the name of the targeted man, informed citizens were immediately able to identify the unnamed party. Savonarola's celebrity simplified the task.

In January 1495, in sermons delivered in the great church of Santa Croce, the turncoat and former admirer of Savonarola, Domenico da

Ponzo, a Franciscan monk, made a sustained assault on his claims. Since he was strongly rumoured – and the allegation was probably true – to be an agent of the Duke of Milan, his real aim was to tear Florence away from its alliance with the King of France. While appearing not to touch this matter at all, he went for the jugular vein: he rejected Savonarola's claim to be a prophet and God's spokesman in Florence, thus undermining the foundations of San Marco's reform programme. No, Savonarola had not been graced with knowledge of God's plans. The gift of prophecy 'had long since ceased to be part of divine revelation', and hence such predicting was 'nowadays impossible'. Since 'God no longer appointed prophets to reveal his will to mankind, Savonarola could not have received from Him the knowledge he claimed to possess'.

From this time on, the Friar's foes and critics would chip away at his claim to be a prophet, especially because his entire standing in Florence and on the European stage rested on this contention. The force of the claim was in its singularity and focus, which also, however, made it easier to target. Perfectly cognisant of this, Savonarola fought back with a short work, published in the late summer of 1495, his *Compendium of Revelations* (*Compendio di rivelazioni*). Here he draws an interesting, but opportunistic, theological distinction between absolute and conditioned prophecies, the second depending in part upon contingent forces in temporal affairs, such as the free will, in theological terms, of the King of France or of the Florentine people. He also runs through his series of prophecies as supposedly realised thus far, thereby seeking to justify and strengthen the primacy of his voice.

First however, back in January, he had been embarrassed by a debate on his principal contention, the claim that he was a prophet, at a meeting held in the government palace and organised by Filippo Corbizzi, Gonfalonier of Justice, and soon to stand out as one of the Friar's enemies. The details of the occasion escape us, but it appears that the city's leading theological minds had been invited to take part in the discussion and that Savonarola himself was not at all impressive in the exchange.

His chief antagonist that day, fra Giovanni Caroli, who hailed from the more conservative branch of the Dominican Order, the Conventuals, was based in the convent and church of Santa Maria Novella, where he had served as Prior for three terms. Caroli enjoyed some fame as a theologian; he had professed theology at the *Studio*, the University of Florence; and he had written biography, contemporary history, and polemic, in addition to theology. But if, as a religious thinker, he was second in the city only to the renowned Neo-Platonist, Marsilio Ficino, his worldly credentials were stamped by the fact that he was known to be a committed Medicean.

The brunt of Caroli's attack was aimed at Savonarola's prophesying and wrongful interfering in the city's political affairs – wrong because his ecclesiastical superiors had not authorised him to meddle in politics. In a subsequent composition, a *Letter . . . to a friend*, Caroli returned to the question of prophecy; and while allowing for its possibility in the present day, he considers it so rare and dubious as to be most unlikely. Besides, how can any modern man offer clinching proof of such a divine appointment? Would it not require a dramatic and incontestable miracle? In effect, he accuses the prophet of San Marco of being an impostor, a deceiver driven by ambition and the desire for celebrity and power. False prophets, he suggests, manipulate the superstitious mob for their own ends and are the generators of civil conflict. Caroli himself was a strict conservative in political and social matters, and had little but 'contempt for the multitude', which even surfaced in his suggesting that Savonarola had emerged from the 'swamps of Ferrara'.

We learn from the Friar – he too had his spies – that in early April, 1495, a secret assembly of high clergymen in Florence had resolved to destroy him, and that they had begun to charge him with heresy, with the promotion of radical monastic poverty, and with being ready to despoil the Church of its vast properties. Savonarola naturally rejected these accusations. Other attacks followed in swift succession, in print no less than in sermons from different pulpits. The basic article of indictment was always the same: he was a spurious, wicked, and seducing prophet. Now, however, there were growing charges of heresy and schism (splitting or dividing the Church); and henceforth he would be forced to spend more and more time defending himself. Even men from Florence's country towns got into the fray. Preaching in the church of Santo Spirito, on the far side of the Arno in March 1496, the Augustinian friar, Leonardo Neri da Fivizzano, while not actually naming Savonarola, characterised his closest supporters as barking dogs, seducers, souls turned to scum, and whited sepulchres. He assailed the 'holy hypocrisy' of the friars of San Marco, who were to be seen about in their 'ignoble' dress, 'wearing their [friarly] tunics half way up their legs'. In fact, Savonarola believed that the long garment of his friars should be skimpy, rather than abundant, costly, and showy.

In the winter of 1498, Angelo da Vallombrosa, a learned monk from a monastery to the east of Florence, offered to kill Savonarola with his own hands, if need be at the very altar, so snarling was his hatred of the man. Angelo saw himself as a Judith killing Holofernes. His monastery at Monte Scalari was split, and the Friar had sided with the losing monks, who had been seeking a more ascetic rule. In a series of letters, each of them individually published, Angelo directed a stream of invective at Savonarola, and called on the children of Florence, in a missive to Florentine women (August 1496), to stone that 'perfidious seducer' and 'evil hypocrite' to death, for having preached against the wealth of the Church. A letter to the Friar himself holds that 'Anyone who speaks ill of men in holy orders is bad-mouthing God.' In other letters, he assails 'modern prophets' who go about claiming that 'God says this and that'. Let them go to Rome, 'not to women and gullible plebeians', to 'explain their visions, prophecies, and divine indignations'. Contrary to Savonarola's claims, the vices were not in Rome but in human nature, hence in all men. And in a letter to the friars of San Marco (11 July 1497), the Vallombrosan denounces 'the fictions, tall tales and dreams of your hypocrite, liar, and false prophet, rebel, and most bitter enemy and detractor of the clergy, prelates, priesthood, Roman See, and the one Holy Catholic and Apostolic Church'. When Savonarola's friars responded with a strong, insulting reply, Angelo called for all of them to be burned, for their 'synagogue' to be sucked down to hell, and for God to make them understand 'that the Apostolic See [the Pope] never errs'.

Angelo's concluding letter, issued probably in early 1498, was addressed to the heads of the Florentine church and is a vehement attack on them for having put up with Savonarola. He is outraged by the 'heretical' claim 'that the excommunication should not be obeyed' because Alexander VI is alleged to be 'a simonist', 'not the true pope', 'of a lascivious and evil life, and of sacrilegious and disgraceful customs'. No, is the short reply to all these claims. And anyway, as Pope, Alexander is not subject to human laws.

Let us look, next, at two other virulent diatribes against the Friar.

The first one, an anonymous attack published early in 1496, purports to answer his circulating letter of 1495, *Epistle to a friend*, in which Savonarola tries to refute the accusations that had been made against him. Chief of these were his meddling in politics and his alleged heresies. In this broadside, the Friar is said to be 'puffed up with arrogance' because he denies the Pope's 'fullness of authority', disobeys him, and affects to be prophetic in a time when such a claim requires the approval of the Church. He is a fraud and a seducer like Mohammed, worse than the barking Cerberus in hell, and a wolf who deliberately dresses down in fake humility. The term 'tyrant', so readily cast about by him, applies to Savonarola himself, who goes through the streets escorted by an outrageous company of armed men. Purporting to be giving vent to the thoughts of the learned clerics who oppose the Friar, the anonymous author also claims that San Marco's head is a man of no mercy, does not understand Aristotle on government, has defamed and abused too many men, including the holders of high Florentine office, and applauded the entry of 'plebeians' to the Great Council. Being riddled with the antagonisms of the Old Testament, he even wants to remove the papacy from Rome.

The second diatribe is more tenaciously political and carries the title, *In defence of the magistracies and laws and ancient religious ceremonies of the city of Florence against the invectives and offenses of friar Girolamo[Savonarola]*. It came from the hand of Francesco Altoviti, a militant republican, born into a respected old family. Offering a cascade of insults and run-on constructions, it bristles with anger and hatred. The Friar's invasive piety, or his campaign against opulence, gambling, and sodomy, had plainly got up Altoviti's nose.

Written just after Savonarola's excommunication, but before the disturbing executions of late August 1497, the diatribe against 'this frenzied and evil little friar', 'such a liar of a man', begins with well-known charges: his building of a divisive political 'sect' and his disobedience to 'the Vicar of God'. Suddenly, however, we get the seeds of a radical new accusation. We are told that most of the 'passionate men' who follow the Friar had 'been assistants and followers of the tyrant [Piero de'

Medici]', and he, Savonarola, 'a foreigner' and 'fully-professed cleric', who is 'blinded and inflamed by the vice and monarchy of his own pride', should not be butting in to act as 'the shield of the tyrant'. Take this government: he has been so publicly insulting about 'our magistracies' that he is guilty of 'lese-majesty'. Not content with this, he runs down our ancient customs and 'does not want us to dance, to play music, or to sing – chastely, like the angels in heaven'. Were he truly a prophet, he would show 'divine simplicity and humility'. Instead, 'many times, in the presence of throngs of people, without trembling or reverence, he has said to the high God, "If I lie, you lie. You told it to me." ' Although Savonarola had claimed that his prophecies were simply a passing on of God's words to him, Altoviti keeps underlining the dramatic remark. It followed that the Friar has 'profaned, rotted, and corrupted' the pulpit of the cathedral 'with lies'. He 'is more horrible than all other sinners and more villainous than all the world's thieves, [alone] in falsely saying, "God said it to me".'

Surprisingly, we are told that Savonarola 'has always been the enemy of the poor', not only by preaching that they not be given alms and instead be made to work, but also by urging 'the rich not to spend money on festivities, weddings, and honest family banquets, with the result that poor artisans have no income'. What is more, the price of grain has risen wildly because of his predicting scarcity and famine.

The polemic rushes forward in Altoviti's run-on style. 'He has never commended or recommended family relations, marriage, widows, orphans, or the dowries of our noble and delightful daughters, but rather, like a capital enemy of the human race ... and more than the infernal Cerberus, he has barked from the pulpit of Moses against our noble and virtuous citizens, those he has called "mad dogs" and "crazies", and has boasted, like a dictator, that he introduced the present government, and that if there were anyone about who could come up with a better one, he [the Friar] would accept it, which means: I can order citizens about by force.' He has even 'railed basely against the men who got the tyrant chased out of the city by risking their lives, blood, and property for liberty'. By his 'temporal sects' and 'assemblies', and by his appeals for 'arms and justice', he has aimed at nothing 'but blood and vengeance and convictions and jailings and executing the citizens of our city'.

Altoviti, astonishingly, has been building up to the most damning and dramatic charge: 'Piero de' Medici has favoured him and worked to keep the excommunication from reaching Florence, and has gone in person to the Pope to beg that he [the Friar] stay in Florence, not go away, so that he may hold the place and use of tyranny for him.' And 'if at first the Friar preached occasionally against tyranny, he has toned this down because Piero became his friend, and yet this has not been believed, because he could not better deceive Florentines than by showing himself, in his words, to be an enemy to the enemy of the people, while in fact and in secret working for the opposite goal'. With all this, and having toiled to hold on to Piero's friends, Savonarola 'can be called the father of the tyrant and defender of the friends of the tyrant. They say that the Friar, using secret contacts, got Piero to come right up to the city gates at much expense and trouble for our city, and if the Signoria and other top officials had not been ready that day [28 April 1497], friar Girolamo would have put us in danger of a great spilling of blood . . . There is not the least doubt that wherever we have the Friar, there too are Piero de' Medici and his followers, and whoever sees the Friar is seeing Piero de' Medici, and so if we want to wipe out the name of tyrant entirely, we must wipe out the name of friar Girolamo, because he is father to the tyrant and is holding his [tyrant's] place [in this city].'

These weird allegations require a brief comment.

The historical value of Francesco Altoviti's tirade rests in the contorted logic and fury of his words. It helps us to see why the Prior of San Marco needed the protection of armed guards when he went into the streets of the city. There were men about who were prepared to kill him, while others – such as the Duke of Milan (Ludovico Sforza) and rich Arrabbiati – were ready to pay for his assassination. And given his ways, Pope Alexander himself would quickly have pardoned the assailants. Unfortunately, we know almost nothing about Altoviti, apart from the fact that he claims to have suffered exile, presumably in the time of Lorenzo the Magnificent, and suggests that the penalty had something to do with his commitment to 'liberty'.

If Altoviti truly believed that Savonarola was Piero de' Medici's secret agent in Florence, we may look upon his rage in wonder and entertain the suspicion that it had borne him to the brink of insanity. More likely, however, he was trying it on: his hatred of the Friar knew no bounds, and he therefore reached out for the wildest accusations by linking San Marco's spiritual primacy to Piero's despotic designs. There was much more sense and reason in Altoviti's desire to take the revolt against the Medici away from Savonarola and his God, and to reclaim it for Florentine citizens. But wherever evidence can be brought to bear on his text, as in his linking the Friar to Piero's armed attempt on Florence in April 1497, his assertions turn out to be fiction.

One of the most simple of the papist arguments against the Friar was succinctly presented in a short Latin dialogue, *Dialogus Tusci et Remi adversus Savonarolam*, published in Rome toward the end of 1497. Girolamo Porcari, the author, was a high Curia official, Bishop of Andria, a some-time governor in papal territory, and one of the twelve judges of the chief papal court, the Rota. Using Remo, one of his fictional inter-locutors, as his spokesman, Porcari argues that Savonarola had foretold 'false insanities', while also causing Florence to topple from its former splendours – and, by the way, the Friar was afflicted by the *morbum gallicum* (syphilis). Yes, a Christian should naturally cleave to the teachings of Christ, but Christ, through Saint Peter, had transferred his powers to his vicars, the popes. Therefore, to refuse to obey them must issue in damna-tion. 'He who does not honour the Vicar of Christ with humility and obedience . . . denies Christ.' Porcari took for granted that he need not even allude to one of the obvious implications of his position, although it was frequently noted by Pope Alexander himself: namely, that however unworthy a holder of the pontifical dignity might be, all Christians owed reverence and obedience to the office, and hence to the man.

CHAPTER THIRTEEN

Excommunication: May–June 1497

Cast Out

ALEXANDER VI WAS a diplomatic and tolerant pope, not surprisingly so, in view of his worldliness and flaunted children. How could he be the one to throw the first stone? And he might even have thrust the whole Savonarolan affair into a corner, save that the Duke of Milan and the Friar's enemies in Florence were ready to move heaven and earth to prevent this. They wanted the case to hold the centre of the Italian stage. So from the winter of 1495 to the spring of 1498, scores of letters and reports poured into the papal chambers, accusing the Friar of every manner of crime, including high treason, theft, sexual perversion, and of course heresy. But this deluge of material was destroyed or allowed to perish. As a recent historian has noted, with a controversial and embarrassing priest like Savonarola, the papal chancellery aimed, if possible, to wipe out the memory of the man, as well as his printed works.

Foremost among the Friar's daunting enemies was Ludovico Sforza, who had usurped Milan's ducal title by pushing a nephew aside. In the effort to make his shady takeover more secure, he was the principal figure in the invitation that drew Charles VIII into Italy. Surrounded by poets, musicians, scholars, and gifted artists – among them Leonardo da Vinci – Ludovico was also flanked, more closely, by courtly adulators who led him to believe that he possessed the keenest political mind in the whole peninsula. Like Pope Alexander, with his Giulia Farnese *la bella*, he also had a mistress: Cecilia Gallerani, one of the loveliest married women in Italy – at all events judging by Leonardo's celebrated portrait of the lady. And, again like Alexander, he had not the temperament to begin to understand a man like the friar from Ferrara.

Realising almost immediately that King Charles's entry into Italy had opened a Pandora's box, especially because the French had a claim – so far dormant – to the Duchy of Milan, Ludovico spun round against the French and into the face of Savonarola's prophecy of the King of France as divine scourger. His agents and ambassadors in Rome and Florence now began to call on every resource to break the new republic's alliance with France; and in this prospect, the Friar had either to disavow that prophecy – yet how could he? – or be destroyed. Politics and brute force were king, not theology. Still, the final assault on the Friar could not be openly or merely political; it had to be made on doctrinal grounds. After all, he was in holy orders; he held no political office; he did not stand at the head of a patronage network, whatever the claims of his enemies; and he had taken a vow of obedience to his Dominican superiors. Here then, in his insubordination, would be the best ground of attack, though this alone would not suffice. The charges of heresy and schism would have to be introduced, resting on the contention that he was guilty of serious and obstinate errors of faith.

How strong or popular Savonarola's position in Florence was on the eve of his excommunication may in part be gauged by the fact that in January–February 1497, one of the most Savonarolan of all Signories held office, with Francesco Valori as Gonfalonier of Justice. In addition, that very season saw the most successful of San Marco's pious 'carnivals', with companies of earnest children more or less in control of the streets, the range of their zealous doings culminating in a great bonfire and burning of 'the vanities'. The Rude Companions could only gnash their teeth.

Valori's Priors proceeded to silence the poets and preachers who were speaking out against the Friar. In the enacting of new measures, according to Parenti, they would call in only friendly advisers, intimidate fellow counsellors, and hammer away at the Great Council by pushing a proposed bill again and again, until its passage was obtained. If true, these were methods that Valori and the Frateschi had gleaned from the notebooks of Lorenzo the Magnificent's government. Former supporters of the Medici, the republican leaders – Valori, Ridolfi, Soderini, Mazzinghi, and others – came from the same backgrounds as their Medicean adversaries. And most of them assumed that the aim in political struggle was to win, not to be fair. Looking to 'the common good' and the importance of the

Great Council, the Savonarolans were ready to copy certain Medicean tactics, doubtless doing so with a better conscience.

Coming on top of Valori's two-month primacy in Florence, and a Carnival season of piety rather than adolescent rioting and rock fights, the Friar's hard-hitting Lenten sermons of 1497, inspired by the prophet Ezekiel, intensified the anti-Savonarolan lobbying around Pope Alexander. Not to be foregotten was the man's silent rejection – it could only be read as 'contemptuous' – of the Pope's order, as given in his brief of 7 November 1496, that San Marco be incorporated in the new Tuscan–Roman Congregation. The time for stern action had come.

Pope Borgia signed the brief of Excommunication against Savonarola on 13 May 1497, and this was then followed by a touch of colour. The brief had to be taken to Florence, where its contents would be publicly proclaimed. Gianvittorio da Camerino, a professor of theology, was chosen to be the bearer of these tidings. However, he had been in Florence in March, and there, publicly assailing Savonarola, possibly in a sermon, he had provoked the anger of the Eight, who issued an arrest warrant and had him expelled from Florentine territory. He was expressly warned not to return or he would make himself subject to the penalty of death. Now, about mid-May, the learned courier made his way into Tuscany and halted in Siena, from where he dispatched letters to the Eight and Signory, requesting a safe-conduct. None came. They knew who he was and what he was carrying, and although the Eight now included enemies of the Friar, and the Signory of May–June was mostly an anti-Savonarolan group, they were trying to avoid a flare-up of civic tensions. Savonarola was still too popular a figure, and announcement of the excommunication would provoke new strains. Yet how could they keep the news out of the city? Fully informed about the Pope's action, the enemies of the Friar – Franciscans, Dominican Conventuals, Mediceans, Augustinians – were doing everything they could to broadcast the information.

The movements of the foiled courier, as we shall see next, followed fast on the heels of Piero de' Medici's intended *coup* of late April, 1497. And at about the same time, under the Gonfaloniership of Bernardo del Nero, the Compagnacci had run a nocturnal campaign of shouted insults and graffiti around San Marco. More: on the night of 3–4 May, in anticipation of Savonarola's preaching the next day, they broke into the cathedral, smeared excrement on the pulpit, and covered it over with the rotting, stinking hide of a donkey. They also drove nails up from under the plane of the pulpit's lectern, hoping that the exposed points would puncture the Friar's thumping hands or hammering fists. Their scurrility was discovered and quickly cleaned up early the following morning; and shortly before noon, despite the fact that angry threats had been made against him, the Friar insisted on mounting the pulpit to deliver his Ascension Day sermon, his last of the season in the cathedral. Alleging the dangers of pestilence, the Signory had suspended all further preaching, everywhere in the city, as from May 5th.

When the Friar was well into his sermon, the velveted Compagnacci suddenly rioted, setting off the fracas with a tremendous din and menacing shouts, then throwing open the cathedral doors and causing people to rush out in fear. Some of Savonarola's defenders hurried off to certain houses on the Via del Cocomero and quickly came back, armed. Others gathered around the pulpit to protect its occupant, and drove away two members of the Eight, known anti-Savonarolans, who had approached in order to assault or kill the Friar, or so the defenders believed. He, in the meantime, had knelt in the pulpit, praying, and then came down to be accompanied back to San Marco by a throng of armed men. That evening, surely, the city reverberated with details of the events.

Since the bearer of the excommunication, the professor of theology, was not allowed to enter Florence, the brief had to go in by a different route, and about a month later, on June 18th, with many friars present at each venue, it was finally proclaimed in five of the city's most important churches, including Santa Croce, Santo Spirito, and Santa Maria Novella. In each of the churches, once the denunciation had been read out, small bells were sounded and two large lighted candles were turned upside down, to have their flames snuffed out on the ground. The light of the Church was henceforth denied to the stricken man. Friar Girolamo Savonarola had been cast out of the community of Christians, until such time as he went to Rome, made his pleas and apologies, and obtained, if possible, the Pope's pardon and absolution.

The brief of excommunication stated that he had been put outside the Church 'because he has not obeyed our apostolic admonitions and commands'. Moreover, on pain of suffering the same penalty, *all* Christians, male and female, laity and clergy, are ordered 'to avoid friar Girolamo altogether, as one excommunicated and suspected of heresy'. These few lines, the heart of the anathema, carry a dire load of meaning. The Friar was cut away from all the Church's sacraments: he could not confess; he could not have holy communion; he could not, if dying, have extreme unction; all churches were closed to him; and he was to be avoided by all Christians. None could even converse with him, without risking the same censure. Yet all this had been anticipated in Florence during the past year, and the Friar had simply carried on with his agenda. Many priests had been urging their parishioners, and friars their penitents, not to attend Savonarola's sermons and not to go to San Marco, frequently alleging that he was a heretic and already an excommunicate. Simple people, it was reported, were often taken in by these claims, given out, as they were, by literate men in holy orders.

The jubilation in Medicean and oligarchic milieux, including Compagnacci circles, was matched by the shock and outrage of the Friar's supporters. Excommunication was a well-known censure in Florence, but it was seldom imposed on leading personalities. The most celebrated case went back to the Pazzi Conspiracy (1478), in the wake of which Lorenzo the Magnificent himself had been stricken with the penalty and lived with it for more than two years. His government, however, had closed ranks around him and stood up to the interdict inflicted on the city, doing so by forcing the clergy to be patriotic and to perform the more essential religious services. In answer to such effrontery, Pope Sixtus IV raged, hurt Florence as best he could, but also had to put up with the city's flagrant disregard of the imposed censures.

In 1497, with the Florentine political class deeply divided over Savonarola and the French alliance, the enemies of San Marco would see to it that all the infamy and dangers of the excommunication were highlighted, with the result that its real impact would depend upon how Florence elected to deal with the ecclesiastical curse, not on the distant powers of the papal monarchy. The first reactions went against the Friar. Within a week of the censure's publication, on 24 June, Florence was to celebrate St John's Day, the holiday of the city's patron saint; and the different religious orders, headed by the Franciscans and Augustinians, informed the government that they would take no part in the traditional religious procession, a great parade through the city, if the Dominicans of San Marco also participated. They were suggesting that with Savonarola living in their midst, those friars were already splashed and tainted by the excommunication. The anti-Wailer Signory gave way to the ultimatum and ordered the friars both of San Marco and of the reformed convent of San Domenico in Fiesole to stay home that day – no parading for them. It was the same Signory which refused to look for evidence against any citizens who had been complicit in Piero de' Medici's attempted *coup d'état* of late April.

Fighting Back

POPE ALEXANDER AND his advisers had been careful. The excommunication stated that the Friar was 'suspected of heresy'. It did not charge him with the crime; doing so would have required an investigation and a trial. The Curia knew all about observing legal procedures, and also about appearing to observe them.

With some in Florence delighted by the anathema, and others angered by it, the city was now more divided than ever, particularly since the Mad Dogs (the Arrabbiati) had the document immediately translated from the Latin into Italian and rushed into print for widespread distribution. The clash was above all a battle of words, as each side jockeyed to win support and to defame or discredit the other. Divisions even in March had already been so acrimonious that the government had assembled the leaders of the main factions, twelve men in all, to have them try to reach some kind of harmony, beginning with peace among themselves. Another attempt at an amicable solution was made in June, but this too ended in failure. No agreement could be reached on the question of what to do about Savonarola, and leaders were also divided by the dispute over France versus the Holy League. Inevitably, too, loquacious Florence was treated to some insulting anonymous sonnets, penned against the Friar and his Piagnoni. Even pictures were thrown about, showing Savonarola in obscene dress or a lurid stance of some sort – an image surely to be counted among the first cartoons in the history of Europe.

The Friar's enemies in Florence always claimed that he had single-handedly divided the city and filled it with discord. This take on events was both true and false. The false part was in the suggestion that Florence's deep schisms were about the man, rather than about politics, issues, and ideas – an analysis, in short, that was no analysis at all but rather gross oversimplification. In the course of 1495, the Friar became the most fearless and important defender of the new republic, with the Great Council as its foundation block and the chief magistracies – Signory, Ten, and Eight – now rendered more responsible to an electorate, thanks to the eyes and electoral input of the Council. But his charisma and his ability to hold the rapt attention of up to 15,000 listeners had also turned him into an icon: a figure whose aura seemed to resolve or simplify the burning questions that swirled around him. We may assume, however, that political leaders – Pierfilippo Pandolfini, Bernardo del Nero, Paolantonio Soderini, Francesco Valori, Bernardo Rucellai, and the rest – never lost sight of the realities of politics, and this also meant using the Friar as an icon, whether to win support or to direct hostility against him and the Savonarolans. The most controversial of men could thus be blamed for everything, at the same time that he was being used to promote or to attack policies that would still be very much there long after he had vanished from the scene.

If we want to say that the leaders – aristocrats all of them – were in politics for reasons of ambition and grandeur, as the diarist Parenti constantly asserts, so be it. But again, to allow this conclusion to sum up events makes for poor history, because it converts politics into personal moral quiddities, such as greed and pride. However it was driven, the political struggle was about ways of getting Pisa back, about war and public spending, elections, patronage webs, and some manner of input from the voice of 'the people' (*il popolo*).

In this light, Savonarola was absolutely right to say in a number of his sermons that the campaign to destroy him was not indeed about him, a lowly friar, but about the Great Council, the new republic, and in effect the *popolo*. Technically, even before the brief of 13 May, he was already an excommunicate, having incurred the penalty by his refusal to take San Marco into the new Tuscan–Roman Congregation of Dominican convents. Pope Alexander had chosen not to make a fuss about this, but he was now dispelling all doubts. Rome wanted the Friar's expulsion from the community of Christians to be nailed to the public mind.

Savonarola learned about the fatal brief within a week of its having been signed and sealed, and reacted with an oblique diplomatic reply to Alexander on 20 May, commencing, 'What is the cause, my lord, of your being so angry with your servant? What bad thing have I in hand?' Less than a month later, however, he drafted a rebuttal of the excommunication, addressing it, in the form of a letter, 'To all Christians and the beloved of God'. Dated 19 June, but already in print and ready for distribution, it was brought out on the day after his lights, so to speak, had been put out in Florence. There was no time to waste in the war of words, and Savonarola was the master of tactics in this field.

An indictment of 'the tepid', the letter declares that he was 'sent by Jesus Christ to the city of Florence to announce the advent of the great scourging (*flagello*) of Italy and above all of Rome, which is then to spread to almost all the world in our days and soon'. The aim of the *flagello* would be to renew the Church. But now here at last is the excommunication that he had foretold years ago. He denies that it can have 'any value for God or the Church', having been 'imposed by the false recommendations of men, so as to do evil and to work against God and the truth. Unable to find a just reason for excommunicating me, they have given the Pope false reasons as the true ones, and say that I am spreading pernicious doctrine and heresies.' Yet 'the whole world is a witness to my preaching only the doctrine of Christ.' In fact, he continues, he has never been disobedient to his superiors in the Church, although he insists that Christians should not obey commands that are contrary to God. Any man who 'issues an order against God is not our superior'. He then reminds readers that he has often explained all this in his sermons and writings, and specifies three of the sermons. The sticking point was San Marco's refusal to join the new Congregation. In fact, he and his friars had offered detailed explanations at the time, and he succinctly rehearses some of them here, but Rome never bothered to reply. At any rate, his friars insist that rather than enter into the new Congregation they would choose 'excommunication, prison, and martyrdom'. Now 'our adversaries' 'shamelessly' retail 'manifest lies to the Pope, and so the consequent excommunications can have no validity'. He closes by threatening that if his claims and reasons are ignored, 'we shall make this truth known to all the world in such a way that no one will be able to deny it'.

With Savonarola already barred from preaching, the excommunication opened a period of intense writing for him, out of which there came a spate of letters arguing that the anathema had no value, and seeking to justify his stand against it. The arguments brought out the theologian and canonist, but also the logician: 'The Pope as pope cannot err in the exercise of his office. But when he errs, he does not err as pope; and if he commands a thing in error, he does not command as pope.' This subtlety was directed against the claim that the Pope had to be obeyed absolutely and at all costs, however much a rotter he might be, because Christian obedience was due to the office.

Savonarola, as it happened, was never willing to meet either of the two conditions that the Curia had laid down for repeal of the excommunication: that is, that he go to Rome to seek the Pope's pardon, or that he and his friars join the Tuscan–Roman Congregation. Rather harmless looking at first sight, these conditions added up to an enormity: they required that Savonarola abandon his life's work – the renewal and reform of the Church.

Since politics and the social virtues that belonged to Christian doctrine had been fused by the new republic in its professed ideals, Savonarolan Signories – and particularly those of July–August 1497 and January–February 1498 – urged their ambassadors in Rome to seek a removal of the excommunication. To no avail. Savonarola and the republic had many more foes than friends in the eternal city. Cardinals Giovanni de' Medici and Ascanio Sforza, the Duke of Milan, the Venetian republic, and Florentine aristocrats continued to demand even more censures against Florence and the Friar.

Icy relations verged on a thaw in the autumn of 1497. There was talk again of Charles VIII's possible return to Italy, and allies of the Holy League, with the Pope at the fore, again sought to entice Florence into the alliance by holding out the promise of restoring Pisa to Florentine hands. For a time, it even looked as if the allies might be willing to bend on the 'problem' of Savonarola. Encouraged to do so by Cardinal Carafa and the Signory, the Friar even sent a strong supplicating letter to the Holy Father in October, seeking to get back into Rome's good graces. It was a slippery rhetorical exercise, and nothing was to come of it.

CHAPTER FOURTEEN

Five Executions: August 1497

Piero at the Walls

O NE OF THE most remarkable politicians of fifteenth-century Florence, Bernardo del Nero (1426–1497), took office on 1 March 1497 as Gonfalonier of Justice, head of the new Signory, for the usual two-month term. He was known to be such a bitter enemy of the Frateschi that Savonarola – it was later bruited – had longed to see him murdered. Bernardo was now to captain a government that split on the fiery monk, although the Frateschi Priors held a slight majority. Hence the Gonfalonier could not hope to summon up the six beans (votes) that would be required to take action against Savonarola. The immediate political climate, in any case, was too uncertain, and therefore Bernardo's hostility to the Friar would have to run along a different route.

The strongest perhaps of all Savonarolan Signories, under the Gonfaloniership of the imposing Francesco Valori, had just left office. They had enacted a few Piagnone measures; they silenced several preachers who had been laying into Savonarola, and they also saw to the arrest and silencing of two poets, who had circulated verses (tantamount to political action) against the Friar. Late-medieval and Renaissance republics did not tolerate dissent, when it was voiced *outside* the inner circles of government. It was felt that insistent, open criticism led to discord and civil strife; and the proudest of all republics, Venice, was particularly brutal about suppressing dissent.

The Friar's excommunication was little more than two months away (13 May), and rumours of his coming disgrace were already snaking through the city, not only because of the frequent arrival of letters from envoys in Rome, but also because San Marco's Florentine enemies, with their lofty contacts at the papal court, were tenaciously pulling strings and working for his destruction. Reports from the Holy City said that Pope Alexander was now resolved to 'get' the Friar.

At that point, accordingly, Bernardo del Nero was the best man to have in the republic's top office. The Friar's adversaries had no cooler head in their midst. A minor guildsman who had been active in the second-hand rag trade, Bernardo was distinctly a new man, having risen under the patronage of Cosimo and Lorenzo de' Medici, in the classic manner of those of modest origins who win the favour of princes or powerful magnates. He became one of the closest collaborators of the Medici. On the day of Piero de' Medici's flight from Florence, 9 November 1494, when he tried the charade of passing himself off as a republican, he was, as we have seen, turned away and physically threatened by the swelling crowd in the government square.

But the elapse of time, Savonarola's appeal for a general pardon, and Bernardo's huge resourcefulness enabled him to slip back into politics; and it may indeed be said that he owed his safety, if not his life, in part at least to the Friar. Besides, Bernardo was a formidable politician, having known for years how best to use his talents. He had held almost every major office in the city at least once, was Gonfalonier of Justice on three occasions, and was judged to be a consummate tactician. Not surprisingly therefore, years after his death, he was to reappear as the leading protagonist in Guicciardini's famous work of political rumination, his *Dialogue on the Government of Florence*. While having little or no Latin, Bernardo had loved the company of literary men, Marsilio Ficino among them, and had enjoyed something of a reputation for learning. But among republicans he was also reputed to be cruel, rapacious, and overreachingly ambitious: in short, the former *rigattiere* (used-clothing merchant) was an intriguing and complex figure.

Piero de' Medici, meanwhile, had never ceased to move about from one court or professed allegiance to another, in search of military support for a triumphant return to Florence. His biggest hopes resided in the King of France, the Pope, and the Duke of Milan. He even got some help from the Venetian republic. And the spring of 1497, with Bernardo del Nero at the head of Florentine republican government, must have struck him as an ideal moment for taking the city by force and by surprise.

Piero, let's remember, was an outstanding athlete and horseman.

Among the many complaints that citizens had secretly raised against him, one of the most acerbic was that he had too often neglected affairs of state in order to show off his physique — for instance, by playing foot-ball in the city squares, and by racing horses just outside of Florence's north-eastern walls. Consequently, once he fled from the city, he turned naturally to the company of soldiers and mercenaries. Contemporaries no doubt said that this ran in his blood. Being an Orsini from Rome on his mother's side, he could look to their grand and long history in the profession of arms, to feel all the more vindicated. And as his younger brother Giovanni was already a rich cardinal, handsomely ensconced in the other great Orsini profession (holy orders near the top of the hier-archy), Piero could be seen as fulfilling a family destiny. As if by a natural process, the two brothers completed a trajectory in the Medici family's relentless climb from business, banking and politics to the domineering business of princely courts.

Piero was now preparing to take Florence by storm and gave all of March to his preparations. Meanwhile, although knowing something about the new soldier's plans, the head of state back in Florence, Bernardo del Nero, said nothing. But just how much more he knew remains a mystery, as we shall see.

As early as 17 March, the government seems to have been alerted to Piero's troop movements, and there was talk about the possible connivance of citizens in Florence. It later emerged that he had raised money, some of it Venetian, to hire Orsini troops and ex-papal soldiers. On the 17th, although some counsellors minimised the likely danger, the jurist Domenico Bonsi and others recommended that the government step up security in Florentine Tuscany. Eleven days later the topic was taken up again. The Florentine towns of Arezzo and Cortona were picked out as points to re-enforce; and the Eight, like the War-Office Ten, were urged to crack down on suspect citizens. On April 7th, in a letter to the Duke of Ferrara, the Ferrarese ambassador to Florence reported on the city's concerns over Piero's military advance into Tuscany. Sources indicated that Piero was in the company of a soldier who had married into the Orsini family, the professional captain (*condottiere*), Bartolomeo d'Alviano, who was in command of more than 400 cavalry and from 1500 to 2000 foot soldiers. Yet by 11 April, owing to 'fresh news' from Rome, again according to Ferrara's ambassador, the *Signori* and their advisers had decided that there was nothing to fear from Piero's manoeuvres, and that little needed to be done to prepare for a possible attack or treachery at the city gates.

This apparent change of mind was surprising, especially as February had released a flood of starving peasants, begging for bread, into Florence. On February 19th the government was forced to confront violent bread riots on such a scale that the Palace of the Signory itself had required additional protection. All the same, the price of grain continued to rise, aggravating the famine, and two months later, on the 18th of April, a crowd of desperate women triggered another violent riot, shocking the city. Yet it was known that Piero and his followers were fond of handing bread out to the poor, with an eye, if the occasion arose, to rallying their support in the streets. This was why the riots of 19 February had resounded with the approving shouts of 'Palle! Palle!', signifying the Medici coat of arms; and some of the rioters had cried out against Savonarola, seeing him as the cause of the harrowing grain shortage. A month later, on 17 March, *Messer* Domenico Bonsi made a clear reference to the opportunism of the Medici lord and his readiness to exploit the famine for political purposes.

Early in April, the Signory touched glancingly on the question of Piero's military movements, but not until the fourth week did the government finally send soldiers out in the direction of Siena, with orders to their commanders to spy out Piero's moves and intentions. To judge, however, by the Signory's recorded discussions, it was only on Friday, April 28th, that the danger was truly confronted, and by then it was on top of them. Piero and his small army were outside the walls of Florence, waiting near the Gate of San Piero Gattolino, at the southern spur of the city, though at a safe distance from the range of small canon fire (*spingarde*).

Suddenly, too, the leading Savonarolans sprang into action inside the city, taking on different tasks. Early that morning, two of the most prominent Frateschi, Paolantonio Soderini and Jacopo Pandolfini, had rushed out to the Gate in question, to see that it remained shut and to keep an eye on its defenders. This was not a job to be delegated. More ominously, in a canny exercise of hostage-taking and on advice from the stern Francesco Valori, the government was talked into summoning an emergency consultation which would include all of Piero de' Medici's friends and suspected allies in the city. They were held in the palace until Piero and his soldiers departed, and the power of visual communication was brought into play. The official executioner was called in to be amongst them, and he arrived, with assistants apparently, bearing 'axes, chains, and a multitude of ropes for hanging men'.

Guicciardini, whose father was an actor in these events, puts the number of hostages at the surprisingly high figure of about 200, but Parenti gives a sum of 'around 50', and this seems a more realistic number, because it would have encompassed the heart of Piero's committed supporters in Florence. Parenti also gives some of their names, and since a few of them will recur in this account, while the appearance of others shatters the notion that Florence was the scene of 'party' politics in the modern sense, we may do well to note them: Piero Alamanni, Andrea Betti, Agnolo Niccolini, Antonio Malegonnelli, Piero Soderini, Niccolò Ridolfi, Jacopo and Alamanno Salviati, Filippo dell'Antella, Piero Tornabuoni, Giannozzo Pucci, Francesco Taddei, Luca di Maso degli Albizzi, Antonio and Filippo Lorini, Cosimo Sassetti, Lorenzo and Francesco Martelli, 'and others of lesser importance'. Let's note the incompatibility of some of these names.

Pucci and Ridolfi would be summarily tried for treason against the republic four months later. And I suspect that Parenti also meant to name another of the men to be accused, Lorenzo (rather than Piero) Tornabuoni, a well-known Medici sympathiser. There is something very odd, however, about his listing the names of Malegonnelli and the two Salviati brothers, because they were known Frateschi, though here, all of a sudden, they appear among Piero de' Medici's alleged sympathisers. The solution is likely to be be in proposing that either the government had thrown its nets widely, in order to include all the city's leading men in the 'consulatation', or that Parenti and others looked upon the three men, at least at that moment, as crypto-Mediceans. So slippery were the boundaries of sects, parties, factions, or whatever we choose to call them.

In the meantime, outside the city walls, the plot itself was swiftly unwinding. On that Friday, 28 April, Piero and his soldiers had been meant to arrive before dawn at the appointed Gate, where the clandestine assistance of armed men was expected. But torrential rains had delayed their progress during the night, and they failed to appear until the afternoon. They now waited around for four hours; no one in the city made a move in Piero's favour; and this was partly due perhaps to the fifty or more hostages being held in the Palace of the Signory. With a view to cutting a deal, Piero even tried to make contact with Florence's mercenary captain, Paolo Vitelli, only to be greeted with a dismissive silence. The small army was suddenly faced with a grave risk, for the tocsin directed at the countryside (*martello di fuori*), which curiously was never sounded, could easily have hastened the assembly of bands of armed peasants for the defence of the city. Yet once more, accordingly, the incompetent Piero had exposed himself to being killed or captured. Having no faith in him, Pope Alexander had expected the failure and could not keep himself from joking about it when the news reached him. That evening, as Piero's troops departed, winding their way towards Siena, Vitelli and his soldiers were ordered to go after them.

In the palace, meanwhile, recognising the impossibility of Piero's venture, the wise old Bernardo del Nero must have seemed to cooperate with the city's defensive stance, but neither he nor the other Priors used their authority to call for the hammering of the alarm bell. His attitude and all his actions (or non-actions) that day would come back to haunt him.

Bernardo and the Priors around him had convened a selection of the city's premier public figures back in March, drawing them from the different factions. They were given the task of bringing peace to the city, as if to show what noblemen of good will could accomplish. They would thus have come close to constituting Bernardo's ideal oligarchy of aristocrats and skilled politicians. Numbering twelve men in all, the group comprised the cream of Florence's most powerful politicians: Bernardo del Nero himself, Tanai de' Nerli, Niccolò Ridolfi, Agnolo Niccolini, Guidantonio Vespucci, Bernardo Rucellai, Piero degli Alberti, Lorenzo di Pierfrancesco de' Medici, Piero Guicciardini, Francesco Valori, Paolantonio Soderini, and Pierfilippo Pandolfini. Of these the first eight were known opponents of the Friar. Lorenzo was a cadet-line Medici. The next three were Piagnoni, and Pandolfini was a Medicean.

This committee of reconciliation was able to agree on a raft of important matters, but when they came to the problem of Savonarola, of whether to cherish or to expel him from the city, the peace initiative fell apart. All their differences came forth; and their desire to settle the supreme question – in the apparent conviction that they, the chief oligarchs, would be able to impose their solution on the Great Council – was stymied. Though probably not thinking of him at all, it was as if they had sought to give flesh to the words of a prominent oligarch, Piero Capponi, uttered in 1495, when he asserted that Florence was best governed by twenty-five to thirty noblemen.

Throughout the April events, and despite his preference for rule by an aristocracy, Bernardo del Nero had held his tongue about the gravity of Piero's designs on Florence. But there was more to this than met the eye. The government's refusal to sound the tocsin on the early morning of 28 April can only be explained as a decision intended to protect the pro-Medicean nobility from the violence of an aroused populace. And we must entertain the suspicion that even the leading Frateschi connived, while at the same time ignoring Savonarola altogether. They had no need to consult him on such a matter. The fact that at least fifty suspects had been rounded up and were being held was already scandalous enough, although they were soon released in the wake of Piero's retreat. If the Signory had sounded the great emergency bell, calling out armed citizens, alerting the neighbouring countryside, dispatching more guardsmen to all the city gates, and putting extra soldiers in and around the government palace, the upsurge of defensive feeling would have endangered the suspect families, while also inflaming the controversies that already split the city. In the event, Bernardo and the Signory decided to handle the crisis quietly, including a muted call for citizens to arm themselves. The outcome seemed to speak for the good sense of their decision. But they had taken a capital risk. The keen witness, Cerretani, was convinced that if the rains had not retarded Piero's march, 'then all was lost, because the counter measures had been put into place [too] late'.

The suspicious Parenti, who saw sinister secret agreements everywhere, had a devious explanation for why many citizens had refused to arm themselves against Piero's threat, despite the fact that they knew about his plans and presence outside the city walls. Those who refused to take up arms, he said, were of a more neutral sort; hence they suspected that weapons would only serve to increase the strength of the rival groups of oligarchs, who would then use Piero's plot as the excuse for grabbing still more power. Parenti also reminds us, of course, that some citizens wanted Piero in the city.

The events of 28 April sharpened conflict in Florence, then suddenly made even worse by the fact that a somewhat anti-Savonarolan Signory, under the gonfaloniership of Piero degli Alberti, took office for two months on the 1st of May. Four days later a rampage in the cathedral, directed against Savonarola's preaching, sparked off a near riot. Rumours and more heated quarrels possessed the agitated city. Then came Savonarola's excommunication; and though the papal brief bearing the anathema did not reach Florence until 18 June, as we have seen, the Pope had actually signed it on May 13th, so that the document had been ghosting through talk in Florence for three or four weeks. News from Rome could reach the city walls by fast courier in less than forty-eight hours.

Seen in the light of these events, Piero's plot took on a more ominous cast. It was already suspected back in March that he had been in close touch with select citizens in Florence, as he prepared his April foray. They were thus assumed to have been privy to his plans. No evidence of treachery had surfaced at the time, but none of this had been forgotten. The Signory of May–June showed no interest in pursuing the question. The next Signory of July–August, however, had a Savonarolan stamp, and the first days of August were to bring forth the desired testimony against a circle of conspirators.

Traitors

THE MAN WHO confessed, offering names and details, Lamberto dell'Antella, came from a Florentine family of ancient vintage, the Antellesi. As an ardent supporter of Piero de' Medici, he had roused the suspicions of the republican regime, and had been previously arrested, questioned, and exiled. At some point, however, he violated the terms of his exile and incurred the penalties of 'rebel' and 'outlaw'. Residing in

Rome, in the midst of other Florentines, as was often the custom of citizens living abroad, he had picked up information about Piero's contacts in Florence and was himself a likely accomplice in the plot of 28 April. But he and his brother, a priest, had fallen out with the Medici brothers and then fled to Siena, where a request from Piero brought about their confinement in that city.

Wishing to return home, and seeking to ingratiate himself with his fellow citizens, Lamberto had written to Francesco Valori, Piero Corsini, and his own brother-in-law, the Savonarolan lawyer *Messer* Francesco Gualterotti, putting out feelers for a permit of safe-conduct, so that he could enter safely into Florentine territory and go before the Signory and Eight to tell his story. He made the mistake, however, of stealing out of Siena and paying a visit to his ancestral lands, only some three or four miles from Florence's walls, without the desired permit. Secretly tracked and arrested there, he was hauled into Florence and – in keeping with the practice of the day – tortured. In the presence of the Eight, of one or two of the Priors, and of members of the War-Office Ten, he suffered a number of strappados. Wrists tied behind his back and hooked to a pulley, he was lifted up high several times and then dropped to a point above the floor. The sudden jerk of a single such broken fall could dislocate the shoulders. I offer these particulars because we shall go on meeting the strappado, the drop and jerk, as the chief instrument of torture.

When Lamberto was caught, he seems to have been carrying secret messages. The first round of questioning induced the Signory to issue a proclamation barring all citizens, of whatever rank or condition, from leaving Florence, unless they had the permission of the War Office. Aside from a single period of one half-hour, the restriction lasted for two days.

Now at last a series of names began to tumble forth, and news of the main ones – eminent men – sent shivers and anger through the city, notably through the ranks of the upper-class families. Contemporary sources accuse Lamberto dell'Antella of malice and evil intentions. He had enemies in Florence; he was in need of money; he was in serious trouble with the rulers of Siena, and had a beloved brother there in prison or under house arrest. But he also possessed a wealth of information concerning Piero de' Medici, including details about his wild spending, dissolute life, financial difficulties – all his valuables had been pawned – poisonous strains with his brother Giovanni (the Cardinal), and even a list of the men and families whom Piero proposed to eliminate on his return to Florence. These included the Valori, Pazzi, Nerli, Giugni, and Corsi houses, in addition to certain branches of the Capponi, Nasi, Rucellai, Albizzi, Gualterotti, and Bardi, as well as a string of individuals, headed by the Savonarolan, Paolantonio Soderini. It went without saying that Savonarola was to be exiled or executed. Overnight the city was talking about nothing else.

On the principle – to use Lamberto's folksy expression – that 'pulling on one cherry brings out others', he produced two names: Giovanni di Bernardo Cambi and Giannozzo Pucci. Let's take them in order.

Born into an old family of silk merchants, and former manager of the Pisa branch of the Medici Bank, Cambi had lost much money in that ancient seaport, in the wake of Pisa's revolt against the Florentines. But he had also been active as a go-between in helping to raise money for the Medici and had been secretly in touch with Piero. This in itself was bad enough, for the laws of the city allowed no Florentine citizen to have any contact with political exiles or political outlaws, unless he or she had the explicit consent of the Signory or the Eight. In serious cases, infractions were punishable by death.

The rich Giannozzo Pucci sprang from a family of upstarts who had been closely linked to the Medici house ever since the 1420s. Climbing relentlessly, they had married into the old lineages. Now head of the Pucci clan and known to have been one of Piero de' Medici's boon companions, Giannozzo was associated, all the same, with the Savonarolan movement. His sudden exposure must have made him look like a spy or a wolf in sheep's clothing. In late February, when Bernardo del Nero was elected Gonfalonier of Justice for the March–April Signory, Giannozzo had been one of the first men in Florence to contact Piero, urging him to make a run at the city, with a view to overthrowing the republican regime.

Encouraged to talk by pulley, drops, and jerks, Cambi and Pucci in turn produced a string of other names – men who had either known about Piero's planned assault on the city or who had offered him their help and money. These names aroused even more fear and anger. At the top of the list was none other than Bernardo del Nero, followed by two others whose social standing in the city no Florentine could ignore: Lorenzo Tornabuoni and Niccolò Ridolfi. More than a dozen other men were also fingered, but most of these were out in their country villas, or had somehow managed to scramble out of the city, either fearing that their guilt would be demonstrable or acting on the advice of friends. Two of the accused, Nofri Tornabuoni and Lionardo Bartolini, were in Rome. They were sentenced to death in absentia, on top of which all their earthly possessions were seized – spoils for the public treasury.

Among the most important of the other suspects were Piero Pitti, Tommaso and Pandolfo Corbinelli, Francesco Martelli, Jacopo Gianfigliazzi, Cosimo Sassetti, Andrea de' Medici, and Gino Capponi, all of them bearers of distinguished surnames. They were stripped of their political rights and exiled; and little more than six weeks later, four other well-known names would be added to the list of exiles – two Tornabuoni brothers (Luigi and Piero), Tommaso Minerbetti, and Piero Alamanni. The Eight, however, ordered the hanging of a few socially-obscure men, a decision that seems to smack of class feeling. They were found guilty of having been the couriers in a secret correspondence.

Fearing the escape of the chief suspects, the Signory and Eight resorted to trickery. Served with invitations, Del Nero, Ridolfi, and Lorenzo Tornabuoni were accompanied to the Palace by messengers of the Signory, and they went along, expecting to attend a consultation or a simple round of questioning. If they went without suspicion, a surprise awaited them, for on ascending the main staircase of the palace and reaching a certain landing, instead of moving on to the audience chamber of the Priors, they were suddenly turned the other way and led into the quarters of the Eight. Their political experience told them at once that something more menacing was in store for them. They knew that they were in the shadow of a new law, according to which merely to think of plotting against the republic, if this somehow emerged, was to risk capital punishment. The law had been enacted early that year, under the Gonfaloniership of Francesco Valori. And Bernardo del Nero, for one, as Gonfalonier back in April, had borne in his consciousness the scene and plan of just such a plot. Yet even in the agony of more than one strappado, the old man (aged seventy-two) seems to have confessed to having known only about Piero's intentions, though this was already enough to merit the penalty of death.

The diarist, Piero Parenti, linked by marriage to the big Strozzi clan and a harsh critic of the Friar, lashes out against Bernardo at this point, characterising him as a ruthless *arriviste* who was ready to cooperate with almost any side, so long as he could go on being a top dog. There was more than a pinch of class jealousy in this view, but Parenti, who detested the arrogance and ambitions of political grandees, also knew Bernardo to be one of the city's keenest exponents of tight oligarchy.

Niccolò Ridolfi's case, in an Italian expression, was 'a different pair of sleeves' altogether. The Ridolfi had been wielders of power in the city for more than a century, and thus had frequently held office in the Signory and other lofty magistracies. Their connections were the stuff of envy. An influential man under the old regime, and one of Lorenzo the Magnificent's most trusted supporters, Niccolò was father-in-law to one of Lorenzo's daughters, Contessina. He had been rather passed over by the new republican government, despite the fact that his brother Giovanbattista Ridolfi belonged to the trinity of top aristocrats in the Savonarolan camp, the other two being Francesco Valori and Paolantonio Soderini. About forty noblemen from the first layer of citizens now filed in to the Signoria to plead for Niccolò's innocence, mostly, it appears, by simply claiming that he had done nothing wrong. He was, however, a known pro-Medicean, and testimony had come in, tying him to Piero de' Medici's designs. As a result, on August 19th, Savonarola himself, seeing the sombre drift of events and fearing the outcome, was moved to write a letter to the suspect's brother, Giovanbattista, calling for his prayers and resigned patience. It was a letter of condolence before the fact.

The case of the fifth leading suspect, Lorenzo Tornabuoni, was the one that most jolted the city and even brought tears to the eyes of the Savonarolan diarist, Luca Landucci. The young man was universally seen, in Florence at least, as the prime model of courtesy, generosity, and gentility. He was sure to have been — or how else account for the views of contemporaries? — strikingly likeable, attractive, and graceful. Although surpassingly rich as well, with assets, it was rumoured, in the range of more than 100,000 ducats (hundreds of millions of euros in our terms), he was so much a partner in the Medici Bank, that part of his wealth had been entangled in theirs. When Medici assets were confiscated to pay off Lorenzo the Magnificent's debts and theft of public monies, the young Tornabuoni had also suffered losses, and only the return to power of the Medici could make up for these. Nevertheless, he was the single suspect — some historians believe — in favour of whom Savonarola may have spoken some kind words to Francesco Valori, seeking apparently to save his life. Valori himself, moved perhaps by the man's reputation, may also have wanted to save him, but could not do so, Guicciardini observed, because he had conspired more than any of the others, and Valori was determined to get rid of Bernardo del Nero.

A Tornabuoni in the direct line of the Magnificent's mother (Lucrezia), Lorenzo was closely related to the fallen ruling house, and had been a riding companion to Piero. He also had grand contacts abroad. Back in November 1494, in the days of the French occupation, friendship had brought the King of France's uncle, Philippe de Bresse, to Lorenzo Tornabuoni's house, where he lodged as a guest. Lorenzo therefore was inevitably seen as a supporter of the Medici. And yet, remarkably, he had sought to pass himself off as a man in sympathy with Savonarola, having been one of the 360 or so signatories of the famous 1497 letter in his support. Sent to Pope Alexander in testimony of the Dominican friar's holy life and orthodoxy, the letter sought to have his excommunication revoked. Now here he was, accused of having conspired to assist Piero de' Medici to overturn the republic, hence to exile families, to execute a select number of men, and to kill the Prior of San Marco or to pack him off to Rome, to end his life in fire or in a prison cell.

It was certainly the case, as affirmed by the diarists of the day, that a number of former Miceceans had joined the Savonarolan movement, in part, it seems, to disguise their political identities, but partly too out of conviction or out of gratitude for the Friar's struggle to get Florence to pardon all collaborators of the old regime. Hostile to Savonarola, with the exception of Landucci, the diarists also allege that he was happy to count on them, because they swelled the ranks of his followers, while also adding honour and weight to his movement by their family ties and exalted connections. But whatever may have been in their minds, the

Friar believed – or wanted to believe – that they had undergone something of a genuine political change of heart. For *his* commitment to the republic and Great Council was indisputable, in spite of any calumny to the contrary; and his incessant polemic against tyranny, knifing through his many sermons, constituted a permanent indictment of the Medici and their regime. He understood only too well that any tyranny, or any return of the exiled house, had to be at the expense of his life and mission, the reform of the Church, with Florence as the starting point. Therefore, in accepting the support of former Mediceans, he needed to believe, and certainly to hope, that they had truly passed over to his army of republicans.

Did he see Giannozzo Pucci and Lorenzo Tornabuoni, endorsers of the letter in his support, as turncoats? Who can tell? Though if he really offered a kind word in favour of that glamorous Renaissance courtier, Tornabuoni, a fetching man who could be all things to all people, the Friar may have wondered about how he, Savonarola, could have been seduced by the arts of worldly charm, now that Florence's most popular man suddenly turned out to be a trickster, a traitor, and – in view of Piero de' Medici's tyrannical designs – an accomplice to future executions.

The Rage of Politics

L AMBERTO DELL'ANTELLA WAS arrested on 4 August. He confessed that very day. All the other men then implicated were arrested, or summoned to appear before the Eight, on the next day. To keep suspects from escaping or colluding, the government struck swiftly. Tornabuoni and Pucci were released after a few hours of questioning, but were soon re-arrested. The interrogation of the prisoners was complete by 17 August, when the Signory gathered 200 citizens, presented them with the confessions of the conspirators, and made the 200 their judges. The case was considered so important, and had so split the political class, that the Signory did not dare restrict the verdict to their own competence and that of the Eight.

No historian, not even the *Arrabbiato* Cordero, has fully told the story that follows. The rage of politics in our own day, or rather our sense of it, may offer us oblique assistance in the effort to assemble the different pieces of that far-away puzzle.

On 6 August, two days after Lamberto dell'Antella's confession, the Signory summoned an emergency *condottiere*, Count Ranuccio da Mariano, along with an additional company of 300 soldiers, to protect the palace and government square. Anti-Savonarolan diarists blame Francesco Valori for this intimidating display. But in view of the government's desperate shortage of money and the extraordinary expense of soldiers, the decision was more likely to have been defensive, and it was taken by the Signory, in tandem with the Eight and War-Office Ten, not by Valori. There was a report about, alleging that Piero de' Medici was gearing up for a new secret attempt on the city, to be made in the middle of the night and with the help of internal plotters.

The confessions of the arrested men had frightened the *Signor* Priors, who were also anxious about a Medicean reaction to the arrests. By hiring Count Ranuccio and more troops, they delivered a warning to the foes of the Friar, while also responding to Piero's reported shifty movements. Meanwhile, it was August, the worst month for deaths from pestilence; an acute famine persisted; the poor were seen collapsing in the streets; and the unemployed remained subject to Medicean blandishments. Most of the upper-class families had retreated to their country villas, with the result that the government could not be sure of the numbers of friends and enemies present in the city.

There was yet another worry for the Signoria. Savonarola lay under a ban of excommunication; he was not preaching; and this had given new courage to his enemies, a change best seen in the mounting combativeness of the Compagnacci. But while bereft of numerous upper-class families, Florence was not without its political men and more active citizens. Although women and children, especially during summers of pestilence, tended to remain in the country, the men frequently returned to look after business and political matters. At the heart of every citizen's social identity was the city. The Milanese ambassador, Paolo Somenzi, reported that the government, running scared, wanted more people back from their villas.

By 17 August, a government summons had got a sufficient number of supporters back into Florence, and the Signory was ready to bring the five men to justice, despite the fact that the ruling class was passionately divided about what to do with them. Strappados had extracted confessions, and although these were read out to the jury of 200 citizens, they were never published, because they contained information, allegedly, that so compromised 'the great powers' – Milan, the Pope, and Venice – that the Florentine government would have been forced into an embarrassing round of foreign accusations. And the Signory had no wish – nor the diplomatic or military muscle – to pull such whiskers. Back in 1478, having foiled the Pazzi Conspiracy against Lorenzo the Magnificent, the Medicean regime suppressed the confessions of all but one of the men involved in the plot (and even parts of this one were deleted), because they made a pope, a king, and the Duke of Urbino complicit in their conspiracy: again, too embarrassing.

The trial of the five men took place in an atmosphere of so much suspicion and accusation that some Florentines believed – Cerretani for one – that Lamberto dell'Antella's behaviour had been a charade. His cooperation, they argued, had been secured beforehand by some of the Friar's Men, and he was not in fact tortured. Nothing, however, in the tight configuration of events lends substance to these allegations.

Read out to the assembled mass jury, the evidence and testimony linked the five men to Piero's arrival outside the walls of Florence on April 28th; and when the case was put to a vote, the assembly found all five of them guilty of treason. In Florentine law, this verdict automatically carried the penalty of death and the confiscation of all the worldly possessions of the condemned. Now, however, taking a lesson from the strong-arm and illegal tactics of Medicean government, the republican regime called for a commitment that was nothing if not a technique of duress: an open vote. 'To proceed in this case in a more united manner,' Parenti noted, 'and so that none would then be able to offer excuses, each man, one by one, was asked for his verdict, and it was recorded by a public attorney. Nearly all of them voted that they [the accused] should die. The jurors used few words, [saying] only that justice should be done, without actually specifying death.' The vote was not quite unanimous, so it has to be said that, in view of the tensions in the city and palace, the few men who dug in their heels and rejected a guilty verdict were unusually brave, as the events of the next few days would show.

No sooner had the vote been taken than the question of an appeal was raised. In accordance with a law of March 1495, enacted under the inspiration of Savonarola's pleas, the five men now chose to appeal to the Great Council over the heads of the Signoria, the Eight, and their appointed jurors. No question at that moment could have been more calculated to split and stir up the government and its opposition. Next, adding to the swell of passions, the premier defender of oligarchy, one of the city's foremost legal minds, *Messer* Guidantonio Vespucci, stepped forward to act as legal counsel for the five defendants. About sixty years old, a man of vast political experience at home and abroad, he was one of the most forceful and frequent speakers in government consultations, and over the previous fifteen years had conducted a large number of major ambassadorial missions. Republicans now faced, perhaps, their leading opponent, a man not as canny, politically, as Bernardo del Nero, but more learned and with fewer enemies.

The guilty verdict of 17 August was followed by four days of intense debate, much of it in streets and private enclaves. Not until 21 August do we get a recorded and final set of deliberations concerning the appeal. The sense and feel of the controversy, as it took shape over the previous four days, has to be gleaned from the letters of foreign ambassadors, from two diaries (Cerretani and Parenti), and from Guicciardini. Anger and disagreement over the case had been rising since 9 or 10 August, but after 17 August the contending sides were borne to the lip of violence by their explosive differences.

Vespucci does not seem to have submitted a written defence of the appeal, in part anyway because there was nothing regular about the case or its proceedings. And while the Priors and their appointees, plus the Eight and the War-Office Ten, were to sit in judgment on the appeal, they were not a court of law and were not bound by ordinary legal procedures. Vespucci, as will be shown, was not even allowed – or did not choose – to address the jurors on the evening of the final discussions. He must therefore have confronted them on the 18th or 19th, before the whole question attained a fever pitch on the 21st. For suddenly, a perfectly rational question in law – had the five defendants the right of appeal to the Great

Council? – turned into a rage in politics. And it is a wonder to see how passion recruited reason in the will to triumph. The interpretation and understanding of the law was battered by politics, precisely as in the 'war against terrorism' in our own day.

The law said that any Florentine citizen condemned to death by the Signory and Eight, including therefore by any appointees acting under their authority, had the right to appeal that sentence to the Great Council. Otherwise – the Friar and the Savonarolan republicans had argued – the power of the Signory, which was neither a court nor a legislature, was too awesome. Six of nine beans (a two-thirds vote in the Signory) could destroy men and their families too, because capital sentences in crimes against the state were automatically accompanied by a second penalty: the sequestration of all the worldly goods and chattels of the condemned. In this seemingly transparent statute, most ironically, the friends of the Medici and secret enemies of the Great Council now found the obvious legal grounds for the appeal of the five defendants. On the other hand, many of those who feared the wiles of the Mediceans and of the five 'conspirators', but who cherished the Great Council and had clipped the wings of the Signory, now wanted the *Signori* – at least in this case – to prevail over the Council. There was bad faith on both sides. Let's have the arguments.

The case for the appeal of the five, as we have seen, was rather straightforward. It only remained for defenders to add that to deny this right to the accused was to put men tricksily above the law, and so to live by the will of men rather than by the rule of law. Moreover, the case was of such moment that the *popolo* in the Great Council, the real 'lord' in this city, should rightly have the final say. Moral and social arguments were also added. When faced with the threat of death, no man should be defrauded of the legal right to defend himself. Death was the supreme loss, and therefore merited particular care and attention. Once inflicted, it could not be undone. In this case, indeed, such considerations gathered additional force, because the reputations, distinguished lineages, and relatives of the accused were such as to cast a troubling shadow over the whole city if they were denied their right to an appeal. The law conferring this right was enacted with just such a case in mind.

Drawing, we must suppose, on some of the preceding arguments, the subtle *Messer* Guidantonio Vespucci went further. According to another lawyer, Francesco Guicciardini, Vespucci argued that the five defendants could not all be put into the same bin; some had done more than others 'and in different ways'; there were significant differences among their individual actions; and indeed some had merely known things, but had not engaged in actions. He also wanted the case to be considered in the light of all other laws in the city that might bear on it. In effect, then, he was adding the argument that the case called for much more time and thought; and letting it go into the Great Council would allow for this.

The other side was no pauper in its store of legal arguments. In fact, the jurists present at the discussions, *legum doctores* all, were entirely split by the case, in a tally of something like five against four, with the majority rejecting the claimed right of appeal. Their argument, intriguingly, was one that migrated from the statute at the focus of the debate out to larger questions of state, of security and public safety, and the expedient avoidance of tumult and scandal. At some point, probably on the 17th or 18th, as one speaker noted, all the statutes regarding treason and the case in question had been read out to the assembled counsellors.

The opponents of the accused men were not so foolish as to deny the validity of the Savonarolan law of appeal. They held, however, that the republic was facing an emergency; that Piero was in Siena gathering troops and hoping to march on Florence; that delay in the case might cause an uprising, because the powerful relatives of the defendants were the sort who could provoke a tumult; and the people, moreover, were calling for the heads of the accused, so great was the anger over their treachery. They added that the request for an appeal was both a delaying tactic and a way for the influential relatives of the five to organise their rescue in the Great Council; and this was 'to put justice under the will of relatives, friends, and weak men [in the Council]'. Speaking for the 'doctors of law', *Messer* Domenico Bonsi even urged that if a swift appeal was granted, 'it would seem right to them to have the relatives of the prisoners held in a well-known place (*in luogo trito*), so that if troubles broke out, they would not be able to exploit them'.

The final discussions, held on 21 August, made it clear, as other sources do not, that sending the case up to the Great Council would have required more time, perhaps a good deal more. Many citizens, after all, were still out at their farms and villas; the Great Council would have to come in with a quorum; and there was no knowing how long this might take. Still, what if the right of appeal was granted, asked another Savonarolan lawyer, *Messer* Francesco Gualterotti, and the Great Council, falling short of a quorum, failed to act? He was speaking for the War-Office Ten. 'We would then have to find another solution, to avoid any outburst directed against our city, both at home and abroad, by the big powers of Italy.' So, as if bending to the humanity of a possible appeal, the lawyers and some other citizens were willing to grant it, but with an all but impossible condition: namely, that the appeal go into the Great Council and be fully handled in a day or two at the most, by 22 or 23 August. The expressed urgency underlined the essence of the legal arguments against the appeal: that is, that Florence faced an imminent danger to the state, and that this must override all particular statutes, including those touching cases of capital punishment.

For all their fatal significance, these abstractions fail to catch the fury and passion that accompanied the arguments. Tempers and strong words reached a peak on the 21st, in meetings that began that morning and ran right through the day, lasting until well after midnight. The case was now in the hands of a more restricted group: the Signory, the Ten, the Eight, and a selection of counsellors. They proposed to hammer out the question of the appeal, but the final decision would rest with the Signoria itself, with the nine votes of the Priors and Gonfalonier of Justice.

On that warm August night, at about 11:00pm, with troops patrolling the Piazza della Signoria, men down in the square heard shouts of anger coming from the open windows far above. Few events had ever produced the like in the history of Florence. Cerretani tells us that 'the Palace that night was like a forge, or rather, a cavern of fury, and all the men present driven by contempt and as if by a mad rage, with weapons in hand, wounding words, and full of quarrels . . . so that a number of noblemen feared for their safety'. The lives of five eminent men were on the line, and all knew that horror would streak through the city if they were executed, despite the applause of a majority of citizens. Yet the opponents of the appeal entertained a vision of all Italy bound together in the Holy League, conspiring against Florentine liberty and against a Florence that was nearly bankrupt, unable at any rate to hire the most eloquent of all voices in foreign affairs, a credible professional army. The city was committed to fighting internal tyranny and to saving its 'God-given' republic.

Now, outrageously, here were five 'perfidious parricides', as they would be known by the Priors: five Florentines who had plotted to over-turn the republic by working with its capital enemy, Piero de' Medici. Speaking for the Eight, another doctor of law, *Messer* Luca Corsini, one of the revolutionaries of November 1494, declared himself 'stupefied' to see that the five defendants had turned into dangerous internal enemies of the republic, despite having figured among the former Mediceans who had been pardoned 'with so much clemency'. Corsini might at this point have asked with Savonarola, if a man deserves death for commiting a murder, what does a tyrant deserve, and therefore his assistants too, for snuffing out liberty and oppressing a whole city and people?

In the hours leading up to the final decision, the Signory was dead-locked, with four or five votes in favour of granting the appeal, and any decision, for or against the appeal, requiring the famous six black beans. Whereupon, in the midst of that furore, with counsellors such as Francesco degli Albizzi menacing and insulting the Signory, or calling out 'Justice! Justice!', the nobleman Carlo Strozzi went up to Piero Guicciardini (the historian's father), who was at the table of the Priors, grabbed him by the shirt or doublet, and threatened to throw him out of the windows, unless he voted to deny the appeal. Strozzi chose the elder Guicciardini because, in social rank and political standing, he was the most distinguished of the Priors who continued to favour the appeal; and if this man could be coerced into bending, then one or two of the others, men of no social weight, would also pass over to those who opposed the appeal. Later, when reporting what he knew about these events, Cerretani flatly asserted that if the lawyer for the defendants, *Messer* Guidantonio Vespucci, had been present there that evening, he would have been hurled from the Palace windows, down to the piazza far below. Strozzi's flagrant crime, collaring and threatening a Prior, marked the high point of the enveloping fury. It was in this nimbus of anger that Francesco Valori, one of the Ten, 'got up, went to the feet of the Signory, with a ballot box in hand, and pounded loudly on the table before them, demanding that either justice be done or all hell would break loose'. He also threw in a fierce ultimatum: either he would die or it was death for the conspirators.

The angry republicans got their way. One or two of the Priors passed over, including that day's reluctant *proposto* (provost) of the Signory, Luca Martini, and this increased the deciding beans to six. The appeal was denied. Valori, reportedly, herewith got his great enemy and rival out of the way, Bernardo del Nero.

It was already after 2:00 in the morning. The next moves followed with such speed as to suggest that the anxiety itself of the *Signori* was the driving force, as all at once they had to think about the execution of the five men. Decapitation was to be the method, a death befitting their station as gentlemen and done out of the public eye. There would be the keening of powerful relatives and friends, especially of the Tornabuoni, Ridolfi, and Pucci families. The old Del Nero, no longer there to lead the strict oligarchs and to stand up to Francesco Valori, would be painfully missed by heavyweights such as Bernardo Rucellai. And there would be horror, rumours, the nursing of secret hatreds, passionate desires for future revenge, and escalating threats from foreign powers and princes. What to do? Better to rush the 'parricides' to their deaths.

Within minutes of the Signory's decision, word went out to the executioner, to the condemned, and to their families. Wives, children, or other close relatives were permitted to make a swift visit to the prisoners; and priests – perhaps already alerted – arrived to hear their confessions. None had yet prepared for his final moments. All five had counted on the appeal, expecting more time. Instead, too soon 'the master of justice', the executioner, led the five men out, one at a time, shoeless and in chains ('like mere villains'), into the courtyard of the Bargello. Here too they were accompanied by priests. Large quantities of hay had been stacked around the point of decapitation, armfuls of which would then be quickly thrown over the signs of each beheading, so that none of the five would see the blood of the others. And by about 4:00am the beheadings had taken place, with Bernardo del Nero the last to die, after five blows of the executioner's axe, one of which, Cerretani hurriedly tells us, had lopped off his chin.

When early risers got up and went into the streets, they soon heard the news. Landucci saw the coffins being borne away. No special bell had been rung, and no town crier had trumpeted announcements, as was the custom in cases of capital punishment. No, this case was notorious enough, and now there was acute discomfort as well. Fearful of a backlash of angry feeling, the government would have preferred to keep the whole bloody business under wraps. In fact, the desire for secrecy went back for days. The 200 citizens who brought in the original verdict against the accused had sworn not to divulge the particulars that led them to convict the defendants. Violations of this oath carried a swingeing penalty of 500 gold florins. The oath had been imposed to save Florence from the appearance of seeking to embarrass the 'foreign powers' that had connived with the Medici.

Blame the Friar

T HE FIVE EXECUTIONS echo through the historical literature on Savonarola and on Florence in the 1490s. If men and women in modern democracies gawp at celebrities and are 'star' struck, is it any wonder that the blood of noblemen and of the prominent figures of past time is stuff for the imagination, or for afterthoughts, in ways that the blood of obscure men can never be? The most democratic of peoples are captivated by the pre-eminent and the celebrated. So what is said about them needs careful sifting.

In the wake of the August executions, there was a rumour about, picked up by Cerretani, alleging that the Friar had sent a message to the Gonfalonier of Justice, Domenico Bartoli, saying that 'God wants justice to be done.' Meaning: kill them. Unless he be one of 'the Rabid', such as Franco Cordero, who believes that Savonarola was capable of just about any crime, no historian who has combed through the life of the Friar can accept the rumoured claim. It was not in keeping with the man and his ways, and I should have to enter a maze of fine particulars to argue this point. It also follows that Savonarola would not have prayed for the execution of the defendants. The death of particular men held no plea in his programme of reform, nor in his heart, as far as we can make out. He lashed out endlessly against the 'tepid', but he would never have said, 'Piero and Roberto are tepid. Therefore, kill them.' He might speak for God, but not in this register. As a would-be prophet, he had to keep to generalities.

Machiavelli, who was in Florence throughout the years of Savonarola's primacy, later opined that the executions marked a turning point for the fortunes of the Friar, that from this moment on he began to lose popularity, owing to his failure to step personally into the case, to try to rescue the accused men from a government which appears to have been dominated by his supporters. But Machiavelli expressed this view more than fifteen years after the events in question; and if indeed the Friar was losing popularity in the autumn of 1497, then that decline has to be ascribed, instead, to his excommunication, to King Charles VIII's failure to return to Italy, and to Pisa's continuing rebellion.

The executions chilled the hearts of some citizens, and would instill a growing mood of regret in many upper-class Florentines, particularly after Savonarola's fall. At the time, however, and for five or six months, the majority of citizens wanted the death of the five men, having worked themselves up against the 'perfidious' traitors. The strength of this feeling may be measured by a vote taken in the Great Council in September. Close relatives of the five lodged an appeal with the Council, requesting that the properties and possessions of the dead men not be confiscated, thus enabling their estates to pass on to their families and legatees. Although approved in the smaller Council of Eighty, this appeal was overwhelmingly defeated in the Great Council, an outcome which tells us that if the five men had won their appeal, the verdicts of the Signory and the 200 counsellors would have been resoundingly confirmed.

Historical critics of the Friar sometimes hold that if he had been what he claimed to be, he would have sought to save the condemned men. This objection ignores the realities and strains of the Florentine scene in 1497. All the evidence at hand cuts against the suggestion that the five were not after all guilty of treason. Politics in the Italian city-states was a brutal, ruthless, life-taking business, in Florence as in Rome, Perugia, Bologna, and even Venice. In his summing-up of the case, the contemporary Guicciardini (a lawyer himself, not solely an historian) ruminates on how dangerous and short-sighted it was for the five to have risked so much in a plot that had little chance of success. He was talking about the baneful extremes of politics.

In holding that the Friar should have been moved by merciful religious feelings, critics enter a field of contradiction. They intimate that he was a hypocrite. Yet the case was stridently political: to step in was to step into turbulent political waters. However merciful, therefore, any intervention had to be a political act too, in this case with a plea to save the willing or passive assistants of an aspiring tyrant, despite the fact that Savonarola had spent the previous thirty-two months fighting the whole order and menace of tyranny. Once only, back in December 1494, had he cried out against the outcome in a particular case, although without naming the man: the case of the modestly-born but influential Medicean official, Antonio di Bernardo Miniati, who had been executed for corruption in the wake of the revolution against the Medici. Savonarola saw that many Florentines would happily have acted as Miniati had, in his profitable labours for Lorenzo the Magnificent. What, then, was the moral justification for his legal lynching? Now, however, in the case of the five men accused of treason, he could not fail to sense the dangerous ambiguities of his position. By electing to keep out of the affair, he was making a political statement, but yet not actively so, while at the same time maintaining his distance as a religious leader. Whatever he did was going to be wrong in the eyes of one interest group or another, and so he chose the way of silence and inaction.

Well, but then what about the Friar's famous pleas for mercy in other cases? He had made these in late 1494 and 1495 for the numerous men who had cooperated with the regime of the Medici, although such a call for reconciliation naturally benefited the prominent personalities most of all. His argument was that unless all collaborators were pardoned, the republican cries for revenge would erupt in bloody civil war. And this judgment still makes sense. It made sense to Guicciardini. Once that crisis had passed, however, he took up the stricter demand for 'justice' and pursued it to the end of his life, in public at any rate. In private, as disclosed by his *Manual for the Instruction of Confessors* (c. 1497), he stressed the need to be tolerant and gentle. Yet when wading in against his severity, critics never call for the Friar's pity in the case of the several 'little' men of no name, the carriers of secret correspondence, who were also executed. They were far less guilty, less responsible, than their upper-class masters, and hence more deserving of mercy, at least in Savonarola's view of the world. Here surely, in having made no attempt to rescue them, he fell short of the humanity in his larger take on things.

The five defendants were accused of complicity in an armed attempt to overthrow their fatherland's free republic. They were put through a summary trial, the norm in such cases; and though the Signory could not indict them for having pounded, swords drawn, on the doors of the government palace, we may assume that the charges against them were sufficiently specific, especially in view of the notoriety of the case. The Friar always said that he never intervened in politics by seeking to favour particular men, and there was something to this — the same point that raises serious doubts about his having approached Francesco Valori with a plea for the rescue of Lorenzo Tornabuoni.

The executions are alleged to have opened a chasm between the Mediceans and Savonarolans, and historians agree that the natural death in September of the top pro-Medici politician, Pierfilippo Pandolfini, rather left Francesco Valori and the Friar's Men as the uncontested political masters of the city. Milan's ambassador, Somenzi, even noted that men did not dare to speak up against the Frateschi — presumably in the councils. This claim, by implication, almost certainly attributed too much unity to the Savonarolans. Soon enough, however, during the coming winter, with the Pope and the Arrabbiati hounding them, they were going to need true measures of unity in order to survive.

The case of the five men underlines the extent to which political Florence had slipped, under the Medici, toward being run by a restricted elite, by men of the sort who came to expect special treatment. Denial of the appeal, therefore, in riding over such men, made the case all the more sensational. But most of the anger and shock really concerned the three aristocrats: Lorenzo Tornabuoni, Niccolò Ridolfi, and Giannozzo Pucci, even if the Pucci rather qualified as parvenus, in having risen only since the 1420s. Cambi was small fry. Bernardo del Nero, though a brilliant politician, was old; it was perhaps considered that he had lived his life; and besides, he sprang from a humble background.

CHAPTER FIFTEEN

Rome Closes In

In Your Face

AT THE END of 1497, the August executions and the Friar's official position outside the community of Christians had not yet turned the tide of Florentine public opinion against San Marco. Indeed, elections in the Great Council returned a Savonarolan Signory for the months of January–February, 1498. But that winter the controversy with Rome blew up again. It was ignited by the outcast himself, who began to preach yet once more. The Priors of the new Signory visited San Marco on January 6th, and kissed Savonarola's 'hand at the altar'. Little more than a month later, on Sunday, 11 February, and again in the cathedral, he launched his *Exodus* sermons.

The lawyer, Domenico Bonsi, one of two Florentine ambassadors to Rome, had continued to sue for the Friar's absolution. A Savonarolan himself, he was following instructions from both the Signory and the Ten, but over the coming weeks he would get cold feet. Very little had changed during the past few months. Rome kept suggesting that if the Florentines would but become 'good Italians', turn against barbarian France and join the Holy League, Pisa would return to their hands – and, who knows, the Pope and Florence might then be able to settle other matters, although the honour of the Holy See would have to be respected.

News of the excommunicate's new sermons reached Pope Alexander's ears on 14 or 15 February, and suddenly all was fury. On the 17th Bonsi dispatched a plea to the Ten, urging them to write to the angry Pope, to explain and to apologise. Back in Florence, meanwhile, the government's commitment to the Friar was so resolute that when *Messer* Lionardo de' Medici, vicar to the Archbishop of Florence (an Orsini), tried to block the Friar's return to the pulpit, the Signory gave him two hours to resign his post and to get out of town, or face 'the penalty of being proclaimed a rebel', which ordinarily meant, in Florentine law, that he could be killed with impunity. Only his being in holy orders would serve to protect him.

Bonsi wrote to the Ten on the 22nd, to say that the Holy Father was so upset by Savonarola's audacity that he refused to meet with Bonsi and the other Florentine envoy, Ser Alessandro Bracci. 'So,' the Pope had said, 'you are allowing Friar Girolamo to preach again. I would never have believed that you would treat me this way', and had then walked out of their last meeting. Meanwhile, more dramatically, Bonsi himself was in considerable danger, probably because he was known to be a supporter of the Friar. On the night of the 21st, at about 3:00am, three men, armed with swords and an axe, had smashed their way into his garden and courtyard, where one of them had mounted the wall to get up to his terrace, to force an entry into the house. In the event, he toppled into the courtyard and broke a leg, whereupon the others fled. Bonsi concluded that their aim had been not robbery but murder, because the injured man came from Montepulciano, an attractive Tuscan town – Poliziano's birthplace – that had rebelled against its Florentine masters with the help of Siena.

Over the course of the next six weeks, life in Rome would become increasingly hard for Bonsi, particularly because Florence provided him with no credible reasons for why Savonarola had resumed preaching. All he could do was to go on offering a pitiable refrain, stating that the Friar was a good and a holy man, that he was prepared to be obedient (!), and that he had the loyal support of the Florentine government. On the 25th, in a letter to the Ten, he emphasised the Pope's anger and wonder at Savonarola's continued preaching, this being proof – Alexander held – of Florence's contempt for the Holy See. Hence he now definitely threatened to impose an interdict on the city, 'to be published everywhere', unless the Friar was silenced or, better, arrested. Having been finally granted another papal audience, the two ambassadors had tried to speak up, but were cut off each time by the Pope or the cardinals in attendance. Bonsi related that a secretary had even read out some scurrilous Florentine sonnets, penned against the Pope, who exclaimed, 'Oh, that I should be put thus into sonnets!' Wordy, literary Florence again! The

Curia also knew that some of the Friar's sermons were aimed directly against His Holiness. Bonsi closes this letter by reminding the Ten that the custom in Rome was for envoys to give letters received from their governments into the hands of curialists and cardinals. He therefore requests that they send him some letters of the sort — careful, respectful, flattering — that could be shown to the Pope.

A papal brief of 26 February to the Signory admonished the Priors to send the Friar to Rome, presumably in chains, or at least to arrest him. The reply from Florence was all apologies and eyewash, as the Priors allowed Savonarola to continue preaching. With the entry of a new Signoria, however, his venue was moved on 1 March from the gigantic space of the cathedral to the pinched confines of San Marco — a concession certainly, but not a surrender. The Pope himself, always the diplomat, was being both seductive and firm by turns, for even now, as conveyed by Bonsi in a letter of 27 February, he was saying that he would be ready in due course to absolve Savonarola, if the Friar would stop preaching and keep silent for a time. Agents, meanwhile, were providing the Curia with copies of the sermons; the Pope had read all of the first one; and detailed knowledge of the contents of the others was widespread in elevated Roman circles, including the corps of foreign diplomats. The Venetian ambassador to Rome used this knowledge to stir the Pope up against Florence; and back in Venice, as we know from his *Darii*, the great chronicler Sanuto was also well informed about Savonarola's doings.

The Signory of January–February 1498 even persuaded the Friar to draw up a statement of his political creed, the *Trattato circa il reggimento e governo della città di Firenze*; and the War-Office Ten warmly seconded this encouragement. But a fresh Signory took office on March 1st, and this group of Priors, it turned out, headed by a foe of the Frateschi, the Gonfalonier, Piero Popoleschi, was more inclined to be critical of Savonarola. Evidently, some change of tactics or feeling in the Great Council had issued in election results that pleased the Arrabbiati. The on-going clash with Rome, and San Marco's flagrant disobedience, had brought about a swing in mood. Nevertheless, this Signory had to test the air first, before trying to introduce any shifts in policy. And anyway the Friar continued to be both enormously popular and greatly revered. For the moment, therefore, the new Priors, working together with the

Ten, threw their weight behind the policies of their predecessors.

The Ten wrote to Bonsi on 3 March, insisting – and he was to pass this on to the Curia – that Savonarola was preaching 'out of zeal to produce good fruit in this city', not to show contempt for the Pope. Furthermore, as soon as he heard about the Holy Father's recent warnings, he had given up preaching in the cathedral and moved his sermons to San Marco.

4 March. A letter from the Priors to the Pope discloses that they had been stung by his reference to Savonarola as 'a son of iniquity'. Passionately defending his goodness and correct doctrine, they denounce his Florentine enemies and highlight his emphasis on civil justice, defence of the city's rights, alerting of citizens to plots against the republic, pleas for the right education of children, such as getting boys to revere the deeds of Christ and the saints, and persuading women to renounce the vanities of dress. In short, the Signory wanted him to go on preaching.

Three days later, 7 March, ambassador Bonsi posted letters to the Signory and Ten. To the Signory he made a point that could not be stressed enough, especially in the gathering crisis: 'we are dealing with someone [Alexander VI] who has a superior grasp of, and a way of subtly considering, every moment' of his current relations with 'us'. Looking back, a modern historian may put this differently, while drawing in the background as well. In a conclave of cunning and powerful cardinals, Rodrigo Borgia had bagged the papal tiara by no other means than those of supreme diplomatic skills (simony included), and this fact was too often ignored by the Ten and by successive Signories in their instructions to Florentine ambassadors. It was Florence's military weakness, however, that also prevented them from expressing more forceful and forthright policies. They had neither the courage nor the soldiers to say something like the following.

> Look, your holiness, we know that as a man in holy orders Savonarola
> is legally under you and the government of the Church. But he is also,
> for better or worse, a public figure of extraordinary importance here.
> He is so popular and so greatly revered that for us to hurt him could
> drive this city toward civil war. What is more, we also happen to believe
> that he is a good man of high and sound doctrine, and the Curia has

yet to demonstrate anything to the contrary. We are the government here and we have a whole people to rule. Therefore, we cannot allow you, nor the head of any other Italian state, to push us around. Knowing about matters of state, you can surely understand this. We have commitments to France; you and the other Italian states see France as the enemy. Very well, then diplomacy and negotiation are what is needed, at least until we have Pisa back under our control. Most of your quarrel with us is about foreign affairs, and you know this. So let's not pretend that heresy comes into the picture. Disobedience is not heresy. We admit that the Friar recently has shown too little respect for the Holy See, and this is surely something that calls for an inquiry and correction. Give us time to try to sort out the problem. We cannot silence him abruptly and brutally without also humbling and demeaning Florence, its people, and its government. Let's negotiate patiently.

Such a statement would never be drafted and dispatched to *Messer* Domenico Bonsi, although in their straining, oblique, and rhetorical way the Ten and the Signory were trying to communicate a message like it.

Knowing that he was addressing a Savonarolan group in the Ten, Bonsi's letter to them of March 7th had much more substance than his letter to the Signory of the same day. He and Bracci had been granted a papal audience that morning, with the Milanese ambassador and the Bishop of Parma also present. The Pope noted that Savonarola had moved his preaching venue to San Marco not by express command of the Signory but out of his own volition. He was amazed, angry, and in a menacing mood; and although he could impose an interdict on Florence now, for the moment he would refrain from doing so. He did not condemn the Friar's preaching good doctrine, but rather the fact that he was thumbing his nose at the excommunication by preaching, by refusing to ask for absolution, and thus 'in evident contempt of him [the Pope] and of the Apostolic See and as a bad example to others'. The Pope and his two secretaries had even agreed that in the most recent letter from the Florentine Signory, 'the dictation was all Friar Girolamo and his style'! Consequently, the best that could be hoped for at the moment, adds Bonsi, was a short delay of the interdict. Later in the day, he and Bracci heard from the Bishop of Parma that after their departure from the audience chamber even he had trembled at the words used by the Pope. In short, Savonarola must stop preaching.

Rome Closes In

9 MARCH. BONSI TO the Signory. He includes a papal brief with his letter, and reports that His Holiness and the cardinals are astonished and disturbed by the Friar's pertinacious preaching, particularly because he speaks out in contumely of the Pope and the Holy See, thereby — interposes Bonsi — supplying fuel to 'your' enemies, 'of whom there are many here of every sort'. The brief itself, also dated 9 March, is an all-out assault on Savonarola, aimed at his arrogance, presumption, illegal preaching, scandalous behaviour, and effrontery in daring to argue that he has not been excommunicated. As a spreader of poison, he must be arrested, held a prisoner in his convent, and have all his conversation with others cut off. In fact, the Pope wants the culprit sent to him, so that if he cooperates, he may be duly absolved and restored both to the Church and to Florence.

Well might Pope Alexander rage, for Savonarola had intensified his assaults on Rome and the Curia in late February and March, not only by scorning the validity of the excommunication, but also by proposing and insisting that the men behind it were 'heretics'. 'Hear me, Rome, whoever contradicts this [my] activity [in Florence] contradicts Christ.' Indeed, 'this excommunication is a diabolical thing' and 'was made by the devil in hell'. He also hits out at Pope Alexander by introducing the example of a notorious earlier pontiff, that 'wicked pope' Boniface VIII (1294–1303), 'who began as a fox and died like a dog'.

Savonarola's return to the pulpit had been greeted by a great multitude with a song of joy, *Te deum laudamus*, and — as if he would again pack the cathedral to its limits with vast throngs — stands for children, set up along the sides, had again gone up. Despite his outcast status, crowds were attending his sermons, and when he was forced to take his preaching back to San Marco on March 1st, his crowd of listeners continued to be so large that the women had to be separated out.

Henceforth fra Domenico da Pescia preached to them in the neigh-bouring church of the convent of San Niccolò, on the Via del Cocomero.

For weeks now, in their verbal fencing with the Pope, the Ten had been plying Bonsi with guff about how to interpret the Friar's sermons. If one realised, they said, that he was using allegorical argument, thereby truly understanding him, then it became clear that he was not attacking the Holy Pontiff and the Curia. In a letter of 10 March, they even give their own words about how rightly to interpret the sermons.

Confronted with an angry and menacing Curia, Bonsi's reply of 16 March simply ignored allegories, despite his learning. The time for refine-ments was gone. Treated to such a reading, Pope and cardinals would have laughed him out of the audience chamber. As if they needed lessons on how to read! Now that some of Savonarola's printed sermons had arrived in Rome, all negotiating had come to an end. The Curia wanted actions, not words. And Bonsi reminds the Ten that the Pope and his curialists hold 'the authority and dignity' of the papacy to be supremely important. They had asked how the rulers of Florence would like it if one of their citi-zens disobeyed, rebelled, and then persisted in his obstinacy.

In fact, the Friar was making nothing easy for his defenders. On 13 March he wrote a final letter to the Pope, boldly warning him to worry about the state of his immortal soul. He was even drafting letters to the kings of Spain and France, and to the Emperor Maximilian, inviting them to convene a universal Church Council, with a view to deposing a man who 'was not a Christian and had no faith of any kind', Pope Alexander VI.

Reaching the end of his tether, Bonsi was living in fear. Seven men, it turned out, had taken part in the attempt to break into his house. The prisoner, the man with the injured leg, had been paid ten ducats for his efforts and wore flashy hose bearing the insignia of Pandolfo Petrucci, tyrant of Siena and an enemy of Florence; but he had been unable, allegedly, to provide the names of the other men. Bonsi next underlined the dangers he lived in, adding that these would become worse if the interdict was imposed. Passing to complaints about famine and soaring costs in Rome, he now begged for permission to return home.

The new Signory meanwhile, on 3 March and then again on the 14th, striving to gain the initiative, had launched a series of talks with their chief counsellors and with well-connected citizens. They focused on the question of what really to do about the Friar — a stance that already hinted at the hostility of most of the fresh *Signori*, although papal anger, it was true, had now risen sharply. What was Florence to do? Dispatch Savonarola to Rome? Arrest and keep him confined? Halt his preaching? Go on protecting him? And what about the threatened interdict, which was likely to hurt Florentine merchants everywhere in Europe, except France?

The first speaker in the consultations of 3 March, Giovanni Mariotti, representing the Sixteen Gonfaloniers, admitted that they had split on the question. Ten of the gonfaloniers, he reported, want to 'satisfy the Pope' and would suspend the Friar's preaching. The other six, according to their spokesman, Luigi Corsi, considered that 'if the Pope knew the fruits of this Friar, they think that he could never have' requested his arrest or committal to Rome, so he is evidently 'ill informed'. Corsi went on to say that the excommunication had been 'obtained against us by the other Italian states'. Any change in the Friar's situation would bring danger to the city and agitate 'the people, something the Pope should never seek to do'.

Filippo Sacchetti, speaking to the Signory for the unanimous Twelve Good Men, seconded Corsi, and added that 'in the days when your republic was sorely afflicted, you were freed by the prayers of this servant of God [Savonarola]; and you know how much he has struggled for your good. Like Luigi [Corsi], therefore, they do not believe that the Pope could have done what he did, unless he was doing so on the basis of misinformation.' The War-Office Ten were also unanimous in standing behind Savonarola. Their spokesman, Giovanbattista Ridolfi, singled out his 'good life and great doctrine', denied that he had ever been anything but good for Florence, and held that unless the Pope was acting out of wrong or false information, then, really, he was in bad faith and working against Florence's welfare.

The spokesmen for each of five rows of citizens spoke next. They sat on long benches and represented particular offices or urban districts. Three of the five benches were split between those citizens who wanted to make concessions to the Pope, mainly by silencing Savonarola, and others, on the contrary, who were ready to concede nothing, while also voicing indignation with the Pope's shaming treatment of Florence, as if this city was one of his subject towns! The other two benches agreed with the Ten in their defence of Savonarola and the need to stand up to Alexander VI. Giovanni Cambi, a Piagnone and speaker for one of the unanimous benches, declared that it would not be honourable to obey the papal brief; that all the trouble had been generated by the Friar's enemies in Florence; hence these men should be found and punished. The brief was based on false information, for 'we have a treasure [in Savonarola] to be desired by everyone', and Rome should be satisfied with the fact that he has stopped preaching in the cathedral.

Wednesday, 14 March. The Signory now held a more committed and heated consultation, as the new Priors began to detect and to encourage a shift in mood. The threat of a papal interdict had widened the splits in the political class, and many citizens, while revering the Friar, were now ready to see him temporarily silenced, in the hope that Rome would refrain from imposing the city-wide anathema. Their feeling that all Italy was against Florence made the threatened interdict all the more ominous. The papal brief of 9 March and Bonsi's letter of the same day were read out to the assembled counsellors, who then broke up into their respective groups and held separate discussions. With all the counsellors present, spokesmen for each group then reported to the Signory.

Seven of the Sixteen Gonfaloniers were now ready to resist the Pope and to let the Friar himself decide whether or not to suspend his preaching. The honour of God, as well as the welfare and honour of the republic, were at stake. However, the other nine saw the letters from Rome as 'all fiery' and feared the interdict, 'because everyone would [then] be able to rob us and to treat us as outlaws'. Therefore, they wanted the preaching halted, or the Great Council to be sounded out on the matter. Almost unanimous, the Twelve Good Men – though they were about to leave office – remained firm in their support for Savonarola against the Pope. But the Signory now went around this group to the Twelve who were soon to take office, and they were strongly pro-papal. So, once again, new elections in the Great Council had registered a marked change in feeling and outlook.

Speaking for the new Twelve, Giovanni Canacci made one of the most hostile speeches ever recorded against Savonarola, at any rate up to that point. He observed that the directive in question came from 'the Supreme

Pontiff, vicar of God, lord of Christians. He has jurisdiction in all the world, above all among Christians. He is commanding this Signory, the least of Italy's five [great] powers, even when it has all its empire. Florence lives from industry, has citizens throughout the world, and cannot live without such activity [hence we should fear an interdict].' The new Twelve had unanimously decided, moreover, that they wanted Savonarola's sermons 'completely stopped and that no citizen should be allowed to meet with him or go to him, and this not only for his own good but also for the good of citizens, because they think that [political] meetings should take place in the Palace and not over there [in San Marco]'. The Pope, after all, had a right to that which was his due: jurisdiction over men in holy orders.

Speaking to an assembly which included numerous men who continued to have an enormous regard for the Friar, Canacci was a brave man. But he knew that he had influential patricians behind him, and there were perhaps some moments of quiet approval and angry silence when he had finished.

The next set of views came from the Captains of the Guelf Party. This ancient, conservative, and patriotic pressure group was frequently consulted. Their speaker, Antonio del Vigna, praised the Friar 'with every reverence', but held, nevertheless, that they should now seek to satisfy the Pope, 'so as not to incur censure or malediction'.

The Guelfs were followed by the War-Office Ten, who were represented by the prominent oligarch, Paolantonio Soderini. His report, however, was rather weak, because the Ten — made up almost entirely of Savonarolans — had absolutely nothing new to add, now that Alexander VI had radically upped the stakes with an ultimatum. Rehearsing most of the old arguments, Soderini held that the papal brief was an insult to Florentine honour, that the Pope's commands aimed to satisfy the wishes of the other Italian powers and to sow dissension in the city. Florence did best to go on trusting in God. 'Friar Girolamo should be cherished as a precious jewel, the like of which was not to be found anywhere else in Italy.' But Soderini said nothing about the ultimatum; he could not afford to, since this would have required balancing that danger against the alleged worth of the Friar. At any rate, he could not have made any impression on the citizens strongly aligned against Savonarola. Nor did the next speaker, who represented the mighty Eight.

This magistracy stood 7 to 1 in favour of letting the Friar continue with his Lenten sermons, but added nothing fresh or different to the discourse.

The debate had turned into a revealing performance. Something subtle was taking place. The Savonarolans were beginning to lose the initiative and vigour, not because their belief in the Friar or in the republic was failing, but because the papal threat was now so strong, so urgent, that it was changing the Florentine political atmosphere. In short, action and fresh arguments were required, if the leaders of the Frateschi were to retain forcefulness in their ranks.

The fight was certainly not yet lost. Florence had recently been under a Savonarolan government in the Signory of January–February. Even though having to preach in San Marco, Savonarola was in the midst of his powerful Lenten sermons. And the next speaker, Lorenzo Lenzi, representing the influential Monte Officials, the rich men in charge of the city's treasury and public finances, made an ardent plea in favour of the Friar. He reminded his audience that Savonarola's doctrine was 'perfect in every way', that they should have more esteem for God than for the Pope, that the Friar and his prayers had brought peace and salvation to the city, that his was the voice mainly responsible for the Great Council and for keeping the grandees in their place, and that he, not the Pope, should be the one to decide whether or not he would go on preaching. Finally, 'if the interdict comes, let it come. Our city has had interdicts before . . . The grace of God has always freed us.'

Lenzi had shown more courage and sparkle than the honourable Soderini.

But one of the most tightly-reasoned and cogent arguments of the day – and the longest – was presented by *Messer* Guidantonio Vespucci, the anti-Savonarolan diplomat and lawyer who had defended the accused traitors of the previous August. Accustomed to addressing princes and powerful men, this self-assured politician, speaking for the majority (5 to 4) in the corps of 'doctors of law' (*pro Doctoribus*), told the Signory that they, the majority, chose to 'obey' the Pope: 'We are what we are in Italy. Your ambassador in Rome is there to request an absolution for the Friar and to ask for the *decima* [a tax on the clergy], which, if not obtained, will mean that we shall not be able to meet our expenses . . . Requesting graces of the Pope [such as the return of Pisa] and then doing things that are offensive . . . strike him [Vespucci] as self-defeating rhetoric. Whether Friar Girolamo is being abusive and defamatory or not, the point is that the Apostolic See holds him to be so . . . If the interdict is imposed . . . your things will be offered up as prey. Merchants have already stopped sending goods abroad, and [requests for] safe-conducts have already been turned down . . . Since he [the Friar] has been forbidden to preach by his superior, no sin is incurred in holding him back from doing so . . . It has been said here that this matter [the ban against Savonarola's preaching] is not all that serious. I have to say, for all my paltry experience, that I do not treat it lightly, because the arms of the Apostolic See are in censures. Take these away and you take away the dignity and the obedience that are their due, and so their censures have to be greatly esteemed because they esteem them, having no other weapons. . . . Again, it has been said that we should care for the honour of God, and speaking for myself, I agree that this should precede every other thing. Yet this also is ambiguous talk, for the Pope is the vicar of Christ on earth and holds his power from God. And he [Vespucci] believes that whoever shall choose to obey the Supreme Pontiff and his censures, whether just or unjust (which I want in no way to judge), will deserve more than by not obeying . . . [Finally,] if we were absolutely certain that he [Savonarola] was sent by God, it would be well to let him preach and to put this before all others things. But not being certain, it would seem to him more fruitful in every way for the city to satisfy the Supreme Pontiff, as you will then be easily able to request favours of him.'

The core of Vespucci's plea was legalistic, and therefore solid and coherent, particularly in the shadow of the threatened interdict. At this juncture the Frateschi had a more difficult position to defend. *Messer* Antonio Malegonnelli, who represented the other four jurists and sided with the Friar, took the floor next, and had to weave between admitting that the Pontiff *was* God's vicar on earth and claiming that Savonarola's life and doctrine were good. He noted that the Italian states were seeking discord in Florence by assailing the Friar, who, moreover, had suffered calumny even before his alleged disobedience. Malegonnelli closed by saying that he was constrained to believe that the Friar spoke for God. To terminate his preaching, therefore, could bring on a greater malediction than anything threatened by the Pope.

The flow of speeches zig-zagged between positions for and against Savonarola, with many still full of praise for him, but also signalling the need to satisfy the Pope by getting the contentious monk to stop preaching, whether of his own accord or by command of the Signory.

The most effective pleas in favour of Savonarola were in the claims that he was a holy man, that he had saved Florence from civil war and ruin, that he was the key figure in the political solidity of the new republic, and that the city owed him a debt of gratitude. In this prospect, Florentines desperately needed the inspiration of his preaching, particularly because all Italy was arrayed against them. Some speakers also observed that it was outrageous for the Pope to intervene with action that violated Florence's liberties and independence. The more modern word 'sovereignty' was of course never used, but Savonarola's defenders came close to articulating this idea.

All this and a little more was contained in a substantial intervention by another jurisconsult, *Messer* Enea della Stufa, who spoke for the majority of his divided bench (8 to 7). He added a special legal and political twist: 'It does not redound to the honour of your Lordships for the Pope to command you, inasmuch as he has authority in spiritual and not in temporal matters; and Friar Girolamo's case may be said to belong to the temporal sphere, owing to the kind of good he has done. Since the Pope has not observed the due measures, they [the bench majority] do not think that he should use you as his ministers . . . If the Pope should obtain satisfaction in this dispute [silencing the Friar], he would then find the opportunity to request something even more dishonourable of you; and though he has made a plea for the assistance of the secular arm, yet he would have us act as if we were his agents and, I may say, his policemen assigned to sending him [Savonarola] all tied up' to Rome. *Messer* Enea's démarche was fully in agreement with the line of a later spokesman, Giovanni Cambi, who said that they should 'flee the ire of God' by honouring the Friar, that they *could* live with an interdict, and that the Pope could do nothing for them about Pisa, because it was in the hands of the Venetians and the Duke of Milan.

An international merchant, Giuliano Gondi, now waded in with a truly remarkable plea. His bench of fourteen citizens had sided vigorously and unanimously against the Friar. These men say, Gondi observed, 'that the [papal] brief should be observed from start to finish and in this manner: that the Friar stop preaching, that he be locked up in that place [San Marco], that citizens not be allowed to go there, and that the guardsmen down below, who are supposed to guard you, be sent instead to guard him. And I would remind you, my Lords, of your dignity and obedience, for you promised your obedience to the Supreme Pontiff. I was one of the guarantors [of your faith] when you took office, and I heard *Messer* Bartolomeo Ciai recite your oath, which included your being faithful and obedient to the Holy Church; and if you are not, then that turns into perjury. This man [Savonarola] preaches that the Pope is not the Pope, that we should have no belief in him, and other things of the sort that you would not even say to a cook. This man will create a sect of *fraticelli* [heretical minorite friars], as happened on another occasion in this city, and it's a sect of heresy you're fostering in this land. Must we be against all Italy and the big powers of Italy and against the Supreme Pontiff as well? The Roman censures mean that we are in rebellion against the Holy Church, and many merchants have not dispatched their goods to Naples and to other places so as not to be robbed or butchered. *Messer* Enea would sing a different tune if he had to suffer losses of this sort. My lords, we will be plundered everywhere, and this is what particularly scares me. The Supreme Pontiff is ready to treat you well if you will let him. Baldassare Brunetti [a business partner] and I have not received a safe-conduct [for travel to a point abroad] because of the censures, a refusal which points to the interdict. I beg you, my Lords, be careful; and if this be not enough [if you are still uncertain], then take the matter into the Great Council. My goods are dispersed all over Italy and beyond. If the interdict is imposed on us, I won't be able to meet my obligations to anyone. And [I think] that on seeing these censures, Friar Girolamo will either humble himself and obey, or come to you and request permission to leave the city.'

Gondi's outburst was a most unusual occurrence in the records of advice for the Signory. He converted the collective opinion of his bench into a pointedly personal plea, while also hitting out angrily at Savonarola, and this, in the emerging climate, he could only have done with the secret support of several leading oligarchs, including the anti-Savonarolan Gonfalonier himself, Piero Popoleschi. We should remember too that the Compagnacci now went about openly scoffing at the pieties of

Savonarola's followers. Public feeling in the city was very much in flux.

No citizen who followed Gondi was as blistering as he, not even the mighty Francesco Valori, who came immediately after him in the roster of speakers. But the conflicted mood of the day, 14 March 1498, may best be caught and pinpointed by singling out a series of statements for and against Savonarola.

Francesco Valori: 'you know how much he has done for your city, sparing neither effort, nor discomfort, nor anything . . . This monastery [San Marco] is a school of [the best in human] nature that will be talked about with even more kindness in fifty years.'

Giuliano Mazzinghi: 'For the dignity of this city, and all that is due from it, I think that we should obey the Pope's brief in order to flee from malediction.'

Antonio Canigiani: 'the excommunication of Friar Girolamo was not willed by the Pontiff; it came from [adversaries] here . . . He has never said that this Pontiff is not the Pontiff . . . [and I would] remind your Lordships that our liberty should not be subjected to a Pontiff.'

Jacopo Schiattesi: 'Fra Girolamo is a worthy man of good doctrine, but seeing that his preaching has divided the city, and that wives are the enemies of husbands . . . [our advice is] that he not preach for now. This done, citizens will join together again for the good of the country.'

Guido Cambi: 'we judge him to be a man of God and sent by God . . . So I advise your Lordships to let this father preach the divine word.'

Giovanni Brunetti: '[we say that those who believe in the Friar] would not be the first deceived into thinking that they have a prophecy, when what they have is something from his fantasy'.

Luigi Venturi [Ventura?]: '[The citizens] on my bench . . . hold that such a man [the Friar] should be guarded and made much of. Still, seeing that the Pontiff represents God on earth, they are afraid to go against any of his commands . . . [and] are inclined to accede to the papal brief and not to place themselves in danger of erring.'

Vieri de' Medici: His bench would by no means have Savonarola arrested and packed off to Rome, but they want him to stop preaching and believe, in any case, that he will himself decide to do so. 'And because the Great Council is the prince of the city, they remind your Lordships to take the question there.'

Giovanbattista Bartolini: 'in view of the sanctity and works of this holy father [Savonarola], let not a hair of his head be hurt, because they [his bench] are certain that this thing is from God'.

Bernardo Nasi: He warned the Signory against the external and internal enemies of the republic, and pointed out that the Friar had 'preached peace, love, the word of God, and right living . . . [And] what I say I say from the heart, because I love my city.'

Jacopo Pandolfini: 'lots of lovely things have been said here, but it seems to me that *Messer* Guido [Antonio Vespucci] has spoken best and confuted the others . . . In short, obey the brief on the matter of making him desist from preaching.'

[Filippo?] Sacchetti: 'it is known that your city was liberated from a tyrant in 1494 . . . I attribute it all to work more divine than human . . . and one can say that to a large extent the instrument was this servant of God . . . This Friar is really the great reason for the government of this city.'

Late that afternoon, or in the early evening, the discussion was concluded by yet another doctor of civil and canon law, *Messer* Ormannozzo Deti, who pared the entire controversy down to two claims: (a) that Savonarola 'has these things' from God, and therefore 'better to obey God than the Pope'; and (b), very simply, that it is better 'to obey the Pope'. Deti then counsels the Signory to choose the more certain of the two routes, namely, to obey the brief, because there is too much uncertainty about the Friar.

Two days later, 16 March. The Signory summoned nearly all of the city's foremost politicians, including the top Savonarolans, to ask for their views again, and now all agreed that the Friar should bring his preaching to an end, although some continued to insist that the brief was an insult to the republic. Informed on the 17th about the brief and ordered to be silent, Savonarola delivered his final *Exodus* sermon in San Marco on 18 March.

The record of advice and discussion, as we have seen it unfold, shows that the papal ultimatum, laid down in the brief of 9 March, so split the opinion of citizens that the field of action was now open for an energetic Signoria to lead the way, unless a dramatic event of some sort suddenly supervened to drive public feeling one way or the other. A republican Signoria would then go with the rushing current.

The letters from Rome, in the meantime, continued to be 'fiery', as one speaker described them. On the 18th the Signory wrote to Bonsi, directing him to tell the Pope that they had ordered Savonarola to stop preaching. Bonsi in turn, on the same day, wrote to the Ten, informing them that having just met with an important group of cardinals, the Pope had shown them reports, quoting the acerbities 'and the terrible terms used by Friar Girolamo in his preaching, in vituperation and to the greatest infamy of His Holiness and of cardinals and generally of all the prelates at this court'. Deeply wounded and angry, Alexander had asked for the cardinals' advice. They replied by encouraging him not only to insist that Savonarola be arrested and dispatched to Rome, but also that he proceed with the interdict, 'lay hands on Florentines [in Rome], see to it that all their merchandise is kept here [not furtively shipped out]', give the republic a deadline for arresting the Friar, 'then imprison the Florentines in Castel Sant' Angelo and have the Apostolic Chamber confiscate all their goods'.

Bonsi's would-be assassin, the intruder from Montepulciano, would soon be executed, but there was no relief for the ambassador from his anxieties, as his masters back in Florence dragged their feet in the face of the papal ultimatum, even though no deadline had been set. On March 19th, with all Florence's enemies in Rome gloating, he reported that Florentine merchants came to see him, desperately worried and begging for action. That day too they sent a letter to the *Signori*, reminding them that the Signoria also had the obligation to defend and protect Florentine citizens abroad. If you fail to act, the merchants wrote, we will be the first to suffer, despite the fact that we bring honour to Florence. His Holiness promises to strike at Florentines everywhere by 'giving out their goods in prey in every part of the world'. The next day Bonsi again wrote to the Ten: 'I await [your reply] every hour, and I pray God that it will meet the needs of the city.' More than dragging their feet, the Ten – heads in the sand – continued to find Pope Alexander's complaints 'truly unpleasant and extremely irksome', while the Signory went on thinking that Savonarola's newly-imposed silence would satisfy the Curia. At the end of the month, Bonsi was still insisting that this would not suffice: the Pope wanted the Friar in Rome.

Back in Florence, all the while, a drama was working itself out behind the scenes. On taking office the new Signory, it seems, entered with a 5 to 4 majority in favour of the Pope against the Friar. The all-important sixth bean remained elusive. However, the debates and discussions of the first two weeks of March, plus the threats from Rome and from the angry anti-Savonarolan lobby, finally drove a sixth Prior, Piero Fedini, into the camp of the Arrabbiati; and this change, in the wake of Fedini's soul-searching, not only enabled the Signory to silence the Friar but also – though not yet – to prepare the way for sterner measures.

The Signory and the Savonarolan Ten were certainly not in agreement at the end of March, but neither was the Signory ready to arrest and send the Friar to Rome, for as Bonsi himself had just said to the Pope, this would lead to 'nothing less than driving the city into some kind of evil tumult'. The republican government was haunted by the fear of a violent civil upheaval. Florence was still too much in thrall to Savonarola. Yet the alternative was the interdict, followed by the arrest and seizure of Florentine merchants and their goods throughout Italy and parts of Europe.

A *coup de théâtre*, promising an ordeal by fire, suddenly spared the anti-Savonarolan Priors from the agony of having to decide.

I have said that the War-Office Ten, all Frateschi, had their 'heads in the sand' when they refused to confront the Pope's ultimatum regarding the interdict.

This was not quite the case. Most of them – headed by Giovanbattista Ridolfi and Paolantonio Soderini, skilled tacticians – were men of considerable experience in public life, and so we must assume that their way of dealing with the Pope was policy. Having sensed a turning of the tide of feeling in Florence, they did not see how they and their movement could survive without Savonarola's voice and charisma. Events were to prove that they were not wrong. They chose, therefore, to ignore the papal threat and to brazen it out by rallying behind the Friar. Their plan, clearly, was to stand up to the interdict when it came, just as Lorenzo de' Medici and his regime, in 1478–1480, had known how to weather the storm of Pope Sixtus IV's interdict. The Ten made a fatal miscalculation. But their decision to take no action in the face of Pope Alexander's threat, even when it meant surrendering the initiative, was politics. It was not the result of moral funk.

Chapter Sixteen

Foiled Fire

The Challenge

C HALLENGED BY SOMEONE to an ordeal or trial by fire, x agrees, like his challenger, to enter a path cut through the middle of a raging bonfire, in the belief that he will emerge safely on the other side. The shield of these brave agonists is expected to be God's grace. To die is proof that grace has been denied. The contestants are volunteers.

So tersely defined and outside any context, such an agreement must strike the modern reader as barking mad, which is why we must make the effort to suspend disbelief, or we shall understand neither the friars of San Marco, nor Florence and its commitment to the spectacle.

The Italian Renaissance was not an age of reason, liberation, and tolerance, unless we choose, perversely, to characterise it by the interests of a miniscule elite of classical scholars and Neo-Platonists, most of whom, in any case and as practising Christians, belonged to the late Middle Ages. It was an age committed to a religion whose supreme heroes were saints and martyrs. Michelangelo was more truly religious than his popes. The subject matter of the great art of the fifteenth and early sixteenth centuries was overwhelmingly sacred rather than secular. Two of the greatest minds of the day, as I have quipped (though it was true), Pico della Mirandola and Angelo Poliziano, died in Dominican dress, all but in the arms of Girolamo Savonarola. And on his deathbed, Lorenzo the Magnificent himself summoned the Friar to his side. The gods and heroes of pagan antiquity, as represented in the art and poetry of the Italian Renaissance, were the figments of learned courtiers and their hired artists and poets. But when the chips were down, the multitudes of Italians reached for their crosses or rosary beads and plunged into fervent prayer, most often to the Virgin Mary.

In March 1498, Florentine citizens sensed that their community was hurtling toward a crisis. The city itself lay under the threat of a collective excommunication. Though Savonarola might be a holy man and good for Florence, his local enemies, relying on powerful support from abroad, now hoped to triumph, to banish him from Florence, and to see his confounded followers shrivel in name and number. Yet once more, accordingly, the political class was beset by anxiety, uncertainty, and anger. Under a Savonarolan Signory, Carnival had again been a time for pious marching through the city, for boys with crosses and olive branches, for the singing of hymns, and for the sounds of bells and trumpets, culminating in another dramatic 'burning of the vanities'. But the harrowing political rifts had turned into a violent dance in the antics of the Compagnacci, who hurled stones, filth, and insults at the pious marchers, snatched crosses or candles from the hands of boys, and sought to break up processions and to prevent the bonfire of the vanities. Now, too, citizens had to contemplate the threats from Rome; and priests throughout the city's parish churches, unless they were forthright supporters of Savonarola, became more strident in their warnings against keeping faith with the Friar or going to San Marco. Yet popular belief in him persisted, especially where it most counted, in the ranks of the middle and upper classes, most notably in the wide sweep of neighbourhoods to the north of the cathedral.

Talk about an ordeal started on March 25th. A Franciscan friar, Francesco da Puglia, preaching in the church of Santa Croce, threw out a challenge, declaring that he was ready to go into fire, although knowing that he would die, in a match with any defender of Savonarola's claims, and first of all the claim that the excommunication had no validity. Having already made such a dare at Prato the year before, he had then left town. But this time the challenge was quickly taken up by Domenico Buonvicini da Pescia, one of Savonarola's top assistants and the current preacher at San Marco. He was substituting for the Friar, who had been silenced. In sermons on the 27th and 28th, fra Domenico accepted the Franciscan challenge, and the subject at once became the talk of the city.

The affair now moved with unnerving speed. And from the moment the Signory became involved, on the 28th, every act would be charged with significance, as if the ordeal was meant to highlight the symbolic

features of Florentine culture. The government saw to it that the arrangements between the contending parties, Santa Croce's Franciscans and San
Marco's Dominicans, were drawn up in proper legal form and notarised,
thus offering a curtsey to the city's mercantile and contractual foundations. Nevertheless, politics, quarrels and bad faith would dog all the
proceedings.

Though he never doubted that he would die in such an ordeal, the
Franciscan friar originally dared any man. But when his dare was accepted,
he spun round and said that he had no quarrel with the taker, fra Domenico
da Pescia, that he was only prepared to enter fire if the other agonist
was Savonarola, who had never proposed himself for the trial and who
reacted instinctively against the whole idea. Once his assistant had accepted
the dare, however, and another Franciscan came forward to take the place
of the original challenger, a great chorus of voices rose up in favour of
the ordeal, including San Marco's followers and friars, adversaries, the
government, and the people of Florence. Now, Savonarola admitted, he
could not get in the way of the fiery duel. He must allow fra Domenico
to go through with it, 'so that the honour of God and his holy truth be
not cast on the ground'.

Suddenly all of San Marco's friars, and thousands of his followers,
including women and children, offered to enter the proposed fire, eager
to prove the truth of Savonarola's claims and the nonsense of the excommunication. In the frenzy of the moment, Savonarolan loyalists entertained no doubts: a miracle *would* take place. Any believer who entered
the fire would surely emerge alive. But Savonarola himself – logician and
theologian, and a man who now and again, in the watches of the night,
must have been gnawed by doubts about himself – was not so sure. It
was not right to tempt God; nor was it up to man to say when and
where the next miracle would occur. Moreover, if San Marco failed to
deliver a miracle, then none but the Friar himself would be stripped of
credibility, and his political and moral weight would immediately evap-
orate. Once trapped, however, he had no choice but to agree to the ordeal
and give himself to prayer.

His adversaries, on the other hand, had little or nothing to lose by
such a trial. They might even gain heaven. If a miracle should take place,
the Franciscans could always change their ways and accept Savonarola as

a true prophet. The laity in the enemy camp, the Arrabbiati and Compagnacci, could also turn to crossing themselves and even to looking upon San Marco as a school for Christian renewal. Politics as such would then be relegated to a secondary position. Instead of fearing a miracle, however, sources suggest (1) that Savonarola's enemies, the Arrabbiati and Compagnacci, pressed Francesco da Puglia to find a substitute for his challenge; (2) they believed that a trial by fire, or even just the effort of trying to stage one, would eliminate the Friar and wipe out the Savonarolan movement; and (3) being in cahoots with the Signory, they took for granted that they would be able to arrange and conduct the affair in such a way that the ordeal would never take place. No Franciscan substitute for Francesco da Puglia need fear that he was actually going to risk his life. The real aim was to destroy the credibility of the Friar, without whom the Savonarolan movement would at once unravel.

Giuliano Rondinelli, another Franciscan, replaced the dithering Francesco, and he signed the agreement on March 30th, while also saying that he knew he would die. Finalised on 6 April, the articles of the agreement were carefully detailed. In the case of the Dominicans, the penalty for refusing to enter the fire would be immediate exile for Savonarola. If both parties burned, Savonarola again would be declared a rebel and given three hours to clear out of the city. But if there was a miracle and fra Domenico da Pescia emerged alive, then, by impli-. cation, the Friar's chief claims would be seen as validated – the imminent scourging and renewal of the Church, the subsequent flourishing of great Florence, the nullity of the excommunication, and the claim that those who had ignored the Roman censures had not sinned. In effect, only a true miracle could now ensure the Friar's survival in Florence. The alternative, exile from the city, would necessarily end his crusade and bring his life as a prophet to a close. No other city-state in Italy had any practical interest in renewing the Church or in reforming papal Rome and Pope Alexander VI.

Rome reacted to news of the ordeal with wonder and displeasure. The capital of Christendom could not look upon such a trial with favour, because the procedures in question lay outside the ordinary boundaries of Church justice and introduced an element of wildness, something uncontrollable and unpredictable. If nothing else, in this case, all of

Savonarola's claims, including his contempt for the excommunication, were to be validated or dismissed as nil by what happened in the fire. A ruling made by the vicar of Christ on earth could suddenly be cast aside by a presumptuous friar. Pope Alexander himself, however spotted his soul, was a true believer and perhaps even somewhat superstitious. Hence he had to entertain and even fear the possibility that a miracle might take place. Then – in view of the Friar's call for a universal Church Council – his pontificate would simply crumble. Yet he did not fire off a brief, forbidding the ordeal. He was hesitating. And after taking no action during the first few days, there was nothing he could do to stop it. Pixilated Florence was caught up in an obsession, and the Signory acted with speed.

But not all Florentines had been carried away with betting, so to speak, on whether or not God would suddenly show them his hand. A number of cool heads were repelled by the whole affair, as Savonarola himself was or would have been, had he been consulted beforehand.

On 30 March the Signory heard from nearly fifty counsellors, Frateschi as well as Arrabbiati. Carlo Canigiani held that the contest between friars was better handled in Rome, where 'they canonise saints', and that 'in this place it is more suitable to talk about war and money'. Girolamo Rucellai scorned 'all this fuss and talk about fire', though 'if this fire could calm the city', he would even favour (sneeringly) the use of 'water, air, and earth'! Giovanni Canacci spoke with angry disenchantment, as he expressed horror at what 'our founding fathers would have thought' if they had known that 'we would become the amusement and disgrace of the whole world'. Another counsellor, Nero del Nero, begged the Signory 'to make these preachers give up these things and get back to preaching the word of God'. While the fed-up Girolamo Capponi simply declared: 'As far as I'm concerned, I'd rather not see any more miracles.'

Capponi was followed by seven experts, doctors of law, all of them well-known names, beginning with the anti-Savonarolan oligarch, *Messer* Guidantonio Vespucci. Though strongly behind the staging of the ordeal, the Priors of the Signoria had some doubts about their legal role in this 'match between friars', and so they requested the views of learned men. The experts found, interestingly, that jurisdiction in the matter really lay outside the competence of the Signory. The *Signori* would be doing little more than lending the government square for the occasion. After all, the friars themselves had proposed the ordeal, and the city was already so strongly in favour of it, that the government would do best to get on with the affair. If nothing else, the outcome of a trial by fire might serve to heal the city's appalling divisions. Two or three of the speakers, including Vespucci and *Messer* Ormannozzo Deti, only regretted that Savonarola himself would not be one of the agonists.

The new vicar of the Archbishop of Florence, Pier Maria da Perugia, an 'ultra Wailer', had been quickly informed about plans for the ordeal, and ambassador Bonsi in Rome conveyed the information to the Pope as soon as he had received the news. There were to be no delays. Since the anti-Savonarolan Priors had suddenly seen a way both to eliminate the Friar at a stroke and to head off the interdict, they seem not to have hesitated about risking their faith. They gambled against the likelihood of a true miracle, even if, as practising Christians (hence ironically), they had to regard it as a possibility that they did not want. Like the Compagnacci, they had no wish to see the city turned into a convent.

The Stand-off

THE ORDEAL WAS set for 6 April, and then moved to the 7th, the Saturday before Palm Sunday, as the Signory saw to last-minute rearrangements. Meanwhile, by about 10:00 on the appointed morning and at some considerable expense to the government, carpenters and masons had built an elaborate platform-like structure in the government square. Made of wooden beams and planks, it was nearly thirty metres long, just over six metres wide, and reached a height of more than two metres. The four sides were enclosed by a low-lying wall of green or unbaked brick, not more than a foot high. Logs were stacked along each side, rising to just under a metre in height and running to a length of about twenty-five metres; and the planks between the two stacks of logs were thickly covered with earth, bricks, and rubble to keep the fire away from the beams underneath. Having then put masses of brushwood, cut branches, and bundles of twigs all around the logs, the workers soaked all the wood with oil, pitch, and resin, adding gunpowder as well, for a fire that would burn all the more fiercely. Running down the middle of the construction was a narrow passage, barely two feet wide, for the rival friars. Death or a miracle had to be the outcome, for as one end was set on fire, the Dominican and the Franciscan were to enter the inferno at the opposite end, which would then be immediately ignited.

At least one of the Signory's advisers, *Messer* Agnolo Niccolini, had doubts about using the government square for a fiery ordeal. In the record, however, no other public space seems to have been considered. Other and more 'sacred' spaces and squares were certainly available, such as the Piazza di Santa Croce, which was often used for games and jousting. Better still, there was all that space outside the city walls, both on the western side, along the river, and along the eastern walls, north of the Gate of Justice, where Piero de' Medici used to run his horse races. But all such sites were rejected, if they were ever considered. The government had chosen to flag a message: the *Signori* were the sponsors and super-visors of the event; the ordeal would take place directly in front the Palace of the Signoria, and was therefore to be seen as a political affair above all, despite the religious claims and the anointed men at the heart of the dispute.

On the day of the ordeal, in the late morning, the mace-bearers of the Signory went to the convents of San Marco and Santa Croce, to inform the parties that all was ready. The Dominicans had spent the morning fasting, in prayers, celebrating a Mass, and taking in a short, inspiring sermon from Savonarola. The meeting point of the contending parties was to be at the southern confines of the government square, in the Loggia of the Signoria, which had been divided in two. Franciscan Santa Croce was assigned the eastern half, the part closer to the palace, and these friars, numbering about 200, arrived first – quietly, heads down, without any pomp or ceremony. But the instigator, Francesco da Puglia, and the monk picked to enter the fire, Rondinelli, were not among them. They were in the palace, holding more talks with the Signory.

All foreigners, with the exception of hired soldiers, had been ordered out of Florence the day before. The arch enemies of the moment, citi-zens of Siena, were most particularly not wanted. And the great gates at the city walls had been locked. That morning, too, all but three 'mouths' (entrances) into the government square were barricaded, and an announcement had gone out, banning all arms there. Groups of soldiers stood guard along the edges of the packed throng choking the square, a multitude made up of supporters and enemies of the Friar. But all were men. No women or children were to be seen. By the sound of trumpet and town-crier, the Signory had proclaimed that they could not attend, and Parenti adds that this was so as to keep 'the weak and ignorant sex' from being 'the occasion of scandal'. In other words, the Signoria feared an explosion of female passion in the midst of a packed crowd of men. Nevertheless, the windows, balconies, and roofs of the *palazzi* all around the square were a dense array of waiting faces, of women and children too.

The contingent from San Marco arrived in a procession about a half-hour after the Franciscans. Leading the march to the government square, and walking two abreast, were about 250 of the convent's friars, including some from Prato and Fiesole. They were followed by the man who seemed to his Dominican brothers so serene and yet so eager to thrust himself into the flames – fra Domenico da Pescia – that at moments, looking on, perhaps even Savonarola was inspired to believe that there might really be a miracle. Flanked by two friars, fra Domenico carried a large crucifix, 'turned toward himself', and wore a long cloak 'of fiery red velvet', as if engaged in an extraordinary and contradictory pantomime of the martyrdom that he believed would not overtake him. He could not possibly have detected the irony – a presaging of his own martyrdom – in the colourful symbolism of that splendid cope. Contemporaries, such as Parenti, were fully aware of the fact that he was playing on the role of martyr.

Behind fra Domenico, in that march to the square, came Savonarola, carrying the consecrated body of Christ in a silver ostensory, and also with a friar at each of his sides, separating him from the people lined up along the way. Next, behind all the monks, came a stream of men, children, and 'a very large number of women' bearing lighted candles and torches – the women, apparently, 'all given up to such weeping and sobbing, that just to look at them filled one with great tenderness'. On reaching the government piazza, however, only the monks continued.

In the square itself, surprisingly, three armed companies, two of them serving as a kind of private guard, took up a good deal of space. Rumours about a possible riot, leading to an attempt on Savonarola's life, had planted fear in the Friar's ranks; and they had reacted by raising a company of 300 soldiers, under the command of a close sympathiser, Marcuccio Salviati, for the protection of the Dominicans. They were posted next to the Savonarolan half of the Signory's Loggia. The Compagnacci, however, also had the authorisation to be there as guardsmen; and several hundred of them, including associates and sympathisers, held the space around the Tetto dei Pisani, on the western fringes of the square. Under the command of their leader, the notorious sybarite Doffo Spini, many of them even wore armour. In addition, the Signory had brought in its own troop of soldiers, led by the Captain of the Square, Giovanni della Vecchia. Although weapons had been banned from that great space, it glittered with steel. The great crowd of spectators, therefore, were massed on the northern side, not only because of the placement of the Compagnacci and of Salviati's men, but also because of the strange construction, the massive stage for the ordeal, which stretched at an angle from the tribune fronting the façade of the palace out toward the western perimeters of the square.

The agonists now locked themselves into a choreography of procedural sticking points, leading to a maddening and dangerous wait. A string of objections was raised by the Franciscans, and first of all against fra Domenico's glorious cope. He could not go into the flames with it, because it was quite possibly bewitched or under a magical spell. Having agreed to give it up, Domenico then had to go into the palace, where he was also stripped of his undergarments for the same reason, and Wailer sources say that the suspicious Minorites even insisted on examining his genitals. He was then made to exchange robes with another monk from San Marco, Alessandro Strozzi. When he returned to his place in the Loggia, fra Domenico, it seems, was now surrounded by Franciscans and not allowed to be near Savonarola, who might, they objected, use incantatory powers to cast a protective shield over him. Wishing to carry his crucifix into the flames, Domenico was obliged to give up this idea too. With Savonarola's encouragement, the harassed friar next decided that he would go through the ordeal carrying the Host, but this also disturbed the Franciscans, and they would not permit it, because burning the bread, the consecrated body of Christ, 'was most wicked' and 'against the Church' and could not be in keeping with the honour of God. The question triggered a brief theological dispute, with the Dominicans proposing that while the accidents (appearances) might burn, the divine substance or essence of the bread would remain intact.

A great public spectacle was hardly the occasion for the subtle ways of philosophy and tricksy language. It was afterwards alleged that the Franciscans sought to blacken San Marco's reputation by spreading the rumour that Savonarola 'had wanted to burn the Sacrament, whereupon the plebeians, ignorant of the mysteries and secrets of God . . . turned against him with indignation and hatred'.

Meanwhile, the hours were passing, and the sea of waiting faces was turning ever more impatient and angry. In that day and age, no announcement would have been made, and none was made, about the reasons for the delay. The expectant throng faced a wall of silence. Francesco da Puglia and Giuliano Rondinelli, the Franciscans at the heart of the controversy, never in fact came out of the palace to join the friars in the Loggia; they were not seen by the waiting crowd; so that San Marco could raise no complaints about whatever Rondinelli proposed to do when he entered the flames. At one point, it seems, a message came out of the palace for Savonarola, requesting that the Dominicans get on with the ordeal, though there was still no sign of the two Franciscans, and the Friar therefore spurned the one-sided invitation.

If the friars of Santa Croce used their objections to help keep their man out of the flames, it was also true that Savonarola and fra Domenico were delaying the trial by arguing for the cope, crucifix, and finally the Sacrament. They were seeking divine favour. The one thing therefore that may be said for them – and it was their saving grace – is that fra Domenico truly intended to go into the fire; and so, understandably, he sought every symbolic or ritual means to help him survive that fiery performance. Rondinelli, on the other hand, never got to that point. Always believing that he would die in such an ordeal, he never intended to go through with it. The question arises, was it possible that all those Franciscans truly believed that the black arts of necromancy, of demonic magical spells, could be superior to whatever powers were lodged in the Host and crucifix? We come away being dubious.

Forced into the fiery gamble by fra Domenico and the enthusiasm of his closest adherents, Savonarola himself had to seem hopeful in the days leading up to the planned ordeal; and that morning, in final words to his friars and the attending laity, he seemed perfectly convinced that fra Domenico would be saved by God's intervention. But he kept adding, 'if the ordeal takes place', thus suggesting that it might not; and the outcome speaks for his instinctive desire to avoid the gamble even at the last moment, if this could be honourably done.

April showers: then a heavy thunder storm broke out, with hail and much lightning, soaking the long, curious stage. And still the vast multitude hung on, some witnesses believing, however, that the lashing rain was a sign of God's disapproval of the ordeal. Parenti noted that the Frateschi looked upon the storm as a miracle, 'heaven [thereby] sending a sign of Friar Girolamo's [Savonarola's] sanctity. Whereas the others reckoned that he managed, by means of magic, a power attributed to him, to compel demons to impede [the ordeal], so as to prevent the discovery of his lies and falsity. In effect, the people had been fooled.' Enemies of the Frateschi made one or two attempts to start disturbances in the massed crowd, but guardsmen restored order, and Salviati drew his soldiers protectively closer to the Dominicans. Resigned or exasperated – after all, the Franciscan challenger, Rondinelli, never even made a public appearance – the Signory finally dismissed the Franciscans. Whereupon, the San Marco group, though ignored by the *Signori*, also took the opportunity to return home, where Savonarola made an exculpatory statement to a crowd of a thousand waiting women.

The procession back from the government square turned into the most dangerous moment of the day for the Friar, as he and his monks, closely guarded by Della Vecchia's troops and Salviati's armed escort, made their way through a hail of insults and vile abuse – 'bigots, excommunicates, hyprocrites, sodomites', and other 'filthy words'. The escorting soldiers were forced to move in a kind of crescent or loop around Savonarola, with Salviati on one side of him and Della Vecchia on the other. The diarists Vaglienti and Parenti claim that the Friar would have been killed, along with some of his 'partisans', had he not continued to clutch the ostensory and Host.

In the course of a few hours, the foiled trial by fire turned the most volcanic part of popular feeling in Florence into raging hatred and contempt for the Friar and his lieutenants. Many Florentines, even Piagnoni, hoping to be living witnesses to a spectacular miracle strictly associated with Savonarola's powers, felt tricked or cheated – all the more so afterwards, according to Guicciardini, when they heard about the quarrel over the Sacrament. The ordeal had turned into a no-win proposition for the Friar. If nothing else, in a great swell of supposition and feeling around him, he should have given orders to light the fire and then, still bearing his Host, walked into the flames himself. He owed this debt to his followers and defenders, who for years had looked upon him as a prophet, a holy man, a saint. The storm of murderous rage that he had so long feared now burst in upon him, as if by his own hands, but also as the crafty work of the Compagnacci, Arrabbiati, and a determined Signory. I say by his own hands, because his very claims had endowed him with an aura that promised miracles, and he could do nothing to dispel this illusion. Even unique and creative Florence could not provide the resources that would enable him to win back belief and regain his vanishing air of holiness.

CHAPTER SEVENTEEN

The Siege of San Marco:
April 1498

A Changed Mood

ACHRONICLE OF VIOLENCE was just beginning to unfold, and while it is not difficult to imagine Savonarola swaying between hope and despair during the next twenty-four hours, we face an insurmountable wall in any effort to get at the conspiring that now went on in the houses of the Compagnacci. Sources are silent about this. Yet it is clear that the 'Ugly Companions' were determined to arouse the populace, relying almost certainly on the connivance of the leading part of the Signory. The mood of the city had changed so dramatically that the new anger in the air seemed to call for a purging; it energised the swelling mob of those who detested the Friar and the pious influence of San Marco.

In the space of an afternoon, it had become dangerous to show Savonarolan credentials. The leaders of the Frateschi – Valori, Ridolfi, Soderini, Mazzinghi – had already been targeted for assault by anonymous scattered or posted bills. Like religion itself, politics too was the ground of finalities, such as in death or in the lofty resurrection of individuals and families; and historians who ignore the political face of Florentine life are unlikely ever to have a firm grasp of that world.

Palm Sunday dawned, and among the waking were the men who had resolved that the exercises of this holy day would exclude and deny the piety of San Marco. One of Savonarola's most devoted assistants, fra Mariano Ughi, was scheduled to preach in the cathedral after evensong; and the anti-Savonarolans knew that despite yesterday's fatal blow to the Friar, many Florentines would still converge on the cathedral to take in

Ughi's words, including whatever he might have to say about the failed ordeal by fire. Popular anger with a materialistic clergy and a cynical Roman hierarchy had not evaporated overnight and would always nourish the Savonarolan ranks. The cathedral canons, although delaying vespers and opposed to the Friar, could find no valid excuse to keep Ughi from preaching.

That day, pacing around the Old Market, well-dressed men sized up passers-by, and when they recognised or detected friarly adherents, they spat into their faces, shouted abuse, and pulled jeeringly at their clothing. Quickening in the early afternoon, such harassment went on in other parts of the city too, along the main streets near the government palace, and all around the cathedral. Worse still, on their way to this church, the worshippers who moved along the Via del Cocomero, in the wake of fra Mariano Ughi, were met by a hail of stones, thrown mainly by boys from the lower classes, and spurred on, or even paid to do so, by their social betters, Arrabbiati and Compagnacci. In these years, stark hunger had sometimes been a spur to public disturbances. Forced to retreat, Ughi, it seems, finally managed to enter the church, where 'the benches were already full'. But before he could get to the pulpit, he was greeted by bellowing cries, shouts, and loud poundings. The whole scene had been organised. Arms were unsheathed; people fled; and men were injured. Ughi's sermon was never given. The action then flowed back into the streets, where armed fights soon gave way to the cry, 'To San Marco! On to San Marco!' Meanwhile, about 400 metres to the south of the cathedral, men had gathered in the government square, and there too the same cry was heard, 'On to San Marco!' Seeming to burst forth as a natural reaction, after yesterday's debacle, this leg of the developing action must also have been preceded by some planning. And that morning, as if scenting his own doom, Savonarola had closed a short sermon by thanking God for being ready soon to take him to Himself — an imminent martyrdom.

A boy and an older man were killed by the rampaging mob of stone throwers in the vicinity of San Marco, where several hundred men and women had been trapped and were afraid to come out, owing to the rain of missiles. But over the next three or four hours, by obtaining safe-conducts or using devious escape routes, nearly all of them managed to

escape before about 7:00pm. A herald had read out a proclamation in
the Piazza di San Marco, ordering all laymen and women to get out of
the convent at once, or face the alarming charge of rebellion, a crime
punishable by the penalty of death.

The Signory had now openly stepped in. Although the Dominicans
had not violated the terms of agreement regarding the ordeal by fire —
and therefore Savonarola had not been admonished at the end of Saturday
— he was now given twelve hours to clear out of the city and Florentine
territory. It was the late afternoon. Sensing an easy victory over the Friar,
the Signory struck, and must have wondered about where the refugee
might go. In an expression of the day, if Florence was 'the rock of scandal'
because it alone wanted the 'barbarous' French army to return to Italy,
then the Prior of San Marco was the outstanding defender of that rock.
Had he taken flight from Florence, he would certainly have been tracked
down and killed by his enemies, or caught and dispatched to the papal
dungeons of Castel Sant' Angelo in Rome. It was a trifling matter to
kill a trouble-making monk, especially if the heads of the Church were
panting for his arrest. Flight, then, was out of the question. And so, in
the midst of a gathering furore outside, and the resounding cries of 'Kill
the traitor!', 'Dead or alive!', Savonarola withdrew into prayer before San
Marco's high altar. In the meantime, the captain of the guard in the
government square, Giovanni della Vecchia, a Savonarolan, was arrested
and taken to the chief criminal magistrate, the Bargello. Order (or
disorder) in the piazza and streets around San Marco now passed into
the control of an angry crowd. They wanted to get their hands on the
Friar and on his top assistants, but it became clear that this would
require a siege.

In the weeks leading up to this day, noting the rising sounds of fury,
as the city tilted toward a mood change, while Rome unleashed its new
campaign against the Friar, a few of the lesser Savonarolan leaders had
begun to fear the very thing that was finally happening, an armed assault
on San Marco. So, with the quiet cooperation of several friars, they had
smuggled a variety of weapons into the convent. The initiative seems to
have been taken by a handful of laymen. The presence of weapons in a
religious house was not altogether outlandish. Some five years previously,
in the Franciscan church and convent of Santa Croce, in a heated clash

over two rivals, each one claiming to be the next General of the Order, the monks had split into two factions and they took up arms. One side suddenly rang the church's alarm bell; a crowd of laymen rushed to the scene and into the armed, bloody fray; several monks were seriously wounded; and the Signory was forced to send out mace-bearers to quell the riot. A political solution had to be sought.

From time to time, in short, even monks were driven to, or seduced into, using weapons. And in the case of San Marco, there was to be the justifying claim of self-defence, above all because the siege was mainly the work of Compagnacci and an angry crowd, even if with government support and a select citizen militia under the command of the rabid anti-Savonarolan, Giovanni di *Messer* Giannozzo Manetti.

On that day of judgment – for Savonarola was being judged by the explosive anger in the city – the deciding six votes of the *Signori* were chiefly on the side of the Compagnacci, but their proceedings were far from smooth. The passions of the street had flooded into that collective leadership. Seeing too much division still among the Priors, the Compagnacci had decided to push things in order to precipitate action. Lanfredino Lanfredini, scion of an important family, was both a Savonarolan and provost of the Signory for that day – meaning that it was his job to draw up and direct the day's agenda. He was doing everything he could to restrain the assault on San Marco, such as by urging his colleagues to get all arms removed from the area. In support of this plea, he must have had the voices of at least two other Priors, for at one or more points their sharp disagreements so flared up that some of them reached for their weapons and threatened each other. When one of the Ten, the Savonarolan Domenico Mazzinghi, dared to go into the palace for a talk with the Priors, almost certainly to try to get them to control the violent commotion around San Marco, he was 'rebuffed with every villainy in the world', said a witness, 'and had it not been for several nobleman, I think he would have been killed'. Two other Savonarolan leaders, Giovanbattista Ridolfi and Pietro Antonio Tosinghi, had also been met with threats and abuse. Later, after the fall of the Friar, Mazzinghi would be accused of having helped to sneak artillery and ammunition into San Marco. He denied the charge, but admitted that a well-known Fratesco, Francesco Davanzati, had warned him that it would be a good thing to get two small pieces of artillery into the convent, in order to protect the monks.

In the three weeks or so before the siege, according to trial testimony, a cache of weapons was borne secretly into that religious house, although some of the lesser items had long been there for use by the armed men who escorted Savonarola whenever he went out to deliver his sermons. One of the chief arms lenders, Francesco Davanzati, provided twelve long battle axes (*partigiane*), ten steel half helmets, five smallish round shields, and ten large shields, seven of which he borrowed from the nobleman, Matteo Strozzi. A hose maker, known only as Niccolaio, one of Savonarola's private guardsmen, was the smuggler of five crossbows, two small stone-throwing instruments (*bombardelle*), one harquebus, thirty firing missiles (*passatoi*, long darts that could also be thrown by hand), and thirteen leather or armour breastplates. He got these from various supporters of the convent. Giovanni di Filippo Cappelli sent in another eight harquebuses, some helmets, three smallish breastplates, a cask of gunpowder, and a load of lead shot. In addition to several other breastplates and helmets, San Marco's defenders would have two *scoppietti*, a weapon that fired arrows, stones, or possibly shot.

The point of this arcane inventory is to indicate that Savonarola's convent had the arms and ammunition to withstand a short siege, provided that there were also the men who knew how to handle the weapons. The harquebuses and proto-mortars required experienced hands, and these were to be found among a few of the laymen who had barricaded themselves in San Marco. At least one of them was a professional soldier from a well-known family of artistic artisans, Agnolo di Andrea della Robbia. Another Robbia, friar Luca, though not one of the San Marco friars, had actually done nocturnal guard duty at the convent over the previous five or six weeks, and, on the day of the siege, he carried a sword, a battle axe, and wore a helmet. On that Palm Sunday too, a hose maker (Niccolaio), a chandler (Paolo), a carpenter (Candela), a miniaturist (Stefano), a shoemaker (Paolo), an unnamed tailor (he was killed), a vendor of used-clothing (Zanobi), and two mercers (Girolamo Gini and Bartolomeo Mei) all carried weapons. At least in some cases they used them effectively when battle was joined.

But the use of arms in San Marco was not confined to a circle of small tradesmen. No one testified to seeing the leading aristocrats with weapons in hand – Valori, Ridolfi, and Soderini, who either had no experience in their use, or were simply too wise, as seasoned politicians, to be carried away by armed passion at the risk of death. In any case, they had all decamped by the time the siege actually began. The honour of bearing arms went, instead, to other men from upper-class families: to Francesco Davanzati, Jacopo Orlandini, Rosso dei Panciatichi (killed), the poetically-named Deifebo della Stufa, Alesso Baldovinetti, Buonaccorso da Filicaia, two members of the Corsi family, and very likely the doctor of law *Messer* Baldo Inghirami. More surprising, perhaps, was the fact that at least six of Savonarola's friars, and possibly as many as sixteen, took up arms on that Palm Sunday, including a young and daring Dominican monk from Germany.

The Assault

THE ASSAULT ON San Marco was unleashed by an angry crowd in the early afternoon of Palm Sunday, 8 April, and for perhaps two hours the Signory did nothing to restrain the attack. It did not at once send soldiers to the convent precincts, nor call up the citizen militias of the city's sixteen different zones. Still less were the Priors interested in any kind of negotiation with Savonarola. There were two reasons for this deliberate refusal to act. First of all, the sixteen companies of armed citizens were likely to include too many men who still sympathised with Savonarola, and who looked upon San Marco as the main pillar of the new republic or as a school for the reform of the Church. Secondly, the Priors wanted an air of menace about, directed against all remaining sympathy for the Friar, and, for the moment, leaving the tumult in the hands of the Compagnacci would accomplish this. The same tactic had been used twenty years earlier, in the bloody reprisals that followed the thwarted Pazzi Conspiracy against 'the Magnificent' Lorenzo de' Medici, when the government allowed gangs of hard men and boys to drag bodies and body parts around the city. It was a policy meant to teach a lesson to the clandestine political opposition, to show off solidarity with the

Medici family, and to satisfy the immediate demands for retribution. The energy of the mob was recruited, directed, and used for political purposes.

As armed men rushed up the Via Larga and the Via del Cocomero to San Marco, shouting insults and incitement, determined to get their hands on Savonarola and his assistants, friars began to hammer rapidly on 'Lady Wailer' (la Piagnona), the convent's great bell, thereby signalling an emergency and constituting a desperate call for help. But the minutes passed, then the hours, and no help came. All who were trapped in the convent, friars and laity, soon understood. The altered political feeling in the city had transformed the psychological ground of action: there was too much anti-Savonarolan violence in the streets, and people were afraid to rush out in the defence of San Marco. The diehards in the convent might be ready for martyrdom, but not the rank and file out in the parishes. The northern part of the city, the heart of Savonarolan Florence, was being overrun by an enemy drawn from all parts of the urban space, and this rush was intimidating the parishes around the Dominican convent.

The enemy, Compagnacci and Arrabbiati, took quick control of the Piazza di San Marco and all the street entries into it. Giovanni Manetti, a district gonfalonier, captained a select company of armed citizens. But Alfonso Strozzi and Jacopo de' Nerli, who were not government offi- cials, also appeared on horseback, helping to direct the start of the siege. The rich Jacopo had paid the expensive curial costs in Rome for the drawing up of Savonarola's excommunication. He and the whole Nerli family were counted among the Friar's most intransigent foes. Angry and aggressive, he rushed into the skirmish with the friars and lost an eye, when struck by a dart fired from inside the convent, or possibly by an accidental blow from someone in his own ranks.

Once the siege began, the Frateschi leaders – Valori, Ridolfi, and Soderini – confronted Savonarola with the question of what he thought they should do. He answered that the moment for physical resistance had come. Someone had to go out of the convent and raise armed support. The claim by his supporters that he advocated prayer and peaceful oppo- sition was almost certainly also true, but he made this plea later, after it became clear that the resounding Piagnona was getting no response and that the government had stepped in decisively on the side of the besiegers.

Savonarola was a fighter; he had often used language shot through with the diction of battle. Now, therefore, with his back to the wall, just as politics was turning bloody and when the outcome of events was still uncertain, it is wholly sensible to accept the claim that he gave his approval for the use of arms. In the war for Christ and the renewal of the Church, weapons too had their function, not only in the French army as a divine scourge, but also in the company of the guardsmen who escorted him about the city. This practice had offended many of his critics, who argued that the escort was there to show off and for the sake of his self-importance. Yet if a resolute attempt against him had been made, his guardsmen would unquestionably have drawn blood.

When the attack on San Marco began, a group of armed men actually emerged from it to join battle. Then and later several men were killed, perhaps as many as a dozen in all, with of course many more wounded. The sums given by the sources are unreliable. But the convent's early bravura was not seen again, as the shouting multitude outside San Marco swelled, and the government followed by asserting its armed presence. The Signoria sent ultimatums into the besieged, commanding all laymen within to leave, and dispatched two stone-throwing machines (*spingarde*) for use in the assault.

All the women and most of the laymen in the convent had left before the enemy closed in on the embattled friars. Among those who fled, fearful of being killed, was the diarist Landucci. Several of the leaders, including Soderini, chose wisely not to go home, and went into hiding with the help of other noblemen. Ridolfi was arrested, but protected from the anger of the mob. The chances were that the *palazzi* of all Frateschi leaders would come under fire.

Francesco Valori was to meet a different fate. With the express intention, like Ridolfi, of going out to collect a troop of armed supporters, some time after about 6:oopm, he escaped through a tunnel that led to the old student college (the *Sapienza*) of the University of Florence and passed out into the fields near Pinti, now the area of Borgo Pinti, a north-eastern stretch of the city. Although recognised, despite taking a very roundabout route, he managed to get home, saw at once that rounding up armed support was out of the question, and tried to hide. A mob attacked his house, began to set fire to the doors, and entered

with a view to sacking it, when two mace-bearers and two other representatives of the Signory arrived to take Valori under their wing, with
the express intention of conducting him safely back to the palace. At
about the same time, his wife, a lady from the prominent Canigiani family,
was spotted at an upper window and killed by a shot to the head, probably from a crossbow. Valori himself never got to the government palace.
The shock and wrath of the previous August, produced by the execution of the five traitors, for which Valori was chiefly blamed, now returned
to clinch his destiny. He and his escorts were surrounded by a crowd of
angry men, including at least three relatives of the condemned traitors.
A stone's throw from the Bargello, and a minute or two from his own
house, just beside the little church of San Procolo, Valori's head was
suddenly split by a billhook, a halberd with finer prongs and points. He
was then dealt three or four other murderous blows, too swiftly, perhaps,
for his guards to intervene. Just before the attack, Parenti relates, the
nobleman Jacopo Pitti 'spat out, Valori, you'll govern us no more, and
Vincenzio Ridolfi split his head open'. The Signory's messengers either
connived or were menacingly pushed aside. In a ritual of pointed indig-
nity, 'plebeians' next stripped the body of its clothing and fought over a
doublet. The naked corpse was carried into San Procolo, the burial site
of the Valori family. It was collected afterwards, ironically, by Franciscans
from the convent of Santa Croce. The killers, Pitti and Ridolfi, were
never even arrested. They were drawn under the protection of a general
amnesty, issued by the government at the end of the month, covering 'all
crimes committed on 8 and 9 April'.

Valori's murder was urgent, because the men eager to avenge the
executions of Niccolò Ridolfi and Lorenzo Tornabuoni rightly feared
that he would be released, once the Signory had questioned him. The
truth was that he had committed no crime, had not even broken the law
against 'intelligences' (the formation of political sects), and would most
likely have enjoyed the benefit of a gradual political rehabilitation, as
was to be the case with Giovanbattista Ridolfi and Paolantonio Soderini.
The murdered nobleman had many enemies, but he had many admirers
too, and was known for his fierce civic integrity.

Back at San Marco, meanwhile, the determined aggressors were
setting fire to its main and side gates. They borrowed ladders from the

Santissima Annunziata, a neighbouring church, and proposed to scale the walls at their most vulnerable point, near the *Sapienza*. In response, the besieged defenders broke through the roof of the convent and began to hurl tiles at the attackers – in vain, for the enemy found their way into the first and then the second cloister. The battle had stand-offs and moments of attempted negotiation, but it went on for about six or seven hours. Using swords and crossbows, friars and Savonarolan laity put up a tremendous resistance, and even repelled the invaders when they smashed their way into the convent. The most effective defensive weapon, fired by gunpowder, turned out to be the harquebus, one of which, being solidly planted on the bookrest of a pulpit, was brilliantly handled by a young German named Herico. In his zeal, this friar seems to have killed a number of the besiegers, but at least two of the defenders also died in the skirmishes. Two other Savonarolans – the chandler Paolo and Jacopo 'the Bientina' – were also seen firing harquebuses. The most intense fighting took place after the friars and their supporters retreated to the choir, located next to the sacristy, in the innermost part of the convent. There they made a truly courageous stand. Aside from Herico, the leading fighters among the friars were the novice Giovanmaria Petrucci and two Florentines, Niccolò Biliotti and Luca della Robbia. The German had clearly been attracted to San Marco by Savonarola's idealistic message, but it is likely that he began his Italian career as a law student at the University of Bologna, where the largest colony of foreign students was German.

Kicked and Punched

S EVERAL SMALL PIECES of artillery had been smuggled into San Marco, but sources say nothing specific about their use. One at least, it is likely, was fired, especially since Parenti claims that the attackers had to approach the siege 'as if they were about to make an assault on a castle'. A lack of trained men was surely what prevented the besieged from making a more effective use of their guns. Friars and Frateschi hoped that the ringing of the great convent bell would bring in some experienced gunners, but this was not to be. With the raging and well-armed strike force outside, and Savonarola himself locked into prayer before the main altar, the friars were finally forced to surrender. The alternative, the government informed them, was the utter destruction and dismantling of the convent itself. A frenzied crowd outside seemed only too willing to do the job. It was now about 1:00 in the morning.

Elsewhere in the city, groups of men had gone out in search of Savonarolan leaders, of Giovanbattista Ridolfi and Paolantonio Soderini above all, but also Andrea Cambini, Domenico Mazzinghi, and Bernardo Nasi. That night, in fact, Cambini's house was attacked, burned, and sacked. An attempt was also made on the houses of Ridolfi and Soderini, but the Signory knew only too well that there was a hungry, ragged mob out there, wanting nothing better than to sack the houses of rich Frateschi. Two years of famine and high unemployment had driven the poor to desperation. The Priors now reaffirmed their class solidarity. They dispatched guardsmen to the threatened *palazzi*, and small mobs, intent on pillage and arson, were held off, until the mania for immediate vengeance passed. The mass theft of private property by riotous crowds could have no place in republican politics. On 8 May, therefore, the Signory even ordered a wide search for everything that had been stolen from Cambini's house on the day of his arrest, a month earlier, despite the fact that he was to be heavily fined and deprived of his political rights for five years.

Some time after the siege began, Savonarola expressed the desire to walk out into the piazza in prayerful action, but he was instantly talked out of this by the horrified leaders, Ridolfi, Davanzati, and the others, who told him that he would certainly be killed, while also admitting unashamedly that without him they would be 'nothing'. They meant that his death would bring their political movement to an end, and that magnates, such as Bernardo Rucellai and *Messer* Guidantonio Vespucci, or rabid anti-Savonarolans, such as the heads of the Nerli family, would push the republic in the direction of a tighter and more traditional oligarchy.

Four government representatives were finally allowed into the convent and led up the stairs to negotiate a surrender: two noblemen, Andrea de' Medici and Guglielmo degli Alessandri, and two citizens of more modest stature, Vieri Riccialbani and Giovanni Bettini. In a meeting with Savonarola, they told him that the Signory wanted him taken to the government palace, together with his two top aides, the friars Domenico da Pescia and Silvestro Maruffi. Savonarola replied that he was ready to go but was afraid that the crowd outside would tear him to pieces on the way. Vowing to surround and protect the three monks with guardsmen, the Signory's envoys even promised, apparently, that the arrested men would soon be returned to San Marco safely and soundly.

Savonarola now went back to talk to his friars in a secluded part of the library. All said final prayers and voiced their resolutions, but fra Silvestro, arrested on the next day, had managed to steal off and conceal himself. Half an hour later the Friar returned to the four men, accompanied by fra Domenico. They descended the stairs and, stepping outside, were at once 'surrounded by a throng of armed men with torches and many other lights'. Owing to the great crowd, guards and prisoners made their way to the Signory not along the narrow Via del Cocomero, the Friar's old beat, but rather up the spacious Via Larga, past the Medici Palace on their right and, farther along, the façade of the cathedral on their left, to the Piazza della Signoria, by way of the Corso degli Adimari. And all the way, moving with the captives, along a path of more than 1,000 metres, there was a shouting and spitting gauntlet. Back at the convent, the Signory had posted enough soldiers to keep the unruly mob from breaking in to wreck and sack it.

With his hands tied behind his back, according to one of the principal sources, Savonarola had stepped into the middle of an angry tumult and a shower of insults, accompanied by attempted kicks and punches, some of which landed on him. One man pushed in between the guards and twisted the Friar's fingers. Another, kicking him from behind, allegedly exclaimed, 'He has his prophecy up his backside!' Others pushed torches toward his face, declaring, 'Here is the true light!' And others still, 'with cries and ugly words, spat into his face or on his back'.

Such a moment, a congealment and a turning point, is rare historically, precisely because it is so freighted with a dramatic history. Savonarola's four years at the forefront of public life had suddenly ended in the shattering disappointment of a few hours, in the abortive fire ordeal, and this was instantly converted into contempt, fury, and cruelty.

Florence's failure to reconquer Pisa, the deceitful and unworthy King of France, the fears and costs and hardships of war, isolation from the rest of Italy, and, oh, the broken promises of the many orisons, fastings, and pious processions – all these resentments streamed into the abuse from that gauntlet of angry men, most of whom wanted nothing better than to get their hands on the Friar. But the explosion of brutality was not solely a 'plebeian' affair, just because it was going on in the streets. The nobleman in the Signory and among the advisers to the government, such as the Nerli men and Doffo Spini, chief of the Compagnacci, had also been driven by anger and disdain, when they insulted or spat on 'the Bigots', snatched candles and little red crosses from the hands of boys in pious procession, and paid or encouraged poor children in the streets to attack Piagnoni with rocks. Now, however, that they had their hands on the hated monk, they could do as they pleased with him, while yet intoning justice, by acting under the wide, wordy, and elastic cover of the law.

Ever since the start of 1495, in the eyes of watchful foreign ambassadors, the Friar and the Frateschi had enjoyed the backing of the greater part, by far, of the Florentine population. This crucial support had now collapsed. Diehard Frateschi lost little faith over time, but in the violence that succeeded the 'Foiled Fire', they had been too terrified to take action in the streets. However deep-rooted and fierce their loyalty, the historical moment went tempestuously against them. And many citizens who had sided strongly with the Friar in his best times now swung over to the Compagnacci, or at any rate moved resentfully away from him. When the dramatic change of mood welled up against Savonarola and the Piagnoni, no social force in the city could be called upon in their defence, all the less so because the government was working hand in glove with San Marco's most implacable enemies.

CHAPTER EIGHTEEN

Confessions of a Sinner

Contemporaries

TWO OF EUROPE'S leading political and historical thinkers, Niccolò Machiavelli and Francesco Guicciardini, saw and listened to the Friar in the cathedral of Florence. Their intellectual formation came from the smithy of the Savonarolan period, with its attendant spectacle of petty states, princes, and oligarchs who quietly honoured the lesson that 'might makes right'. Machiavelli, disabused and dubious about the wide claims of the Church, sided with Savonarola's enemies in the 1490s. Later, however, from about 1515, if not much earlier, he reconsidered the fact that the monk was able to win the support of most of a whole city – and what a city. 'The people of Florence', he noted, 'were persuaded by friar Girolamo Savonarola that he spoke with God. I do not wish to make a judgment about whether or not this was true, for one should speak with reverence of such a man as that. But I do want to say that a vast number of people believed it, because his life, his doctrine, and the issues he took up sufficed to make them have faith in him.' The author of *The Prince* had given lots of thought to Savonarolan Florence.

Guicciardini was one of the believers. He saw the Friar as the real thing – a holy and virtuous man, inspired by God, good for Florence, and right about the need for a fundamental renewal of the Church. In the *Storie fiorentine*, he concludes his pages on the man in this manner: 'his accomplishments in effect were so good, the more so as some of his prophecies turned out to be true, that a multitude long believed him to be a true messenger from God and a prophet, despite the excommunication, the trial, and his death. I am doubtful, and hold no fixed opinion on the matter . . . but I do say this. If he was good, we have seen a great prophet in our time; if bad, we have seen a very great man, because for years . . . he knew how to feign in public so remarkable an enterprise, without ever being found in a falsehood, that one must confess that he had the most profound judgement, genius, and imagination.'

Only much later, looking back from the 1530s, did Guicciardini modify his conception of the Friar and move to a more critical position. By then, however, he had spent years in the service of the papacy; Italy had passed into a new political universe; and Savonarolan republicans were again in hiding. Guicciardini had lost the ardour of his youth, but the older man, if more disenchanted, was not necessarily more 'right' about Savonarola.

A False Prophet

I F THE SIGNORY made promises regarding the Friar's safe and sound return to San Marco, the first sign of any secret orders given to the four 'commissaries' was not promising. Like a common criminal, he was taken off with his hands bound behind his back, as if there were danger that he might assault his captors. Once they got to the palace, the Priors and the Gonfalonier of Justice, having not yet gone to bed on that convulsed night, must have come out of their audience chamber to set eyes on him, as he was led up the stairs to the *Alberghettino* ('the Little Inn'), the prison cell located high up in the palace bell tower. Here guardsmen handcuffed him and put his feet in irons, before he was taken to the Bargello to be questioned. Once upon a time, back in 1433, Lorenzo the Magnificent's grandfather, the banker Cosimo de' Medici, had spent some distressing hours in the Little Inn, anxiously waiting for the Signory to decide, in the midst of a *coup d'état*, whether to exile or to execute him. He would die in his own bed, many years later.

Florence again verged on a *coup d'état*. A single Prior's change of allegiance, giving the anti-Savonarolans the decisive sixth bean in the Signory, had enabled the government to stop the Friar from preaching, to parry the abortive ordeal by fire into an assault on San Marco, and to arrest Rome's outcast. All this, however, had required an abrupt change of feeling in the city, or the Signory would not have had the heft and moral authority to go so far with things. Suddenly the Priors could take yet another leap and crush the Savonarolan movement, but this would call for such a purging of government as to result in a *coup d'état*.

Talks with leading citizens of all sorts were a fundamental feature of everyday government in Florence. This now came to an end: the government had no intention of soliciting the advice of known Savonarolans. All politicians who were known to be defenders of the Friar were either driven out of the palace – if they dared to put in an appearance at all – or they simply stayed away, fearing arrest, if not indeed a lynching. They knew that in the incandescence of the moment the Signory would offer them little protection from sudden assault. Francesco Valori's bloody end loomed in their thoughts. Yet the purge was only just beginning. It cut next into the vitals of government. The War-Office Ten and the mighty magistracy of Eight, a political and criminal tribunal, working together with the Signory, completed the basic structure of daily government in Florence during most of the 1490s. And the Priors seldom if ever took an important step without the close co-operation of the Ten, the Eight, their ordinary 'colleagues' (the Twelve and Sixteen), and the city's most expert citizens, called in as advisers.

Ordinary procedure, however, now ran into a road block. The current Ten and Eight were all, as it happened, Savonarolans, and all were frightened or striving to keep low profiles. They dared not even assemble, though, if they had, the Signory would have invalidated their proceedings. In crises or emergency situations, the Priors of the Signory – if they could bring it off – might suddenly seize and exercise a kind of absolute authority, acting 'from the fullness of power' (*de plenitudine potestatis*). Roman law, the training ground for Italian lawyers, referred to such might as the power of the prince, and only the Signory got anywhere near to having this role in Florentine law.

Now, therefore, seeking to normalise procedure, the Signory simply cast aside the current Ten and Eight, held new elections in the Great Council, and came forth, in the altered climate of opinion, with a new Eight and Ten, comprised entirely of anti-Savonarolans. The members of the Great Council either had no difficulty identifying San Marco's adversaries, or, exceptionally, the Signory was able to limit the names that went up for election. From this moment on the Savonarolans lost their voice in government. With the Friar in chains and the leaders in hiding or under arrest, San Marco ceased to exist as a political centre. Only the moral inspiration would remain, but it would prove to be astonishingly strong in the next generation of Florentine republicans.

Meanwhile, parading through Florence, the Compagnacci were making a display of San Marco's captured weapons, mockingly saying that these were testimony to how loving, caring, and peaceful those friars were. And Milan's ambassador Somenzi, seeking to make his reports more lively, observed that with its crossbows and small artillery pieces (*spingarde*), 'that monastery seemed a well-supplied fortress'.

The eyes of the city were now fixed on the Signory. Would the Friar be dispatched to Rome or be tried in Florence? There was no talk of a third way, such as exile from Tuscany or strict confinement in a convent. And most Florentines – to judge by the political class – wanted him held and judged in Florence, the scene of his supposed crimes. The local populace had been too greatly in thrall to his announced agenda to allow the case to be taken out of their hands. A foreigner, yet he was somehow all theirs, and they wanted, perhaps needed, the whole spectacle of his fate to unfold and be seen in their city.

The Signory appointed an inquisitorial commission of seventeen citizens; but the most combative current of feeling in Florence at that moment had already judged him. He was guilty: a liar, a cheat, a heretic, and a dangerous troublemaker. Parenti, who was bitterly opposed to the Savonarolans, insists that the Friar's Florentine enemies were determined to kill him and therefore rejected any idea that he be put out of the city, even for committal to Rome. In the expanding ethos of revenge, repression, and fear, there was no one to speak up for a proper trial, though even the five traitors, back in August 1497, had been allowed a defence counsel. The commission of seventeen was packed with men who loathed Savonarola, beginning with one who had been recruited from the new Eight, the leader of the Compagnacci, Doffo Spini, and three others selected from the new War-Office Ten: Piero degli Alberti, Giovanni Canacci, and Benedetto de' Nerli, a brother of the man who had lost an eye in the siege of San Marco.

The commission was not set up until 11 April, but the interrogation of the Friar actually began on the 9th, possibly even in the late morning, and went on, with breaks, until 24 April, to be picked up again by two papal envoys on May 20th. He was given three so-called trials, two in April and the third in May, but they were little more than question-and-answer bouts, punctuated by the drop-and-jerk mode of torture. Of 'Weeper' or Piagnone stamp, one of the earliest biographies of the Friar, and the most complete, alleges that his feet were burned, but this smacks of fiction, especially because Landucci would very likely have mentioned it.

The matter of documentation raises a critical question, about which a single warning must suffice. In the field of Savonarolan studies, no source is more contested than the record of the Friar's three trial proceedings — a treacherous sequence of texts. Detailed Piagnone sources, the manner in which the three trials were conducted, and the record itself all suggest that Savonarola's testimony was doctored. Two attorneys drew up the trial papers, but the suspicion falls on Ser Francesco Barone, who seems to have worked as a spy for San Marco's enemies.

To add to the suspicion, all the original trial transcripts vanished. The earliest record of the trials, dated 1498, is a printed one — the product of one edition in Florence and two in Venice; and the oldest manuscript copies, reflecting the 1498 printed text, date from the second quarter of the sixteenth century. The result is that there is no sure way to validate or challenge the printed record, no certainty about what Savonarola actually signed when he endorsed the papers put before him, and no reliable knowledge about the words of the confession actually read out to the Great Council on 19 April. But one of the more revealing bits of duplicitous evidence is lodged in the record itself, in the recurring flat phrase (or variations thereof), so unlike the Friar, saying that he had done things in order to achieve worldly fame and reputation (*per darmi riputatione*) — a turn easily insertable at numerous points in the printed testimony.

It was a record already polluted by the fact that much of Savonarola's testimony was obtained by means of torture, despite the fact, as the trials revealed, that he was notoriously vulnerable to pain. Yet there is no agreement among historians about the nature and extent of the fraudulent changes in the record. The question has not even been properly debated. For better or worse, we must rely on the judgment and prejudices of the historical narrator.

If the purge of Savonarolans required a dramatic change of popular feeling and a *coup d'état*, we must bear in mind that the same change of mood pervaded the interrogation of the Friar, of his two assistants (friars Domenico da Pescia and Silvestro Maruffi), and of the suspect citizens who were arrested and also tortured. Anger, partisan ardour, and fear prevailed. To pick and assemble a jury of impartial judges was out of the question just then, and, anyway, the Signory and Arrabbiati had no interest in such a body. At least a dozen men had been killed in the siege of San Marco; many more had been wounded; and the murder in the streets of two Piagnoni had preceded the siege. On 8 and 9 April, a number of Savonarolans had fled from Florence, going as far as Bologna, Siena, and beyond, hiding in the Florentine countryside, or even in the city, in the houses of friends. Others were put under house arrest. The *palazzi* of the most eminent Savonarolans were in danger from gangs roaming the streets. Landucci noted that on the day of Savonarola's arrest, adversaries kept shouting 'thief and traitor', and no one dared to defend him, 'or they would have been killed'. On the same day, Franceschino degli Albizzi went to the Signory and said: 'Your lordships know about what happened to Francesco Valori. What do you now want done with Giovanbattista Ridolfi and Paolantonio [Soderini]? Thus all but saying, if you want, we will go out and kill them.' Not least of all, there was the release at last of the years of accumulated resentment, bitter and galling, in the men now at the head of state and among the Friar's interrogators. So much for the framework of strain around the trials.

Not counting the inquiries of 9 and 10 April, Savonarola's first trial commenced in a rush, was spread over seven days and completed on the 18th. It began before the Signory had the legal right — not received from Rome until 12 April — to try him, unless we count a face-saving gesture of the *Signori*, who supposedly obtained the immediate consent of the vicar to the Archbishop of Florence.

Savonarola's inquisitors used torture. The resulting confession, as it has come down to us, was signed by him and by eight witnesses, all of them important priests, on the 19th. Conducted by 'the fiercest of his enemies', as Guicciardini describes them, the interrogation touched on religious matters, but concentrated on questions in the realm of politics, the primary ground of their anger. The questions rotated around six topics: (1) his posturings and mendacity in religious matters; (2) his heavy-handed meddling in Florentine politics; (3) the claim that there was an organised and purposeful (hence illegal) political party (*intelligenza*) based in San Marco; (4) the Friar's determination to have this party dominate the Great Council; (5) the charge that he obtained political secrets, acquired in the confessional, from fra Silvestro Maruffi; and (6) his readiness to use arms in the political struggle with his enemies.

I propose to highlight a string of passages in the record of the first trial, beginning the sequence with an opening statement.

'On the 10th of the said month [April], he [Savonarola] was questioned in . . . the Bargello, first with words, then with threats, then by means of torture, and he was given two strappados.' Thereafter, he was examined 'without any torture or injuries to his body'. But having twice experienced the drop-and-jerk procedure, the mere threat of it was coercion enough to break the prisoner's will, and he could not fail to know, as he brought out his words, that the sixteen men gathered around him (one was absent) figured among the most uncompromising of all his Florentine foes.

He was pressed, first of all, into confessing that his prophetic claims did not come from divine revelation; nor, despite his frequent assertions, had he ever held conversations with God. Was it not the case that his vanity had lured him into making those bold claims? 'Regarding my aim or ultimate purpose, I say, truly, that it lay in the glory of the world, in having credit and reputation; and to attain this end, I sought to keep myself in credit and good standing in the city of Florence, for the said city seemed to me a good instrument for increasing this glory, and also for giving me name and reputation abroad.' The theme of Savonarola's earthly glory was then made to run right through the confession, because the questions, as put to him by the commission, kept driving the testimony that way, forcing him to return again and again, in passing, to his alleged true purpose, namely, his own fame and glory, not the renewal of the Church.

The Friar easily granted that he had approved of the new republic from its very beginnings, 'because it seemed to me to go best with my aims. I sought to shape it accordingly . . . I intended that those who called themselves my friends should rule more than the others, and this is why I favoured them as best I could.' He threw his weight behind the

Great Council, pushed for the appeal against the six beans, and promoted the law against the summoning of general assemblies (*parlamenti*), because these steps also conduced to his larger purpose. Next, since unity among his political 'friends' was important, this required a chieftain of some sort. Consequently, he talked up Francesco Valori, but discovered that none of the other leading Frateschi could work with him as boss; they found him too intractable and big for his boots.

'As for the making of secret political agreements (*intelligenze*) . . . in San Marco with our help, I say that no such thing was done that I know of, but that in general this had to do with the men who went to [my] sermons. They all knew each other by sight, and I knew them, and this was the motor of the thing. All the sermons tended toward the indicated end [my self-glory]; so too the processions and devotions observed in San Marco, and the [religious] hypocrisies and familiarities and friendships among citizens, as well as the confessions and prayers with songs; and all other such things were also done so as to help advance my work.' Moreover, 'I knew well that there were' citizens who frequented the convent 'for their own profit', but he expected to get around this obstacle with the help of Valori, Ridolfi, and Soderini. And speaking of these leaders, 'it was enough for them to have me as an emblem and instrument, and to cover themselves with my mantle'.

Savonarola reeled off the names of the citizens whom he called on as messengers and intermediaries. Andrea Cambini was his chief go-between, the man who usually contacted Valori with messages from the Friar. He also named his other socially-prominent supporters, among them Francesco Gualterotti, Domenico Bonsi, members of the important Salviati family, Luca degli Albizzi, Francesco del Pugliese, and Amerigo Corsini. But the protecting of '[my] name and fame for living a virtuous life lay in my firm proposal never to intervene in particulars, knowing well that the citizens who supported me handled that sort of thing better than I and knew much more about it. For me it was enough that they should do whatever it took to maintain the government I desired.'

'We never expressly spoke about the election of new officials, least of all regarding elections to the Signory, the Ten, and the Eight, such as by saying elect this one or that one, because I didn't know all citizens.

[251]

In my sermons, I encouraged good citizens in general, but when the friars told me about someone who was good for our cause, I would commend him in a general way to the friars and citizens who often came to our cloisters, such as by saying this man would serve our cause well.' Turning next to other political matters, the Friar's interrogators got him to admit to having had a private correspondence with the Florentine ambassadors in Rome, Domenico Bonsi and Alessandro Bracci; but he emphasised that it was all about the Pope's threats against him. Moreover, Bonsi reproached him when he began to preach again in February. Savonarola also confessed that fra Silvestro had occasionally provided him with the secret of the names of the new Priors just after election time, but he knew nothing, he said, about where or how Silvestro had obtained such secrets.

Asked about why he had supported the hiring of a company of guardsmen for the government square, a change much resented by the enemies of San Marco, the Friar confessed that they were intended for 'our security, and so that those who were against us would be kept down and not have the temerity to attack us, as we feared'. Defensively, at any rate, he was prepared to have his men resort to arms. But he denied an apparent rumour, in further questioning, that he would ever have coun-tenanced the throwing of Bernardo del Nero out of the palace windows, during the old politician's term as Gonfalonier of Justice in March–April, 1497. Exile from the city would have sufficed.

Savonarola's replies to the questions about his role in the ordeal by fire mingle politics and religious considerations. He was absolutely opposed to the ordeal; he scolded fra Domenico for accepting the chal-lenge, and 'would have paid a huge price' to get himself and his friars out of the snare, because he saw such a fiery trial as 'a big and dangerous affair'. Indeed, had he been preaching at the time, 'I would have laboured to call it off by arguing that those conclusions [to be revealed by the ordeal] could be established by natural reason.' In the end, however, he had sought to bring the power of God into the ordeal, for when confronted with the prospect on the appointed day, 'I wanted him [Domenico] to enter [the flames] with the Sacrament – yes, I had hope in it, hope that it would keep him from burning, and without which I would not have allowed him to go.'

The Signory's inquisitors had no idea just then that Pope Alexander would send out his own prosecutors, a decision not taken until the second week of May, and therefore they broached religious questions too, intent on exposing him as an unholy impostor. Here again Savonarola's replies would be elicited so as to invest them with political consequences.

He disobeyed the Pope's command that he go to Rome because, as he had so often claimed, he feared assassination on the way. Regarding his excommunication, he believed he said, unlike many of his followers, that it 'was true and ought to be observed, and I observed it for a time. But then, seeing that my work was being destroyed, I decided to observe it no longer, and even to argue openly against it by adducing reason and facts, and I was obstinate about this for the sake of my honour and reputation and the good of my work.' As for his decision to begin preaching again on 11 February, despite complaints from friends, 'such as Alamanno and Jacopo Salviati, and Domenico Mazzinghi', this was spurred on by the Pope's refusal to restore that right, 'whereupon, seeing my work going to ruin, I resolved to resume my preaching in order to support my work'.

More damning were some other admissions. 'Speaking of the renewal of the Church and the conversion of infidels, which I predicted would come about, I say that I got and have this from sacred scripture, and I certainly believe it on the basis of scripture alone, without any particular revelation. But [the claim] that it will happen soon, this I don't specifically have from scripture or revelation. Of course I tried to prove it with many reasons . . . and though I asserted, apart from these reasons, that I had it from revelation, this was only said to give myself reputation and credit.' He then added: 'The strict life I lived and got others to live, the solitude that came from letting myself be little seen by others, was all for the sake of reputation and [having] the honour of the world, and to remain high in the opinion and thinking of men of sanctity.'

Savonarola went on to cap these admissions with an absurd reason for seeking a universal Church Council.

'Turning to the Council, about which I have been questioned, I say that being greatly disdainful of the Roman Curia, because it had persecuted me for having criticised it, and also because of their customs, I planned to do something about this by assembling a [Church] Council, and I considered having five letters drafted by different persons.' Addressed to 'the [Holy Roman] Emperor [Maximilian I], the King of France, the King of Spain, the King of England, and the King of Hungary', the letters were to say, in effect, that given the well-known vices of the Church, and the presence in Italy of a preacher (Savonarola) who was prophesying future events, they, as the heads of Christianity, should attend to these matters and prepare to summon a Church Council. Savonarola would have followed these letters with individual letters of his own. A string of gratuitous admissions came next: 'Everything that I have done or planned to do, as I have said above, was directed to my being famous in the present and future, and to my building up such credit in the city of Florence that nothing of the first importance would be done here without my consent. Once this had been achieved, I then intended to do great things in Italy and outside Italy by acting through the [great] lords with whom I would have made friendships and nego- tiated grand affairs, such as the Council. Next . . . we would have thought about other matters, above all regarding my intention, after the Council, to get the Christian princes, and especially those outside Italy, to subju- gate the infidel . . . As for making myself a cardinal or pope, never did I think this, for once I had carried out this work [of religious reforma- tion and the conversion of infidels], it would have seemed to me that I was more than a cardinal or pope because, in conducting such affairs without being pope, I would have been the first man of authority and reverence in the world. Still, if I had then been made pope, I would not have refused it [the dignity].'

Savonarola's testimony here is so remarkable that it cries out for commentary, which must rest partly on remarks concerning his tone, diction, and style. I reserve this commentary for later.

The second trial, a new round of interrogation, stretched from 21 to 25 April and was conducted by the same interrogators, 'without torture or any bodily injury'. But this claim is contradicted by the diarist Landucci, a close observer of the scene, who notes that 'on 23 April 1498 they tortured the Friar'.

The Friar now made a sensational admission: he 'never' went to confession, 'despite the fact that I consecrated [the bread] every day and took communion, and my reason for not confessing was so as not to disclose [my secrets] to anyone and because I would not have been absolved, not wishing to give up my undertaking. But I didn't care, given the great end toward which I was steering. When a man has lost his faith and his soul, he can do whatever he wants and go after every great thing. I now indeed confess to being a great sinner, and I want very much to confess rightly and to do heavy penance.'

In short then, not being confessed, his communions and consecrations added up to a long string of deliberate impieties and sacrilege. In its cold calculation, the implied stance touched on something almost diabolical. Yet how was this possible in such a man, to act, as it were, violently against everything that he had said and stood for over the previous seven or eight years?

On the morning of the 23rd the commissioners got fully back to politics. The first question put to Savonarola asked about his secret and true aims in matters of state. He replied: 'My intention, as I have said at other points, was that the citizens whom I called good should govern all, or at least by a majority of three to one, and that the others, known as the Arrabbiati (although, to preserve my honour, I was careful not to style them thus), should be kept out of government as much as possible.' When urging his followers to work for 'the common good', the Friar specifically meant *his* 'government' and 'the keeping down of the others'. If the topic concerned public life, he always spoke to Francesco Valori and to other Frateschi 'in general terms', yet 'they all understood that this expression, the common good, meant that they should favour those who went along with our aims'. As it happened, however, all the prominent men in the ranks of the Frateschi wanted to be leaders. Here was one of the main reasons for their resentment of Valori, and this was why Savonarola had never wanted the Arrabbiati to be wholly excluded from government: 'I greatly valued having an obstacle in the way of the important men on our side, because I suspected that these top citizens . . . might in the end acquire such weight that they would fashion a narrower regime of their own and wreck the [Great] Council.'

The Friar's acute political sense flashes forth in the last of these observations.

Lunch for the inquisitors imposed a break, but they resumed their commission in the afternoon. Savonarola was taken briefly back to his starting point: 'Again, I say that my plan was to reign in Florence so that I could be more effective in all Italy with the help of the Florentines.' The questions now took a new turn: was he prepared to see his side control the Great Council by the force of arms? Reply: '. . . if it had been necessary, I would have approved. It is certainly true that I wanted my men to have weapons ready . . . and to be able to respond with them every time the others made a move. But that my men should make the first move, no, not unless they were provoked. And I planned for Francesco Valori to be the head of them all, and for the others to go to his house, because I sought to bind them all to him in unity.' His words from the pulpit, he reminds the commission, calling for action 'with clean steel, and other such expressions', were meant 'to animate our men and to strengthen and embolden all those who called themselves mine, so that come what might they would remain superior to all the others'.

Having got a string of rather grey admissions in the last session, the commissioners returned to their inquiries the next day and took up three topics: the threatened interdict, the matter of arms again, and the siege of San Marco. Their procedure was to lead Savonarola through a question. Once they got an answer that satisfied them, one tantamount to a self-indictment, they would then have him sum up and repeat his reply.

'If the interdict had been imposed, I say again that my intention was that it should not be observed . . . I looked mainly for this, to have a Signory in our favour and then, by this route, to compel everyone to ignore the interdict. And even if we had failed to get the whole Signory our way, I wanted in some manner to unify the citizens so that the Signory would be under them, and to force it with words and threats not to observe the interdict.'

He remembered that when the siege began, on Palm Sunday, he had encouraged Valori and Ridolfi 'to go out [of the convent], to take up arms, and to rally friends, so as to stand up to the people who had risen against us'. They replied by saying, 'we will stand together'. When, however, they failed to return with arms or friendly help, and hearing that the numbers outside San Marco were swelling, he became frightened, took hold of a crucifix, and was set to go outside, 'to see if I could resist with friends or die'. But he was stopped by Francesco Davanzati and others. Finally, 'Since you ask me to get everything else off my chest . . . I answer that there remains nothing more for me to say. Having said things for which I merit a thousand deaths, don't imagine that I would now hold back lesser things.'

It was in signing this second confession (25 April), which seems to have been mostly in his hand, that Savonarola noted: 'in places [here] there are some marginal notes from the hand of Ser Francesco di Ser Barone'. He was the attorney (*notaio*) afterwards suspected of having falsified the trial record; he was also a devoted friend of the Compagnacci's chief organiser, Doffo Spini, one of the Friar's inquisitors.

Rome's Hand

THE INTERROGATION OF the Friar was not resumed for more than three weeks, not until May 20th. Although jubilant about the arrest, Pope Alexander continued to press Florence for the prisoner until the end of the first week of May. He was resolved to have him within reach, and perhaps wanted to set eyes on the man; but he was also asserting the Church's undeniable jurisdiction in the case.

The Florentine ambassador in Rome, *Messer* Domenico Bonsi, received the first notice of Savonarola's arrest some thirty-six to forty hours after the event, and replied to the Signory at once, on April 10th, informing the Priors of the Pope's great pleasure. On the 11th he relayed the news of a papal pardon for all penalties incurred during the tumults in Florence. Pope Alexander seems not to have been in the least disturbed by the assault on San Marco. On the 12th, he wrote a letter to the Signory, expressing his 'utmost delight' and thanking them 'for suppressing the madness and frenzy of this son of iniquity, friar Girolamo Savonarola', who had not only deluded the Florentine people 'with empty and bombastic promises but had also, with armed accomplices, persisted in his perversity and condemnation of our mandate and yours'. Next, however, while granting a plenary indulgence to the city, he made it clear that he wanted the three prisoners turned over to his agents for transportation into papal territory.

There was more: a dickering over money. For weeks now Bonsi had been trying to secure papal consent to the imposition of a tax, a *Decima*, on the Florentine clergy. Florence proposed by this means to raise 50,000 gold florins. The Pope had asked for his cut, twenty-five per cent of the sum. Florence countered with an offer of twenty per cent, and there had been some haggling. But the whole question was now held up by the Signory's refusal to ship the Friar to Rome. For different reasons, as we have seen, the Priors neither dared nor wanted to let Savonarola out of their hands. In the end, the Florentine plea was so strongly put, that the Pope, always the diplomat, finally gave way early in May. Invited to send out his own agents to try the religious part of the case in Florence, he dispatched two well-chosen deputies: one for show and the other for real muscle behind the scenes. An air of super legitimacy attached to the person of the Venetian, Gioacchino Torriani, the General of the Dominicans, an old man (aged about eighty-two) with a doctorate in theology from the University of Padua. The mission was bound to be a melancholy affair for him, because he was called upon to try the most famous of all living Dominicans, one whom he himself had openly supported until the spring of 1496.

The other papal envoy, the heavyweight and a countryman of the Pope, was Francisco Remolins, aged about thirty-six, a careerist with a double doctorate in law, a former professor, now a top-flight judge in Rome, plus the holder of four bishoprics (Sorrento, Fermo, Palermo, and Albano), and later on a cardinal. He was a protégé of the Pope and the Pope's son (Caesar Borgia), the true prosecutor and judge in the third round of questioning under torture; and for this, when leaving Florence, he was to be handsomely rewarded by the Signory with a fancy basin and a two-handled silver vessel. He seems to have got at least one other prize as well, procured most likely by one of the Compagnacci – a beautiful widow, who then went on with him to Rome.

The papal emissaries conducted their inquiries in the presence of five Florentines, sitting in for the Ten, the Eight, and the regular advisers to the Signory. Remolins was the sole interrogator. He began by asking if everything that the Friar had confessed thus far 'to these lords' was true. Furthermore, had he confessed 'for the truth and not because of torture?'

Reply: 'It is true.' Though here, revealingly, was the prosecution's implicit admission that there might be a clash between the truth and forced testimony.

In answer to another question, Savonarola went on to swear 'before God' that he had only ever talked about his future plans for the Church, and particularly about a Council, with three men in holy orders: friars Domenico da Pescia, Silvestro Maruffi, and his personal secretary during the past three years, Niccolò Seratico of Milan. The only exceptions among the laity were the several men he had recruited to write letters to the five monarchs. He trusted, he said, only the foreign princes previously named and none of 'the princes or lords of Italy, because I held them all to be my enemies'.

After touching briefly on the Friar's excommunication, and hearing him reaffirm that he obtained no confessional secrets from friars Domenico and Silvestro (Domenico did not hear confessions), Remolins suddenly ordered the guardsmen to undress him and 'to give him some rope [a strappado]. Showing terrible fear, he kneeled down and said: *Now listen to me. God, you have caught me. I confess that I have denied God. I have told lies. Florentine lords, be my witnesses. I have denied him from fear of torture. If I have to suffer, I want to suffer for the truth. I did get from God what I have said. God, you are giving me penance for having denied you from fear of torture. I deserve it . . .* At this point he was undressed and again he kneeled, showing his [limp] left arm, saying that it was useless [it was probably dislocated] and continually repeating: *I have denied you, I have denied you, God, from fear of torture, fear of torture.* Yanked up high, he kept saying: *Jesus, help me, this time you have caught me.*'

Asked, 'as he hung from the pulley, why have you answered this way now? He replied: *To appear good. Don't hurt me. I want to tell the truth, really and truly.* Then why did you deny things just now? *Because I'm a madman.* When he was taken down, he said: *As soon as I see [the tools of] torture, I lose myself [go out of my mind]; and when I am in a room with just a few people and things are calm, I speak up better.* Asked if what he had confessed [thus far] was completely true, he replied: *It is true, and because it is true, I will confess it always.* Asked [again], why he had denied it a little while ago, he replied: *I denied it, thinking that you might then be afraid to lay hands on me. This is why I spoke those words.* Asked if friar Silvestro betrayed confessions to him, he said that Silvestro revealed no particulars, but that in general and by chance he perhaps narrated a few things, not, however, that he ever said he'd got them in a confession. And he added that to know things about

Florence, he didn't need friar Silvestro's confessional secrets, because nothing happened in Florence that he could not have found out about in other ways. Asked how, he replied: *from citizens and from friar Silvestro, who used to be amongst citizens a great deal,* and by this means he [Savonarola] could come to know things without confessions. Besides, he added, he would not have trusted friar Silvestro or friar Domenico in such affairs, in order to keep them from finding out about him, especially friar Silvestro, who was much too open about things and whom he judged to be inconsiderate and not too good a man, whereas he thought of friar Domenico as good and sincere. Next he said: *I was the worst of them. Because of my subtle pride and vainglory, I wanted to be considered a prophet and a holy man, and I did not confess this sin so as not to expose myself. Nevertheless, I knew I was erring and doing wrong.'*

Remolins then had the Friar read the bill of indictment listing the accusations against him. He was asked to reply to each, one by one. The following selections, with his answers, include the major and most revealing of the charges. Savonarola's first-person statements appear in italics.

1. That in his sermons he had abused and insulted the Pope and the Holy See in ways that tended toward heresy. 'Reply: he had never named the Pope, but had used references that could be taken to mean that he was talking about the Pope.'
2. 'That he had not observed the excommunication. He said: *true.'*
3. 'That he, Silvestro and Domenico revealed confessional secrets to one another. Reply: he himself did not hear confessions . . . but it is true that every now and then he would needle friar Silvestro, to get some secrets from him about current matters. But never did he say, *tell me about some confessions,* because he didn't want to expose himself.'
4. That he had claimed to have visions from God and to have talked to him. Yes, he admitted to having made this claim 'for the sake of his honour and to give himself a reputation'.
5. That 'he had preached, introduced, and sought to impart a new form of Christian life and of sacrifices, doing so as a heretic and a schismatic, and dividing the seamless robe of the Church of God. Reply: this he had not done, unless it was a matter of some ceremony that he had talked about in a sermon and of something to do with the

ascetic life of his friars and nuns. He remembered nothing else of this sort, apart, again, from his not having feared censures and excommunications.'

6. That 'he had said the Pope is not a Christian, not baptised, and is not Pope.' Reply: he had previously answered this charge, declaring, in effect, that he had never publicly said such a thing.

7. That he had written letters shaming the Pope by seeking to convene a Council. Savonarola had already admitted the main charge in this accusation, and now corrects minor details.

8. 'Asked about what he really thought he was doing, and whether or not he saw the many scandals that he had got close to provoking, he replied: *My pride, my madness, my blindness got me embarked on this. I was so crazy that I didn't see the danger I was in, and I have realised it here.'*

9. 'Regarding the death of the five citizens who were killed in August, he says he was satisfied that they should be either executed or exiled, but he did not intervene in the case.'

10. On the question of 'his wanting to send friar Domenico into the fire with the Body of the Lord in his hand, he confessed that this came from his madness and crafty pride and presumption. Asked if the bread was consecrated, he answered yes . . . and about his not [normally] consecrating, let there be no doubt [it was true], because not consecrating, he says, was a major and double sin, and so say the doctors [of theology and canon law].'

11. 'About the scandal that followed on the day he was attacked and arrested, he says he was beside himself, seeing his men being too cold, and added: *Do you want to see that I was crazy? Having been given twelve hours to flee by the Signoria, I did not go.'*

12. 'About having said to God, If I lie, you lie, he said . . . *if it is written* [in the published sermons], *then I said it. My pride blinded me, although I know that when I said it, I tried to say it as something true.'*

A few minor items came next. Remolins then halted the proceedings with a warning to the Friar that he think during the night about telling the whole truth on the following day, as if the testimony had not yet yielded enough culpability for Pope Alexander's man to carry out his commission.

The next day was 21 May. Yet once more Savonarola took an oath administered by Remolins, who again, putting all the questions, began the interrogation by asking 'if everything that he had confessed to the Florentines and to him yesterday was true. He replied: *Most reverend Monsignore, the words of denial that I spoke yesterday I spoke as a passionate* [most disturbed] *man; I wanted* [suddenly] *to free myself from a great mess, inasmuch as these earthly passions, just to see them, are like ten strappados for me. Everything I wrote and signed the first and second times was true, and I should thank those citizens who went easy on me. And if I did not tell all at first, it was because I was veiling my pride, but then seeing that they were gentle with me, I decided to tell the whole truth; and if it seems to you that I have said* [admitted] *few things, don't be astonished, because my things were big but few. All great things are few. What I said yesterday, in denying and then recanting, came from fear. I did wrong and I beg your Lordship's pardon. I have been a bad man; I want to save my soul and unburden my conscience.'*

Remolins got a few lesser items out of the way, then moved to a sequence of more important matters.

Returning to the question of a Church Council, and threatening the use of torture again, the inquisitor ordered the Friar to tell all, meaning with regard to particulars about his contacts. Savonarola answered: '*O friar, where have you been led?* And he began to weep and lament and he said: *When I think about how I got into this, I can't keep from grieving, for I got into it I don't know how. It seems to me I dreamed it.* And he finally recounted the thing in this manner. *I first took up this thing of the Council only three months ago, not before; it came out of my great pride. And once this fantasy occurred to me, I thought about how I would conduct it.'*

Savonarola then proceeded to repeat much of what he had already said regarding the Council. On this topic, however, Remolins's insistence betrayed a desire to collect evidence on any cardinals who had favoured a Council and who hence were secretly ready to work against Pope Alexander. In his readiness to resort to torture with such alacrity, Remolins was looking after his all-important boss. Yet he got no more, in the end, than was already known to him. Savonarola implicated the cardinals who were closest to the King of France, Giuliano della Rovere and Guillaume Briçonnet, but it was well-known that they would have supported a Council, particularly Alexander VI's great adversary, Cardinal Della Rovere, later Pope Julius II. Remolins, however, was especially interested in the

Cardinal of Naples, Oliviero Carafa, San Marco's former protector. Eager to have more evidence against him, he ordered that Savonarola be given another hoisting and jerk on the pulley. Now for a moment the Friar seemed to compromise Carafa: yes, '*I had some exchanges with the Cardinal of Naples.*' He was then abruptly asked again about confessional secrets, to which he replied much as he had before.

Threatened with yet another pull, drop, and jerk, the Friar said that he could 'talk better' with just a few people present. Mockingly reminded 'that he used to speak so daringly in the presence of many thousands, he replied, *I was lord then*. Asked if he believed in Christ, [Remolins] indicating that he doubted it, in view of what he had done', Savonarola replied that it was perfectly possible '*to believe in Christ and do what I did*'. After all, 'the Demon' himself believes in God. Even with another strappado Remolins was unable that day to extract anything more of real interest. To a question about his use of magic or magical spells, the Friar answered 'that he had always laughed at the like'.

Remolins's last round of questions began at 5:oopm on the next day, 22 May. The General of the Dominicans, Torriani, was not present. A short session, it began, strikingly, with Savonarola confessing that what he had said about Cardinal Carafa was not true. He said it out of 'fear', referring to the claim that he had 'held exchanges with the Cardinal of Naples or with other cardinals about the Council'. Nothing of the sort had ever directly or specifically taken place, and he offered his three assistants – friars Niccolò, Silvestro, and Domenico – as witnesses who could provide evidence of this. The rest of the interrogation concerned a secret visit made to the Friar by Cardinal Orsini and the question, once again, of demon possession in the convent of Santa Lucia.

An hour later, at 6:oopm, back at the palace, in the Little Inn, Savonarola was briefly questioned by three Priors and other top officials, regarding political matters. He answered 'that he and the citizens of his *setta* (sect) were chiefly interested in three things. First, that the [Great] Council should be well supplied with their partisans, so that they could have offices their way . . . and especially the six beans of the Signory, the Ten, and the Eight. *And I myself did not meddle in particulars, because of my pride. I carried on like a lord who has a captain on whom he leans, and my captain was Francesco Valori, and I leaned on him. Second, that strong measures be taken against our adversaries, but only when they erred, although very little error on their part was to be alertly noted, and this under the name of justice. Third, they [the sect] should be united, informed and provided with weapons, not so they should make the first move, but so that they could respond if the others should wish to strike.'*

The proceedings were now at an end. Finding Savonarola, Silvestro Maruffi, and Domenico Buonvicini da Pescia guilty of heresy and schism, Rome's emissaries ordered the three men to be handed over for punishment to the government of Florence, but first they were to be defrocked and degraded, and the anointment of priestly ordination removed.

Some version of Savonarola's composite confession had already been read out to the Great Council on 19 April, to the horror and anger of many of its members.

CHAPTER NINETEEN

Fire Again: Three Executions: May 1498

Treacherous Words

L OOKING BACK TO his words and actions over the previous six years, what shall we make of Savonarola's confessions? Was he an imposter and a criminal, or a holy man who had been forced to lie about his experiences by torture, humiliation, insults, and threats? In a withdrawn and furtive scene that could not have been more degrading for the Friar, and speaking Latin, so as to conceal the real subject from guardsmen outside the door, one of his most rabid enemies, Giovanni Manetti, insisted on feeling his genitals, in order to confirm or disprove the rumour that he was an hermaphrodite. Manetti was a member of the seventeen inquisitors, and son to one of the greatest Florentine scholars and intellectuals of the fifteenth century, Giannozzo Manetti, who had been knighted by Pope Nicholas V.

The trial records put neither Rome nor Florence into a good light. Florentine office-holders and important clerks, like Roman curial officials, were tenacious and punctilious record keepers. We may therefore ask, what happened to the official transcripts of Savonarola's trials? After all, there is a sea of fifteenth-century material, even of a minor sort, in the Vatican archives and in the archives of the old Florentine republic. Remolins is alleged to have returned to Rome with the papers of his proceedings, and these should have been deposited with the materials of one of the papal courts, or copied and certified for deposit in a special collection, the usual procedure in such cases. Nothing like this was done, or, if it was, that record was later removed to help salvage the honour, or obscure the shameful truth, of Remolins's work in Florence.

Records of the trial proceedings conducted by Florentine officials are said to have been in the archives of the city's treasury accounts (*Camera del Comune*), only to be destroyed, allegedly, in 1530, under the last Florentine republic. This seems unlikely, because the last republicans would have had a vested interest in Savonarolan truth. Accordingly, the whole record, such as we have it, goes back to the incunables of 1498 and to unofficial sixteenth-century copies. Yet even so, these do not fully veil what seems to have gone on. Suffice it to add that poor friars Silvestro and Domenico went to the gallows and the consuming fire with little more than the pretence of trials.

In the history of Florence, major political trials, as in the case of the famous Pazzi Conspiracy, were usually accorded meagre documentation, because it was not in the interest of the prosecuting regime to preserve a full record of the evidence that had sent the accused to the gallows, or hurling through the windows of the government palace. It was too often the case that the trial itself had been a flawed and rushed affair, or that the evidence as such was flimsy and inconclusive. And what the matter comes down to, in the case at hand, is that we do not know, really, how Ser Francesco Barone's annotations, the ones pointed out by Savonarola, were used in the account that was read out to the Great Council, striking Savonarolans like the diarist, Luca Landucci, as deeply distressing. There is no knowing what might have been added to, or deleted from, the overall confession. What we have then are the words of treacherous texts, and all we can do is to strive to make sense of them in the context of Savonarola's doings in Florence.

One of the most striking features of the three texts is that they sound so little like the Friar himself, the Savonarola of the sermons, letters, and tracts. Of course he is under dreadful duress, disoriented or terrified, and he is being pelted by the words and expressions of his examiners. But he was a speaker of such invention and allusion, and the owner of so rich a vocabulary, that something of the sparkle should have surfaced at various points, and it rarely does. Such a moment tumbled forth when Remolins deridingly reminded him that he had been a bold and brash speaker in front of many thousands, whereupon the Friar shot back, 'I was lord then.' On the other hand, the expression 'my work', which runs through the first two texts, referring to his overall religious and political agenda, seldom turns up in his writings. It is a foreign importation.

Nearest to his own idioms and turns is the confessional language regarding the political side of his activities; but very little is actually new here. Savonarola had loudly supported the Great Council for years; he had preached the 'common good'; he had encouraged citizens to elect 'good' and 'prudent' men; and his opponents had long claimed that San Marco was the centre of an illegal political sect. But even under torture the Friar denied that there was ever any such organisation. Men came to San Marco, or went to his sermons, and got to know each other by sight. This did not constitute a conspiracy, and nor was there a policy of telling citizens how to vote. What is more — and his enemies knew this — he himself had attacked the formation of *intelligenze* in his sermons. Now, however, the Arrabbiati at the head of state needed more evidence to turn the charge of conspiracy into a serious indictment. They were looking for the confessed spine of an organisation: the names of men, a concern for group 'unity', the 'common good' as an ideological slogan, Savonarola's regular access to confessional secrets, the numbers of supporters he sought to have in the Great Council, and the ways in which he supposedly coordinated matters with Francesco Valori by working through Andrea Cambini or others. Here were the components of an organisation, and the inquisitors pushed the Friar relentlessly in this direction, so that by 6:00pm, on the evening before his execution, they had him calling his supporters the 'partisans' of a 'sect', while he himself was 'lord' of that illegal association, with a 'captain' under his supposed command.

The siege of San Marco, and the discovery there of defensive weapons, gave his accusers another idea. To emphasise the militancy and violence of the Savonarolan 'party', they hammered the Friar with the whole arms question, as in his support for a company of guardsmen in the government square. Yet on that final evening, the best they could get out of him on this score was an admission regarding his desire that the Frateschi be prepared to resort to arms if they were attacked first. Strangely, they failed to make anything of his easy acceptance of the armed escort that had customarily accompanied him to and from his sermons.

Behind the anger of the Arrabbiati over this protean question of 'party' lay their own frustration, the sense of their failure to come up with alliances to oppose the spontaneous and natural weight of the Savonarolans.

The trial proceedings highlight Savonarola's hitching of the authority of the Great Council to his broader vision of renewal, and there can be no doubt that a republican polity, as epitomised by that Council, best served his aims. But he had never concealed this. A fiery preacher, with a revolutionary programme of reform, operated best under the wings of a republic such as Florence's, with its taste for a measure of experimentation. The Venetian republic was too restrictive, staid, and oligarchical. Only in Florence could the Dominican aspire to be top dog, and his accusers certainly moved in on this point, so as to convert his Florentine success into a proud and evil quest for worldly glory.

Savonarola's alleged access to friar Silvestro's confessional secrets had political and religious features. His accusers were determined to find a man who had both violated holy vows and darkly amassed political information for wicked ends. Instead, his believable claim was that in exchanges with Silvestro he might occasionally have picked up items that came from confessions, and it was not beyond him to try slyly to ferret out additional details. He pointed out, however, that he never asked for identities, owing to the risk of his losing name and reputation — that is, moral authority — with Silvestro. But this was not good enough for his inquisitors: they needed active collusion, illicit and immoral, and refused on this point to accept the very motivation that they looked for in almost all of Savonarola's other doings, namely, his vainglorious quest for a reputation.

Remolins does not seem to have raised the question of the Friar's attitude toward the threatened interdict, possibly because he was already leaning on points that were too suppositious. But it was a question that looked two ways, to Savonarola's view of papal censures, and to how he had proposed to handle the interdict as a problem for government and politics. The Friar's reply to his Florentine inquisitors revealed the political animal more than the religious reformer, and has about it the ring of truth, because it is wholly consistent with the rest of his over-arching enterprise. He planned to resist the interdict by manoeuvring to get the Signory on his side. This done, the *Signori* would then lead the city in its refusal to observe the censure, just as the government of Lorenzo the

Magnificent had done, when facing up to Pope Sixtus IV in 1478–1480, in the aftermath of the Pazzi Conspiracy against the Medici. But our man was also prepared to go farther, and here suddenly we see the revolutionary. If the Signory had chosen to cooperate with Pope Alexander, the Friar would have been ready to fight the Priors and Gonfalonier by arousing citizens and getting them to resist. He provides no details, but his choices were these alone: (a) to win over the Great Council and get it to exert pressure on the Signory, or (b) to organise, in a show of force, massive religious processions in the streets of Florence. The gamble, as it flicked through the Friar's mind (and this thought he almost certainly shared with no one), must have struck him as a risk worth taking, because it would be done in the name of his final goal, the renewal of the Church and the Christian faith. God would be on his side.

Exactly here, in this ultimate purpose, we come to the ideal that the prosecution was determined to deny him. In the final analysis, for Savonarola, politics was meant to serve a higher good – God and the needs of Christians – but his enemies argued, on the contrary, that he had turned things around by subjecting God and religion to his gigantic thirst for worldly honour, reputation, and the politics of power. Here was the heart of the case against him. Yet there was nothing new in it: his critics had been arguing it since 1495.

The task of the prosecutors was immediately obvious: to establish that Savonarola was not a prophet, had no divine revelations, and that God had never talked to him. If this was so, then what was he really all about? The answer came almost of itself: he was either a self-deluded madman, or an imposter motivated – in modern cant – by the colossal force of his egotism and narcissism, as Franco Cordero has put it. For the prosecution there could not be a mingling of two truths: (a) the Friar's worldly ambitions, and (b) his true commitment to a spiritual mission. This would dilute any indictment.

The Friar's ways and the magnitude of his message proclaimed that he was extraordinarily ambitious. There can be no doubt of this. An orator, a leader, and an innovator – how could he not be ambitious, or even 'a narcissist'? If he was going to get anything done, he had to stand out, and he had to have things his way. Yet precisely here, in *his* terms, lurked pride: a perception that certainly tormented him and that his interrogators, Remolins and the others, knew how to exploit. The question was, were his ambitions tied to anything other than his vaulting self? And here again the answer comes of itself: he had not endangered his life for years solely to satisfy an ego, but rather, as he believed, however shakily at times, to serve Christ and to revivify faith.

Savonarola seems to have said in the second trial that he 'never' went to confession. If Remolins had come across this statement in his version of that trial, he would surely have pounced on it and pressed the point. Instead, all we find in the third set of proceedings is that the Friar's 'vainglory' impelled him to want 'to be a prophet and a holy man', but 'I did not confess *this* sin [author's italics] so as not to expose myself.' In other words, ordinarily he did go to a confessor; he had to in that enclosed community, San Marco; but there were certain things that he held back and did not confess, despite knowing that it was wrong to refrain so, and those things had to do with doubts about his relation to God and about his motivation. Now, however, stripped of the convent's protection, sometimes hanging from a rope, seeing none but hard and mocking faces around him, threatened with more strappados, and feeling that God had abandoned him, as he says in one of his final prayers, his doubts must have come like dense flights of birds. Just here is where we need the supposed science of psychodynamics, at the point where he was ready to accuse himself, to comply with the demands of his inquisitors, and to disavow his claimed relation to God.

That brute force had frightened him into lying, thus rescuing him, he hoped, from more pain, comes forth in his final session with Remolins, when he confessed to having wrongly compromised Cardinal Carafa out of fear. Stricken in conscience, he now withdrew the lie and admitted that he had never held any exchanges with Carafa, nor indeed with any other cardinal, about a Church Council. But even in his first encounter with Rome's man, in a startling moment, just before he was undressed to be given 'some rope', he blurted out a recantation. Speaking of the first two trials, he said that he had denied God 'from fear of torture' and reaffirmed his access to divine revelation ('I did get from God what I have said.'). He kept repeating, more than likely in cries, the reason for his denial of God. The tone of the exchange then shifted to another aspect of the real Savonarola — a quick, intuitive, and clever personality.

Hanging from a pulley, and terrified of being dropped with a jerk, he is repeatedly asked about why he had answered that way. The imaginative Friar quickly produced three different answers: 'To appear good.' 'Because I am a madman.' And so 'that you might then be afraid to lay hands on me [on account of my truly being God's spokesman]'.

Savonarola's testimony is riddled with other problems. Heretics hold obstinately to mistaken doctrine, not to disbelief in God. Yet Remolins, who would charge the Friar with heresy, asked whether or not he believed in Christ, and all the way to Venice there were men, including the great diarist Sanuto, who accepted the claim that the fallen Domincan was an atheist. At the time, however, atheism was not an idea that had been well-defined. In the second trial, the Friar indicated that he had lost his faith as well as his soul, but here again Remolins failed to single out this deeply damning admission, and we are forced to wonder about which trial transcripts were actually turned over to the papal envoy. In testimony to Remolins, Savonarola said that he wanted to save himself, his soul; hence it follows that he continued to have faith in his salvation. He even believed – and this is more evidence contradicting his supposed loss of faith – that fra Domenico might be saved from burning and death by bearing the Sacrament into the flames.

There is a striking poverty of diction in Savonarola's testimony – another of the features that casts doubt on the scope of its authenticity. Most telling in this regard is the reductive and simple-minded assertion, repeated ad nauseam, that everything he had done was fuelled by pride, from his asceticism and vision of religious renewal to his defence of the Great Council and even a bizarre lie, it seems, about having the name of Jesus and a cross carved on his chest. The motor for all this, supposedly, was his desire for earthly honour and glory, although the colourless words *reputation, credit,* and *my honour* are made to do nearly all the work.

The difficulties posed by the Friar's confessions may be traced to the following causes:

1. Sources indicate that the Roman Curia and the Signory had found Savonarola guilty even before he was tried. The question was, what had he been guilty of?

2. When the evidence first came in, the findings were too skimpy to justify the penalty of death, although capital punishment was what his enemies were resolved to inflict. Torture, it was decided, would get the desired evidence, despite the fact that it was seldom used on men of the first importance. Soderini and Ridolfi, the foremost Savonarolan leaders, were not subjected to torture after the fall of the Friar. Lesser men were. But in the Friar's case, the prosecutors were driven to extremes.

3. Made out to be the head of a conspiratorial political sect, he nonetheless never held temporal office. Men in holy orders were barred from doing so. Savonarola's embassies to the King of France were not offices as such, and he was pressed into that service by the Signory and Ten. Remarkably, too, no Savonarolan political leader went to his death because of having participated in the conspiracy of a clandestine sect, an *intelligenza*. The murder of Francesco Valori was an act of vengeance, stemming from his role in the execution of the five traitors, and had nothing to do with his prominent place in a political faction. Therefore, how to execute Savonarola on grounds that were even more applicable to Paolantonio Soderini, Giovanbattista Ridolfi, and Domenico Mazzinghi, who was Gonfalonier of Justice in March–April, 1496? In short, what exactly was the Friar's capital crime in law? Some of his opponents suggested that his very existence posed a serious threat to the security of the Florentine state. Perhaps so, but none of the charges says this. It followed that other grounds had to be found for putting him to death, and they must be religious.

4. Consequently, his prosecutors drummed away at his being a false prophet, a dangerous liar, a heretic, and a schismatic. But when seeking to establish the truth of these accusations, the prosecution was compelled to produce testimony that was rife with contradictions. Most feeble of all were the charges regarding heresy and schism. Although he had published many sermons and numerous works on religious practice and doctrine, his accusers refused or were unable to cite a single item from his writings to help establish these most grave of accusations. The best they could do was to declare flatly that he had 'sought to impart a new form of Christian life and of sacrifices, doing so as a heretic and a schismatic, and dividing the

seamless robe of the Church of God'. But there is nothing specific in this declaration. It is a tautology, no more than a mere restatement of his supposed crimes.

5. Of the other charges levelled by Rome, the most serious concerned (a) his reaction to the excommunication, (b) his readiness to move Europe's major princes into convening a general Church Council, and (c) his fearless indictment of the corruption and careerism of men in holy orders, above all of the episcopal and cardinal clergy. The first of these was an act of disobedience, not heresy. The second was entirely in line with a strong conciliar movement earlier in the century, and looked back to the resolutions of the Council of Constance (1414–1417), which finally healed the Great (papal) Schism. In the wake of the Pazzi Conspiracy (1478), King Louis XI himself had threatened Pope Sixtus IV with such a council. The third item, Savonarola's fierce criticism of the corruption of the Church, might have been used in pleas to help establish his schismatic intentions, but no such argument could be made without some open consideration of the charge itself, and hence a look at simony and 'pluralism' (the holding of several or many income-bearing benefices). Neither Remolins, nor the cardinals around Pope Alexander, could afford to have any interest, not a serious one, in a public inquiry of this sort. That was the way of scandal and division.

Rope and Fire

WITH HIS MESSAGE of peace and reconciliation, Savonarola had rescued scores of eminent Mediceans from destructive fines, exile, and even lynchings; and numerous Florentines believed that in November 1494 he had saved Florence from being sacked by an occupying French army. But nothing now could rescue him from the teeth of his Florentine foes and the 'cleansing' fires of Rome. The ordeal by fire, the aborting of which had disappointed thousands of Florentines, would now be played out, though the outcome was foreordained: none would emerge from the flames.

On 22 May, in the government square, up again went a long platform, heaped at one end with a circular mound of firewood, and over-
hanging it was the gallows for the hanging of three friars: Silvestro Maruffi,
Domenico da Pescia, and Girolamo Savonarola. Since the gibbet looked
too much like a great cross, the protruding top of the vertical beam was
sawn off, and the arms of the crossbar were also cut and shortened. The
government wanted no Christ-like martyrs, real or symbolic.

On their final night, the three friars were attended by comforting
citizens, one each, all come from the city's Black Company in the
Confraternity of St Mary of the Cross at the Temple, the group responsible for providing spiritual support and solace to condemned men or
women, especially on the night before their execution. By his demeanour
and piety, Savonarola seems to have gained the sympathies of his attendant, Jacopo Niccolini, who persuaded the Signory to allow the
condemned friars to have a last meeting together. Now it was the Friar
who comforted the other two and dissuaded the impassioned Domenico
from requesting death by fire for himself, rather than hanging – so keen
was his desire for martyrdom. How we die, Savonarola told him, is not
for us to choose; the manner belongs to the will of God. At dawn the
three men came together again to hear Mass and take communion.

The final arrangements for their execution took an hour or two, and
would include preparing them to be defrocked and degraded. Thereafter,
although the mark of holy ordination was considered to be indelible,
they could be returned to the ranks of ordinary laymen. On that morning
of 23 May, 'the ceremonies [of degradation] lasted for the space of two
long hours', between about 8:00 and 10:00, as noted by one witness, Piero
Vaglienti, who described the spectacle as 'a beautiful thing'. But only the
most summary descriptions come down to us.

The ritual had its origins in the practice of expelling soldiers from
the Roman army of the ancient world; and the steps were set forth in
Roman law. Having been fully dressed in fresh Dominican garb, the three
friars were escorted down the palace staircase to the tribune out front,
where they faced a great and expectant throng. Also present on the tribune
were the representatives of church and state: the papal envoy (Francisco
Remolins), the General of the Dominican Order (Torriani), canons and
diverse monks, as well as the Eight, the Colleges (counsellors to the

Signory), and the man who was to conduct the defrocking, the Bishop of Vasona, Benedetto Paganotti, a former San Marco friar and one-time admirer of Savonarola. Remolins read out to the accused and to the sea of faces the ecclesiastical sentence: the three friars stood condemned as 'heretics, schismatics, and contemners of the Holy See', and he concluded by inflicting removal of the rank and dignity of priest. With the assistance of Tommaso Sardi, a Dominican conventual from the friary of Santa Maria Novella, who performed the actual divesting or stripping, Bishop Paganotti then spoke the words to go with the defrocking, intoning the charges of heresy and schism with the peeling off of each sacred vestment. From their hands were taken the scapular and perhaps a book, or even the chalice and paten, the 'instruments' that had been put into their hands at the time of their ordination. In addition, their hands, faces and heads were shaved, in action symbolising both the elimination of the tonsure and the removal of the holy oil that had been used to anoint their hands. And since everything was being solemnly said and done, the ceremonies proceeded slowly.

Once the degradation was complete, Remolins turned the three men over to the secular arm of the law, the government of Florence; and if he did things in the usual manner, he would then have added a plea for lenience. But he knew that the Eight, acting for the Signory and supposedly for the Florentine people, had their sentence ready, the one that all had been expecting for weeks, and which probably he had been commissioned to obtain. A member of the Eight now announced it. Suddenly, too, however, an act of kindness from Pope Alexander was made known. The good pope had sent them a plenary indulgence, rescuing them from the sufferings of purgatory. Remolins wanted to know, did they accept it? All three nodded their heads. And now, dressed in flimsy white tunics, one at a time, Silvestro first, followed by Domenico and then Savonarola, they were led out to the gallows, near the end of the wooden platform poking far out into the piazza. There each was led up a ladder and hanged, and then all were burned to ashes.

Angry spectators, it seems, in an unslaked desire to inflict pain, tried to ignite the pile of firewood before the friars were dead, but were repulsed. Silvestro and Domenico were heard repeating the name of Jesus, while being strangled by their halters; but Savonarola, whose praying lips never stopped moving, perished in silence. He was imitating Christ. Iron collars were then attached to their necks and gibbet, to keep their bodies from dropping into the fire with the burning of the halters. When all three were dead, or moved no longer, the executioner set fire to the great mound of straw and firewood, setting off 'sharp sounds of rockets and cracking'. Gunpowder had been added to the combustibles. For some moments a wind seemed to turn the flames away from the hanging bodies, but they were soon enveloped. The fire was fuelled for an hour or two, until the hangman and his assistants, commanded by Remolins, pulled down the big vertical beam, getting embers and fire all over the human remains, as they tried to reduce everything to 'powder'. Surprisingly, in issuing orders just then, Remolins was doing the job of the Eight.

Witnesses reported that once the fiery bodies had started to shed legs and arms, as they were burned away, with most of the remains still hanging from the chained iron collars, boys began to direct a volley of stones at the shrivelling corpses, to the screaming accompaniment of insults. Their aim was to make the stumps fall, so that they would then be able to drag the blackened things, the charred flesh and bones, around the great piazza. Cambi claimed that the boys came from the 'scum' (*prebaccia*, sic), the poorest and hungriest parts of the populace. More wood, however, was fed into the fire, so as to leave nothing for the relic mongers in the gawping multitude. The crowd had not even called out 'Jesus! Jesus!', in the customary manner at executions, as each man was hanged. In that rebarbative atmosphere, spectators who remained loyal to the Friar and to San Marco did not dare reveal themselves by crying out in sympathy. As soon as workers could get safely at the embers and ashes, they swept everything up, heaped it all into carts, and rolled the lot to the Ponte Vecchio, to be dumped into the Arno River. The carts were flanked by the Signoria's mace-bearers, signalling the government's watchfulness and determination to be rid of every remaining bit of the friars, ashes as well. There were to be no relics, nor even the pretext of one.

The siege of San Marco and the arrest of the Friar were converted, we have noted, into a government purge that would also have echoing and important symbolic features. On the day after the triple execution, San Marco was ritually cleansed, giving it a new beginning. A party of three – the General of the Dominicans, Remolins, and Bishop Paganotti – went out to the convent to bless it and its inmates. The cause of heresy had now been extirpated. Vaglienti records that the General of the Order had thirty-six of the friars transferred to the Dominican house in Ferrara, and that the security police, the Eight, exiled fourteen others, most of whom sprang from noble families, such as Sacramoro Malatesta of Rimini, Mariano Ughi, Roberto Ubaldini, Cosimo Tornabuoni, Bartolomeo Cavalcanti, Roberto Salviati, and two men from the Medici lineage.

The ideological cleansing continued. On 27 May, an announcement was made in all Florentine churches, stating that anyone in possession of Savonarola's writings, *any* of his writings, had four days to turn them over to the papal agent, Remolins, in the church of San Piero Scheraggio (now the entrance to the Uffizi), located just beside the government palace. Failure to do so incurred the penalty of excommunication.

The execution of Savonarola set off a widening and more sustained cleansing of minds, which would be carried out in part by angry voices in the populace itself. Church and state mounted a campaign to wipe out the Friar's influence and block all efforts to turn him into a martyr. San Marco was sealed off for nearly three months, until 4 July, and all laymen and women were barred from entry. The new Signory, which had taken office on 1 May, confiscated the convent's great library, the core of which – none other than the former Medici collection itself – had been acquired by the friars for the huge sum of 3,000 gold florins, and testified to the Friar's ambitious programme of learning and re-education. The old university building, a student college or dormitory, the *Sapienza*, was also taken from them, and they were forbidden ever to mention Savonarola's name. To destroy the convent's fraternal sense, there were to be no further processions, no prayers in common, no singing of their favourite hymns, and no nonsense about little red crosses. Their mode of dress was also changed, in a spurning of the Friar's more austere ways. They were now required to wear longer and more ample robes.

Obscene and insulting songs, targeting Savonarola and his followers, echoed everywhere in Florence, and came from the mouths of children and women as well. Painted sheets of paper did the rounds, with pictures showing the Friar in a sodomite's stance with a novice monk. And one night the Compagnacci, or a random group, hung the stinking corpse of a donkey on San Marco's doors. The festivities for the city's patron saint, San Giovanni (24 June), included a float with ugly figures, one of them allegedly representing 'the dead giant', Francesco Valori, and another, a pig, was for 'that pig of a Friar', Savonarola.

For the rest of the year, pranksters committed acts of sacrilege and impiety in different churches, calculated to outrage and sneer at the continuing or former admirers of Savonarola. Their message was unmistakable: Florence had been overly and wrongly pious for too long. Hence Carnival of 1499 saw a wholesale return to rock fights, roistering, lewdness, masks, and small bonfires. But two incidents of late June and December, 1498, reveal the scope of the anti-Savonarolan furies.

Lobbied by members of the Nerli family, intransigent opponents of the whole Savonarolan movement, the Signoria ruled on 29 and 30 June that San Marco should de deprived for fifty years of its resounding bell, *la Piagnona* (Lady Weeper or Wailer), which had been used to ring for help on the evening of the siege. In ceremonies that smacked as well of jocularity as of something grave and even tragic, the bell was removed from its tower and subjected to a spectacle of public infamy. With jeering and laughing onlookers in attendance, it was carted through the city streets and literally whipped by the official hangman on the way to its new site, outside the city walls, in the Franciscan church of San Salvatore al Monte. No longer would it send out a distinctive language of sounds to believers in the renewal or reformation of Holy Mother Church.

Six months later, on Christmas night, erupting riotously into the middle of Mass in the cathedral, a gang of murderous revellers ran a poor old horse through the nave, shouting out abuse so vile, says Landucci, that it would have been 'unspeakable in a whore house'. They clubbed the horse mercilessly, even poking staves into its backside, bloodied the floor of sacred space, and finally abandoned the dying animal outside the main front portals, facing the Baptistry. In their jubilant frenzy, they also threw excrement at the pulpit and poured ink into the holy-water basins. On that same night, other pranksters ran goats through the grand church of Santa Maria Novella.

For some Florentines at least, removing Savonarola had been the lifting of a lid. And major holidays elicited their contempt or longing for revenge, expressed chiefly in forms of symbolic action. The timbre of their rage indicated that the Friar's reign had affected not only abstract religious and political matters, but also daily life itself – gambling, drink, sex, dress, forms of profit-taking, and even fasting, as well as prayers, Carnival, and alms-giving.

Meanwhile, the settling of political scores – venerable Florentine and Italian practice – had not been overlooked. In late April, shortly before elections for the May 1st Signory, 200 known Savonarolans were temporarily purged from the Great Council, with a view to assuring an electoral victory for the Arrabbiati. On 27 April, having arrested a good number of the Friar's fervent followers, the new Eight saw to it that they got strappados, and all that day, from morning until night, incessant cries were heard around the Bargello, although none of the victims, with the possible exception of Domenico Mazzinghi, seems to have been the bearer of an important name. On the Via Por Santa Maria one day, near the New Market, the Savonarolan magnate, Paolantonio Soderini, was caught and assaulted, and would have been killed, it seems, but for the fact that he was rescued by a passing group of noblemen. He soon took himself quietly off, for a short time, to the little neighbouring republic of Lucca, where he could walk the streets without danger. In June, twenty-eight more citizens were stripped of their office-holding rights, and the Bargello again hosted the whipping or torture of another group of modest men.

Special treatment, however, was reserved for prominent Savonarolans, all of whom came from leading families. The really big men faced the penalty of punitive loans. They were forced to lend large sums of money to the government of Florence, but were not stripped of the right to hold office, whereas Piagnoni from well-known families of the second rank were fined and deprived of political rights for periods ranging from two to ten years. The different types of penalties made for a very Florentine solution, in the observing of subtle class and rank distinctions, and the favouring of the top men both because of their skills in politics and their family webs of influence.

The obligatory loans levied on the leading Savonarolans, in April 1498, ranged from the 800 gold florins each for Jacopo Salviati and Antonio Canigiani to the 1500 florins for Bernardo Nasi, topped only by the 3,000 for Soderini. Curiously, but owing again to his connections, Ridolfi was assessed a mere 500 florins; and more curious still, or rather revelatory, was the fact that in due course they were meant to collect interest on their loans! More damaging by far were the penalties inflicted on Frateschi who were not nearly so eminent, as indicated by the following examples, which list the outright fine (*not* a loan) and the years of their suspended political rights:

> Francesco del Pugliese, 500 florins, two years.
> Andrea Cambini, 150 florins, five years
> Domenico Mazzinghi, 300 florins, three years
> Giovanni Cambi, 200 florins, three years
> Simone del Nero, 200 florins, two years
> Lionello Boni, 50 florins, two years
> Francesco Davanzati, 50 florins, two years.

Davanzati, the last of these, also lost a lucrative post, the governorship of Cortona, for which he had only recently been designated.

I have referred to distinctions of class and rank. Astoundingly, in this regard – and the fact all but beggars modern belief – in February 1499, a mere nine months after the Friar's execution, two of his most distinguished adherents, Paolantonio Soderini and Giovanbattista Ridolfi, were back in the political limelight as the Florentine republic's new ambassadors to Venice. Ridolfi, in fact, rose to the top again, in the office of Gonfalonier of Justice for November–December, 1499. Such was the influence of the city's most illustrious houses. One of the lessons seemed to be that danger to life and to family estates could breathe cynicism into the front line of even the Frateschi. There is a startling note in this connection: striving to keep a foot in the enemy camp, Soderini allowed his son Tommaso – indeed, encouraged him – to join the ranks of the Compagnacci.

The purge that followed Savonarola's death was never to be complete. Florentines continued to read and revere him. His impact had been little short of overwhelming, but only because his vision met the needs, politics, and piety of citizens. Landucci reported that within hours of Savonarola's execution, women had vases torn from their hands and shattered, as they sought to collect pinches of his supposed ash; and a few days later, other women were found on their knees, praying at the supposed point in the Piazza where he had been executed. Nuns in certain convents, especially at

Santa Lucia, fell into swoons or frenzies; and reports of miracles, occasioned by bits and pieces that had allegedly belonged to the Friar, began to circulate almost at once, quickly spreading as far as Venice.

The years passed, but not the memory of the Friar's politics. The message of his faith in citizens, as in the Great Council, and his detestation of 'great lords' (*gran maestri*), lived on in a tenacious republican legacy. The constitutional innovations that he was prepared to defend with his life, the Great Council and the suppression of demagogic *parlamenti*, were the very points targeted by those who aspired to despotism, or to office for themselves, under the mantle of the Medici. After 1500, the Mediceans and their allies bided their time. Their opportunity came in September 1512. Falsely alleging the threat of a Spanish army, which had just sacked the neighbouring town of Prato, Giuliano de' Medici, the Cardinal's younger brother, and a band of diehard Mediceans, flooded the palace square with their hired soldiers and overthrew the republic. They summoned – illegally of course – a supine Parlamento, set up a dictatorial *balìa*, and simply shoved the Great Council aside. The Council's grand hall, built with Savonarola's inspiration, was soon turned into a barrack and horse stables. The Medici were back.

Yet the ideals of a free republic, mingling aristocratic and popular features, remained the elemental stuff of underground Florentine politics. And fifteen years later – in May 1527 and in new circumstances – the dramatic roles that we have already seen were replayed, again passionately. Seeing Pope Clement VII, the second Medici pontiff, battered by foreign armies and the Sack of Rome (May 1527), Florentine republicans took heart and easily overturned the Medici regime by forcing the Medicean governor to retire. Straightaway they brought back the Great Council, as well as aspects of the Friar's morality, and even the idea of Christ as Lord of Florence. The city rose in their support and grateful songs resounded through the streets.

But the flash of steel – in the form of Spanish and German armies – had become the decisive voice in Italian affairs; and three years later, in August 1530, the last Florentine republic went to the wall, dispatched by a besieging imperial army which now put power back into the hands of the Medici.

CHAPTER TWENTY

The Conscience of a City

Terrorist

S AVONAROLA'S GRASP OF politics had a good deal of hard realism, particularly in his stress on the supremacy of the Great Council, much or most of it comprised of citizens from the city's wide middle class. He was relying here on a vigorous tradition: the entry of a large swathe of Florentines into public life, a practice that went back to the middle of the thirteenth century and continued strongly until the 1430s, when the new Medici regime began to undermine the legislative councils. The Friar found a large constituency in the old class of citizens. They cherished the Great Council. They also needed a core of ideals to keep them united, and the Savonarolan movement provided this. Only a determined unity would enable them to defend the Council against experienced Mediceans and oligarchs. The coming struggle would go on in a deeply deferential Italy, where power, as in northern Europe, was in the hands of princes and prepotent elites – the very people whom the Florentine republic would have to deal with in its continuing relations with other states. All the dangers were here, in a setting that nourished relations between Florentine magnates and foreign princes. Even after the Friar had been eliminated, right up to 1530 and beyond, his core ideals continued to inspire republicans, who became the prey of spies for the first Duke of Florence. The return of the Medici, in late 1512, splintered and frightened the republican families of aristocratic and high bourgeois caste, vitiating their allegiance to the Great Council. In that world of princes, dynasts, warlords, and hired soldiers, the men of the middle classes – not having the contacts, poise, or social weight – could not go it alone: could not rescue the Council from internal conspiracies, ineptitudes, and foreign soldiers. They needed a Savonarola, and he came at the price of a stricter morality.

In their call for a moral cleansing, the Friar and his followers are occasionally accused of having terrorised Florentine citizens. Let's take the bull by the horns and consider the claim that he was a 'terrorist', as one historian, writing in the 1980s, has put it.

A watered-down charge of this sort was already implicitly about in the 1490s, whenever his critics contended that Savonarola wanted to turn Florence into a convent, that is, that he yearned to bend Florentines to his ascetic ideals. His campaign against 'superfluities', against gaudy wealth, saw the self-indulgence there as the denial of charity to the poor. Such wealth was also an emblem of wordly ambition – testimony to a man's being devoted to his pride, pleasures, and to sin, rather than to God and to the care of his soul's proper destiny. These values stood at the heart of late-medieval Christianity, and hard though it was to live by them, they animated many Florentines in the climate of the 1490s. To speak, therefore, of a reign of terror would be humbug. If anything, the ballooning fear in the city's Medicean circles was deflated by Savonarola's fight to win a pardon for all former collaborators of the banished house.

At the height of the Friar's influence, 'his children' certainly stepped out of line by aggressively confronting richly-dressed women in the city streets, or even by knocking too urgently on doors. The hue and cry raised against such effrontery, however, came swiftly, and Savonarola had to warn the children in sermons to be more gentle and civil in their ways. He had no trouble living with this.

More intimidating were the Friar's appeals to citizens, calling for harsher policies against blasphemers, sodomites, and gamblers, the last of whom could tear families apart by their losses. Launched from the pulpit in fulminating tones and to rapt throngs of 12,000 to 15,000 approving listeners, Savonarola's words must have come through as disturbing to any who felt themselves accused. In some instances, for example, echoing the law codes of the age, he would have had the tongues of persistent blasphemers pierced. But all the great preachers of the fifteenth century could be stern in calling for the punishment of blasphemy. To insult God was no picayune crime. Yet time and again, Savonarolan Signories stubbornly refused to take anything like the action called for by the city's unarmed prophet. For a year or so, street gamblers scampered at the approach of the Friar's children. A backlash, however, soon set in, and the children themselves, threatened with violence, backed away from confrontations. The older boys were particularly afraid; and gamblers, like blasphemers, got their way again in the widening shadow of the Compagnacci.

Savonarola's fight against the practice of anal intercourse was directed against compliant women as well. He knew that this 'vice' was honoured in marriage, as well as in female prostitution. Homosexual males held no monopoly. Florence's reputation for sodomy was so widespread that in the Germany of that day, to sodomise 'was popularly dubbed *florenzen* and a "sodomite" a *Florenzer'*. Savonarola reacted by insisting, in a number of his sermons, that sodomites deserved to be stoned or burned alive in public. He was a Biblicist, determined to keep to the letter of the Bible, and his inspiration was the Old Testament's horror of sodomy. The act in question, in seeking sexual pleasure as a thing frankly divorced from the will to procreate, seemed to sum up carnal debauchery. Everywhere in Italy, therefore, urban law codes prescribed harsh penalties against the crime, including capital punishment and death by fire for persistent offenders. Earlier in the century, San Bernardino and other popular preachers had often called for the fiery elimination of sodomites; and certain cities – among which Venice and Genoa – had seen the arrest and execution of groups of homosexuals. In practice, at Florence, capital punishment for sodomy was more likely to be reserved for homosexual rape.

In his fight to clean up the Church and clergy, Savonarola continually picked out simony, a tepid faith, greed, fornication, and sodomy as the chief vices that had corrupted organised Christianity. When he promised glory, wealth, and more power to the citizens of Florence, he based his promise on their repentence and good behaviour, and therefore he urged them to be severe judges of the city's worst sins. He wanted a kind of contract with the Florentines: God would give, but they too must honour their side of what he, God's ambassador, had negotiated; and this meant trying to purge the city of wicked priests, blasphemers, and sodomites.

But the Friar also knew his Florence. He raised his voice in a campaign to eliminate sodomy, while also recognising – he had taken the measure of their realism – that Florentines would not build bonfires

for such 'sinners'. And there is really no knowing how he himself would
have reacted, had he actually been confronted with the spectacle. In the
event, one sodomite alone seems to have been executed in Savonarolan
Florence, but only 'because the man was also said to be an infamous thief
and bandit, for which the penalty was normally death'. Even in the face
of a strong commitment to the Friar, Florence had too much political
wisdom to witch-hunt active homosexuals and sodomised women.

Savonarola's 'terrorism' was political too, and was related to his larger
battle for a reformation of the spirit. In different sermons, throughout
the years of his dominant ministry, he invited Florentines to enact severe
measures against those who entered into illegal political 'sects' and who
were sharply critical of the new republic or the Great Council. The alternative was a 'tyranny', a Medicean principate, and the suppression of the
right of citizens to control their own political destinies.

At one point in a sermon, as we have seen, in a fictitious give-and-
take, he lashed out with a wild declaration: 'I want the citizens who are
against this [republican] government to perish.' Did he mean it? In his
trial proceedings, on the contrary, he claimed to value the political opposition to the Frateschi, because he considered that it kept the leaders of
his movement from gaining too much (corrupting) power. There was no
doubt of it: Savonarola's eloquence could be dangerous. He provoked
hotheads both for and against him; but his rhetoric bent with the times,
and should be read in the light of the windings in Florentine politics.

The triumph of the Medici in sixteenth-century Florence guaranteed that the historical record would be stacked against Savonarola, as
neatly encapsulated in the chilling words of advice offered to a Medici
lord in 1512: *omne nefas victis, victoribus omnia sancta* ('all crimes to the losers,
to the winners all things pure'). The Friar came to stand for the republic,
for ordinary citizens (*il popolo*), for all the forces that had humiliated
Lorenzo the Magnificent's family in the 1490s. He had to be cast as a
villain, and we have largely inherited this view of the man.

Yet the climate of opinion now, since September 2001, is even worse
for the Friar. The different fundamentalisms of our day, with their cargoes
of fury, or criminals who purport to act under the banner of a religious call, affect us in such a way that we are almost destined to pull
Savonarola out of his historical context, the more angrily to condemn

him. He is such an easy target, that vile bonfire-burner of beautiful 'vanities', even if such activity rested on recent precedents in Florence and elsewhere. And if we judge by what the diarists actually tell us, it may be contended that far less was burned of beauty than has often been suggested.

The real burners – and the point calls for emphasis – were the people of Florence, their children, and the men in public life. The city fostered a changed climate in the mid-1490s, but only because the Friar succeeded in highlighting some of its own basic assumptions, so that they would be taken more seriously. It is likely that certain painters, such as Filippino Lippi and Sandro Botticelli, edged their way into the ranks of the Piagnoni, not to mention most of the circle of Florentine intellectuals. So, more than condoning, the Florentine people applauded and lit the fires themselves. We may seek to brush this aside, and wipe the face of history and of Florence, by singling the Friar out as the great villain, but this has nothing to do with the study of history. Like Luther and Calvin, or indeed like Pope Alexander himself, Savonarola was steeped in the values of his age, so that, in grappling with him, we grapple with his world as well. To cut the man away from his cultural surroundings may be the way of popular biography, but it is a flawed historical proceeding and an act of pandering.

Guicciardini said, as we have seen, that if the Friar was good, he was a great prophet indeed; if bad, 'we have seen a very great man . . . [of] profound judgement, genius, and imagination'. Looking back now, it strikes me as more fitting to say that if there was something hugely disturbing about Savonarola's claim to be a messenger from God, then this impression has to be weighed against the infamy of the Church which he chose to challenge. Under Pope Alexander, cardinalships were sold for a minimum of 15,000 gold ducats; a few years later, the Medici Pope, Leo X, sold them for not less than '25,000 ducats per head'. The Friar, in short, had taken on a Church that was about to fracture the unity of Western Christendom by helping to spawn the different churches of the Protestant Revolution.

'Florence is a Friar'

F LORENCE'S ENCOUNTER WITH Savonarola was a meeting with much
of its own soul: with its piety, anticlerical attitudes, patriotism,
eloquence, republicanism, and even its rationalism. The living context of
this encounter was therefore not just the 1490s; it was also the history
of Florence's shaping ideals, reaching back to the explosive commune of
the thirteenth century, when the city fought princes, prelates, neighbouring towns and lords, and itself as well, in civil strife that pitted old
families of magnates against a flourishing new class of merchants. In
that century too, men often crossed the lines of social class, seeking the
elusive, yet profound, satisfactions of politics.

A meeting with its own soul? There could be no doubt of Florence's
religious bent. The city had more than 100 pious confraternities; new
ones sprang easily into being; and its great cathedral, paid for by the city
and by citizens, finally neared completion in the fifteenth century. Seventy
parish churches served the spiritual needs of the populace, along with a
rich assortment of other religious houses, including twenty-one convents
for friars and forty-four for nuns. Long processions, arrayed behind crosses
and pictures or statues of the Virgin Mary, were a common sight, and
they moved with a visual magnetism that easily dominated street scenes.
Famine and fear also brought out the slow-moving, stately processions,
which could be organised against any threat to the community. In addition, Florentines issued a stream of devotional poetry, and it is almost
certainly the case that fifteenth-century Florence produced more religious
plays than any other Italian city. Consistently enough, therefore, Florentine
bankers and merchants often sought to make amends for their ill-got
('usurious') gains by making large donations to churches and friaries.
Although frequently impelled by 'low' motives such as pride and social-
climbing, the rich men who displayed their family coats of arms in church
chapels, seeking to assert status and moral worth, were also driven by
piety and the desire for Masses to be said in perpetuity, there in the
semi-private space of their chapels. They were paying to purge sin and
guilt.

Florentines were pious, but not uncritically so, like, let us say, the

Venetians, who produced no legacy of anticlerical literature in the four-teenth and fifteenth centuries. Florence, instead, nursed a strain of acid censure of the clergy, running back to the thirteenth century and unmatched elsewhere in Italy. A dramatic episode in this history was Florence's anti-papal War of the Eight Saints (1375–1378), when the city, in a fighting mood and under an interdict, seized and sold large quantities of Church property to help pay for its soldiers. The experience inflicted scars in rela-tions between 'church and state', and contacts between clerics and politi-cians became more difficult. More demonstrably, Florentine poetry, tales, and memoirs began to carry heavier loads of anticlerical criticism which impugned cynical priests and a power-hungry papacy. Most of this liter-ature came from the pens of educated men of the upper classes – lawyers, humanists, merchants, and the occasional statesman. In the early fifteenth century, one of the city's foremost public figures, Gino Capponi, offered some chilling private advice to his sons: 'Don't get mixed up with priests: they are the scum of the earth.' Even Lorenzo the Magnificent looked upon high-clerical Rome as a moral cesspool and longed, at times, to see it smashed as a political force in Italy. Accordingly, at the beginning of the sixteenth century, the Florentine anticlericalism of Italy's two great polit-ical minds, Machiavelli and Guicciardini, was rooted in a rich local tradi-tion.

I need hardly add that Savonarola's diatribes against a 'tepid' clergy – careerist, money-grubbing, simonist, nepotistic, and cynical – found a ready and approving audience in Florence, and they were not just the 'credulous' multititude. He could thus ring out in a sermon: 'Do you want to make your son bad? Make him a priest.'

Eloquence too was part of the city's innermost self. With Dante, Petrarch, and Boccaccio at the head of its outstanding constellation of writers, followed by the likes of Leon Battista Alberti, Lorenzo de' Medici, Luigi Pulci, and Angelo Poliziano, Florence was the literary city *par excellence*; and it teemed with many other writers as well – poets, histo-rians, translators, diarists, humanist scholars, and compilers of antholo-gies. Florentines had a peninsula-wide reputation for wit and words. They trafficked in a rich circulation of poems, stories, meditations, and other compositions, frequently passed on in manuscript form, even after the printed book made its appearance. They were therefore bound to study and weigh the words of a phenomenal preacher, while drawing on standards of eloquence that were exacting. In this test, Savonarola's sermons and delivery conquered the city even more, much more, than San Bernardino had in the 1420s. His flow of galvanising words, in sermons that often lasted for more than two hours, touched something deeply receptive in the Florentine people.

Next there was patriotism. Italian cities – Venice, Genoa, Milan, Rome, Bologna, Ferrara, and so forth – had long and irresistible traditions of local patriotism, backed up by founding myths or by stories about their early heroism. The emotional ties to birthplaces had been deepened by pitiless wars between urban communes, such as between Venice and Genoa, Milan and Pavia, Florence and Milan, or Pisa and Florence. And citizens could be passionately attached to their cities, a true fatherland or *patria*. In this regard, looking back to the ancient Romans as its founders, proud and eloquent Florence was second to none. The city had fought despots, warlords, and the Church; it abounded – Florentines asserted – in grand churches and palaces; it looked out beyond its great walls to the splendid villas of its citizens; its merchandise, especially in the cloth trade, filled inhabitants with pride; and they believed that the city was blessed with such healthy and beautiful natural surroundings, that even the air over Florence was somehow superior!

Savonarola tapped into this well of patriotism and local pride, so much so that his critics accused him of being pander to Florentine self-love. Once the Medici had been banished, he told *fiorentini* that they were unique, that their city had been chosen by God to be the forerunner in the coming renewal of the Church; and he repeatedly announced that Florence would be richer, mightier, and more glorious than it had ever been.

This was heady stuff, and so of course many Florentines took the Friar to their hearts. He was telling them what they wanted to hear. But we may readily infer from his trial record, regardless of the tampering, that his promises had troubled him: he was too knowing, too suspicious of the ubiquity of pride, not to see that lashings of flattery had helped to establish him in Florence.

He touched Florentines in yet another way. Tight or syllogistic reasoning may be one thing, and meticulous book-keeping something else, but both proceed by movement in which each step follows more or less strictly from the one before. The operations of Florence's many banks, business companies, and small shops were tracked in well-kept accounts, sometimes in the double-entry mode; and Florentines were careful accountants, as attested to by the great quantities of their extant business diaries, ledgers, and family log-books (*ricordanze*).

Long passages in many of Savonarola's sermons are characterised by tightly-reasoned argument, in which each step, each claim, follows from the previous proposition. Although he shared this feature with some of the best preachers of the age, I would propose that it also enabled him to win over many of his Florentine listeners, as he marched along a line of reasoning just as numbers and transactions marched across their ledgers.

Again: God and Politics

I N HIS CONCERTED pleas for a revitalised republic, Savonarola drew the conscience of the city into a unified vision. He argued that the new republic and the Great Council, founded on the broad participation of citizens, were sent by God. Piety and civic allegiance to the Council thus flowed together in a form of Christian republicanism. To support the Council was an act of religious faith. It was also an expression of *florentina libertas*. A new form of patriotism came of itself: it lay in the rejection of sinful tyranny and the proud, militant defence of the new republic. The mingling of piety and republicanism was also present in the Friar's vision of Florence as the New Jerusalem and spearhead of reform. Here was the place for Savonarolan anticlericalism. The purging of unscrupulous priests, of men who had no business being in holy orders, became a major theme in his broad message. His goal was a puri-fied clergy, fit to serve the spiritual needs of a converted republican laity. There was to be no untravelled gulf between civic life and the life of the spirit. Was it not obvious that to attain its proper end, the human soul also required salutary social and political conditions? But why polit-ical? Because leadership in public life, as in the Church, stood as the prime model for men and held the levers of social organisation. All the strands of a public conscience were thus brought together.

Though we may laugh at Savonarola's claim that the revival of the republic had been willed by God, our amusement and scorn have no bearing on the case. The point is that many citizens in his serried ranks of supporters were ready to believe the claim; and the political importance of this, at first unseen, has to be fetched out by the historian.

The new republic was besieged by internal and external enemies. On the outside were the Pope, the Duke of Milan, and Venice, all determined to see a change of regime in Florence, and best of all with the return of a Medici boss, whether from the main or the cadet line. The next step would have been to draw Florence into the Holy League against France. Pope and Duke felt personally threatened by King Charles VIII; and the Venetians, once France was counted out of the picture, expected to be able to throw their weight around more successfully in their far-flung zones of influence. The internal enemies of the Savonarolan republic were both the oligarchs who detested the Great Council and the circle of crypto-Mediceans, some of whom, in scrambling for political safety, had stolen into the Friar's camp, although their true commitment lay with the Medici cause.

In the face of these dangers, it was clear that the survival of the Savonarolan republic required the spirited support of citizens, and if this came with a dose of religious zeal, then so much the better, at all events in the eyes of those who feared the return of the Medici. The belief that God had intervened to favour the new republic led to the view that Florentines who gave it their loyalty were necessarily more virtuous in office – more likely, too, to spurn privileged interests and to look to the greater good of the community. Here was a movement to endow politics with ideals and even morals. Francesco Valori said to Savonarola, you do your part – that is, work up zeal for the republic – and we shall do ours, the practical political part. Each man understood the value of the other.

Never mind, as we have seen, that Soderini and perhaps Ridolfi, Savonarolan leaders, were in the Frateschi camp in order to wield power, to stand out, and even to further their own family interests. The point is that they were compelled, time and again, to pay open tribute to the value of the Great Council; and they came very close to losing their lives for the Savonarolan republic.

The effort to inject morality into politics returns us to the heart of the Friar's republican enterprise, which even included the curtailment of the Signory's power to crush opponents, notably in the right of appeal to the Great Council. Cutting into the authority of the Signory in this fashion was seen by many aristocrats as an attack on themselves, and rightly so. Savonarola had not pulled these policies out of thin air. He saw what was needed; he had studied local chronicles and the history of Florence; and he knew that factions and factional conflict had always tended to issue in the practice of putting the part before the whole, with the victorious faction taking over the entire city. This is what had happened under the Medici in the fifteenth century, a stealthy seizure of power that seemed to turn into a permanent takeover.

The colossal banking fortune, ruthlessness, and political know-how of Cosimo de' Medici had opened the way to the triumph of his faction, and this constellation of men and families then became the ruling force in Florentine government. In the past, factions had exercised authority by placing men in the top offices and eliminating, when possible, their principal opponents: that is, they manoeuvred and trafficked. But after 1434, with the victory of Cosimo and his satellites, the new winners began to suppress the opposition altogether and to secure control of office by the exile of opponents, by stripping citizens of their political rights, manipulation of the electoral system, fines, punitive taxation, the blackballing of possible candidates, and a general air of menace. Much of the old structure of public offices was retained, but by using powerful ad-hoc councils (*balìe*) and by inflating the authority of the executive offices, the Mediceans gathered power into the hands of a narrowing elite. By the summer of 1480, Lorenzo de' Medici was boss of the city, if not yet the outright lord.

Rooted in the old republican commune, a political system which had endured for more than 200 years was on the verge of destruction. The best jobs, offices, honours, lighter taxes, favour in the law courts, Church benefices, and the coveted marriage matches went to close Medici supporters. And the most eminent of these – often the bearers of distinguished family names – had, in turn, their own clients. Free debate in the councils became a thing of the past. With its web of spies, the security police (the Eight), an arm of the oligarchy, reached out for more authority and came to be hated by the silent opposition. Increasingly, in the face of a crystallising Medicean ruling group, Florentines outside this clique had to obey, to bend the knee, to keep silent, to acquiesce. Here in the making was an ever more deferential society, but with something completely new: a ruling figure at the centre of public life, with circles of servitors and collaborators around him. In time, a growing number of prominent families – Soderini, Tornabuoni, Ridolfi, Salviati, Martelli, Pucci, Pandolfini, Albizzi, etc. – made their peace with this political arrangement and were ready to serve the ruling house, provided that they could stand above all other families and be rewarded with the most honourable offices: embassies, lucrative governorships, and places in the Ten, the Signory, in special commissions, and as counsellors to the Magnificent Lorenzo. The whole idea of the common good, except as eyewash, was discarded. If what was good for the Medici was good for Florence, including even Lorenzo's theft of public money, then what was good for the pro-Medici aristocrats and for jumped-up servitors was also good for the city.

The significance of the new (Medicean) arrangements was not lost on an alert Florentine population. An undercurrent of resentment and disapproval ran through the citizenry. It had taken two *coups d'état*, in 1458 and 1466, backed up by companies of soldiers and demagogic assemblies, to rescue the regime from rebellious councils. On top of this, the Medici had carefully courted and bought the friendship of the Sforza lords of Milan, becoming their bankers, with a view, if ever the need arose, to being able to call on their armed might, as indeed happened in the Florentine political crises of 1458, 1466, 1469, and 1478. For Cosimo, as for his son and grandson, nothing spoke so eloquently as Milan's troops.

Yet in November 1494, no Medicean arrangement was able to rescue the young heads of the Medici family from the contempt and fury of the Florentine populace, or from an aggressive circle of high-ranking citizens. More than mere anger with Piero de' Medici's appalling ineptitudes, the burst of passion and revolution on 9 November, casting out the Medici, issued from a deep well, a history, of rancour and frustration. Interloping Medicean councils and Lorenzo the Magnificent's theft of public monies were now quickly denounced; 'collaborators' had to face calls for revenge; angry men attempted to lynch the 'creatures' –

important secretaries — of the Medici; enemies of the collapsed regime were called back to the city from political exile; scores of men, including artists, stepped forward to sue the Medici for debts, many stretching back to the time of Lorenzo; and Savonarola was now able to place himself at the moral forefront of the cry to bring back 'liberty'. The cry came spontaneously.

In practice, at least, politics in Florence had long since been stripped of its moral ideals. When the friends and heads of the Medici regime spoke of the common good, or of whatever served 'the people' of Florence, none but they and the ill-informed were taken in; and even they, the collaborators, knew that politics was a world in which their own personal and family interests came first.

Savonarola's explosive entry into public life carried the promise of something fresh and revivifying. He was not, after all, a politician; he lived and slept in a convent; he had no web of dependants clamouring for favours; no ambitious and proud family to prop up; and he had no 'earthly' axe to grind. Yes, he purported to speak for God, but he also spoke passionately and feelingly of the people of Florence, of that which would benefit the entire community, and of the values that rose up above all worldly passion. He laid into tyranny, tyrants, unprincipled bosses (*gran maestri*), the insolence of office, partisan government, selfish politicians, lukewarm commitments, bent priests, and careerist prelates. A complete outsider, both as a priest and a non-Florentine, he talked his way into politics with a voice that was disinterested, at all events in his charismatic prime, as he raised it against every kind of evil.

In a world of inveterate privilege, government could not cleanse itself; the self-interest of groups and leaders could not simply be wished away. If nothing else, the cynicism, connivance, and secret habits planted by the Medici and their cronies went too deep. Christianity was everywhere, to be sure, but it was chiefly in trappings, in external or ceremonial forms. And there was certainly no charity or Christian brotherhood to be found in politics. Consequently, if Florentines were to reform the political life of their city in the crucible of a new republic, how were they to do it, if there exactly, in the rank struggle for worldly honours and prizes, is where the corruption of the Medicean regime was born? Evidently, the revitalising ideals had to come from outside the arena of politics and government, from beyond purely temporal considerations. The Age of Reason was still more than two centuries away.

Here again we see the magnetic force of Savonarola's appeal, launched into the midst of a Christian society. There was nothing alien or strange about the message itself, his message. The great preachers of the fifteenth century, while never appropriating the name of prophet, now and then declared that God spoke through them. This is not generally known and is seldom highlighted. The novelty in the Friar's case was in his claim to be a prophet and to be speaking for God. Yet this too lost its strangeness, because he was greeted with approval when he stepped into the middle of an epochal crisis not only for the Church, but also for Italy and Florence, as attested to by the French invasion, the overthrow of the Medici, civil strife, war; and the frightening incidence of pestilence, unemployment, and famine.

A frightened populace went to the cathedral to listen to Savonarola, to find solace in his words, and to draw in around him. They needed to believe in him.

The Savonarolan Problem

A NY MAN OR woman who really wants to change the world, seeking more than mere readjustments, may be regarded as an extremist. Moses, Jesus, Napoleon, Lenin? In this sense, Savonarola was extreme, but so too were Luther and Calvin, who risked their lives for the sake of revolutionary change. In 1524–1525, the leaders of the rebellious German peasantry, in revolt against their overlords, appealed to Luther, fully expecting his approval and support. They had perceived his violent invectives against a corrupt Church as part of a larger operation against injustice. Luther at once recoiled, fearing the reaction of the German nobility, and seeing his Reformation suddenly thrust into danger. He turned savagely against the peasantry and called for their bloody repression. They were slaughtered by the thousands.

Savonarola had no such blood on his hands. Indeed, Florence rallied so strongly behind him for several years, that its acclamatory reception blunted the edges of his extremism, and his programme came to seem viable. The allegiance and zeal of his multitudes of listeners spurred him on, heightening his courage; and he, in turn, fought to lead them toward a better Christian life. When we see him in this light, we may say that Florence not only connived with him, it made him.

The public man in Savonarola was very different from the private one-on-one individual. Most of his friars always saw him as kind and gentle; and his handbook for confessors advised understanding and tolerance. But the public man, locked into a battle for the soul of Florence and Italy, could not afford to seem anything less than a fighter, because his capital enemies were Italy's *gran maestri* – in the Church first of all, and then those in high temporal places. They had the troops, guns (artillery), law courts, prisons, skills, and gallows. Being at war, his constant task was to inspire his supporters, whenever he saw them losing spirit, patience, or bravery. No wonder his enemies agonised to silence him.

This is no place for a discourse on the separation or joining of religion and politics in the history of the West. To get Savonarola right, however, and to grasp him in context, it may be useful to turn to a wider vista.

Over the past 5,000 years, and as much work in anthropology has shown, the separation of earthly power from the power of gods or higher spirits has been exceedingly rare. Western political theory since the Renaissance, with much input from Aristotle's *Politics*, introduced a complete break between the two, a break that is first seen dramatically in *The Prince* by Niccolò Machiavelli – ironically, one of Savonarola's contemporaries who was fascinated by the man and who took notes on a number of his sermons. Nevertheless, the detailed notion of a link between God and political power survived strongly in European thinking and feeling until the late seventeenth century.

In the period around 1500, Italian statesmen, bred to the brutal realities of politics, knew all about the ploys and pleas of power in public life. Despite the wide claims of Christian theory, they knew and saw politics as an activity divorced from anything religious. When pursuing their ends, they quietly pushed religion to one side. As Cosimo de' Medici put it, the state is not run by paternosters. Thinkers who were close to Florentine statesmen, or who worked in their midst, like Machiavelli and

Guicciardini, were pushed toward drawing the obvious lesson: that is, that a political theory could be spun wholly outside the perimeters of religion. Yet right down to our day, in ritual, as in the kind of patriotisms demanded by the most secular of states, the separation between God and government has never been complete, as attested to by ceremonies for soldiers killed in war, in the words of national anthems, in patriotic national prayers, and mottos on certain currencies ('In God we trust'), and so forth. Even in so-called Marxist states, the metaphors that have frequently attended the concept of 'Party' have often turned it into something transcendent, something luminous, standing above all conflict or divisiveness, and representing a kind of ultimate value, as if filling in a void caused by the removal of God.

When the subject is the power of the state, with its colossal resources, thinkers have often found it difficult, for good or ill, to separate it altogether from the 'higher powers'. A reserve sets in. Something in the spin of language itself seems to call up odd feelings. And then strange things begin to happen, above all the sliding in of *a priori* suppositions, or even of the transcendental.

If such matters are so now, then we must reconsider them when they are taken in the context of early-modern Europe: a world in which cardinals and bishops commonly served as ambassadors and political advisers, and where governments often had a hand in organising religious processions, with all the top men of state taking part. Religious turns of phrase pervaded preambles and the language of laws and constitutions, not to mention oaths taken by officials, while the reasons for the very existence of the state were taken back to the 'God-given' need for order, harmony, and justice. The divinity that hedged kings and handed power down to rulers was more than empty rhetoric. Monarchs, ministers, lawyers, and churchmen believed the claim, or wanted to believe in it; and they most assuredly wanted subjects and citizens to believe it.

Savonarola could not be put to death for seeking worldly glory, nor for being, as alleged, an imposter and a 'seducer' of the Florentine people. These were not capital crimes, all the less so in view of the fact that he never held public office. His message, however, had infuriated political leaders in Rome, Florence, Milan, and even Venice. By harnessing the intensity of religious feeling to his declared battle for a renewal of the

Church, the Friar posed a fundamental threat to authority and to the self-interest of rulers, including religious ones. His plea for morality menaced the most powerful vested interests – the papacy itself, as well as cardinals, princes, political bosses, and tight oligarchies.

If the lines of my analysis in this book have any validity, then I trust that my own rationalism flashes forth in such a way as to make clear that I personally am opposed to all mystifications. When, however, political power is irresponsible and spurns being accountable, or when it passes into the hands of ruthless elites, it opens the way for those who contend that they speak for justice, morality, and God. And we must be prepared to read and study such contenders, not because they speak for God, but because they are likely to be saying something significant about current politics.

NOTES

These notes provide sources and more detail. The numbers on the left, in bold type, refer to pages in the book, and are immediately followed by the first words of a paragraph on the page indicated. References thus refer to material *in* the paragraph. All names and abbreviations may be squared with entries in the Bibliography.

Attention: in the following notes, Sav = Savonarola

CHAPTER ONE
CHORUS

1 *In the final months.* Source detailing the plot: Violi, *Giornate,* 73–74.
2 *Of small to medium.* The earliest and most reliable descriptions of the man are in: Luschino, *Cedrus,* 74; and *Vulnera,* 18.
6 *Savonarola threw.* Mary, Renaissance whore: Sav, *Amos,* II, 26 (5 March 1496).

CHAPTER TWO
VILE BODIES

The essential biographers of Savonarola are Villari, Schnitzer, and Ridolfi. They draw heavily on the ('Pseudo'-) Burlamacchi, Luschino, Cinozzi, Filipepi, and Della Mirandola. Cordero's recent work calls for a longer statement: see the Bibliography.

8 *He knew luxury.* On Savonarola's family: Schnitzer (1931), I, 1–7.
9 *The young Girolamo's.* For the Este executions: Martines (2001), 222–23.
9 *Something of his.* The remark about bastardy: Luschino, *Vulnera,* 23.
10 *His poem on.* The poem quoted here and following: Sav, *Poesie* (Martelli), 3–5. All his verse was written before the autumn of 1484: Cattin, 191.
11 *At the age of.* On the anticlerical tradition in Florence: Martines, 'Raging against Priests in Italian Renaissance Verse.' In Connell, *Society,* 261–77.
11 *Here, speaking to.* The poem: Sav, *Poesie* (Martelli), 6–9.
12 *Honoured father.* The letters here: Sav, *Lettere* (1984), 3–6, 7–8.
15 *Looking back.* Quotation: Ridolfi (1952), I, 20.
17 *On his first.* His early preaching, evidence: Ridolfi (1952), I, 26–27.
18 *The death in 1484.* Poem: Sav, *Poesie* (Martelli), 13–15.

CHAPTER THREE
THE FRIAR RETURNS

19 *Prodigious irony.* Best on Lorenzo's relations with Savonarola: Martelli, 'Savonarola e Lorenzo'; and Garfagnini (2000), 'Firenze tra Lorenzo'.

20 *The roots of.* Italy at the end of the Middle Ages: Jones; Martines (1979).

21 *In 1490, accordingly.* The Florentine building craze: Goldthwaite, *Building*.

22 *At that moment.* Background to the 1490s: Guicciardini, *Dialogue*, 25–31; Brown (essays, as listed); Fubini (essays, listed); Martines, *April Blood*.

22 *Brought back to.* Lorenzo's words: Burlamacchi, 24.

23 *Delivered in San Marco.* Quotation (6 Jan. 1491): Sav, *Sermones*, 252.

24 *One day, five.* Savonarola's five visitors: Burlamacchi, 26–27.

25 *The Latin outlines.* Quotations: Sav, *Quaresimale*, xxv, and 10 (16 Feb. 1491).

25 *The succeeding.* The Friar's words: Sav, *Quaresimale*, 76 (27 Jan. 1491).

25 *He singled out.* Citations: Sav, *Quaresimale*, 114, 130, 172.

26 *But his bravest.* Citation: Sav, *Quaresimale*, 300.

26 *His theme was.* Citations: Sav, *Quaresimale*, 300, 302.

26 *How Savonarola pitched.* Quotation (20 March 1491): Sav, *Quaresimale*, 212.

27 *In the end.* Genazzano: Schnitzer (1931), I, 126–27; Gutierrez, 'Testi'.

28 *All the same.* Old Wailer claim: Burlamacchi, 32–33; Della Mirandola, 18–19.

CHAPTER FOUR
THE WAIT

29 *Sorrow in Florence.* On Piero: Guicciardini, *Dialogue*, 31–32.

30 *Within a year.* Contents here: Guicciardini, *Storie*, 71; Rubinstein, *The Government of Florence under the Medici.* 230-31; Bertelli, 'Un magistrato'. 476; and Fubini, 'Politica', 587–88.

31 *Meanwhile, he had.* Savonarola and Piero: Schnitzer (1931), I, 146–47.

31 *Accounts of the.* Relations with the Lombard Congregation: Schnitzer, I, 137–61; Ridolfi (1952), I, 81–98.

32 *The Savonarolan struggle.* On the whole question of simony: Hallman, *Italian Cardinals.* M. Pellegrini, 'Turning-Point', 18–19, gives 'red-hat' prices.

32 *In the wake of.* Bentivoglio affair: Burlamacchi, 30–31; Cordero, I, 229–30.

33 *At the beginning.* The French invasion: Abulafia; Denis; and Labande-Mailfert.

CHAPTER FIVE
FEAR AND LOATHING

Essential sources for this chapter: Parenti (*Storia*), Cerretani, Landucci, Guicciardini, Nardi, and Vaglienti. To these should be added the epistolary reports of ambassadors, especially Manfredi (under Cappelli), Sozmeni (under Villari and Del Lungo), and Ghivizzano (under Portioli).

34 *There were omens.* Quotation: Cerretani, 200.

35 *The Signoria and its.* On Tornabuoni and troop numbers: Vaglienti, 13, 16–17.

35 *There was now.* For these and the succeeding events: Cerretani, 197–206; Parenti, *Storia*, 116–25; Landucci (1927), 58–62.

37 *Knowing that Piero's.* Jacopo de' Nerli: Cerretani, 206. Shakespeare, *Romeo and Juliet*, I, i, 42–46, specifies the 'thumb'.

37 *Piero returned to.* Quotation, Parenti, *Storia*, 122.

39 *Calls went up.* Piero's request for clothing: Parenti, 130.

39 *On that day.* Attacks on private houses: Cerretani, 207–08; Parenti, 126; Landucci (1927), 62; Portioli, 331; Dorini, 1–2.

39 *The moment had.* For the Mediceans here: Guicciardini, *Storie*, 98.

40 *Over the next.* The return of exiles to Florence: Martines (2003), 252, 280, n.252.

41 *One of the most.* Quotations: Guicciardini, *Storie*, 99–100.

43 *It was late.* The King's entry: best described by Parenti and Cerretani.

43 *Charles was to be.* For items here: Praticò, 217; Cerretani, 201, 212.

44 *In a gathering.* Cerretani, 212; Parenti, 133.

45 *His route took.* Cerretani, 213.

47 *By picking up.* The diarists: chiefly Parenti and Cerretani.

47 *Two days before.* Quotation: Parenti, 131.

48 *Meanwhile, Piero's.* What Piero said: Parenti, 132.

48 *According to contemporaries.* Alfonsina and the young Tornabuoni: Cerretani, 217; Parenti, 135; Nardi, 50.

49 *As if, back in.* Parenti, 136–37.

50 *The city's thickening.* Some contemporaries felt that the King dishonoured the other envoys by favouring Savonarola: Vaglienti, 15–16.

50 *Savonarola told the king.* Citations: Cordero, I, 315–20.

51 *On 21 November.* Parenti, 137–38, 238.

52 *On 24 November.* The fracas: Vaglienti, 22; Cerretani, 218–19; Parenti, 142.

52 *Spurred on by.* Quotations: Cerretani, 219; Parenti, 142; Guicciardini (1931), 105.

53 *Apart from the.* Details in: Parenti, 141.

53 *Charles entered Italy.* The King's army: Labande-Mailfert, 257–59; and Guidi (1988), 59.

54 *An indicator of the.* On smuggled weapons: Cerretani, 218.

55 *The Friar, meanwhile.* On looking back: Sav, *Compendio*, 51.

55 *Savonarola's central metaphor.* The sermons in question: Sav, *Aggeo*.

55 *He addresses Florence.* Citations, in text's order: Sav, *Aggeo*, 6, 21, 12, 16.

56 *In his fourth.* Citations: Sav, *Aggeo*, 74, 80, 81, 82.

CHAPTER SIX
HOLY LIBERTY

58 *Creative Florence.* Artistic commissions: Hall, 'Savonarola's Preaching'.

60 *Unhappily for the.* Everything in this paragraph and the preceding ones in this

chapter is extrapolated from primary sources. For more on backers of the cadet- line Medici, see Bertelli, 'Un magistrato', 476; and Fubini, 'Politica', 587–88.

61 *A revolution was.* The preceding and subsequent events are narrated in part by Cerretani and Parenti. Guicciardini is too sketchy. The best detailed history of the changes of Nov.–Dec. 1494 is Guidi, *Lotte*, I. For the documentation: Cadoni, *Provvisioni*, 1–57. Gilbert, 52–55, offers a digest of the events.

62 *Let's put our.* On the group of protesters: Parenti, 150; Guidi (1988), 72.

63 *Yet the great and.* On 20 December: Manfredi, in Cappelli, 337.

66 *He always stressed.* References in text's order: Sav, *Aggeo*, 105, 35–38, 290, 145.

67 *Again and again.* The claims here: *Aggeo*, 244–47, 256; and in sermons 1, 14, 15, of this preaching series.

67 *One of his most.* Claims here: *Aggeo*, 290, 133–34.

67 *On the following.* Sunday, 14 December: *Aggeo*, 209–28.

67 *Moving quickly.* Quotations: *Aggeo*, 211–12.

68 *'O Florence,' he exclaims.* Quotations: *Aggeo*, 212-13.

68 *Conspicuously implicit.* Quotations: *Aggeo*, 215, 220.

69 *Turning to the.* Quotation: *Aggeo*, 223–24.

69 *Seeing his announced.* Quotations: *Aggeo*, 224, 226.

69 *He passes next.* Quotations: *Aggeo*, 226.

70 *All of a sudden.* Quotation: *Aggeo*, 226.

70 *He moves toward.* Quotations: *Aggeo*, 228.

71 *In the remaining.* Quotations: *Aggeo*, 232, 234–35, 247.

71 *His sermons often.* Quotations: *Aggeo*, 321, 326, 327, 329.

72 *Christ reminds him.* His words: *Aggeo*, 329.

72 *The sermon of Saturday.* On the tepid: *Aggeo*, 398–99.

73 *The final sermon.* Quotations: *Aggeo*, 420–21, 425–26, 427.

CHAPTER SEVEN
STAMPING OUT TYRANNY

This chapter brings another major source into play: Fachard, *Consulte e pratiche* (2002). Since Fachard is unfamiliar with Florentine political personalities of the 1490s, he is occasionally unreliable about names. Thus, in *Consulte* (1993), 27, 'Messer Guido' is not Guido Mannelli; he is *Messer* Guidantonio Vespucci, jurist and top politician. The same is true of Fachard, *Consulte* (2002), 1.

76 *Manfredo de' Manfredi.* Manfredi's letters: in Cappelli, 'Fra Girolamo'.

77 *Was Savonarolan Florence.* On parties: Bertelli, essays listed in Bibliography.

78 *The fight for the.* Controversy over the Twenty Electors: Cerretani, 222–23; Parenti, *Storia*, 151–52; Guicciardini, *Storie*, 106–07; Guidi (1988), 65–73.

79 *The anger of.* On Salviati and abolishing the Twenty: Parenti, 214–15; Cadoni, *Provvisioni*, 155.

80 *Savonarola took it.* First mention of six-bean controversy (6 January, 1495): Sav, *Salmi*, I, 10. The controversy: Fachard, *Consulte* (2002), 2–19.

81 *On 19 March.* Law enacted: Cadoni, *Provvisioni*, 118.

81 *Two months after.* On electing the Ten: Cadoni, 132–37.

81 *Florence, in the meantime.* The Ten: Cadoni, 275–86.

83 *For more than 200.* Parlamento question: Sav, *Salmi*, II, 173–75 (28 July 1495).

84 *The Savonarolans got.* Parlamenti eliminated: Cadoni, *Provvisioni*, 177–85.

84 The jingle: Sav, *Salmi*, II, 196.

CHAPTER EIGHT
GOD AND POLITICS

85 *The crisis in.* Palaces: Goldthwaite, *Building*; Bucci, *Palazzi*.

86 *One of the first.* Propaganda wars: Martines (2003), 179–84.

86 *In Florence, as it.* The new technology: Barberi, *Per una Storia*, 1–52.

87 *To reach the largest.* Data here: Garfagnini, 'Savonarola e l'uso della stampa', in *Girolamo* (1999); Rhodes, *Annali*; and Schutte, 329–52.

88 *Yet the foregoing.* The sums here: Rhodes, 100–12.

88 *An 'intellectual' then.* Quotes: Sav, *Aggeo*, 304, 392; *Salmi*, I, 85–86, 256.

89 *Trained in medieval Christian.* Quotations: Sav, *Aggeo*, 30; *Ezechiele*, II, 71; *Amos*, II, 212.

90 *Drawing from Aristotle.* Quotations: Sav, *Ezechiele*, I, 168.

92 *For nearly four.* In sermons given in the great church of Santa Maria Novella (1400–1406), the friar, Giovanni Dominici, ripped into the corruption, greed, and warmongering of Florentine politicians: see Debby, *Renaissance Florence*, 225–312, especially 207–08, 240–42, 255, 260, 288.

93 *Savonarola's life passed.* The Pope and Gatto: Manfredi, in Cappelli, 372.

94 *His sermon of 21.* References and quotations: Condivi, *Vita*, 98; Ridolfi (1974), I, 118; Sav, *Amos*, II, 109.

94 *We begin to make.* Antoninus: Howard, 'The Preacher and the Holy,' in Kienzle, *Models*, 365–66; and Machiavelli (1971), 94, in *Discorsi*, Bk. I, Chap. 11.

95 *When Renaissance preachers.* Foremost preachers: Zafarana, 'Per la storia'.

95 *Savonarola's failure as.* Cinozzi, *Epistola*, 11.

95 *Since sermons might.* Bench singers and other references: Sav, *Salmi*, I, 238; *Quaresimale*, 276.

96 *Halfway to being.* Caracciolo: Visani, 861.

96 *The desire to.* Quotations: Sav, *Aggeo*, 253; *Ruth*, I, 351 (19 June 1496); again *Aggeo*, 22–23.

97 *O Florence, O Italy.* Source here: *Aggeo*, 98.

97 *Savonarola had just.* Sav, *Salmi*, I, 180, 182.

97 *Come now, friar. Salmi*, II, 181,

98 *Do what I've said.* Sav, *Ruth*, I, 145.

98 *You [Florentines] seem.* This and the next three paragraphs: *Ruth*, I, 353, 464; II, 56, 252–53.

98 *Up now, Satan.* This and the next two paragraphs: *Amos*, I, 24, 343; II, 262.

99 *Having pointed out.* Four paragraphs: Sav, *Ezechiele*, I, 46, 291; II, 79–81.
100 *Well, you'll say.* Three paragraphs: Sav, *Esodo*, I, 24, 65, 67, 307–08.
101 *For him, therefore.* The four ages: *Aggeo*, 234–35. On the 'millenarian pattern', see Weinstein (1970), 33.
102 *Almost everything else.* The gambler's cry: Sav, *Ruth*, II, 318 (28 Oct. 1496).
102 *Well now, what are.* Quotation: Sav, *Amos*, III, 33.
103 *A man of his.* Not a leveller: *Aggeo*, 80–82; *Sermones*, 122; Sav, *De simplicitate*, 101-02.
103 *The Friar's conception.* On Genazzano: Zafarana, 'Per la storia', 1050.
105 *Savonarola would have.* Spring, 1495: Sav, *Giobbe*, I, 261.
106 *We have seen.* Quotations: Sav, *Trattato*, 13.
107 *Savonarola's vision of.* On Parenti: Matucci, 'Savonarola'. On 'prudent' rather 'good' men: Prodi, 'Gli affanni', 31, 44.
108 *Every Florentine citizen.* Quotation: Sav, *Trattato*, 43.
109 *God had set up.* Quotations: *Salmi*, II, 26, 191.
109 *In the tract.* Quotations: *Amos*, I, 217; *Trattato*, 23; again *Amos*, I, 217–18.

CHAPTER NINE
ANGELS AND ENFORCERS

111 *Florence had never.* Famine and poverty: Cambi, 97–102; Landucci (1927), 116; and Tognetti, 'Prezzi', 275–82, plus his tables, showing the crunch in the last decade of the fifteenth century.
111 *Religious companies.* Children: Trexler, *Public Life*, 368–87, 474–90; Polizzotto, *Children*, chaps. 1–3; and Taddei, *Fanciulli e giovani: crescere a Firenze nel Rinascimento*.
112 *Working as a foil.* Attacks on old men: Sav, *Amos*, II, 344; *Ruth*, I, 135, 202, 331–32; II, 203.
112 *On 3 September.* The letter: Domenico, *Epistola*. I used the British Library copy, 1A 27347. See Terreaux-Scotto, 'La place', 99–103, for an edition.
115 *The main sources.* More scholarship on the children's companies: Benvenuti; Ciappelli; Niccoli; Taddei; and Terreaux-Scotto.
115 *The most condensed.* See especially the two essays by Ciappelli.
115 *The boys of San.* On 'vanities' and street rimes: Manzoni, *Sull'abbruciamento*.
116 *In one composition.* Quotation: Manzoni, 11–30. See a version in Macey, 74–78.
117 *The apothecary, Landucci.* Citations: Landucci (1927), 102; Parenti, *Storia*, 311; Cerretani, 232; for the Milanese ambassador, Del Lungo, 9; and Villari (1930), II, the appendices here.
118 *By transcending.* On the Purification company: Polizzotto, *Children*.
119 *Owing to the religious.* Male homosexuality in Florence: Rocke, *Forbidden*. On the caged priest, Landucci (1883), 155.

CHAPTER TEN
POPE AND FRIAR

121 *The name of Rodrigo.* For 'más putas que frayles': Cirillo Sirri, 'Il tempo'. Pasquino and the anonymous poems, Martines, 'Literary Crisis'.

122 *Spain had a minor.* Sources: Iradiel and Cruselles, 'El entorno eclesiástco'; Picotti, 'Rodrigo Borgia'; Mallett, 51–83.

123 *With the knowledge.* Franceschetto's marriage: Bullard, *Lettere*, 481–92.

123 *Every papal election.* Quotations: Pastor, V, 385; De Matteis, 'Alessandro'.

123 *If bribe monies.* Quotations: Pastor, V, 363, 386–87; Mallett, 81.

124 *And then there were.* The 'cries of anguish': Mallett, 142.

125 *Alexander VI did.* On the Pope's tricky position: M. Pellegrini, 'Turning-Point'; and Fubini, 'Politica', 576–79.

126 *Meanwhile, the Lord.* Quotations: Del Lungo, 'Fra Girolamo', ii, 6–7.

127 *Eight months after.* The Friar's words: Sav, *Lettere* (1984), 73–74.

128 *The brief quickly.* The brief: Sav, *Lettere* (1933), 75–90; and Scaltriti, 51–53.

129 *Savonarola's reply.* Letter of 29 Sept.: Sav, *Lettere* (1984), 75–79.

130 *The men of the.* Quotation: *Lettere* (1984), 89.

131 *A remarkable reversal.* Papal brief of 16 Oct.: *Lettere* (1933), 233–35.

133 *Savonarola was to.* Support for the Friar and quotations: Ridolfi, I, 209–10, 222–23. Marchese, 'Documenti', 146–47; Gherardi, *Nuovi documenti*, 123–33.

134 *All too soon.* Complaints to Becchi: Gherardi, 134–35.

134 *In a letter to.* To Becchi: Marchese, 148; Gherardi, 137–38.

134 *On 18 and 20.* From Becchi: Gherardi, 139.

135 *Becchi then winds.* Becchi's letter: Gherardi, 141–42.

136 *Savonarola's enemies.* The sermons: Sav, *Amos*, I, 3–4, 24–25, 45, 151–56 (for the Great Council), 216–30 (against tyranny), 309–10 (corrupt clergy), 374 ('Rome, you will be made a horse stable'); II, 1–27 (mainly against the 'tepid'), 433 ('Stop writing to Rome').

137 *Having delivered his.* Source: De Maio, 72–74 .

137 *Was a new phase.* Reasons, quotation: De Maio, 75–77; Sav, *Ruth*, II, 126.

137 *The year 1496.* Based in Venice, but well informed, Sanuto offers a grim picture of conditions in Florence: Sanuto, I, 138, 184, 237–38, 491.

138 *The Friar's relations.* The papal letter: Villari, I, cxlii–cxlv; Scaltriti, 108–10.

138 *Savonarola now held.* The Friar's letter: Sav, *Lettere* (1984), 271–76; Scaltriti, 110–11.

139 *What Savonarola did.* On this question: De Maio, 99–106.

CHAPTER ELEVEN
THE SAVONAROLAN MOMENT

140 *Florence was his.* Carnival, 16 Feb., 1496, the songs: Macey, 64, 68. On the Great Hall and 'holy liberty': Polizzotto (1994), 28–29.

141 *If there were.* Quotations: Macey, 54, 68.

142 *As the Friar's.* The armed escort: Parenti, *Storia*, 324; Ferrara, 'Sonetti', 42.

142 *His ranks of.* Guicciardini and father: Cordero, IV, 27; Brown's notes in Guicciardini, *Dialogue*, 184; and Martines (2001), 79.

142 *His ranks of.* Father's diary: B. Machiavelli, *Libro*.

142 *Before the middle.* Medici money for San Marco and friar numbers: Schnitzer (1931), I, 76–78; Cordero, I, 219; Polizzotto (2000), 59, 61; Kent, *Cosimo*, 171–78; Verde, 'La Congregazione'.

143 *San Marco was.* The hostile Florentine clergy: Parenti (Schnitzer), 115; Polizzotto (1994), 53.

144 *The city's leading.* Points about fasting: Sanuto, I, 184; Praticò, 217.

145 *The story of.* Sources here: Burlamacchi, 64–67; Della Mirandola, 33.

150 *In June 1496.* About Ser Giuliano: Parenti (Schnitzer), 125–28.

152 *Supremely talented.* Remarks on the Soderini: Bertelli (1987); Clarke, *The Soderini*, 133–34; and Guicciardini, *Dialogue*, 191–92.

152 *Francesco Valori.* Description of Valori: Cerretani, 248.

153 *The charge that the.* Savonarola regarding 'intelligences' and on how to vote: *Amos*, I, 172, 334; *Salmi*, II, 171–72.

153 *The shifting anatomy.* On crypto-Mediceans: Parenti, *Storia*, 317–18; and Parenti (Schnitzer), 181–82.

155 *In the last year.* On Compagnacci: Cerretani, 241–43; Violi, *Giornate*, 64–74.

CHAPTER TWELVE

WAILERS AND BIGOTS

156 *Savonarola had foes.* Of 'little women': Sav, *Compendio*, 76.

156 *A poetry of.* Sonnet in Sanuto, I, 759; also Ridolfi, 'Poesie inedite', in *Studi*.

157 *One anonymous poem.* The four verse citations: Ferrara, 'Due sonetti', 137ff.; Ridolfi, *Prolegomeni*, 47; and Bacci, *Notizia*, 27, 29.

158 *In January 1497.* Muzi and Cei: Ridolfi (1952), I, 276–77; II, 178–79; Schnitzer (1931), I, 448, 458; and Cei, *Canzoniere*.

158 *But the most.* Genazzano: Gutierrez, 'Testi'; Schnitzer (1931), I, 126–27.

158 *In January 1495.* Domenico da Ponzo: Schnitzer (1931), 247–51.

159 *From this time.* The Friar's claims here: Sav, *Compendio*, 155–56.

159 *His chief antagonist.* Giovanni Caroli: Polizzotto (1994), 59–75.

160 *The brunt of.* Contents here: Polizzotto (1994), 61–62; Weinstein (1970), 235.

160 *We learn from.* The secret assembly: Sav, *Giobbe*, II, 164, 245, 310–11, 433. The Augustinian: Polizzotto (1994), 82–83; Neri, 'Un avversario', 481.

161 *In the winter.* Vallombrosa, *Lettere*, 94–95, 19, 25, 41, 46, 84, 86–88, 90.

161 *Angelo's concluding.* Reference: *Lettere*, 92–97.

162 *The first one.* Attack and quotations: Anonymous, *Epistola responsiva*, 124–39.

162 *The second diatribe.* Source: Altoviti, *In Defensione*.

162 *Written just after.* Quotations: Altoviti, 140. 141, 143, 145.

163 *The polemic rushes.* Quotations: Altoviti, 145–46.

164 *Altoviti, astonishingly.* Quotations: Altoviti, 146–47.
165 *One of the most.* Quotations: Miglio, 'Savonarola', 110–11.

CHAPTER THIRTEEN

EXCOMMUNICATION

166 *Alexander VI was.* The recent historian: De Matteis, 'Alessandro VI'.
167 *Valori's Priors proceeded.* For items here: Parenti (Schnitzer), 154–58; and Cordero, III, 500–08.
168 *Pope Borgia signed.* The courier, Gianvittorio da Camerino: Parenti, 192–93.
168 *The movements of.* Events of 3–4 May: Villari, II, xxviii–xxix, xxxvii; Parenti, 182–83; Cerretani, 236; Landucci (1927), 118–19; Burlamacchi, 107–08.
169 *Since the bearer.* A witness: Landucci (1927), 122–23, was present at the excommunication ceremony in the church of Santo Spirito.
169 *The brief of.* The brief: Villari, II, xxxix–xl.
170 *In 1497, with the.* The Franciscans and Augustinians react: Parenti, 197.
171 *With some in.* Lurid pictures: Parenti, 193.
173 *Savonarola learned.* His letter: Sav, *Lettere* (1984), 271–76.
173 *An indictment of.* Source here: Sav, *loc. cit.*
174 *With Savonarola already.* Quotation: Sav, *Esodo*, I, 308 (7 March 1498).

CHAPTER FOURTEEN

FIVE EXECUTIONS

175 *One of the most.* On Del Nero: Arrighi, 'Bernardo'; Rao, *Processi*, 120; and Brown's sketch in Guicciardini, *Dialogue*, 189–91.
176 *But the elapse.* Republicans against Del Nero: Parenti (Schnitzer), 208–09; and Rinuccini, *Ricordi*, cxxxvii.
177 *As early as.* Sources here: Fachard, *Consulte* (2002), 439–41, 453–58; Ferrara's ambassador, Cappelli, 'Fra Girolamo', 376–77; and Bertelli, 'Machiavelli', 36.
178 *This apparent change.* Sources: Carnesecchi, 'Un tumulto'; also Parenti (Schnitzer), 165; and Cordero, IV, 6.
178 *Early in April.* Military movements: Fachard (2002), 462.
178 *Suddenly, too, the.* City gates and the executioner: Cerretani, 234–35.
179 *Guicciardini, whose father.* Guicciardini, *Storie*, 132; Parenti, 181.
180 *Bernardo and the.* On the twelve: Parenti, 171–78; Guicciardini, 133–34.
181 *Throughout the April.* Quotation: Cerretani, 235.
181 *The suspicious Parenti.* Reference: Parenti, 180.
183 *Wishing to return.* Dell'Antella's confession: Villari, II, iii–xv.
184 *Encouraged to talk.* Cambi and Pucci: Cerretani, 236–37; Parenti (Schnitzer), 206–07; Landucci (1927), 125; Manfredi, In Cappelli, 382–85.
186 *Niccolò Ridolfi's case.* On Ridolfi: Bullard, 268. His nephew Piero was married

to Lorenzo the Magnificent's youngest daughter. See also Rao, 75–76, 82.

186 *The case of.* On Tornabuoni: Landucci (1927), 126; Cerretani, 236–37; Rao, 166–67; Guicciardini, *Storie*, 143: Villari, II, xxxii–xxxiii (letter, Somenzi to Sforza); and De Roover, 367, 370, on the partnership with the Medici.

189 *The confessions of.* Citizen villas, famine and poverty: Nardi, *Istorie*, 130–33.

190 *The trial of.* Cited: Cerretani, 236–37.

190 *Read out to the.* Quotation: Parenti (Schnitzer), 207–08.

191 *No sooner had.* On Vespucci: Bullard, *passim*; Martines (1968), 494.

192 *The law said.* Enacted 19 March 1495, the law is in Cadoni, *Provvisioni*, 111–18; see also Guicciardini, *Storie*, 139–44.

192 *Drawing, we must.* Quotation: Guicciardini, *Storie*, 141.

193 *The other side was.* One speaker noted: Martines (1968), 441–45; Fachard, *Consulte* (2002), 509.

193 *The opponents of.* Quotations: Cerretani, 238; Fachard (2002), 511.

193 *The final discussions.* The record of the debates: Fachard (2002), 509–14.

194 *On that warm.* The shouting and anger that night: Cambi, 113; Cerretani, 239.

195 *Now, outrageously, here.* Quotations: Villari, II, xlix; Fachard (2002), 511–12.

195 *In the hours.* Cerretani, 237; Parenti (Schnitzer), 211; Guicciardini, *Storie*, 141–42.

196 *Within minutes of.* Sources: Cerretani, 238–40; Landucci (1927), 125–26.

196 *When early risers.* Secrecy imposed on the 200: Manfredi, in Cappelli, 386–88.

197 *The five executions.* The trial and executions: Cordero, IV, 102–24.

197 *In the wake.* Quotation: Cerretani, 238.

198 *Machiavelli, who was.* Machiavelli, *Opere*, 127 (in *Discorsi*, Bk I, chap. 45).

199 *Well, but then.* The Friar's handbook for confessors: Weinstein, 'The Prophet'.

200 *The executions are.* On Milan's ambassador and the effects of the executions: Bertelli, 'Machiavelli', 39–40.

CHAPTER FIFTEEN
ROME CLOSES IN

201 *At the end of.* On 6 January and papal relations: Landucci (1927), 129; Gherardi, 175–77.

201 *News of the.* Papal reaction and the archbishop: Marchese, 164–65.

202 *Bonsi wrote to.* On Bonsi and Bracci: Gherardi, 178–79.

202 *Over the course.* Bonsi's reporting: Gherardi, 180–82.

203 *A papal brief of.* Sources here: Gherardi, 183–85, 186; and Sanuto, I, 899–900, 905, 920. Villari, II, lxvi–lxvii, has the letter threatening the interdict.

204 *The Ten wrote to.* Letter of 3 March: Gherardi, 187–88.

204 *4 March. A letter.* The Priors' letter: Marchese, 165–67.

204 *Three days later.* Bonsi's words: Gherardi, 192.

205 *Knowing that he.* Bonsi's words: Marchese, 167–70.

206 *9 March. Bonsi.* Quotation: Gherardi, 192–96.

206 *Well might Pope.* The Friar's words: Sav, *Esodo*, I, 27, 40, 71, 179.

207 *For weeks now.* Letter of 10 March: Gherardi, 198.

207 *Confronted with an.* Bonsi's reply: Gherardi, 198–201.

207 *In fact, the Friar.* Letter of 13 March: Sav, *Lettere* (1984), 226–27.

207 *Reaching the end.* Source: Gherardi, 201. There was an obvious cover-up, clearly the work of *gran maestri.*

208 *The first speaker.* On 3 March: Fachard, *Consulte* (1993), I, 42–43.

208 *Filippo Sacchetti.* Quotations: Fachard, 43–44.

208 *The spokesmen for.* Source: Fachard, 44–45.

209 *Seven of the.* Source: Fachard, 45–46.

209 *Speaking for the.* Canacci: Fachard, 47.

210 *The next set.* Vigna: Fachard, 47–48.

210 *The Guelfs.* Soderini and the Eight: Fachard, 48.

211 *The fight was.* Lenzi: Fachard, 48–49.

211 *But one of the.* Vespucci: Fachard, 49–51.

212 *The core of.* Malegonnelli: Fachard, 51.

213 *All this and.* Della Stufa and Cambi: Fachard, 51–52, 53.

213 *An international merchant.* Gondi: Fachard, 53–54.

215 *Francesco Valori.* The source for this and the twelve paragraphs that follow: Fachard, 54–60.

216 *Two days later.* Source: Fachard, 60–61.

217 *The letters from.* Bonsi's reports: Marchese, 171; Gherardi, 204.

217 *Bonsi's would-be.* Bonsi again: Marchese, 172–73; Gherardi, 204–11.

217 *Back in Florence.* Fedini: Ridolfi (1959), 223–34; Cordero, IV, 199.

218 *The Signory and.* Quotation: Gherardi, 212.

CHAPTER SIXTEEN
FOILED FIRE

220 *Talk about an.* For a more complete picture: Schnitzer (1931), II, 60–67; Cordero, IV, 379ff.

221 *Though he never.* Savonarola's words: Rao, *Processi,* xlviii.

222 *Giuliano Rondinelli.* Sources: Marchese, 173–75; Villari, II, xci–xcii.

222 *Rome reacted.* The Papal reaction: Gherardi, 217–18.

223 *On 30 March.* Quotations: Fachard, *Consulte* (1993), I, 64–65.

223 *Capponi was followed.* What the advisers said: Fachard, *Ibid.,* 65–67.

224 *The new vicar.* The 'ultra-Wailer': Cordero, IV, 389.

224 *The ordeal was set.* The 'stage' for the ordeal: Vaglienti, 44–46; Landucci (1927), 135; Parenti (Schnitzer), 256.

225 *At least one.* Niccolini: Fachard (1993), I, 65–66.

225 *On the day of.* The proceedings: Burlamacchi, 140–54; Violi, *Giornate,* 75–84; Parenti, 256–59; Cerretani, 244–45; Landucci (1927), 135–36.

225 *All foreigners.* Women banned: Parenti, 258.

226 *The contingent from.* On fra Domenico: Parenti, 257. Cordero, IV, 381, calls Domenico 'the idiot'.

226 *Behind fra Domenico.* Quotations: Parenti, 257.

228 *A great public.* Quotation: Burlamacchi, 154–55.
229 *April showers: then.* Quotation: Parenti, 259.
229 *The procession back.* Quotations: Parenti, 259; Cordero, IV, 434.

CHAPTER SEVENTEEN
THE SIEGE OF SAN MARCO

232 *That day, pacing.* Insulting and assaulting the Frateschi: Burlamacchi, 155–56;
     Cerretani, 246; Cordero, IV, 437.
232 *A boy and.* Source: Burlamacchi, 156.
233 *The Signory had.* The banishment order and Della Vecchia: Parenti (Schnitzer),
     261; Cerretani, 247.
233 *In the weeks.* The Franciscan riot: Parenti, *Storia*, 51–54.
234 *On that day.* The Priors' clash, and Mazzinghi: Parenti (Schnitzer), 265; Portioli,
     349.
235 *In the three.* Three paragraphs: names and weapons come from the confes-
     sions of friar Maruffi and of the Piagnoni: Villari, II, ccxxv–cclxxxvi.
237 *The enemy, Compagnacci.* On Manetti, Strozzi, and Nerli: Parenti (Schnitzer),
     262; Cerretani, 247.
238 *All the women.* The diarist: Landucci (1927), 137.
238 *Francesco Valori.* His murder: Parenti, 263–64; Landucci (1927), 137; Guicciardini,
     Storie, 151–52. The amnesty: Polizzotto (1994), 207.
239 *Back at San Marco.* The battle: Parenti, 265–66; Cerretani, 248–49; Landucci
     (1927), 138; Burlamacchi, 156–62; Filipepi, 488; Luschino, *Cedrus*, 82–86.
240 *Several small pieces.* Quotation: Parenti, 265.
241 *Elsewhere in the.* Cambini's house: Rao, *Processi*, 87; Cerretani, 248.
242 *Savonarola now went.* Quotation: Cerretani, 249.
242 *With his hands.* Quotations: Cerretani, 249; Burlamacchi, 163–64.

CHAPTER EIGHTEEN
CONFESSIONS OF A SINNER

244 *Two of Europe's.* Quotation: Machiavelli, *Opere*, 94 (*Discorsi*, Bk. I, Chap. 11).
244 *Guicciardini was one.* Quotation: Guicciardini, *Storie*, 159. For his later views:
     (in his *Storia d'Italia*), *Opere*, 530–33; and especially Gusberti, 'Il Savonarola'.
246 *Now, therefore.* Held new elections: Parenti (Schnitzer), 268–69.
247 *Meanwhile, parading.* Quotation: Villari, II, 181.
247 *The Signory appointed.* New officials, and burning feet: Rao, *Processi*, 52;
     Burlamacchi, 165–66; Della Mirandola, *Vita*, 47.
248 *To add to the.* The whole record is best treated by Rao, *Processi*, xv, ciii–cxi.
248 *If the purge.* Quotation: Guicciardini, *Storie*, 155.
249 *Not counting the.* Quotation: Guicciardini, *Storie*, 153.
250 *On the 10th of.* Quotation: Rao, *Processi*, 4.

250 *He was pressed.* Quotation: Rao, 5–7.

250 *The Friar easily.* This and next paragraph, quotations: Rao, 7–10.

251 *Savonarola reeled off.* This and next paragraph, quotations: Rao, 10, 11, 15, 20.

252 *Asked about why.* Two paragraphs: Rao, 14, 16, 22.

253 *He disobeyed.* Two paragraphs: Rao, 14–15, 18–19.

253 *Turning to the.* Quotations: Rao, 20–21.

254 *The second trial.* Two paragraphs: Rao, 25–31; Landucci (1883), 174.

255 *On the morning.* Two paragraphs: Rao, 26, 27–28.

255 *Lunch for the.* Quotations: Rao, 29.

256 *If the interdict.* Two paragraphs: Rao, 30–31.

257 *It was in signing.* Quotation: Rao, 31.

257 *The Florentine ambassador.* The Bonsi–Signory exchange: Marchese, 177–80; Gherardi, 226–30.

257 *There was more.* About the *Decima*: Marchese, 180–81; Gherardi, 239–42, 257.

258 *The other papal.* On Torriani and Remolins: Gherardi, 264; Rao, 152–54.

258 *The papal emissaries.* Three paragraphs, quotations: Rao, 33.

259 *After touching briefly.* Since the quotations run seriatim, so also the following citations: Rao, 33–43.

CHAPTER NINETEEN
FIRE AGAIN: THREE EXECUTIONS

266 *In the history.* The diarist: Landucci (1927), 139.

271 *There is a striking poverty.* The bizarre lie: Rao, *Processi*, 26.

274 *On their final.* Contents here: Schnitzer (1931), II, 138–45; Ridolfi (1952), I, 399, 401.

274 *The final arrangements.* Vaglienti, 48.

274 *The ritual had.* On the proceedings: Parenti (Schnitzer), 280–82; Cerretani, 251; Landucci (1883), 176–77; Schnitzer (1931), 145–47. Degradation and defrocking: *Catholic Encyclopedia*, IV, 677–78.

275 *Once the degradation.* The vertical beam and other matters: Cambi, 126–27.

276 *Witnesses reported.* Sources: Burlamacchi, 184; Cambi, 127; Parenti, 280–82.

276 *The siege of.* As cited: Vaglienti, 49–53; also Parenti, 283–84.

277 *The ideological.* Sources: Vaglienti, 52; Landucci (1927), 143–44.

277 *The execution of.* Sources: Burlamacchi, 189–95; Villari, II, 248–50; Filipepi, 497; Landucci (1883), 180–81.

278 *For the rest of.* Carnival, 1499: Cambi, 136–37.

278 *Lobbied by members.* San Marco's bell: Landucci (1883), 181; Cambi, 134; Schnitzer (1931), II, 432; Polizzotto (1994), 170.

278 *Six months later.* Horse, pranksters: Landucci (1883), 190–91; Cambi, 135–36.

279 *Meanwhile, the settling.* The purge, arrests, torture, and Soderini: Rao, 84–86 (on Soderini); Landucci (1883), 174.

279 *Special treatment, however.* Of Soderini and Ridolfi: Parenti, 275–76; Rao, 75–76 (Ridolfi).

279 *The obligatory loans.* Fines and loans: Parenti, 275–76; Nardi, 156; Cambi, 131–32; Landucci (1883), 180.

280 *I have referred.* Soderini's son: Guicciardini, *Storie*, 147.

281 *The years passed.* September 1512: Butters, *Governors*, 166–86. The legacy of Savonarolan republicanism has been expertly treated by Polizzotto (1994).

281 *Yet the ideals.* The Medici toppled in 1527: Stephens, *The Fall*, 203–241.

CHAPTER TWENTY

THE CONSCIENCE OF A CITY

284 *Savonarola's fight.* Homosexuality in Florence: Rocke, *Forbidden Friendships.* Venice: Ruggiero, *Boundaries*, 109–45. Rocke is much checked and modified by Cohn (1999). Quotation regarding Germans: Rocke, 3.

284 *But the friar.* Quotation: Rocke, 208, 321, n.63.

285 *The triumph of.* The secretary, Bernardo da Bibbiena, schooled in the classics, voiced the Latin proverb: in Butters, *Governors*, 183, n.77.

285 *Yet the climate.* There were many precedents for the burning of 'vanities': see Chiappini, 'Un bruciamento'.

286 *Guicciardini said.* Quotation and costs: M. Pellegrini (2002), 18–19.

287 *A meeting with.* Numbers, parish churches: Peterson, 'Religion', 77; religious houses, Schnitzer (1931), I, 291; devotional poetry, Martines (2001), 37–81.

287 *Florentines were pious.* Eight Saints' War: Peterson, 'The War'. Capponi's advice, in Martines, 'Raging against Priests in Italian Renaissance Verse', 273.

288 *I need hardly.* Quotation: Sav, *Esodo*, II, 18.

289 *Savonarola tapped:* Essential here: Weinstein, *Savonarola and Florence*.

296 *The Public Man.* On the confessors' manual: Weinstein, 'The Prophet'.

BIBLIOGRAPHY

Scholarship on Savonarola is rich, complex, and more than usually erudite. Readers, therefore, looking for some assistance may find the following comments useful. The best and most complete overall narratives are to be found in Villari, Schnitzer, Ridolfi, and Cordero, though the last of these calls for a note apart. Weinstein and Polizzotto provide superior thematic narratives.

In the preparation and editing of primary source material, the leading scholars are again Villari, Schnitzer, and Ridolfi; plus Verde, Lionardi, Garfagnini, Ricci, and Romano (all entered below under Savonarola and his works). Historians of Florence, and more particularly of the 1490s, merit a separate classification. Here I would single out the labours of Cadoni, Brown, Guidi, and Pesman-Cooper. The recent edition of Savonarola's three trials (*I processi*), by Rao, Viti and Zaccaria, is superb.

The following diarists, chroniclers, and historians are absolutely fundamental: Cambi, Cerretani, Filipepi, Guicciardini, Landucci, Nardi, Parenti, and Vaglienti. They offer priceless detail and convey a crucial, dense atmosphere. Of these, only Filipepi was a full-blooded 'Wailer'. Landucci's allegiances were occasionally split, such as over the executions of August 1497.

The most ambitious study in recent times, Franco Cordero's *Savonarola*, in four volumes, was well researched and is often brilliant, as in the tracking of Savonarola's canny rhetorical dodges. But the entire work is also self-destructive, because Cordero so detests the Friar that he is constantly, so to speak, in the ring with him, punching away and hoping for a knock-out blow. This puts Cordero continually on the brink of losing all objectivity, as he scorns, derides, and highlights Savonarola's alleged posturing, inconsistencies, illogicalities, egomania, bad faith, and rhetorical violence. Furthermore, his Freudian approach trammels him all the more in the sustained abuse of his subject, as he labels the Friar an 'exterminator', a 'terrorist', an '*homme de théâtre*', a 'holy condottiere', an 'energumen', 'demagogue', 'meglomaniac', 'pyromaniac', 'narcissist', and '*gaffeur*'. And the children of the Savonarolan movement were 'storm-trooper units' (*Sturm-Abteilungen*, Cordero, III, 37). He matches the hatred of Savonarola's contemporary foes, the Compagnacci.

Abbreviations

ASI Archivio storico italiano
DBI Dizionario biografico degli italiani. Rome, 1960–

Abulafia, David, ed. 1995. *The French Descent into Renaissance Italy, 1494–95*. Aldershot, UK.

Alessandro VI e Savonarola. 1950. Issued by the Accademia d'Oropa. Turin.

Altoviti, Francesco. *In defensione de' magistrati e delle leggi e antiche cerimonie al culto divino della città di Firenze contro alle invettive e offensione di Fra Girolamo.* In Garfagnini (2000): 140–147.

Ames, T. L., Green, E. A., Kienzle, B. M., eds. 1989. *De ore domini: Preacher and Word in the Middle Ages.* Kalamazoo.

Anonymous. *Epistola responsiva a frate Ieronimo da Ferrara dell'Ordine de' Predicatori da l'amico suo.* In Garfagnini (2000): 124–39.

Arrighi, V. 1990. 'Bernardo del Nero'. *DBI,* 38, 170–73. Rome.

Bacci, Peleo. 1894. *Notizia della vita e delle rime inedite di Tommaso Baldinotti (Poeta pistoiese del xv sec.).* Pistoia.

Barberi, Francesco. 1981. *Per una storia del libro.* Rome.

Benivieni, Domenico. 2003. *Trattato in difesa di Girolamo Savonarola.* Ed. G. C. Garfagnini. Florence.

Benvenuti, Anna. 'I Bruchi di Frate Gerolamo: L'eversivo anacronismo del Savonarola'. In Garfagnini (1997).

Bertelli, Sergio. 1987. 'Di due profili mancati e di un bilancino con pesi truccati', in *ASI,* 145, 4: 579–610.

———. 'Un magistrato per a tempo lungo o uno dogie'. In *Studi di storia* (1980).

———. 'Machiavelli e la politica estera fiorentina'. In Gilmore, *Studies* (1972).

Brown, Alison. 1992. *The Medici in Florence: The Exercise and Language of Power.* Florence.

———. 'The Revolution of 1494 in Florence and its Aftermath: A Reassessment'. In Everson and Zancani (2000).

———. 1997. 'Partiti, correnti o coalizioni: un contributo al dibattito'. In Fontes, Fournel.

———. 2000. 'De-Masking Renaissance Republicanism'. In Hankins.

———. 'Uffici di onore e utile: la crisi del repubblicanesimo a Firenze', in *ASI,* 161, 3 (2003): 285–321.

Bucci, Mario, and Raffaello Bencini. 1973. *Palazzi di Firenze.* 4 vols. Florence.

Bullard, M. Meriam. 2003. *[Lettere] Lorenzo de' Medici: Lettere (1486–1487),* Vol. 10. Florence.

Burlamacchi, Pseudo. 1937. *La vita del Beato Ieronimo Savonarola, scritta da un Anonimo del secolo xvi e già attribuita a fra Pacifico Burlamacchi.* Ed. Piero Ginori Conti. Florence.

Butters, H. C. 1985. *Governors and Government in Early Sixteenth-Century Florence, 1502–1519.* Oxford.

Cadoni, Giorgio. 1994. *Provvisioni concernenti l'ordinamento della repubblica fiorentina, 1494–1512.* Rome.

———. 1999. *Lotte politiche e riforme istituzionali a Firenze tra il 1494 e il 1502.* Rome.

Calzona, Arturo, and F. P. Fiore, A. Tenenti, C. Vasoli, eds. 2002. *Il Principe Architetto.* 'Atti del convegno internazionale', Mantova, October 1999. Florence.

Cambi, Giovanni. 1785. *Istorie,* II. Vol. 21 of *Delizie degli eruditi toscani.* Ed. I. di San Luigi. Florence.

Cappelli, Antonio. 'Fra Girolamo Savonarola, e notizie intorno al suo tempo'. In *Atti e memorie delle RR. Deputazioni di Storia patria per le province modenesi e parmensi, IV* (1869): 321–406.

Caracciolo, Roberto. 1993. *Opere in volgare.* Ed. Enzo Esposito and Raul Mordenti. Galatina.

Carnesecchi, C. 1902. 'Un tumulto di donne', in I. Del Badia, ed., *Miscellanea fiorentina di erudizione e storia*, II, 45–47. Florence.

Catholic Encyclopedia (The). 1907–1918. Vol. 4. New York.

Cattin, Giulio. 1973. *Il primo Savonarola. Poesie e prediche autografe dal Codice Borromeo.* Florence.

Cei, Francesco. 1994. *Il Canzoniere.* Ed. Marta Ceci. Rome.

Centi, Tito S. 'L'Itinerario spirituale di fra Girolamo Savonarola'. In Garfagnini (1999).

Cerretani, Bartolomeo. 1994. *Storia fiorentina.* Ed. G. Berti. Florence.

Chiabò, M., and S. Maddalo, M. Miglio, A. M. Silva, eds. 2001. *Roma di Fronte al Europa al Tempo di Alessandro VI.* 3 vols. Rome.

Chiappini, Luciano. 'Un bruciamento delle vanità a Ferrara nel 1474'. In *Atti e Memorie della Deputazione Provinciale Ferrarese di Storia Patria.* 7, 3 (1952): 55–59.

Chittolini, Giorgio. 2001. 'Città, Istituzioni ecclesiastiche e "Religione civica" nell'Italia centrosettentrionale alla fine del secolo xv'. In Fragnito, Miegge.

Ciappelli, Giovanni. 'Il Carnevale del Savonarola'. In Garfagnini (1996).

——. 'I bruciamenti delle vanità e la transizione verso un nuovo ordine carnavalesco'. In Fontes, Fournel (1997).

Cinozzi, Placido. 1898. *Epistola.* In Villari, Casanova.

Cirillo Sirri. 'Il tempo che a Roma "havía más putas que frayles en Venecia" '. In Chiabò, Maddalo (2001): II, 387–96.

Clarke, Paula C. 1991. *The Soderini and the Medici: Power and Patronage in Fifteenth-Century Florence.* Oxford.

Cohn, Jr., Samuel K. 1999. Review of M. Rocke's *Forbidden Friendships* (see below), in *Speculum: A Journal of Medieval Studies*, 74, 3: 481–83.

Condivi, Ascanio. 1927. *Vita di Michelangiolo.* Florence.

Connell, William J., ed. 2002. *Society and Individual in Renaissance Florence.* Berkeley and Los Angeles.

Cordero, Franco. 1986–88. *Savonarola.* 4 vols. Rome and Bari.

Corsini, Carlo A. 1996. 'La demografia fiorentina nell'età di Lorenzo il Magnifico'. In *La toscana al tempo.*

Debby, Nirit Ben-Aryeh. 2001. *Renaissance Florence in the Rhetoric of Two Popular Preachers: Giovanni Dominici (1356–1419) and Bernardino da Siena (1380–1444).* Turnhout, Belgium.

Delcorno, Carlo. 1982. 'L' "ars predicandi" di Bernardino da Siena'. In Maffei, Nardi.

——. 'Medieval Preaching in Italy (1200–1500)'. In Kienzle (2000).

Della Mirandola, Giovanfrancesco Pico. 1998. *Vita di Hieronimo Savonarola (Volgarizamento anonimo).* Ed. Raffaela Castagnola. Florence.

Del Lungo, I., ed. 'Fra Girolamo Savonarola'. In *ASI*, 18, 1–2 (1863): 3–18, 3–41.

De Maio, Romeo. 1969. *Savonarola e la curia romana.* Rome.

De Marchia [Della Marca], S. Jacobus. 1978. *Sermones dominicales.* 3 vols. Ed. Renato Lioi. Ancona.

De Matteis, Maria Consiglia. 'Alessandro VI: alle origini di un mito negativo'. In *Roma di fronte al Europa* (2001).

Denis, Anne. 1979. *Charles VIII et les Italiens: Histoire et Myth.* Geneva.

De Roover, Raymond. 1966. *The Rise and Decline of the Medici Bank.* New York.

Domenico da Pescia. 3 Sept., 1497. *Epistola di frate Domenico da Pescia mandata a' fanciulli fiorentini.* Florence. British Library, IA 27347. Also in Terreaux-Scotto.

Dorini, Umberto. 'Le disgrazie di un nemico del Savonarola'. In *Rivista storica degli archivi toscani*, 1 (1929): 186–98.

Enciclopedia dei Papi. 2000. 3 vols. Rome.

Everson, Jane and Diego Zancani, eds. 2000. *Italy in Crisis 1494.* Oxford.

Fachard, Denis, ed. 1993. *Consulte e pratiche della repubblica fiorentina, 1498–1505.* Geneva.

——. 2002. *Consulte e pratiche della repubblica fiorentina, 1495–1497.* Geneva.

Ferrara, Marco. 'Due sonetti contro il Savonarola'. In *ASI*, 80 (1922): 135–155.

Filipepi, Simone. 1898. *Estrato della cronaca.* In Villari and Casanova, pp. 453–518.

Fontes, A., J.-L. Fournel, and M. Plaisance, eds. 1997. *Savonarole: Enjeux, Débats, Questions.* Paris.

Fletcher, Stella and Christine Shaw, eds. 2000. *The World of Savonarola: Italian elites and perceptions of crisis.* Aldershot.

Fragnito, Gigliola, and Mario Miegge, eds. 2001. *Girolamo Savonarola da Ferrara all'Europa.* Florence.

Fubini, Riccardo. 1998. 'Politica e profezia in Savonarola', in *Frate Girolamo Savonarola e il suo movimento*, vol. 29 of *Memorie domenicane*: 573–92.

——. 'Lorenzo de' Medici, architetetto costituzionale? Disegno principesco e reggimento cittadino nella Firenze del secondo Quattrocento'. In Calzona, Fiore (2002).

Garfagnini, Gian Carlo, ed. 1996. *Studi savonaroliani. Verso il V centenario.* Florence.

——, ed. 1997. *Savonarola e la politica.* Florence.

——, ed. 1998. *Savonarola: Democrazia Tirannide Profezia.* Florence.

——, ed. 1999. *Savonarola e la mistica.* Florence.

——. 1999b. 'Savonarola e l'uso della stampa'. In *Girolamo Savonarola* (1999).

——. 2000. *'Questa è la terra tua': Savonarola a Firenze.* Florence.

——, ed. 2001. *Una città e il suo profeta: Firenze di fronte al Savonarola.* Florence.

Gasparri, Laura. 'Nove prediche inedite in volgare di Roberto da Lecce'. In *Aevum. Rassegna di scienze storiche linguistiche e filologiche*, 66, 2 (1992): 361–417.

Gherardi, Alessandro. 1887. *Nuovi documenti e studi intorno a Girolamo Savonarola.* Florence.

Gilbert, Felix. 1965. *Machiavelli and Guicciardini: Politics and History in Sixteenth- Century Florence.* Princeton.

Gilmore, Myron P., ed. 1972. *Studies on Machiavelli.* Florence.

Girolamo Savonarola: l'uomo e il frate. 1999. Spoleto. In 'Atti del xxxv convegno storico internazionale', held in Todi, October, 1998.

Goldthwaite, Richard A. 1980. *The Building of Renaissance Florence.* Baltimore.

Guicciardini, Francesco. 1931. *Storie fiorentine.* Ed. R. Palmarocchi. Bari.

——. 1953. *Opere.* Ed. Vittorio de Caprariis. Milan and Naples.

——. 1994. *Dialogue on the Government of Florence.* Trans. Alison Brown. Cambridge.

Guidi, Guidubaldo. 1988. *Cio che accadde al tempo della Signoria di novembre dicembre in Firenze l'anno 1494.* Florence.

——. 1992. *Lotte, pensiero e istituzioni politiche nella repubblica fiorentina dal 1494 al 1512.* 3 vols. Florence.

——. 'La politica e lo stato nel Savonarola'. In Garfagnini (1996).

Gusberti, Enrico. 'Il Savonarola del Guicciardini'. In *Nuova rivista storica,* 54 (1970): 581–622; and 55 (1971): 21–89.

Gutierrez, David. 'Testi e note su Mariano da Genazzano (+1498)'. In *Analecta Augustiniana,* 32 (1969): 117–204.

Hall, Marcia B. 1990. 'Savonarola's Preaching and the Patronage of Art'. In Verdon.

Hallman, Barbara M. 1985. *Italian Cardinals: Reform and the Church as Property, 1492–1563.* Berkeley.

Hankins, James, ed. 2000. *Renaissance Civic Humanism: Reappraisals and Reflections.* Cambridge.

Howard, Peter. 'Entrepreneurial Ne'er-do-wells: Sin and Fear in Renaissance Florence'. In *Memorie* (1994).

——. 'The Preacher and the Holy in Renaissance Florence'. In Kienzle *et al.* (1996).

——. 'The Politics of Devotion: Preaching, Piety and Public Life in Renaissance Florence'. In Howard and Troup (2000).

Howard, Peter, and Cynthia Troup. 2000. *Cultures of Devotion: Studies in Medieval and Renaissance Religion.* Clayton, Australia.

Iradiel, Paulino, and José M. Cruselles. 'El entorno eclesiástico de Alejandro VI. Nota sobre la formación de la clientela politica borgiana (1429–1503)'. In Chiabò, Maddalo (2001): I, 27–58.

Izbicki, Thomas M. 'Pyres of Vanities: Mendicant Preaching on the Vanity of Women and its Lay Audience'. In Ames, Green, Kienzle (1989).

Jones, Philip J. 1997. *The Italian City-State: from Commune to Signoria.* Oxford.

Kent, Dale. 2000. *Cosimo de' Medici and the Florentine Renaissance.* New Haven and London.

Kienzle, Beverly Mayne, ed. 2000. *The Sermon.* Turnhout, Belgium.

Kienzle, Beverly Mayne, *et al.,* eds, 1996. *Models of Holiness in Medieval Sermons.* Louvain-La-Neuve.

Klein, Francesca. 'Il mito del governo largo: Riordinamento istituzionale e prassi politica nella Firenze savonaroliana'. In Garfagnini (1996).

——. 'Obtenere la provvisione cimentata. Cenni intorno al procedimento legislativo nel periodo savonaroliano'. In Garfagnini (1997).

Labande-Mailfert, Yvonne. 1975. *Charles VIII et son milieu (1470–1498): La jeunesse au pouvoir.* Paris.

Landucci, Luca. 1883. *Diario fiorentino.* Ed. I. del Badia. Florence.

——. 1927. *A Florentine Diary from 1450 to 1516.* Trans. Alice de Rosen Jervis. London and New York.

La toscana al tempo di Lorenzo il Magnifico. Politica Economia Cultura Arte. 1992. 3 vols. Pisa.

Leonardi, Claudio. 'Savonarola e la politica nelle prediche sopra l'*Esodo* e nel Trattato circa il reggimento e governo della città di Firenze'. In Garfagnini (1997).

——. 'La profezia di Savonarola'. In *Girolamo Savonarola* (1999).

C. Lupi, ed. 'Nuovi documenti intorno a Fra Girolamo Savonarola', in *ASI*, 3, 1 (1866): 3–77.

Lunetta, Loredana. 'La figura del profeta in Angelo da Vallombrosa, Girolamo Savonarola e Giorgio Benigno Salviati'. In Garfagnini (1996).

Luschino, Fra Benedetto [da Firenze]. *Cedrus Libani*. Ed. P. V. Marchese. In *ASI*, Appendix, Vol. 7 (1849): 59–95.

——. 2002. *Vulnera diligentis*. Ed. Stefano dall'Aglio. Florence.

Macey, Patrick. 1998. *Bonfire Songs: Savonarola's Musical Legacy*. Oxford.

Machiavelli, Bernardo. 1954. *Libro di ricordi*. Ed. Cesare Olschki. Florence.

Machiavelli, Niccolò. 1971. *Tutte le opere*. Ed. Mario Martelli. Florence.

Maffei, Domenico, and Paolo Nardi, eds. 1982. *Atti del simposio internazionale Cateriniano-Bernardiniano*. Siena.

Magia, Astrologia e Religione nel Rinascimento. 1974. Warsaw. The proceedings of a conference held in Warsaw, Sept. 1972, sponsored by the Polish Academy of Sciences.

Mallett, Michael. 1971. *The Borgias: The Rise and Fall of a Renaissance Dynasty*. London.

Manzoni, Luigi. 1881. *Sull' abbruciamento delle vanità fatto in Firenze negli anni 1497 e 98*. Bologna.

Marchese, Vincenzo, ed. 'Documenti intorno al Savonarola'. In *ASI*, Appendix, vol. 8 (1850).

Marks, L. F. 'La crisi finanziaria a Firenze dal 1494 al 1502'. In *ASI*, 112 (1954): 40–72.

Martelli, Francesco. 'Alcune considerazioni sull'introduzione della "Decima" a Firenze in epoca savonaroliana'. In Garfagnini (1997).

Martelli, Mario. 'Savonarola e Lorenzo'. In *Memorie* (1998).

Martines, Lauro. 1968. *Lawyers and Statecraft in Renaissance Florence*. Princeton.

——. [1979] 2002. *Power and Imagination: City-States in Renaissance Italy*. London and New York.

——. 'Literary crisis in the generation of 1494'. In Fletcher, Shaw, *The World*, 5–21.

—— 'Raging against Priests in Italian Renaissance Verse.' In Connell, *Society*, 261–77.

——. 2001. *Strong Words: Writing and Social Strain in the Italian Renaissance*. Baltimore and London.

——. 2003. *April Blood: Florence and the Plot Against the Medici*. London and New York.

Matarrese, Tina. 2001. ' "Come parli, frate? . . . ": sulla lingua e lo stile del Savonarola'. In Fragnito and Miegge.

Matucci, Andrea. 'Savonarola nella *Storia Fiorentina* di Piero Parenti'. In *Girolamo Savonarola* (1999). *Memorie Domenicane*. (1983), volume 14; (1994), volume 25; (1998), volume 29.

Miglio, Massimo. 'Savonarola di fronte ad Alessandro VI e alla curia'. In Garfagnini (2001).

Nardi, Iacopo. 1842. *Istorie della città di Firenze*. 2 vols. Ed. Lelio Arbib. Florence.

Neri, Achille. 'Un avversario di Girolamo Savonarola'. In *ASI*, 5 (1880): 478–82.

Niccoli, Ottavia. 1995. *Il seme della violenza. Putti, fanciulli e mammoli nell' Italia Tra Cinque e Seicento*. Rome and Bari.

——. 'I Bambini del Savonarola'. In Garfagnini (1996).

Pampaloni, Guido. 'Il movimento Piagnone secondo la lista del 1497'. In Gilmore, *Studies* (1972).

Parenti, Marco. 2001. *Ricordi storici, 1464–1467*. Ed. Manuela D. Garfagnini. Rome.

Parenti, Piero. 1994. *Storia fiorentina I: 1476–78, 1492–96*. Ed. A. Matucci. Florence.

———. 1910. [Schnitzer] *Savonarola nach den Aufzeichnungen des Florentiners Piero Parenti*. In Schnitzer, *Quellen und Forschungen*, Vol. 4.

Pastor, Ludwig. 1950. *The History of the Popes*. Vols. 5–6. Ed. F. I. Antrobus. London.

Pellegrini, Letizia. 'La predicazione come strumento di accusa'. In *Girolamo* (1999).

Pellegrini, Marco. 'Il profilo politico-istituzionale del cardinalato nell'età di Alessandro VI: persistenze e novità'. In Chiabò, Maddalo (2001): I, 177–215.

———. 'A Turning-Point in the History of the Factional System in the Sacred College: The Power of Pope and Cardinals in the Age of Alexander VI'. In Signorotto and Visceglia (2002).

Pesman-Cooper, Roslyn. 2002. *Piero Soderini and the Ruling Class in Renaissance Florence*. Goldbach.

Peterson, David S. 'Religion, Politics and the Church in Fifteenth-Century Florence'. In Weinstein, Hotchkiss (1994).

———. 'The War of the Eight Saints'. In Connell, *Society* (2002).

Picotti, G. B. 'Alessandro VI, il Savonarola ed il Cardinale Giuliano della Rovere in una publicazione recente'. In *Archivio della società romana di storia patria*, 3rd ser., 83 (1960): 51–72.

———. 2000. 'Rodrigo Borgia'. In *Enciclopedia*, III, 13–22.

Polizzotto, Lorenzo. 1994. *Elect Nation: The Savonarolan Movement in Florence, 1494–1545*. Oxford.

———. 2000 'Savonarola and the Florentine Oligarchy'. In Fletcher and Shaw.

———. 2004. *Children of Promise: The Confraternity of the Purification and the Socialization of Youths in Florence*. Oxford.

Portioli, Attilio, ed. 'Nuovi documenti su Girolamo Savonarola'. In *Archivio storico lombardo*, 1 (1874): 325–54.

Praticò, Giovanni. 'Spigolature savonaroliane nel Archivio di Mantova'. In *ASI*, 398, 1 (1952): 216–35.

Prodi, Paolo. 'Gli affanni della democrazia: La predicazione del Savonarola durante l'esperienza del governo popolare'. In Garfagnini (1997).

Quaglioni, Diego. 'Tirannide e democrazia: il momento savonaroliano nel pensiero giuridico e politico del Quattrocento'. In Garfagnini (1998).

Rao, Ida Giovanna, Paoli Viti, and Raffaella Maria Zaccaria, eds. 2001. *I processi di Girolamo Savonarola (1498)*. Florence.

Rhodes, Dennis E. 1988. *Gli annali tipografici fiorentini del xv secolo*. Florence.

Ridolfi, Roberto. 1935. *Studi savonaroliani*. Florence.

———. 1959. *The Life of Girolamo Savonarola*. Trans. Cecil Grayson. London.

———. 1974. *Vita di Girolamo Savonarola*. Florence. 2 vols. Florence.

———. 2000. *Prolegomeni ed aggiunte alla vita di Girolamo Savonarola*. Florence.

Rinuccini, Alamanno. *Ricordi*. In Rinuccini, Filippo.

Rinuccini, Filippo di Cino. 1840. *Ricordi storici dal 1282 al 1460, con la continuazione di Alamanno e Neri suoi figli*. Ed. G. Aiazzi. Florence.

Ristori, Renzo. 'Un mercante savonaroliano: Pandolfo Rucellai'. In *Magia* (1974).

Rocke, Michael. 1996. *Forbidden Friendships: Homosexuality and Male Culture in Renaissance Florence*. New York and Oxford.

Rubinstein, Nicolai. 1966. *The Government of Florence Under the Medici*. Oxford.

Rucellai, Fra Santi [Pandolfo]. 2004. *Epistolario*. Eds. A. F. Verde and E. Giaconi. Pistoia. In *Memorie Domenicane*, Vol. 34.

Ruggiero, Guido. 1985. *The Boundaries of Eros: Sex Crime and Sexuality in Renaissance Venice*. New York.

Sanuto, Marin. 1879–1902. *I Diarii*. 58 vols (Vol. 1). Ed. R. Fulin *et al.* Venice.

Savonarola, Girolamo. 1933. [*Lettere*] *Le Lettere*. Ed. Roberto Ridolfi. Florence.

——. 1955. [*Ezechiele*] *Prediche sopra Ezechiele*. 2 vols. Ed. R. Ridolfi. Rome.

——. 1955–56. [*Esodo*] *Prediche sopra l'Esodo*. 2 vols. Ed. P. G. Ricci. Rome.

——. 1957. [*Giobbe*] *Prediche sopra Giobbe*. 2 vols. Ed. R. Ridolfi. Rome.

——. 1959. *De simplicitate christianae vitae*. Ed. Piero Giorgio Ricci. Rome.

——. 1961. *Triumphus Crucis*. Ed. Mario Ferrara. Rome.

——. 1962. [*Ruth*] *Prediche sopra Ruth e Michea*. 2 vols. Ed. V. Romano. Rome.

——. 1963. *Trattato circa il reggimento e governo della città di Firenze*. Ed. Luigi Firpo. Torino.

——. 1965. [*Aggeo*] *Prediche sopra Aggeo, con il Trattato circa il reggimento e governo della città di Firenze*. Ed. L. Firpo. Rome.

——. 1968. *Poesie*. Ed. Mario Martelli. Rome.

——. 1969–74. [*Salmi*] *Prediche sopra i Salmi*. 2 vols. Ed. V. Romano. Rome.

——. 1971–72. [*Amos*] *Prediche sopra Amos a Zaccaria*. 3 vols. Ed. P. Ghiglieri. Rome.

——. 1974. *Compendio di rivelazioni, testo latino e volgare, e Dialogus de veritate prophetica*. Ed. A. Crucitti. Rome.

——. 1984. *Lettere e scritti apologetici*. Eds. R. Ridolfi, V. Romano, and A. F. Verde. Rome.

——. 1989. *Sermones in primam divi ioannis epistolam*. Ed. Armando F. Verde. Rome.

——. 1996. *Compendio di revelazioni. Trattato sul governo della città di Firenze*. Ed. Franco Buzzi. Casale Monferrato.

——. 1997. *Verità della profezia. De veritate prophetica dyalogus*. Ed. Claudio Leonardi. Florence.

——. 1999. *Il Breviario di Frate Girolamo Savonarola: Postille autografe*. Ed. Armando F. Verde. Florence.

——. 2001. *I processi*. See under Rao.

——. 2001a. *Il Quaresimale del 1491: La certezza profetica di un mondo nuovo*. Ed. Armando F. Verde and Elettra Giaconi. Florence.

——. 2003. *A Guide to Righteous Living and Other Works*. Tr. Konrad Eisenbichler. Toronto.

Scaltriti, Giacinto A. 1976. *L'Ultimo Savonarola. Esame giuridico-teologico del carteggio (brevi e lettere) intercorsi tra Papa Alessandro VI e il Frate Girolamo Savonarola*. Torino.

Schnitzer, Joseph. 1931. *Savonarola*. 2 vols. Milan.

——. Ed. 1902–10. *Quellen und Forschungen zur Geschichte Savonarolas*. 4 vols. Leipzig.

Schutte, Anne Jacobson. 1983. *Printed Italian Vernacular Religious Books: 1465– 1550*. Geneva.

Signorotto, Gianvettorio, and Maria Antonietta Visceglia, eds. 2002. *Court and Politics in Papal Rome, 1492–1700*. Cambridge.

Stephens, J. N. 1983. *The Fall of the Florentine Republic, 1512–1530.* Oxford.

Studi di storia medievale e moderna per Ernesto Sestan. 1980. Florence.

Taddei, Ilaria. 2001. *Fanciulli e giovani: crescere a Firenze nel Rinascimento.* Firenze.

Terreaux-Scotto, Cécile. 1997. 'La place des enfants dans la réforme savonarolienne de la cité'. In Fontes, Fournel.

Tognetti, Sergio. 'Prezzi e salari nella Firenze tardomedievale: un profilo'. In *ASI*, 563, 1 (1995): 263–333.

Trexler, Richard C. 1974. 'Ritual in Florence: Adolescence and Salvation in the Renaissance'. In Trinkaus and Oberman.

——. 1980. *Public Life in Renaissance Florence.* New York.

Trinkaus, Charles, and Heiko A. Oberman, eds. 1974. *The Pursuit of Holiness in Late Medieval and Renaissance Religion.* Leiden.

Vaglienti, Piero. 1982. *Storia dei suoi tempi, 1492–1514.* Eds. G. Berti, M. Luzzati, E. Tongiorgi. Pisa.

Valerio, Adriana. 2001. 'La predica sopra Ruth, la donna, la riforma dei semplici'. In Garfagnini (2001).

Vallombrosa, Angelo da. 1997. *Lettere.* Ed. Loredana Lunetti. Florence.

Verde, Armando F. 'La Congregazione di San Marco dell'Ordine dei Frati Predicatori'. In *Memorie* (1983), 164–201.

——. 'Girolamo Savonarola: tra profezia e condanna'. In *Memorie* (1998).

——. 'La presenza della cultura scolastica nelle opere di fra Girolamo.' In *Girolamo Savonarola* (1999).

Verdon, Timothy, and John Henderson, eds. 1990. *Christianity and the Renaissance: Image and Religious Imagination in the Quattrocento.* Syracuse, New York.

Villari, Pasquale. 1930. *La storia di Girolamo Savonarola e de' suoi tempi.* New ed. 2 vols. Florence.

Villari, P. and E. Casanova, eds. 1898. *Scelta di prediche e scritti di Fra Girolamo Savonarola con nuovi documenti intorno alla sua vita.* Florence.

Violi, Lorenzo. 1986. *Le giornate.* Ed. G. C. Garfagnini. Florence.

Visani, Oriana. 'Roberto Caracciolo, un imitatore di Bernardino da Siena'. In Maffei, Nardi (1982).

Weinstein, Donald. 1970. *Savonarola and Florence: Prophecy and Patriotism in the Renaissance.* Princeton.

——. 'The Prophet as Physician of Souls: Savonarola's Manual for Confessors'. In Connell, *Society* (2002).

Weinstein, Donald, and V. R. Hotchkiss, eds. 1994. *Girolamo Savonarola: Piety, Prophecy and Politics in Renaissance Florence.* Dallas.

Zaccaria, Raffaella Maria. 'Pandolfo Rucellai da mercante fiorentino a frate domenicano e savonaroliano'. In Garfagnini (1996).

Zafarana, Zelina. 'Per la storia religiosa di Firenze nel Quattrocento. Una raccolta privata di prediche'. In *Studi medievali*, ser. 3: 9, 2 (1968): 1017–1113.

——. 'Caracciolo, Roberto'. In *DBI*, 19: 446–52.

Zancarini, Jean-Claude. 1997. 'La question de l'ennemi dans les sermons et écrits de Savonarole'. In Fontes, Fournel.

INDEX